COMPETITIVENESS OF THE SINGAPORE ECONOMY

COMPETITIVENESS OF THE SINGAPORE ECONOMY
A Strategic Perspective

Edited by

TOH MUN HENG
TAN KONG YAM

SINGAPORE UNIVERSITY PRESS
NATIONAL UNIVERSITY OF SINGAPORE

World Scientific
Singapore • New Jersey • London • Hong Kong

Published by

Singapore University Press Pte. Ltd.
AS3-01-2, National University of Singapore
3 Arts Link, Singapore 117569

and

World Scientific Publishing Co. Pte. Ltd.
5 Toh Tuck Link, Singapore 596224
USA office: 27 Warren Street, Suite 401-402, Hackensack, NJ 07601
UK office: 57 Shelton Street, Covent Garden, London WC2H 9HE

British Library Cataloguing-in-Publication Data
A catalogue record for this book is available from the British Library.

COMPETITIVENESS OF THE SINGAPORE ECONOMY
A Strategic Perspective

ISBN-13 978-9971-69-214-8
ISBN-10 9971-69-214-7
ISBN-13 978-9971-69-221-6 (pbk)
ISBN-10 9971-69-221-X (pbk)

CONTENTS

ACKNOWLEDGEMENTS

We would like to express our gratitude to the participants of the "Workshop on the Competitiveness of the Singapore Economy" held on the 9 December 1997, for their valuable comments and suggestions to revise and improve the chapters in this volume.

We are thankful to the Department of Business Policy (NUS), Centre for Management of Technology (NUS) and Singapore Confederation of Industries (SCI) for jointly organising the "Symposium on the Competitiveness of the Singapore Economy" held on 8 January 1998, to enable the authors to share their research findings with researchers and practitioners from the private and public sectors. We are grateful to Mr Robert Chua, the President of SCI, and Professor Shih Choon Fong, the Deputy Vice Chancellor of the NUS, for their welcoming addresses and support for the symposium.

We are also thankful for financial support provided by National University of Singapore (NUS) Research Grant (RP3972035) in conducting the research project.

Last but not the least, we like to thank Ms Rittu Khattar, Ms Sally Han, Mdm Teo Woo Kim, Ms Woo Ka Meng and Ms Lim Sin Ying for their patience and speedy efforts in providing editorial and word-processing assistance.

ABOUT THE AUTHORS

Anthony T.H. Chin is Sub-Dean of the Faculty of Arts and Social Sciences and Senior Lecturer with the Department of Economics and Statistics at the National University of Singapore (NUS). His current areas of research include financing and cost recovery of transport infrastructure investments, regional port and airport competition, use of economic instruments and externalities from land transport and the impacts of road pricing on travel behaviour. He is also the Principal Researcher, Centre for Transportation Research at the Faculty of Engineering, NUS, Council Member of the Land Transport and Economic Development Committee of the Transportation Research Board of the USA, and Member of the Air Transport Research Group in Vancouver, Canada. He has been a consultant to various institutions such as Singapore Airlines, Port of Singapore Authority, the Automobile Association of Singapore and UNDP.

Björn Bjerke, a Scandinavian, has travelled widely and he has worked at several universities. Since 1991 he has held a position as a Senior Teaching Fellow at the National University of Singapore. Bjerke's main interests are entrepreneurship and cross-cultural studies. He has published several books on these subjects.

Ho Kong Chong is a senior lecturer in the Department of Sociology at NUS. Dr Ho received his doctorate from University of Chicago. He recently co-authored *City-States in the Global Economy: Industrial Restructuring in Hong Kong and Singapore* (Westview, 1997), and is co-editor of *Culture and the City in East Asia* (Oxford, 1997). Dr Ho is current a resource person for the Government Parliamentary Committee for National Development. He is also a member of the Advisory Panel on Youth Research, National Youth Council, and a member of the Publications Advisory Panel, Ministry of Information and the Arts.

William Koh is a Senior Lecturer in the Department of Organisational Behaviour at the Faculty of Business Administration, NUS. His research interests are in the areas of leadership, motivation, job design, stress management, human resource management, and general management. His work has been published in the Journal of Organisational Behaviour, Research and Practice in Human Resource Management, International Journal of Human Resource Management, and various international Conference Proceedings. Besides undergraduate teaching in NUS, Dr Koh also teaches at the various Executive Development Programmes organised by the Faculty of Business Administration. He has also done consulting work with various organisations around the region such Motorola, Johnson and Johnson, and the Singapore General Hospital.

Lawrence Loh is currently Vice-Dean of the Faculty of Business Administration, NUS. He received a PhD from Massachusetts Institute of Technology (MIT) in the field of information systems. He has published in internationally-refereed journals such as Management Science, Journal of Business Research, Information Systems Research, Journal of Management Information Systems, etc. Dr Loh has been a consultant to many well known international companies like IBM and Anderson Consulting (USA), as well as government agencies like National Science & Technology Board (NSTB), National Computer Board in Singapore. He is presently in the National Productivity & Quality Council and contributes as a resource person for the Committee on Singapore's Competitiveness.

Lim Guan Hua is currently a lecturer in the Graduate School of Business and the Department of Finance and Accounting, Faculty of Business Administration, NUS. He has a PhD in finance from the Wharton School, University of Pennsylvania. Dr Lim's research interests are varied and include the IPO market, cost & profit efficiencies of banks, operations & behaviour of financial markets, gray marketing, warranties, SMEs, and signalling & game theory. His papers have been or will be published in the Journal of Business Finance and Accounting, Journal of Global Marketing, Review of Pacific-Basin Financial Markets and Policies, Singapore Management Review, and the SES Journal.

Tan Kong Yam is the Head, Department of Business Policy, Faculty of Business Administration at NUS. He is a graduate of Princeton and Stanford University. Prior to joining NUS, he has worked at the Hoover Institution, World Bank, the Monetary Authority of Singapore, and was the Director of Research at the Ministry of Trade and Industry in Singapore. His research interests are in international trade and finance, growth and development in the Asia Pacific region and economic reforms in China. He has consulted for many organisations including Citibank, IBM, ATT, BP and Mobil, etc. Currently, he is an economic consultant to the Ministry of Trade and Industry and a resource person for the government Committee for Singapore's Competitiveness.

Toh Mun Heng is an Associate Professor in the Department of Business Policy, NUS. He obtained his doctoral degree in Economics and Econometrics from the University of London, London School of Economics. His research interests and publications are in the areas of econometric modelling, input-output analysis, international trade and investment, manpower studies, transportation economics and household economics and development strategies for emerging economies in the Asia Pacific. He has been engaged as an economic consultant by international agencies such as the UN ESCAP, Asian Development Bank and ASEAN Secretariat, private companies and governmental ministries. Currently, he is an economic consultant to the Ministry of Trade and Industry and a resource person for the government Committee for Singapore's Competitiveness.

Jose L. Tongzon is a Senior Lecturer at the Department of Economics and Statistics, NUS. He specialises in international economics and maritime transport. Areas of research interest include ASEAN economies, transitional economies of Southeast Asia, and port efficiency. Before joining NUS, Dr Tongzon was Chief Economist of the Port of Melbourne Authority and worked as an academic and public servant in Australia and the Philippines for several years. At NUS he has published articles in the area of port performance, efficiency and international benchmarking for such journals as Transportation Research and Maritime Policy and Management. He is an active member of the Chartered Institute of Transport (CIT) and International Association of Maritime Economists (IAME).

Wong Poh Kam is an Associate Professor at the Faculty of Business Administration, NUS. He is currently the director of a research centre, the Centre for Management of Technology (CMT), and deputy director of the Graduate School of Business. He obtained his doctoral degree from the Massachusetts Institute of Technology. He has consulted widely for international agencies such as the World Bank/EDI, Asian Development Bank, UNESCAP and ASEAN Secretariat, various government agencies in Singapore such as EDB, NSTB, NCB and TDB, as well as numerous private companies in the region such as Southern Steel (Malaysia), HP Singapore and Singapore Telecoms. His current research interests include Management of Technological Innovation, Technology Strategies of East Asian Firms, National Science and Technology Policy, and National Information Infrastructure Policy.

Wong Poh Poh is an Associate Professor in the Department of Geography, NUS. He has a PhD in geography from McGill University and was trained as a coastal geomorphologist. Over the last decade, he has extended his research to coastal tourism in Southeast Asia, Taiwan and Reunion Island. He initiated and taught a course on Geography of Tourism for nearly 20 years and currently offers a new course on Tourism in Southeast Asia. He published widely on geography education, coastal geomorphology, tourism and coastal zone management and is the author of "Coastal Tourism in Southeast Asia" (1991) and editor of "Tourism vs. Environment: the Case for Coastal Areas" (1993). He has served as consultant to local and international organisations on environmental impact assessment, coastal tourism development and coastal zone management.

INTRODUCTION

Toh Mun Heng

After 37 years as a nation, Singapore is at another important turning point of economic history: the challenge in enhancing and maintaining its competitive edge in the international economy. The international economy has also undergone fundamental changes during the last two or so decades. Economic activity is becoming not only more internationalised but also more significantly, it is becoming increasingly globalised in a world of increasing complexity, interconnectedness and mobility[1]. We live in a rapidly changing and increasingly competitive world in which global competition is making it essential for regional economies to develop the capacity and capability to make rapid adjustments to changing conditions if they are to remain competitive.

Globalisation has become a familiar theme in social sciences, particularly in the field of international economics. Globalisation can be defined generically as the growth of economic activity spanning politically defined national and regional boundaries. A number of forces are operating simultaneously to create a worldwide market in goods and services. The most important of these forces include: (1) technological diffusion, which allows a growing club of middle- and even low-income countries to produce an increasing range of sophisticated products that were formerly monopolised by a few suppliers; (2) decreasing cost and increasing speed of transportation, especially by air freight, allowing world markets to be reached within a few hours; (3) increasing diffusion of information, accompanied by the movement of capital (FDI) to facilitate the development of complex networks of production across international frontiers; (4) declining trade barriers to trade through GATT or WTO agreements, and trade liberalisation initiatives by regional trade blocs such as the North American Free Trade Agreement and ASEAN Free Trade Agreement and international forum like APEC;

[1] More extensive discussion can be found in Dickens P. (1992) *Global Shift: The Internationalisation of Economic Activity*, New York: Guilford Press.

and (5) government policies and behaviour such as the deregulation of financial or other markets, the lowering of barriers to competition, trade, and investment.

Concurrently, the scope of competition is no longer limited by national boundaries nor by the definition of a particular sector — hence the term *global.* In essence, competition is about internalising on a worldwide scale key assets such as knowledge, finance, production experience and market access, that can lead to the development and to the effective commercialisation of a wide variety of product and services. As a small and extremely open economy, Singapore long term survival is very much dependent on the ability to maintain its viable position and remain afloat in the sea of global competition.

This book is intended to provide an intensive review of the several aspects of competitiveness in the Singapore economy. It is hoped that the present study will help to design an operational analytical framework to identify the strategies which will allow the economy to retain its competitive advantage in an increasingly globalised economic environment for the future years. It is a timely exercise in view of the fact that the international trading and investment climate has liberalised considerably, and the regional economies are achieving remarkable economic growth and development which begin to challenge Singapore's competitive edge as an regional transportation hub, international financial centre and a primary regional centre for technology and education. It is also a concerted effort of the academic community to complement the work of the government committee: Competitiveness of Singapore Committee (CSC) which will be releasing the report and recommendations in early 1998. The current study on national competitiveness will be a continuation of the research effort of the researchers and targeted to yield useful findings, which will be of interest to policy makers as well as researchers interested in socio-economic development strategies.

The chapters in this volume study will address the issue of national competitiveness from three perspectives:

(a) macro economic policies for continued growth and sustainability;
(b) micro-economic strategies for promoting and sustaining

competitiveness in economic sectors: manufacturing, financial services; tourism, construction and others;

(c) the interface of social — cultural and economic dimensions on competitiveness.

Brief Overview of Chapters

In the first chapter, Tan Kong Yam and Toh Mun Heng provides a survey of factors which determine the competitiveness of firms and nations. A framework for competitiveness analysis is suggested. The importance of infrastructure facilities as a weapon of competition for city states is highlighted and the role of government in maintaining the nation's competitive edge is reviewed. It is recognised that the continued viability and prosperity of Singapore as a city-state nation will need it to be adaptable to ever changing competitive terrain in the world. It will have to vie for the development and status of a global city — a particular type of production site for the production of specialised services, for the production of financial innovations and making of markets. The oligopolistic structure of the world economy and increasing information content of production, coupled with a trend away from integration and mass production *a la* Ford and Taylor, and towards flexible networks of producers, implies that command and control functions become even more important, and these activities are apparently becoming concentrated in a decreasing number of cities and regions.

The strategic importance of technology in maintaining competitiveness is the theme of the second chapter authored by Lawrence Loh. It tracks the establishment of a dominant thinking in technology policy management within the country rooted on an economic imperative and highlights some observations in terms of technology inputs, throughputs and outputs. The chapter also articulates several challenges for Singapore's technology policy to strive beyond economic upgrading as an over-arching goal as well as to sharpen the focus on basic sciences. The use of information technologies and the ability to innovate in terms of products and process can be encouraged with appropriate policies implemented at a national and company level.

Singapore has won several accolades for being an efficient

international transportation hub. In the third chapter, Tongzon Jose and Anthony Chin evaluate the current situation and consider measures in which Singapore's airport and seaport can further improve and maintain the competitive advantages nurtured over the years. The manufacturing sector has been a major locomotive of industrialisation and economic growth since Singapore obtained its Independence. Being flexible in adapting to an international trend of foreign investment and technologies, the manufacturing sector is responsible for about a quarter of the nation's GDP and is a major production base for electronic products in Asia. However, that its importance has not diminished over the years is due as much to continuous upgrading in the composition of industries as to the production processes and products. In Chapter 4, Wong Poh Kam presents a framework for identifying alternative routes the Singapore manufacturing sector can retain its catalytic role in economic development. It suggests the establishment of Singapore as a world product charter for selected niche products; as a "process technology transfer station" for the region and as a regional supply chain integrator, to further enhance the competitiveness of Singapore's manufacturing sector. Furthermore, the experience of successful high-tech firms in the four Asian NIEs of Korea, Hong Kong, Taiwan highlighted in the chapter can provide useful lessons for Singapore.

The construction sector is often considered as a sector with little opportunity for externalisation, and that it is technologically backward and low-skilled intensive. Contrary to this perception, the construction industry in its developed form can be an important foreign exchange earner and employer of professionals and technocrats. It is an industry which can provide high value-added jobs for the skilled workers and professionals like engineers, architects, lawyers and financial analysts. In Chapter 5, Toh Mun Heng discusses some major issues related to the restructuring of the construction sector to meet higher level of demand for efficiency and international competitiveness. These include the introduction of new management techniques, the problem of productivity improvement, the role of technology, the constraints pose by labour scarcity and the need for regionalisation and bidding for international contracts.

The tourism industry has been an important foreign exchange earner for Singapore since the 1960s. Over the years, the industry has undergone several structural changes in tandem with changing international demand and shifting consumers' tastes. However, the growth in the number of visitors coming to Singapore appears to be dwindling in the few years. Wong Poh Poh in Chapter 6 reviews the state of the tourism industry in Singapore. It examines the notion of *New Age Tourism*, regional tourism and other issues relevant to industry's competitiveness. Very much like the manufacturing industries, innovations in product, process, technology and management are required in the tourism industry to create growth and positive feedback effects on other sectors in the economy.

The development of Singapore as a world-class financial centre is critically assessed in Chapter 7. Lim Guan Hua, supported by evidence of international practices and rational arguments, puts forth several proposals for restructuring the financial sector in Singapore so as to achieve higher level of competitiveness and growth. Some of the strategies for sustaining and improving competitiveness in the industry include maintaining the distinction between domestic and offshore banking market; encouraging internet banking; merging finance companies with commercial banks; merging Sicom with SIMEX; and extensive liberalisation of the ways in which CPF moneys can be invested.

Despite the prominent presence and contribution of foreign companies to the national economy, there is still a substantial number of small and medium enterprises (SMEs) in the economy. Totalling about 80,000, these SMEs function as an important bedrock for local entrepreneurship in the economy. The role of entrepreneurs and the importance of SMEs are reviewed in Chapter 8 by Bjerke Bjorn. Contrasting the Western practices of entrepreneurship with that found in Singapore, Bjorn provides a list of advice and suggestions that would improve the entrepreneurial environment in Singapore.

The social aspect of globalisation and competition is a much neglected area of study. In Chapter 9, Ho Kong Chong examines the effects of globalisation and its impacts on the social structure of Singapore society. The author considers whether Singapore's increasing embeddedness in the global economy, with the consequence of exposure to foreign culture and practices, development of contractual relationships and new social-cultural forms, would dampen the nation's competitiveness.

Globalisation, massive technological change and international competition have led to greater emphasis on quality, and changes in the nature of work. In the final chapter of the book, William Koh considers how these pose new challenges for the human resource professionals in the way they carry out their traditional functions such as recruitment and selection, training and development, performance appraisal, pay and compensation, and career development.

The studies reported in this book are not the ultimate prognosis on the competitiveness of the Singapore economy. Nevertheless, it is sincerely hoped that they would encourage even more researchers and practitioners to explore in greater depth other competitive issues and strategies. Competitiveness of the Singapore economy is very likely to be a perennial concern for every Singaporean.

PART I

MACROECONOMIC STRATEGIES

1

The Macroeconomic Perspectives of Competitiveness

Tan Kong Yam and Toh Mun Heng

1. Introduction

The debate over the sources of national wealth and prosperity is as old as the economic profession itself. In the modern globalised economy, this debate has evolved into the search for the economic system, institutions, policies, and proper role of the government, that can sustain international competitiveness and generate prosperity over the long term. This paper has two objectives. The first is to provide a brief survey of the factors which determine the competitiveness of firms and nations. The second objective is to consider the role of government in fostering the competitiveness of an economy in the new international environment where information technology is pervasive and globalisation has become a dominant facet of international business.

While a multiplicity of factors, some of which are non-economic in nature, could plausibly affect the performance of an economy from period to period, a country's growth over a reasonably long period of time is ultimately determined by the application, accumulation and acquisition of productive resources. Given the state of technical know-how, the more efficiently existing resources are utilised, the higher would be the output. An economy will be able to expand its output when productive resources, which include both human and physical capital, are accumulated to bolster the productive capacity. Finally, the potential efficiency level and consequently the economic output, will be increased with technological progress associated with technology transfer, adoption, adaptation and innovation.

2. What is Competitiveness?

One problem in facing up to the issue of competitiveness is that the term has been abused to mean almost anything. Clarification of the issues of competitiveness requires some definition or concept, which recognises the problem both at the economic and business level.

A well known management guru, Michael Porter, defined competitiveness as "the degree to which a nation can, under free and fair market conditions, produce goods and services that meet the test of international markets while simultaneously maintaining or expanding the real incomes of its citizens."[1] However, this definition appears to be made merely from the angle of production and marketing. A wider coverage is desirable, as the "value-added" chain extends beyond production and marketing. Thus it may be better to consider competitiveness broadly to refer to the *ability of a business, group of businesses, or indeed a country's economy as a whole, to sustain future growth.* At the level of the firm, competitiveness may be defined by a business sustainable growth rate relative to actual or likely competitors. This same definition can also be extended to a group of businesses, such as a business sector in a country comprising its economy, in which case the issue is one of economic growth relative to that of rival countries.

At all levels, the concept of sustainability is important, because it is this that rules out superficial analysis and forces deeper examination of fundamental factors underlying the strength and weaknesses of an economy or of a particular business. In either area, it is not difficult to obtain a temporary boost to performance. Demand policy can stimulate faster economic growth in the short term, and this incidentally can improve the immediate prospects even of businesses or whole business sectors facing underlying competitive problems. Similarly, a company in a weak position can even succeed in increasing market share for a short while. The problem in all these cases, however, reduces to sustainability. Competitiveness is about the ability to sustain the growth of living standards.

---

[1] Porter, Michael E., (ed.) (1986) *Competition in Global Industries*, Boston: Harvard Business Press, p. 3.

Some of the most powerful economic principles for improving competitiveness were already laid down in classical economics. Adam Smith in his "Wealth of Nations" and later classical and neo-classical economists have argued that sustained growth in the wealth of a nation depends on the accumulation of capital. In classical economics, competitiveness depends on people's economic choices, particularly with respect to immediate pressure on living standards. If, as happened in Japan after the War, people are prepared to forego immediate consumption, the benefit is reflected in lower costs, higher savings, lower real interest rates, encouraging investment not only in plant and equipment, but also in less tangible forms of business development such as product and process development, marketing, distribution and so on. Such choices considerably enhance prospects for sustained growth.

In the classical economic framework, government's most constructive role (apart from urging people to moderate real wage demands) is viewed as one of non-intervention. According to this argument, government should not create distortions by attempting to support businesses or business sectors, advancing their particular vested interests. However, the Great Depression of the early 1930s had cast doubt on the economy being in a continuous state of equilibrium to ensure full employment of resources. Keynes, in particular, has argued that economic systems actually operate in the real world, and could result in disequilibrium phenomena not allowed in classical economics. He advocated the use of fiscal policies (the intervention of the government in the economic system through deficit budgeting) to "fine tune" the economy, and create sufficient effective demand to ensure the full employment of resources.

Several economists have attacked both the classical and Keynes' theoretical models as artificial and have argued for more pragmatic intervention. The main problem is too much reliance on economic policies based on such over-general theoretical approaches has distracted policy makers' attention from other real and urgent problems concerning manufacturing performance, R&D, investment, engineering and education inputs to that performance. We shall return to the role of government in the discussion of endogenous growth theory.

3. A Framework of Competitiveness

Competitiveness, though it can be assisted by better economic choices, ultimately depends on appropriate national and company policies. Competition is the crux of economics. It represents the interplay of companies, sectors, and nations as they battle for market share at home and abroad. In a recent publication, Michael Porter noted the changing currents of international competition and the growing similarity of industries across countries. This growing similarity in available infrastructure, distribution channels, and marketing approaches — a long term trend — is continuing, as more and more products and brands are available everywhere, indicating similar buyer needs in different countries. Liberal capital markets and falling tariff barriers are also contributing factors to these trends of parallel development across nations. Nonetheless, government policy, history, supply constraints, demand factors and a myriad of other influences differentiate national economic systems.

Free markets will in theory lead to intensification in competition (exacerbated by new entrants) and eventually destroy any possibility of profitability, unless companies can achieve defensible niches offering potential for some degree of monopoly. Porter (1980) utilises principles of imperfect competition to draw up ground rules so that companies can manage this situation and direct themselves to areas of less intense competition. He distinguishes three main "generic" competitive strategies: overall cost leadership, differentiation, or focusing on narrow segments of the market. Successful companies, he argues, follow consistently any of these three approaches but avoid being "caught in the middle". Strategies must also be coherent in the context of an industry's competitive dynamics, and Porter details the factors behind five major sources of competition — the threats from substitute products or new entrants into the industry, from increasing customer power on the one hand or from increasing power of one's own suppliers on the other, and finally internal rivalry among existing competitors. The framework of competition is extended to consider the competitive position of a nation (Porter, 1990).

Porter's framework is useful but it does have some limitations. Porter (1980) ignores the issue of real wage (unit labour cost) not being the same for all competitors. This is particularly important in the context of global competition. The whole basis of international trade theory in economics, the concept of comparative advantage is that over long periods of time real exchange rates in competitive countries will move to offset competitive advantage achieved by one country over another. It is well recognised that considerable productivity differentials exist between countries offset by real wage adjustments (Carr, 1990). By discounting such factors, Porter's position seems inconsistent with international trade theory. Porter's approach may therefore risk underplaying the role that real wage variations can play in sustaining competitiveness. Moreover, the key strategic issues on which he focuses attention are how a company can achieve less-intense competition, rather than the key issues it needs to face in order to improve its own performance and effectiveness relative to that of the competitors. Thus, Porter's approach is more suited for short term tactical evaluation rather than long term survival strategy.

The contribution of Porter's ideas, which are richly supported by examples, lies in sensitising those concerned with strategy to the need to find a coherent niche in the longer term; companies may otherwise become indecisive and merely reactive in the face of immediate competitive pressure. The danger with any such general approach to competitive strategy is, however, that it risks underplaying the importance of more mundane contextual issues such as production/operations and changing technology.

More recent literature, while endorsing the usefulness of Porter's framework, has been modified and extended to cover the role of technology and trade policy. We identify six elements to competitiveness relevant for a city-state. The first four form the domestic portion of the equation; the latter two the international portion. Obviously, the domestic and the international interact to produce overall competitiveness. Briefly, the six elements are:

Technology embodies knowledge in advanced machinery and superior systems of management and administration. In engineering, it translates into greater potential for undertaking projects and greater efficiency in completing them.

Human resources measure the abilities of people: their level of education, capacity for operating and using new technologies, and adaptability to new problems and situations. Human resource requirements are probably as high in engineering as they are in any other industry.

Capital reflects the ability to finance upgrades in technology and human resource levels. It is especially important in international engineering work because firms must be able to extend their resources over long distances.

Infrastructure in the form of transport and communication facilities, together with appropriate institutional supports such as legal enforcement of contracts and respect for property rights.

Trade policy is a two-way street. One way is the support provided to exporters to sell their goods or services overseas (i.e., subsidies); the other way is the openness of the domestic markets to importers. Trade, as propounded by Ricardo, Samuelson and other economists, is based on comparative advantage. However, comparative advantage is not invariant over time. It can be created/altered by human efforts, as in the accumulation of technological expertise and human capital. Goods as well as services can be transacted across countries to improve human welfare.

New competition reflects the state of the art in the industry. Competitor abilities are the sum of the technology, capital, human-resource and trade policy elements. Hence, competitiveness must be seen as a relative phenomenon rather than an absolute one.

These six elements and how they interact to form competitiveness are shown in Figure 1. All are also affected by national macroeconomic conditions such as domestic rates of growth or exchange rates.

4. Measuring Competitiveness: With Particular Reference to Southeast Asian Economies

While economists and management experts have provided much

Figure 1 A Framework of Competitive linkages

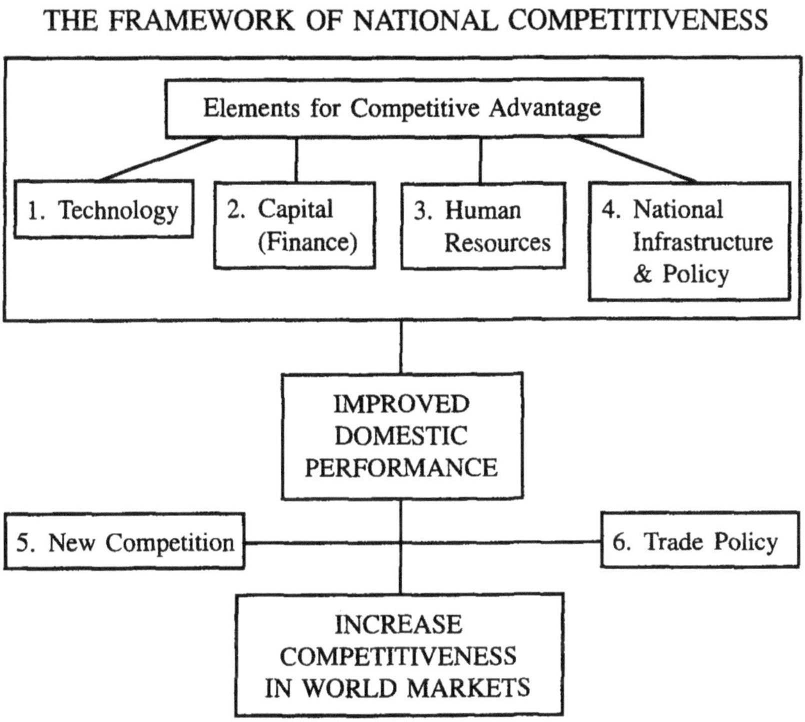

Source: Adapted from James Lee (1993)

theoretical and analytical foundations on competitiveness, the task of measuring competitiveness of economies can only be a meaningful exercise if the determining factors can be quantified adequately. The two leading surveys on national competitiveness at the global level are the Global Competitiveness Report by the World Economic Forum (WEF) of Geneva, Switzerland and the World Competitiveness Yearbook by the International Institute for Management Development (IMD) of Lausanne, Switzerland. The WEF defines international competitiveness as the ability of the country to achieve sustained high rates of growth in GDP per capita on the basis of suitable policies, institutions and other economic characteristics. Thus the focus is less on the short term fluctuation of the business cycle and more on the fundamental trend rate of growth of the economy over the medium term. Eight clusters of structural

characteristics are deemed to contribute to competitiveness:
(a) openness of the economy to international trade and finance
(b) role of the government budget and regulation
(c) development of the financial markets
(d) quality of infrastructure
(e) quality of technology
(f) quality of business management
(g) labour market flexibility
(h) quality of judiciary and political institutions.

Each of the cluster of structural characteristics is then assessed via a host of criteria. Some of the indicators are based on quantitative data while others are derived from survey data based on the perception of 2000 international business executives about the country they are operating in.

In much congruence with the broad definition of competitiveness discussed in the earlier section, the IMD defines competitiveness as the ability of a nation's environment to sustain the creation of value added, and, by extension, the competitiveness of their companies. The eight major factors of competitiveness identified are domestic economy, internationalisation, government, finance, infrastructure, management, science & technology and people. Each of the factors is a weighting of hard statistical data and soft survey data compiled from an executive opinion survey.

These clusters of structural characteristics deemed to be critical for international competitiveness are based on the results of theoretical and empirical research of modern economic growth theory (Barro and Sala-I-Martin, 1995). For example, the importance of openness to international trade and finance in enhancing international competitiveness have been supported by Sachs and Warner (1995), Dollar (1992), Frankel and Romer (1996). The importance of political stability, size of government and role of education have been empirically supported by Barro (1991). The significance of efficient financial institutions is confirmed by King and Levine (1993). The empirical support on the important contribution of quality infrastructure to international competitiveness and growth can be found in Munnell (1992). Evidence of the importance of technology, research and development and technological diffusion can be found in Coe, Helpman and Hoffmeister (1995). The importance of the quality of political and judiciary institutions to international competitiveness and sustained development can be found in Knack and Keefer (1995). Evidence on the importance of labour market flexibility is highlighted in Abowd, Kramarz, Lemieux and Mangolis (1997), and Coe and Snower (1997).

The significance of the WEF Competitiveness Index in explaining cross country differences in economic growth is confirmed by the strong statistical correlation between the competition index (after adjusting for income levels or stage of development) and the recent growth in GDP per capita between 1992-1995 (see Chart 1).

Comparing the ranking of East Asian countries between the WEF and IMD (see Table 1), it is clear that apart from Japan, the other East Asian countries are generally ranked significantly lower by IMD, particularly for Southeast Asian countries like Malaysia,

Chart I Growth is positively associated with the Competitiveness Index, after controlling for initial GDP per capita

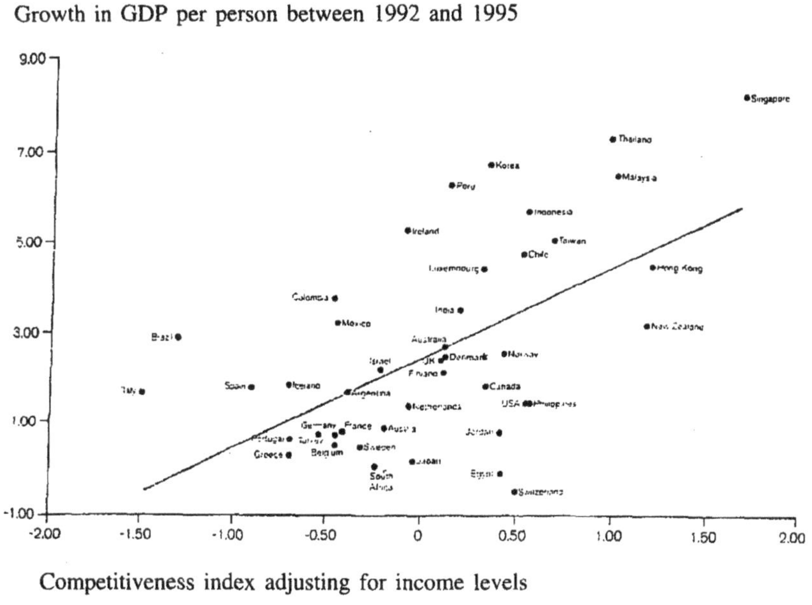

Table 1 Comparison of WEF and IMD Ranking

	WEF	IMD
Singapore	1(1)	2(2)
Malaysia	9(10)	17(23)
Indonesia	15(30)	39(41)
Korea	21(20)	30(27)
Thailand	18(14)	29(30)
Philippines	34(31)	31(31)
China	29(36)	27(26)
Japan	14(13)	9(4)
Taiwan	8(9)	23(18)

Note: Ranking for 1997 with ranking for 1996 indicated in bracket.
Source: Global Competitiveness Report (1997) by WEF and World Competitiveness Yearbook (1997) by IMD.

Indonesia, Thailand as well as Korea. In view of the currency crisis and decline in growth in these four countries since mid-1997, it appears that the IMD ranking is more predictive of the latest development in East Asia.

As indicated in Table 2, a clear trend over the past five years is the gradual deterioration of international competitiveness of Southeast Asian countries, especially in Indonesia and Thailand as well as in Korea and Japan. A significant trend is the clear substantial improvement of international competitiveness by China. In particular, relative to Southeast Asia, China has improved significantly in internationalisation, government, infrastructure, management, science and technology and people (see Table 3). This deteriorating trend in Southeast Asia against China has significant implications for the long term industrialisation and development in Southeast Asia, even after the present currency turmoil has stabilised.

Another worrying trend is the relative deterioration of national competitiveness of Southeast Asia against the Latin American countries which have been undergoing rapid economic reform. As indicated in Table 4, the relative competitive position of Brazil,

Table 2 Trends in Ranking (IMD)

	1993	1994	1995	1996	1997
Singapore	3	2	2	2	2
Malaysia	14	18	23	23	17
Indonesia	38	36	34	41	39
Korea	28	32	26	27	30
Thailand	26	26	27	30	29
Philippines	35	37	36	31	31
China	–	34	31	26	27
Japan	2	3	4	4	9
Taiwan	11	22	14	18	23
USA	1	1	1	1	1

Source: World Competitiveness Yearbook (1997) by IMD.

Argentina and Chile have been improving steadily against Indonesia and Thailand over the past five years. Both Brazil and Argentina have improved significantly in internationalisation, government, management, science and technology as well as people.

The key conclusion is unmistakable. Southeast Asia, particularly Indonesia and Thailand, have declined steadily in international competitiveness against the rapidly emerging China and Latin American countries like Brazil and Argentina. This is a key fundamental factor in the currency crisis and turmoil in Southeast Asia since July 1997.

At the global level, it is noteworthy that various regions have performed differently due to substantial differences in institutions and policies. Based on the classification by the WEF, Table 5 compares the competitiveness index, average economic growth for the period 1992–95 as well as all the eight clusters of structural characteristics. It is clear that the small open, entrepôt economies like Hong Kong, Singapore, Luxembourg and Switzerland are the most competitive group of nations. They scored high in openness, government, finance, labour and civil institutions. The Anglo-Saxon countries of UK, Australia, Canada, New Zealand and the US are

Table 3 Relative Competitive Ranking of China, Indonesia and Thailand

		1993	1994	1995	1996	1997
Domestic Economy	China	–	3	2	2	14
	Indonesia	23	20	22	25	11
	Thailand	7	8	9	12	12
Internationalisation	China	–	41	34	23	29
	Indonesia	35	33	33	37	35
	Thailand	33	28	29	33	25
Government	China	–	14	12	9	6
	Indonesia	20	21	21	25	27
	Thailand	7	6	7	8	18
Finance	China	–	39	38	37	40
	Indonesia	36	36	29	36	39
	Thailand	24	22	24	26	29
Infrastructure	China	–	43	43	40	40
	Indonesia	35	38	36	36	39
	Thailand	34	34	39	42	42
Management	China	–	45	41	30	34
	Indonesia	33	33	36	42	41
	Thailand	22	20	28	31	31
Science & Technology	China	–	23	27	28	20
	Indonesia	33	33	33	40	41
	Thailand	40	43	29	44	32
People	China	–	38	37	35	31
	Indonesia	44	44	45	45	44
	Thailand	36	34	34	40	37

Source: The World Competitiveness Yearbook (1997), IMD

Table 4 Relative Competitive Ranking of Southeast Asia Against Latin America

	1993	1994	1995	1996	1997
Indonesia	38	36	34	41	39
Thailand	26	26	27	30	29
Brazil	44	43	38	37	33
Argentina	–	33	30	32	28
Mexico	33	29	42	42	40
Chile	19	24	20	13	24

Source: World Competitiveness Report Yearbook (1997), IMD

much more competitive and hence performed better than the EU. They tend to score much higher in openness, labour market flexibility, government, management and technology. The weakness of the EU is clear, particularly in labour market rigidity and government policies arising from high tax rates and expenditure as well as state provision of pensions. It is noteworthy that Asian manufacturers, that include Japan, Korea, Taiwan, Malaysia and Thailand, are relatively weak in openness, labour market flexibility, quality of judicial and political institutions, as well as management.

The key lessons appear to be that in a globalised economy driven by technology and increasingly dependent on information and knowledge as the important factors of production, openness, labour market flexibility, strong management, finance and technology are crucial for sustained competitiveness and growth. These are critical lessons relevant for Southeast Asia, Korea and Japan — that are presently groping for a strategy to climb out of the financial crisis and economic slump over the next few years.

5. City State in Global Competition

Critics have argued that unlike firms which compete over a given market in a zero sum game, nations can increase its standard of living without undermining the growth in the standard of living of

Table 5 Relative Competitiveness of Regional Grouping

Country	Growth (%) 1992-1995	Competitiveness Index	Openness (Index)	Government (Index)	Finance (Index)	Infrastructure (Index)	Technology (Index)	Management (Index)	Labour (Index)	Civil Institutions (Index)
Entrepot	4.2	1.7	0.6	0.9	1.0	0.9	0.6	0.8	0.7	1.0
Anglo-Saxon	2.4	1.1	0.5	0.3	5.0	0.7	0.5	0.7	0.5	0.8
EU	1.5	0.0	0.2	-0.4	0.0	0.4	0.2	0.1	-0.3	0.2
Asian manufacturers	5.2	0.7	0.0	0.6	0.6	-0.0	0.4	0.4	0.4	0.1
Reforming Developing	2.1	-0.9	-0.5	-0.1	-0.5	-0.7	-0.6	-0.3	-0.3	-0.7

Source: Global Competitiveness Report(1996),WEF

other countries in a positive sum game (Krugman, 1994, 1994a). While this is undoubtedly true, some zero sum competition might be a reality, especially for a city-state servicing a regional hinterland. The economic agglomeration effect is relevant in Singapore's competitive environment to be the region's pre-eminent financial centre.

Information technologies, often thought of as neutralising geography, actually contribute to spatial concentration. They make possible the geographic dispersal and simultaneous integration of many activities. At the same time, globalisation of economic activity has raised the scale and complexity of economic transactions, thereby feeding the growth of top level multinational headquarters functions and the growth of services for firms, particularly advanced corporate services. Global cities are a particular type of production site for the production of specialised services, the production of financial innovations and the making of markets in the new information age (Sassen, 1995). *First mover* advantages are particularly important for the long term entrenchment of the pre-eminent position of a global city. Singapore has to strive to be one of these few global cities in the world.

The key clusters of structural characteristics like quality of infrastructure, quality of judiciary and political institutions, openness to international trade and finance, and labour market flexibility, are important for Singapore's competitiveness in attracting the limited pool of direct foreign investment as well as its striving become a regional hub for multinational headquarters. In addition, for a small open economy that depends critically on international trade and the inflow of direct foreign investment, medium term international competitiveness indicators of exchange rates, business cost as well as profitability index are extremely important. These would include indicators like unit business costs index, relative unit labour cost index against the other NIEs, ASEAN countries as well as the OECD countries, profitability index like the rate of returns of US investment in the non-oil manufacturing and services sector compared to the other regional countries.

The unit business cost (UBC) index of the manufacturing sector measures the total business cost per unit of real output. It is divided into unit labour cost (49.4%), services cost including utilities, port, warehousing charges (48.3%) and government rates and fees (2.3%). As indicated in Chart 2, the UBC index has been rising steadily between 1987 and 1992, largely driven by rising unit labour cost and services cost. It has stabilised since 1992. Government rates and fees has risen at a much faster rate in the past decade. However, due to its low percentage share in UBC, its contributing effect is not significant. It is noteworthy that prior to the recession in 1986, unit labour cost rose by 44% between 1980 to 1985, contributed significantly to the rising cost of operation, a substantial fall in profitability, a loss in international competitiveness, eventually leading to the recession in 1986. This UBC index is thus a useful international competitiveness index for the manufacturing sector in the medium term.

The UBC index does not incorporate the relative competitiveness of the manufacturing sector against competitor countries. To do this, we need to include the effect of relative movement of the exchange rates. The relative unit labour cost index (RULC) for the manufacturing sector, incorporates the effect of labour cost, productivity and exchange rate movements against competitor countries.

Charts 3 and 4 indicate the RULC of Singapore manufacturing sector against the other three NIEs and the two ASEAN countries, Malaysia and Thailand. It indicates that while the relative competitive position against Taiwan has remained somewhat stable over the past 15 years, Singapore's competitive position has deteriorated against Hong Kong and Korea, due largely to a strong exchange rate and higher labour cost increase. Measured against Thailand, Singapore's relative competitive position has also remained stable but it has deteriorated against Malaysia, again due largely to a stronger exchange rate and higher labour cost increase.

Chart 5 indicates the rate of return of US investment in the non-oil manufacturing sector in the regional economies, compiled by the US Department of Commerce. It is noteworthy that despite a steady decline since 1980, Singapore remains a highly profitable site for US direct foreign investment. For the services sector, again Singapore remains a highly profitable location, though in recent years Malaysia and Indonesia have overtaken Singapore (see Chart 6).

Chart 2 Unweighted Components of Unit Business Cost of Manufacturing 1980–1996

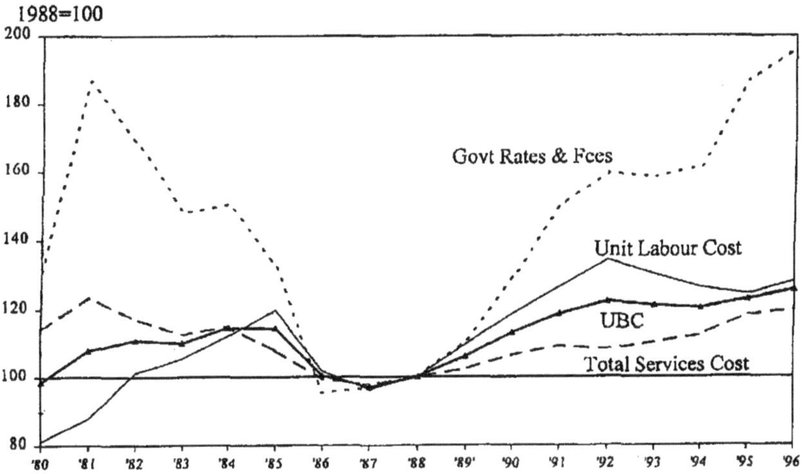

Source: Department of Statistics

Chart 3 Singapore's RULC in Manufacturing Against the Other NIEs

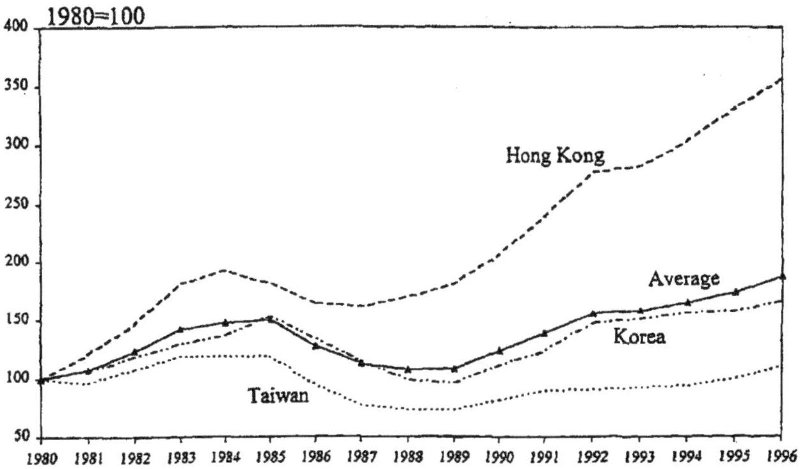

Chart 4 Singapore's RULC in Manufacturing Against Malaysia and Thailand

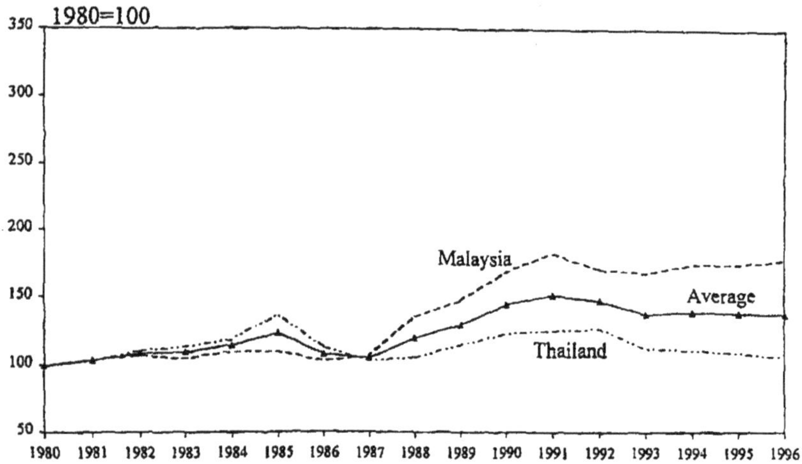

6. Existing Competitive Strengths and Weaknesses in Singapore

The key strengths in Singapore are well known. As indicated in the IMD and WEF reports, for the government sector, key assets are the lack of government subsidies, competence of personnel in the public sector, the clarity and transparency of government regulations, the lack of sectional interest group influences on government policies, low tax rates, an effective tax system, strong budgetary position as well as efficiency in government spending. For the infrastructure sector, key strengths are in air transport, port facilities, road infrastructure, government investment in infrastructure, advantage of geography, telecommunications facilities as well as infrastructure financing. For institutions, it includes the effectiveness of anti-corruption regulations, continuity of legal and political institutions, effectiveness of police protection, and effective enforcement of contracts. In addition, a consistent policy of openness in terms of minimal tariff and non-tariff barriers, as well as emphasis on exports and foreign direct investment has been a crucial competitive strength. In the labour market, flexibility in labour regulations, hiring

Chart 5 Rate of Return of US investments in NIEs: Non-oil Manufacturing

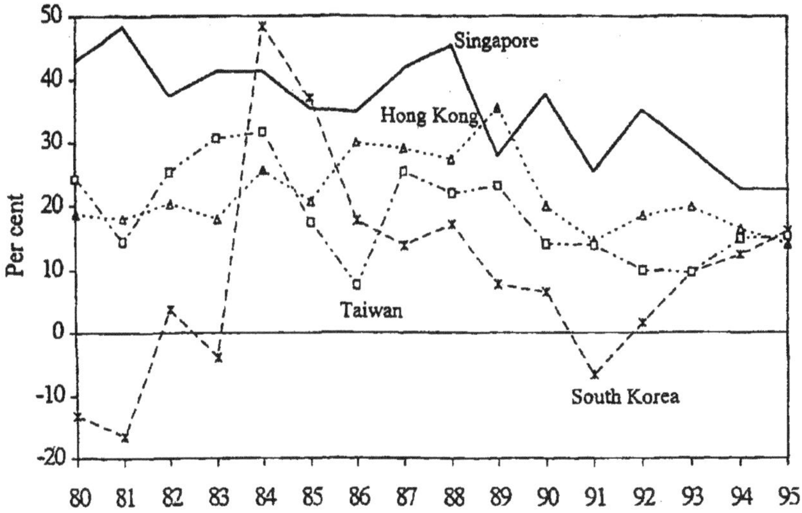

Rate of Return of US investments in Singapore, Malaysia & Thailand: Non-oil Manufacturing

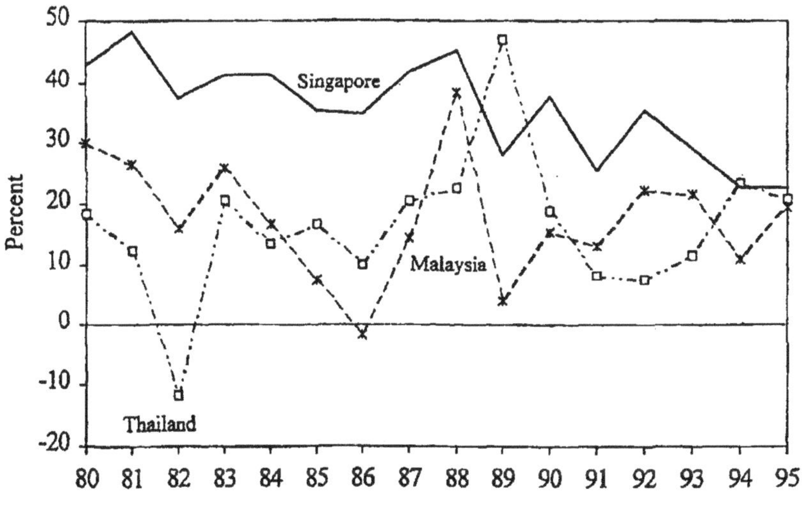

Chart 6 Rate of Return of US investments in NIEs: Services

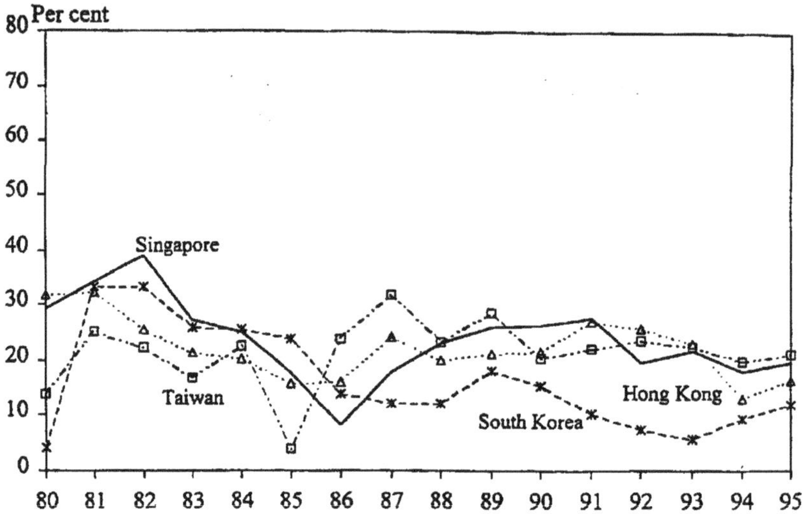

Rate of Return of US investments in Singapore, Malaysia & Thailand: Services

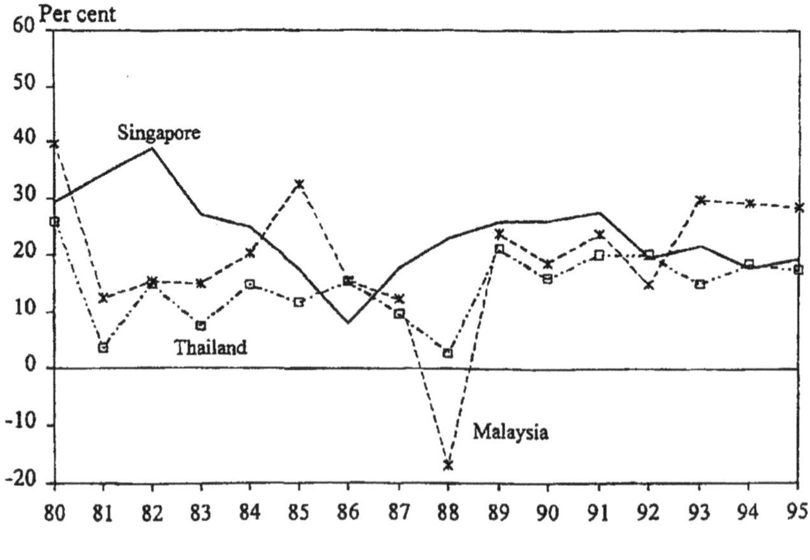

and firing practices, a limited social welfare system, and good labour management relations have been critical in enhancing international competitiveness.

Based on the WEF and IMD reports, it is clear that a key existing weakness in the Singapore economy is the lack of availability of skilled manpower such as qualified engineers, competent senior managers and consequently, their relatively high remuneration. In addition, the weak skill and educational profile is indicated in the relatively high illiteracy rate (8.9%) as well as low secondary enrollment (70%). The other key weakness is in the area of science and technology, with low expenditure on R&D as a share of GDP, low number of patents granted and low domestically established brand names. Reflecting the problem of land constraint, the high cost of living as well as high rentals for apartment and office space are also cited as key competitive weaknesses.

It is clear from Table 6 that the key competitive strength of Singapore against the regional countries derived directly or indirectly from the quality of the people. In particular, the strong international competitiveness index of Singapore is largely contributed by the people related factors like management, people, science and technology, and government. It is noteworthy that there is a wide gap between Singapore and Thailand, Indonesia, a gap that has actually widened over the past five years. Malaysia, however, has been catching up on Singapore, particularly on factors like government, domestic economy and internationalisation. Malaysia, however, is still weak in management, science and technology, infrastructure and people.

7. The Role of Government in Sustaining Competitiveness

We believe that government policy is highly influential in shaping competitiveness. While regulation, publicly sponsored R&D, trade policies, worker training, and education are all relevant, the government's ability to leverage the resources to provide infrastructure and creating a pro-business environment for enterprises as a crucial element to engender competitiveness. In conjunction with declining rates of domestic savings, the public

Table 6 Ranking By IMD (1997)

	Singapore	Malaysia	Thailand	Indonesia	Hong Kong
Domestic Economy	3	2	12	11	9
Internationalisation	2	17	25	35	3
Government	1	4	18	27	2
Finance	6	19	29	39	12
Infrastructure	11	27	42	39	19
Management	1	17	31	41	2
Science & Technology	8	25	32	41	18
People	5	33	37	44	13

Source: The World Competitiveness Yearbook (1997), IMD

sector dissaving (e.g., budget deficits) prevalent in the industrial world, limits the capital that can be converted into growth- and competitiveness-enhancing investments.

The Growth Experience of East Asian Economies

The traditional dominant explanation for the enormous success of the East Asian capitalist economies has been to ascribe it to the efficient resource allocation effect of the free market, economic openness, the provision of a stable macroeconomic environment and a reliable legal framework, "getting the prices right" and the limited role of the government. Adherents of this neo-classical view included Chen (1979), Patrick (1977), Friedman (1980) and Fei (1983). Over the past decade or so, however, a new stream of literature has increasingly emphasised the directive and developmental role of the state in the economic success of East Asia. This revisionist view emphasised the significance of the government-business relationship, resulting in the government not merely being a referee and setting the broad rules of the game, but often acting as a major participant with determining influence on business decisions through direct manipulation of incentives and disincentives in promoting industrial development (Mason 1980, Johnson 1981 and 1982).

These literature emphasised that international competitive advantage in specific products and industries could be deliberately and purposefully created and nurtured in the relentless process of skill, technology and product upgrading in the course of economic development. While from a short run and static perspective, these intervention policies in the factor and product markets appeared to conflict with the operation of the free market and economic rationalism, interventions that nurture industries of rapid technological progress, rising labour productivity and high income elasticity of demand, could be dynamically efficient from a long term perspective (Johnson 1982, White 1988). This view also emphasised the significance of the numerous formal and informal institutions and channels for consultation and coordination between the elite economic bureaucracy and the private sector in the process of policy formulation, implementation and modification.

These interventions using fiscal incentives, socialising of risk and direct credit control mechanism, could result in a very high level of productive investment in specific key industries, far higher than would have occurred in the free market situation (Amsden 1989). Efficiency was maintained, either in ruthless competition among protected domestic firms or eventual exposure to international competition for the industries. The supporting institutional and organisational arrangements in making such interventionist structure possible were a soft authoritarianism and corporatist political structure which allowed for market guidance (Johnson 1982, Wade 1991).

In the report on "East Asian Miracles", the World Bank (1993) noted that since 1960, the eight high performing Asian economies (HPAE) (Japan, Hong Kong, Korea, Taiwan, Singapore, Malaysia, Indonesia and Thailand) have grown at about 5.5% in per capita terms, more than twice as fast as the rest of East Asia (2.4%), roughly three times as fast as Latin America (1.8%) and South Asia (1.9%), and five times faster than Sub-Sahara Africa. The report noted that the HPAEs maintained important fundamental policies like macroeconomic stability, the principle of shared growth, high savings rate and heavy investments in human capital, stable and secure financial system, limited price distortion as well as openness to foreign technology. In addition, they also actively promoted selective interventions like mild financial repression as keeping real interest rates positive but low, directed credit, selective industrial promotion and export promoting trade policies.

These interventionist policies were deemed necessary largely because they helped to address the critical problem of a class of market failures i.e. coordination failures, particularly in the early stage of development. The complementary key ingredient to ensure success, however, was that the government distributed rewards, often in the form of privileged access to credit or foreign exchange, on the basis of competitive performance rather than encouraged rent seeking activities. Thus selective interventions were disciplined by competition via either markets or contests. In addition, the existence of a high quality civil service that was insulated from political interference and had the capacity to impartially monitor performance has been crucial to such selective intervention and to ensure contest-based competition.

On the other hand, various economists, including Paul Krugman (1994b), Alwyn Young (1993, 1995), as well as Kim and Lau (1994, 1996) have used growth theory and accounting to show that growth in East Asia could be largely attributed to sheer increase in the inputs of labour and capital and very little to total factor productivity or more productive use of these inputs. Recent evaluations of the empirical evidence, however, have indicated that Young's number was subject to large measurement errors. Studies by the Union Bank of Switzerland (1996), and the International Monetary Fund (Sarel, 1996), have shown stronger total factor productivity gains, amounting to around 2–2.5% between 1978 and 1996, compared with a weaker 0.3% for the US. However, despite the controversy over measurement errors, it is clear that total factor productivity for East Asian countries, have not been strong in their early stage of industrial takeoff,[2] indicating certain fundamental

[2] Incidentally, this is not too different from the early stage of industrial development of the US and Japan. For example Abramovitz and David (1973) have shown that TFP growth for the US between 1853–1907 has been around 0.5%. Similarly, Hayami and Ogasawara (1996) have shown that real growth for Japan between the Meiji Restoration and World War I could be largely attributed to physical capital accumulation.

weaknesses in the structure of firms, lack of technology and brand names, weak R&D as well as product and process development capability, non-competitive product and factor markets, weak and poorly regulated banking and financial sector as well as the high cost burden of an economy based on patronage and cronyism.[3]

Endogenous Growth Theory

The significance of government policies, human capital development, endogenous technological change in affecting national competitiveness and long run growth rate has received increasing support from the theoretical and empirical literature in endogenous growth theory. The conventional neo-classical growth model was developed by Solow (1956) and Swan (1956). It is built upon an aggregate, constant-returns-to-scale production function that combines labour and capital (with diminishing marginal returns) in the production of a composite good. Savings are assumed to be a fixed fraction of output, and technology improves at an exogenous rate. There are three key results of the neo-classical growth model. Firstly, the growth rate of the output in steady state is exogenously determined by the sum of rate of population growth and the rate of technological progress. Secondly, the steady state rate of growth of output is independent of the saving rate, though raising the saving rate does not increase the steady state level of income. Finally, the model implies that countries with similar production technologies as well as comparable saving and population growth rates should converge to similar steady state levels of per capita income.

In the neo-classical growth model reviewed above, capital exhibits diminishing marginal returns in the production process. This feature of the model prevents it from providing an explanation for the wide variations across countries in either per capita income or growth rates, and for the fact that poor countries do not seem to grow faster than rich ones. In addition, output growth is independent of the saving rate and is determined only by demographic factors (the rate of population growth) and the rate of technological progress. But since population growth and technological change are assumed

[3] The recent currency crisis showed up some of these weaknesses.

exogenous, the model does not explain the mechanisms that generate steady state growth, and therefore does not allow an evaluation of the mechanisms through which government policies can potentially influence the growth process. The new growth literature addresses these limitations of the neo-classical model by making the rates of technological change and/or population growth endogenous, thereby proposing a variety of channels through which steady state growth arises endogenously[4]. The proponents of endogenous growth theory are driven by the view that government policy and economic behaviour more generally must be able to affect the growth rate in the long run, and thus seek theories that will permit that to happen.

Endogenous growth models typically exhibit increasing returns to scale in contrast to the constant returns to scale assumed in the neo-classical growth theory. The phenomenon of increasing returns to scale can be easily perceived with reference to the models with endogenous technological change. In the traditional theory, a proportionate increase in labour and capital will simply lead to a proportionate increase in output. In the new formulation, the increases in capital and labour will, in addition, advance the economy wide technology, which in turn leads to an additional rise in output beyond the proportionate increase.

It follows that with endogenous technological change and therefore increasing returns to scale, policies that affect saving rate and rate of capital formation will affect the long run equilibrium growth rate. Since many government policies have potential effects on these variables, what the government does now matters for long run growth rate.

Consequently, policy options that a country can adopt to increase growth rate include:

1. Increase in investment by reducing budget deficits to crowd in private investment and by providing tax incentives.
2. Reduce unnecessary regulation;
3. Encourage investment in human capital;
4. Increase infrastructure investment;
5. Provide tax incentives for research and development spending.

---

[4] Well known models in the literature include Romer (1986), Lucas (1988), Rebelo (1991), among many others.

The economic success of Singapore in the past three decades demonstrated both the power of the neo-classical view and the importance of the revisionist perspective as well as the insights from endogenous growth theory to complement the explanation on high growth. As the neo-classical view correctly pointed out, Singapore's growth was characterised by high savings rate (34–45% of GDP since the early 1980s), heavy investment in human capital, fiscal and monetary prudence leading to macroeconomics stability, minimal price distortion, stable and secure financial systems and extreme openness to international trade, investment and technology transfer. In addition, as the revisionist stressed, the story of Singapore also demonstrated the necessity and capacity of a country with no natural resources to create national competitive advantage through selective industrial promotion and infrastructural development and continuously renew it in a relentless process of upgrading of industrial structure and living standard.

State as a Factor Creator

The traditional justification of public sector involvement is that of externalities and other forms of market failures. To the extent that much basic research, manpower training, infrastructural support for national competitive advantage and technology diffusion have public goods characteristics, they create significant positive externalities that cannot be easily appropriated by the investing parties. Consequently, the private sector would tend to under-invest compared to what is deemed socially desirable. Another usual justification for public sector intervention is the failure of capital market in allocating finance and pooling risks for major R&D projects involving high fixed costs, long time horizon and great uncertainty. On the other hand, public sector involvement may also be socially inefficient due to agency problem, rent seeking by special interest groups, and other sources of government failures.

In the context of Singapore, the government has involved itself as a key player in the economy largely on the justification of weak institutional structure in the early stage of development, co-ordination failures, positive externalities and perceived pervasive market failures in a small open economy. It assumes the function of factor creator, such as human resource development, investment in research and development and internationally competitive infrastructure in national hardware and software. The approach adopted by the government is often strategic and proactive, not ad hoc and reactive. The lead time needed in factor creation is frequently taken into account, so institution building often occurs with a view to the future.

This creation of national competitive advantage is more crucial for Singapore as it has very little natural factor endowments besides its human resources and geographic location. As such, foreign and domestic investments will only stay in Singapore if it is able to offset its natural resource disadvantage with a man-made advantage: superior national infrastructures. In the early stage of development, Singapore's geographic location gave it a natural base to build sea and air transport facilities that served to establish its competitive position as a regional hub for physical production and transport (manufacturing, entrepot trades and distribution). The recent development of information and telecommunications infrastructure is a logical next step to further strengthen Singapore's role as a regional hub for information production and communication (financial and business services, regional headquarters operations, R&D, design, regional marketing, training and technical support services, etc.).

Government and Technology Policy

There is no doubt that the state will continue to play a central role in shaping the composition and prospects of industries in the economy. There are several key policy areas that cannot be safely neglected by governments intent on creating the conditions for exploiting new technological opportunities[5]. These include policies to: strengthen indigenous technology development and absorption capabilities; develop the human resource base needed for industrial development and upgrading; provide environment in which flexible adjustment of production structures in the face of changing demand conditions is possible; and facilitate access to information about, and the acquisition of, new technologies by domestic firms.

[5] See Chapter 2 for further discussion on technological policies and competitiveness.

Driven by the need to establish and strengthen their presence on international markets in an increasingly competitive and protectionist climate, to secure access to technological innovations, and to share the very high cost of R&D and production, firms are seeking ways to supplement traditional linkages of outsourcing. These new avenues include mergers, joint ventures through equity participation, non-equity collaborative arrangements and other forms of strategic alliance. The state through its various affiliated corporations and government linked companies may have to take an active part in such activities.

R&D resources are still quite scarce, especially in terms of highly qualified scientists and technologists, so importation and pooling of resources may be desirable, assuming they are employed effectively and managed properly. Great care needs to be given to human resource planning so as potential skill bottlenecks can be anticipated and the educational and training programmes can be adjusted accordingly. Forging closer links between industries and universities will also have beneficial effects. In the first place, it makes more effective use of the expertise within the universities to strengthen industrial technological capabilities. In addition, it reduces the risk that growth of industrial R&D will siphon off valuable intellectual resources from the universities.

Promoting Trade in Services

In recent years there has been a distinct trend towards greater externalisation of previously in-house services. Explanation of this phenomenon emphasises three principal factors: the rise in disposal income, policy reform, and technological advancement. As economies become richer, individuals and firms can afford to purchase more products and services. Demand saturation can occur more frequently with respect to goods (especially durable ones) rather than with respect to services. Demand for services are in general more income elastic. A prime example is the growth of insurance services. The growth of demand enables providers to reap economies of scale and supply more services at lower prices.

Changes in prevailing policies and regulations may induce and enhance externalisation. Trade liberalisation promotes specialisation across countries and economies of scale at an international level (e.g. the establishment of global financial market in the 1980s). Second, trade liberalisation and deregulation increase competition nationally and internationally (as happened with air transportation in the US and telecommunication in UK). Third, liberalisation by other countries facilitates access to more foreign markets. Entry into new markets, however, normally requires prior gathering of market information, establishment of links with distributors, etc. Therefore, expansion of merchandise trade also provides a positive stimulus to trade related services such as shipping, merchandise insurance and distribution. Technological innovations raise productivity and improve the quality and quantity of output.

Services benefit from and contribute to economic growth and technological progress. Since services cannot exist independently, they reflect their providers' skills, experience and technical knowledge. Advancement in services is ultimately the result of growth in human capital. It is for this reason that education and training are vital for the growth of services. Services "naturally" expand as more people attain higher levels of education.

Singapore has recognised the importance and benefit of a liberal trading regime for services. In recent years, Singapore, together with other countries, has made significant effort to extend international trading rules supervised and enforced by the World Trade Organisation (WTO) to cover trade in services. As a global city, transaction in services will be a major income earner for the economy. Brokerage of all kinds of transactions, financial, goods, investment banking, advertising, accountancy, architectural and engineering services, data processing and access to databases, management and economic consulting, is becoming increasingly internationalised.

Plugging into the Global Information Infrastructure

The information technology revolution has profound and wide-ranging impact on almost all aspect of socioeconomic transactions in the world. Over the years, one can observe the explosion of communication breaking both physical and cultural barriers that have existed before. In particular, the urge to communicate has led to the development of a Global Information Infrastructure (GII) which feature the Internet and many customised networks and information highways linking all parts of the world.

The growth of new interactive and network based multimedia services such as that provided on the Internet — and particularly via its World Wide Web or (WWW) component — raised the question of the extent to which new technologies create grounds for employment and economic growth, and on what basis this ground can be developed by companies and nurtured by governments. There is an often expressed fear about the rapid pace of new service development, and the manner in which these developments increase competitive pressures on the older industries and raise productivity without creating widespread employment. Research[6] indicates that the survival of existing industries, and the development of new growth industries, depends upon organisational capabilities in the face of dramatic globalisation of competitive forces which is already occurring but which the GII further stimulates. In this regard the *best policy practices by governments are those which support highly adaptable and vigorous "clusters" of a range of inputs (venture capital, skilled personnel, social and physical infrastructure) rather than those narrowly focused on government subsidies, ownership or protectionism.* The government can support this process by assuming a leading role in the organisational change and learning to ensure that structural barriers to job creation are minimised and growth optimised. Information and computer technology has a pervasive impact on demand for labour and operations by firms. Within this context, governments have to redirect their policies, adopting a new overall approach which is known as promotion of learning (Tarabusi, 1997). This consists of meshing elements of a number of different policy areas, including education and learning policies, labour market policies, technological policies, industrial policies, macroeconomic policies and monetary policies.

Wherever possible the market mechanism should be allowed to play the primary role. The principle of competitive neutrality insists on the need to apply the principle of technological and regulatory neutrality — at least as a strategic longer run objective.

[6] See for example OECD, 1996 *Technology, Productivity and Job Creation.*

Government Needs to be Competitive

If we accept that the state has an important role to play in the economy, then the action of the state should be no less efficient and competitive than any other sector in the economy. Developed countries and the NIEs recognised that competitiveness in the marketplace is becoming increasingly dependent on the competitiveness of governments, i.e. the latter's ability to offer an attractive business setting which involves not only a stable sociopolitical and macroeconomic environment, but also the effective provision of public services and public infrastructure at a reasonable cost to business, as well as good research and educational facilities. The changing dynamics of technology and global competition are forcing enterprises and governments to seek alternative strategies and policy instruments that will enable them to respond more effectively.

In the more traditional view, industry, banks and government link up with specific sectors in mind, and set the parameters (quality, price, etc.) which they believe will enable the sector(s) in question to perform well on world markets. Domestic firms are encouraged to compete among themselves, in some cases sheltered from foreign competition. However, industrial targeting can also be seen as a complex set of interactions in which industrial conglomerates, in collaboration with the government, function as insurance policies. The key factor is not so much that this partnership is better able to forecast market and technology trends accurately. Rather, it is that if a mistake is made, then the loser is forced to withdraw and the costs are spread, which encourage risk taking in a longer term perspective. This contrasted with the view that it is a fallacy to focus too strongly on the specific nature of the cooperation between corporations and the government. Instead, the focus should be on the broader context of competing socioeconomic systems. One needs a highly effective combination of macro- and microeconomic policies with emphasis on the strategic outlook.

8. Conclusion

In justifying government intervention in fostering economic development, a key rationale is the pervasive existence of imperfect market and incomplete information, leading to pervasive market failure. As noted by Stiglitz (1989), while traditional literature characterised market failures as exceptions to the general rule that decentralised markets lead to efficient allocation, in the new view, the presumption is reversed. It is only under exceptional circumstances that markets are efficient. This makes the analysis of the appropriate role of government far more difficult as the issues become one not of identifying market failures but of identifying large market failures where there is scope for significant welfare-enhancing government interventions.

In the case of Singapore, the unique feature of smallness and compact size could have made government intervention more effective and manageable, leading to less government failure. In addition, being small, the law of large numbers does not apply as readily and hence it can be argued that pervasive market failure for competitive factor and product markets call for a more interventionist approach.

It is, however, significant to note that the emphasis on government intervention in Singapore is largely geared towards production rather than consumption or redistribution. Instead of intervening or deploying resources to create a welfare state, the emphasis of intervention was in actively creating national competitive advantages through physical infrastructural investments, national information infrastructure, R&D subsidy, manpower development to strengthen long term productive capability.

Government interventions in the factor market have been more controversial and have not produced the expected success. For example, intervention in the labour market has proved to be counter productive. In addition, some of the interventions in the capital market, like the central provident fund forced savings scheme that led to a savings and investment rate of above 40% of GDP, has resulted in weak capital productivity and poor total factor productivity performance (Young 1993, Toh & Low, 1992).

It is noteworthy that the public sector in Singapore is strong, non-corrupt and run in a much more commercial manner compared to that of most other countries. Civil servants have a market oriented evaluation and reward system, with bonus and performance system built in. In addition, the public sector as a whole has its annual bonus tied to the overall performance of the economy. With the public sector's bottom line tied directly to fostering economic growth, the incentive system has been able to galvanise the public sector in servicing private sector interest in growth and development. In addition, the market based system has also significantly injected market rationality into public sector intervention, helping to avoid large and wasteful public sector projects, as well as vast rent seeking activities. Hence, interventions tend to be more market facilitating, correcting and enhancing rather than distorting. In addition, Singapore has the advantage of a small open economy constantly under the check of international competitive forces so that policies or interventions that are too market distorting would be fairly rapidly overwhelmed by international competitive forces.

Competition itself is undergoing far reaching changes. Whereas in the past it was predominantly price driven, it has now become technology driven. Moreover, competition is perceived as increasingly imperfect, as being conducted between giant oligopolists at the one extreme and regional low cost competitors at the other, against a background of multiplying joint ventures, liaisons, cross licensing and other forms of inter-corporate cooperation. Much as a result of this trend, competition in key economic sectors such as automobiles, semiconductors, and consumer electronics appears to be moving increasingly towards worldwide market sharing arrangements.

The cultural element that facilitates government intervention and leadership in East Asia is the greater emphasis on the interest of the group, community or state over that of the individual. Under this cultural milieu, it is considerably easier for the government to harness resources and mobilise the private sector to pursue major development goals, more so when the process of recruitment of the public sector allows it to capture a large share of the best and dedicated minds in the country.

It is not clear, however, whether some of the success in government intervention in Singapore and the other NIEs are merely a function of their stage of development. As a follower in the process of economic catching up, it is not as difficult to identify the priority in industry, infrastructure investment, R&D expenditure, manpower development etc. However, as the case of Japan shows, when these countries gradually reach the technological frontier and are also in the process of pushing forward the frontier, the same policy success of government intervention could no longer be replicated. The art of economic steermanship has yet to be perfected by any government.

References

Abramovitz, M. and David, P.A. (1973) "Reinterpreting Economic Growth: Parables and Realities", *American Economic Review*, Vol. 63, pp. 428–439.

Abowd, J., Kramarz, F., Lemieux, T. and Mangolis, D. (1997) "Minimum Wages and Youth Unemployment in France and the United States", *NBER Working Paper 6111.*

Amsden, A. (1989) *Asia's Next Giant: South Korea and Late Industrialisation*, Oxford: Oxford University Press.

Barro, Robert (1991) "Economic Growth in a Cross Section of Countries", *Quarterly Journal of Economics*, Vol. 106, pp. 407–44.

Barro, Robert and Xavier, Sala-I-Martin (1995) *Economic Growth*, New York: McGraw Hill.

Brotchie, J., Batty M., Blakely, E., Hall, P. and Newton, P. (1995) eds. *Cities in Competition*, Melbourne: Longman Australia.

Carr, C. (1990) *Britain's Competitiveness*, London: Routledge.

Chen, E.K.Y. (1979) *Hyper-Growth in Asian Economies: A Comparative Study of Hong Kong, Japan, Korea, Singapore and Taiwan*, London: Macmillan.

Coe, D. and Snower, D. (1997) "Policy Complementaries: The Case for Fundamental Labour Market Reform", *IMF Staff Paper*, Vol. 44, No. 1.

Coe, D., Helpman, E. and Hoffmaister, A. (1995) "North-South R & D Spillovers", *NBER Working Paper 5048.*

Dollar, David (1992) "Outward Oriented Economies Really do Grow More Rapidly: Evidence from 95 LDCs, 1976–1985", *Economic Development and Cultural Change*, Vol. 40, pp. 523–44.

Fei, J.C.H. (1983) "Evolution of Growth Policies of NICs in a Historical and Typological Perspective", paper presented during *Conference on Patterns of Growth and Structural Change in Asia's Newly Industrialising Countries (NICs) and Near-NICs in the Context of Economic Interdependence*, East-West Center, 1983.

Frankel, J.A. and Romer, D. (1996) "Trade and Growth: An Empirical Investigation", *NBER Working Paper 5476.*

Friedman, M. and Friedman, R. (1980) *Free to Choose: A Personal Statement*, New York: Harcourt Brace Jovanovich.

Hayami, Y. and Ogasawara, J. (1996) *Changes in the Sources of Modern Economic Growth: Asian NIEs in Japan's Historical Perspective*, paper presented at the Department of Economics, Stanford University, March (mimeographed).

Johnson, C. (1981) "Introduction: The Taiwan Model", in J. Hsiung *et al.* (eds) *Contemporary Republic of China: The Taiwan Experience*, New York: Praeger and the American Association for Chinese Studies.

Johnson, C. (1982) *MITI and the Japanese Miracle: The Growth of Industrial Policy 1925–1975*, Stanford, CA: Stanford University Press.

Kim, J.I. and Lau, L.J. (1994) "The Sources of Economic Growth in the East Asian Newly Industrialised Countries", *Journal of the Japanese and International Economies*, Vol. 8, pp. 235–27.

Kim, J.I. and Lau, L.J. (1996) "The Sources of Asian Pacific Economic Growth", *Canadian Journal of Economics*, Vol. 29, Special Issue, pp. S448–S454.

King, R. and Levine, R. (1993) "Finance and Growth: Schumpeter Might be Right", *Quarterly Journal of Economics*, Vol. 108, pp. 717–38.

Knack, S. and Keefer, P. (1995) *Institutions and Economic Performance: Empirical Tests Using Alternative Measures of Institutions*, Association of Economics and Politics, New York.

Krugman, P. (1994a) "Competitiveness: A Dangerous Obsession", *Foreign Affairs*, March/April, pp. 28–44.

Krugman, P. (1994b) "The Myth of the Asian Miracle", *Foreign Affairs*, Vol.73, No. 6.

Lee, James (1993) "Information Technology and International Competitiveness in Consulting and Engineering Design Services: Perception of Firms from the United States", in *Information Technology and International Competitiveness: The case of construction services*, published by United Nations, New York.

Lucas, R.E. (1988) "On the Mechanics of Economic Development", *Journal of Monetary Economics*, Vol. 22, pp. 3–32.

Mankiw, G., Romer, D. and Weil D. (1992), "A Contribution to the Empirics of Economic Growth", *Quarterly Journal of Economics*, Vol. 107, pp. 407–437.

Mason, E. *et al.* (1980) *The Economic and Social Modernisation of the Republic of Korea*, Harvard University Press.

Munnell, Alicia H. (1992) "Infrastructural Investment and Economic Growth", *Journal of Economic Perspective*, Vol. 6, No. 4, pp.189–198.

OECD (1996) *Technology, Productivity and Job Creation*, Paris.

Patrick, H. (1977) "The Future of the Japanese Economy: Output and Labour Productivity", *Journal of Japanese Studies*.

Porter, M. (1980) *Competitive Strategy: Techniques for Analysing Industries and Competitors*, New York: The Free Press.

Porter, M. (1990) *The Competitive Advantage of Nations*, New York: The Free Press.

Rebelo, S. (1991) "Long Run Policy Analysis and Long Run Growth", *Journal of Political Economy*, Vol. 99, pp. 500–521.

Romer, P.M. (1986) "Increasing Returns and Long-Run Growth," *Journal of Political Economy,* Vol. 94, pp. 1002–1037.
Sachs, Jeffrey and Andrew M. Warner (1995) *Economic Reform and the Process of Global Integration,* Brookings Papers on Economic Activity.
Sarel, M. (1996) *Growth and Productivities in ASEAN Economics,* International Monetary Fund (IMF) Economic Issues, No. 1.
Sassen, S. (1995) "Urban Impacts of Economic Globalisation", in Brotchie J. et. al. (eds) *Cities in Competition,* Melbourne: Longman Australia.
Solow, R.M. (1956), "A Contribution to the Theory of Economic Growth", *Quarterly Journal of Economics,* Vol. 70, pp. 65–94.
Stiglitz, J. *et al.* (1989) *The Economic Role of the State,* Oxford: Basil Blackwell.
Swan, T.W. (1956) "Economic Growth and Capital Accumulation", *Economic Record,* Vol. 36, pp. 51–66.
Tarabusi, C.C. (1997) "Technology and Employment: The Role of Organisational Change and Learning", OECD, *Science Technology Industry Review,* No. 20, pp. 89–119.
Toh, M.H. and Low, L. (1992) *Total Factor Productivity in Singapore: Some Myths and Issues,* Mimeo.
The World Competitiveness Yearbook 1997, International Institute for Management Development (IMD), Lausanne, Switzerland.
The Global Competitiveness Report, (1997) World Economic Forum (WEF), Geneva, Switzerland.
Union Bank of Switzerland (1996) "The Asian Economic Miracle", *UBS International Finance Issue* No. 29, Autumn issue.
United Nations (1993) *Information Technology and International Competitiveness: The Case of the Construction Services Industry,* United Nations Conference on Trade and Development (UNCTAD), New York.
Wade, R. (1991) *Governing the Market — Economic Theory and the Role of Government in East Asian Industrialisation,* Princeton: Princeton University Press.
White, G. (1988) *Developmental States in East Asia,* London: Macmillan.
World Bank (1993) *The East Asian Miracles: Economic Growth and Public Policy,* Oxford: Oxford University Press.
Young, A. (1993) "A Tale of Two Cities: Factor Accumulation and Technical Change in Hong Kong and Singapore", *NBER Macroeconomics.*
Young, A. (1995) "The Tyranny of Numbers: Confronting the Statistical Realities of the East Asian Growth Experience", *Quarterly Journal of Economics,* Vol. 110, pp. 641–680.

2
Technological Policy and National Competitiveness

Lawrence Loh

1. Introduction

More than ever before, competitiveness has received intense attention and been extensively operationalised amongst policy makers and scholars. However, it is a controversial notion and has often provoked strong criticism as a non-tenable concept. Krugman (1994) has, in particular, touted competitiveness as a meaningless idea and a misleading underpinning for policy decisions at the national level. Nevertheless, competitiveness appears to be deeply entrenched over time as evidenced by the influential studies such as the Global Competitiveness Report of the World Economic Forum (WEF) and the World Competitiveness Yearbook of the International Institute for Management Development (IMD).

This paper discusses the role of technology policy for economic development within an overall perspective of national competitiveness. The technology policy development of Singapore is used as a case illustration. As this policy depends heavily on its co-evolution with national economic strategy, the paper traces the critical economic policy milestones that shaped the thinking underlying the substance of Singapore's technology strategy. An assessment is also made and several key issues are articulated for further consideration. This is based on a framework that covers technology inputs, throughputs and outputs. The paper then recommends that the technology policy intent may extend beyond economic upgrading as the core guiding philosophy, as well as cover the basic sciences. Further, a review of the current national institutional setup for science and technology policy may be necessary and timely to gear the country towards the future.

This paper is predicated on a view that technology is not competitive *per se*. Only using technology makes it competitive. In other words, a "means" perspective rather than an "ends" perspective is employed. In line with extant literature, the paper posits that economic competitiveness of a nation rests principally on how technology, amongst other factors, is being exploited. It also recognises the strong influences of an institutionalised context on the formulation and implementation of technology policies that are often path dependent. Along such a vein, it emphasises the pivotal role of mission oriented agencies and policy mechanisms in shaping the content and process of policies to attain desired outcomes.

The paper focuses on technology policy that conventionally covers areas within the strategic management of R&D and innovation. The scope of this paper does not include the various policy initiatives of Singapore in the specific arena of information technology (IT), such as the National IT Plan and the IT2000 vision.

2. Technology and Competitiveness in Perspective

Competitiveness Revisited

A widely accepted understanding of competitiveness is based on the definition provided by the influential US Competitiveness Policy Council. Accordingly, the term refers to the national economy's ability to produce goods and services that meet the test of international markets while citizens earn a standard of living that is both rising and sustainable over the long run. The OECD (1996a), in an examination of member countries' policies, characterised competitiveness initiatives as those supporting the ability of companies, industries, regions, nations or supra-national regions to generate, while being and remaining exposed to international competition, relatively high factor income and factor employment levels. The conceptualisation of competitiveness goes beyond a supply side efficiency perspective, where advantages accrue to attractiveness of input factors and output markets, towards a more contemporary view that systemic influences create advantages in an evolutionary yet conscious manner.

With a strong slant towards measurement feasibility, IMD (1997) articulated four forces of competitiveness: (1) proximity and globality; (2) attractiveness and aggressiveness; (3) assets and processes; (4) individual risk taking and social cohesiveness. Operationalising the model, eight factors of competitiveness were derived — domestic economy, internationalisation, government, finance, infrastructure, management, science and technology, and people.

Drawing on modern economic growth (see Barro and Sala-I-Martin, 1995), WEF (1996), in a parallel vein with the IMD project, adopted a measurement based framework to arrive at eight factors of competitiveness — openness, government, finance, infrastructure, technology, management, labour and civil institutions. This is rooted in an argument that competitiveness is a manifestation of a set of unique characteristics of an economy that drive economic growth, besides the initial income level.

Despite the popularity of competitiveness thinking and studies, the often cited Krugman's (1994) criticism of the concept of national competitiveness appeared to have created a worldwide stir. However, countries appear to be taking competitiveness policies even more seriously. Far from being a dangerous obsession, the pursuit of competitiveness is a healthy prerequisite for a prosperous nation. Krugman's sweeping thesis has been attacked as an attempt to "throw the baby out with the bath water" (Clark and Lam, 1995). In fact, competitiveness is argued to be meaningful at even the national level. It is not a mere single holistic index of the economy but a complex aggregate of widely varying indicators that are easily constructed and measured at the firm and the industry levels.

Competitiveness is often understood in terms of a narrower notion, comparative advantage. To this end, it is commonly accepted that such advantage no longer accrues simply because of low labour costs and natural resources, but derives significantly from knowledge intensive value added technology that creates new products and services (Simon, 1993). In other words, the entire notion of comparative advantage within the framework of pure neo-classical economics has expanded to encompass a broader spectrum of considerations that now belong to an omnibus concept of competitiveness. Although relative factor costs do make nations competitive, they alone do not constitute the full picture. The very process of converting these inputs into outputs that create value for consumers seems to be more critical and it is technology that constitutes the underpinning for this process.

Context of Technology Policy Thinking

The interest in technology as a core component of national competitiveness policies has perhaps been a consequence of several structural developments in the global business environment over the past decade or so. A worldwide consumerism movement has resulted in a convergence of demand preferences. This has allowed for a fresh perspective in the way nations have approached the world market. The globalised marketplace is a crucial enabler for the realisation of scale economies, which in turn leads to an increasingly transnational production environment. The natural outcome is a resultant shift in locations of corporate R&D functions, where technology development is fast becoming context free and place invariant.

R&D have traversed from being rooted solely in a few advanced Western countries, particularly the United States, to a prevalent spread across the globe. There is, in fact, a rapid dispersion of technology related activities, especially to East Asia. The locus of technology trade also appears to be progressing in favour of some newly industrialised economies (NIEs), along with the creation of a new growth region within Asia itself. It has been argued that the origins of research into technology globalisation are mirrored by the broader process of globalisation itself (Howells, 1997). In the emergent technology axis within the Pacific basin, countries have been also moving away from a strict zero sum mode of competition to one in which there is a solid focus on complementary technology advancement. Once considered technocentric expansion of the source countries where benefits accrue only to the providers, R&D relocation has indeed been received gladly by recipient countries.

Technology policies have also been often juxtaposed into the invariably sensitive trade debate involving the US and East Asia, especially Japan. A new trade theory at the turn of the decade has cogently proposed that government can determine the structure and outcome of global competition and industry (see Zysman, Tyson, Dosi and Cohen, 1990). Indeed, it has been put forth that, in a path dependent way, technology evolves in nationally rooted trajectories. Policies shape these trajectories with the effect of either speeding or slowing them. Within the context of such thinking, technology policy has become a critical defining feature of national competitiveness, with profound implications not only for international economics but also for politics and diplomacy (Inman and Burton, 1990).

Technological Capability and National Competitiveness

As a broad term, competitiveness is elusive enough. It is unsurprising that a seeming subset of the omnibus concept — technological competitiveness — is an even more amorphous construct. This paper is based on a premise that technology cannot be competitive *per se*. Only using technology makes an economy competitive. In other words, in thinking about competitiveness, technology should not be put as an end by itself. It is a means to achieving a wider systemic competitiveness such as that at the firm, industry, sector or national levels. It is not the substantive content of technologies that requires focus but it is the underlying process of application that will have a direct bearing on performance (see Kotler, Jatusripitak, and Maesincee, 1997).

Technology is a core element of economic policies, whether it is considered as a raw input or as an intermediate facilitator (Haque, 1995). Also, technological competence and change have been viewed as key determinants of sustained economic growth. In the increasingly knowledge centred economy, the act and diffusion of innovation do make a big difference in the relative performance of nations. For instance, in Porter's (1990) model, technology surfaces as a crucial ingredient, especially in strengthening the factor conditions for national competitive advantage.

Before R&D can be translated into productive benefits, it must undergo a critical transformation process (Englander, Evanson and Hanazaki, 1994). There must be successful innovation that can lead to commercialisation and subsequent adoption. While pointing to an actual decline in R&D effectiveness, Englander *et al.* (1994) suggest that such a decline is industry specific and one has to differentiate between the industry using the new technology and the industry creating it. The policy implication is that nations have to utilise an industry differentiated approach to target technology effectiveness and more significantly, foster diffusion by also assisting in the exploitation and not just innovation.

In sum, the issue of technology policy and competitiveness is primarily a question of capability, which captures the ability to scan, assess, select, use, assimilate, adapt, improve and develop technology that is appropriate to changing circumstances (Dahlman, 1991). Technological capability is a more critical concept than technology in its own right. In fact, it is the use of tacit and codified knowledge that is central to the technological competitiveness issue rather than the hardware embodying the knowledge.

National Innovation Systems and Institutions

Adopting an institutionalist structuralist approach (March and Olsen, 1989), institutions are the primary policy drivers underlying the quest for competitiveness. As Clark and Lam (1995) aptly put it, nations compete with one another to provide the most effective set of institutional arrangements to facilitate certain desired outcomes and hinder undesired outcomes. In other words, nations do compete, but this competition is substantially conditioned by the overriding institutional context under which they are embedded.

The fostering of an institutional bedrock for the furtherance of technological capability is manifested in a country's national innovation systems (Nelson, 1993). Dahlman (1994) defines an innovation system to include policies towards foreign direct investments, arms length technology transfer, intellectual property rights and importation of capital goods. In particular, it consists of the network of public and private institutions and agents supporting or undertaking science and technology activities, including R&D, technology diffusion and creation of technical human capital. Accordingly, the system is influenced by the artifacts of institutional conception, namely the macro policy environment that emphasises specifically the incentive regime in place.

An institutional context for technology policy does not

necessarily entail only a local operating environment. In fact, precisely because of the institutional foundation for policy, the whole host of internationally oriented and often diplomatically motivated factors do exert significant influences. Englander and Gurney (1994) argue that countries can benefit to a large extent from foreign R&D through the purchase of patent rights, franchises and goods that embody technology. An enlarged institutional policy space therefore shapes a national technology strategy, beyond piecemeal economic considerations in pursuit of competitiveness.

3. The Evolution of Singapore's Technology Policy

Within the backdrop of emerging perspectives on technology policy and competitiveness as discussed earlier, particularly the roles exuded by systems and institutions, this section provides an overview of the evolution of technology policy thinking in Singapore as a case example. It will be readily observed that path dependencies of technology policy are deeply rooted within an overarching philosophy of economic growth as a key vehicle for national progress.

Early Policy Underpinnings

The need to exploit technology as a leverage for Singapore's economic development has been a long recognised paradigm guiding national competitiveness policy. Although the immediate emphasis in post-independent Singapore in the 1960s was on job creation and import substitution, the 1970s saw the nation adopting an aggressive path for automation. In moves to encourage an even heavier utilisation of technology, a wage restructuring strategy was pursued to reduce the dependence on labour and to raise the relative attractiveness of using technology as a factor input. Under a wage correction policy, salaries were increased by 20% annually across the board, to price labour at a closer level with market forces. At the same time, aggressive tax incentives were instituted to foster a more rapid substitution of capital for labour via mechanisation and computerisation.

Economic Policy Directions

A significant turning point in Singapore's economic development was during the recession of 1985 and 1986. For two decades before these years, the nation had enjoyed phenomenal growth despite the oil crises and global recessions. From 1980 to 1984 itself, the real GDP growth had averaged 8.5% per annum. In a significant departure from normal performance, the economy registered a negative growth of 1.7% in the real GDP of 1985.

To renew the progress and to restore the long term viability of the Singapore's economy, a high level Economic Committee was formed in April 1985 (see Ministry of Trade and Industry, 1986). As part of the review efforts, eight subcommittees and many working groups were convened. Inclusive of broad-based contributions from representatives in all sectors of Singapore, the report of the Committee put forth various policy recommendations that constituted a consensual view on how the economy could be propelled forward to address the challenges of the future.

Amongst various key policies for economic enhancement, the technology- and innovation-related aspects deserve a closer discussion. In the report, a high-tech policy was articulated to encourage a pervasive application of new advances in technology. In addition, suggestions were mooted for Singapore to attain competence in selected new technologies as well as to position high-tech industries as an area for growth.

The core guiding principle of Singapore's use of technology was laid out in no uncertain terms: "Our goal should be to achieve higher value-added content, not high technology *per se*" (Ministry of Trade and Industry, 1986: p 147). This principle has been a basis for policy thinking in national technology management ever since. Furthermore, a dual-dimensional approach was apparent. First, across a horizontal dimension, technology served as a bedrock for upgrading industries across the economy. Second, along a vertical dimension, new technology based industries were identified to be nurtured, including IT, biotechnology, microelectronics, robotics and artificial intelligence, lasers/optics and communications technology.

Running the Competitive Race

The pressing need for technology strengthening surfaced again as one theme in a national level synthesis of key aspirations known as "The Next Lap" drawn up by a Committee of Ministers of State formed in 1989. It laid out, in simple language, broad directions for the long term national development of the country. In the shared vision, amongst the various key messages, it was stated: "For the next phase, we will have to be more focused in what we do. This means specialising and becoming leaders in specific niches and doing more research and development" (Government of Singapore, 1991: p 69).

The First Formal Technology Plan

Technology policy in Singapore went through a critical watershed in 1991, with the formation of the National Science and Technology Board (NSTB). With a stated mission "to develop Singapore into a centre of excellence in selected fields of science and technology so as to enhance our national competitiveness in the industrial and service sectors", the linkage of technology to economic imperatives appeared to be continued.

Immediately after its inception, NSTB unveiled a first ever comprehensive National Technology Plan for Singapore (NSTB, 1991). The intent was to put Singapore closer to the NIEs and ultimately the advanced countries in terms of technology development. In tandem with the emerging phase of global competition that is increasingly innovation rooted, the plan would be a leap forward for Singapore to continue in its path of economic growth.

Supported by a S$2 billion fund to drive R&D in Singapore over a five-year period as well as a host of grants, assistance and fiscal incentives, the plan sought to attain three broad targets by 1995: (1) gross expenditure for R&D (GERD) to be at least 2% of GDP; (2) private sector to account for at least 50% of GERD; (3) number of research scientists and engineers (RSEs) to reach a minimum of 40 per 10,000 labour force.

NSTB, armed with a strong mission orientation, was to

spearhead and be accountable for the deliverables of the National Technology Plan. Its primary focus would be in the area of "industry driven" R&D, where the contribution towards economic upgrading and growth is clearer. Accordingly, the immediate thrust was on downstream research that is economically relevant. Niche areas of technology development were consciously highlighted and fostered. For instance, the plan stipulated focal areas of R&D in the following key technology programmes: IT; microelectronics; electronic systems; manufacturing technology; materials technology; energy, water, environment and resources; food and agrotechnology; biotechnology; and medical sciences.

Strategic Plan Towards a Developed Country

Further continuing and reinforcing the work accomplished by the Economic Committee in 1985, an Economic Planning Committee was formed in 1989. A Strategic Economic Plan was delivered in 1991 (Ministry of Trade and Industry, 1991). In the plan, a vision for Singapore transforming itself into a developed country in the first league was promulgated. Based on both optimistic and pessimistic scenarios, the Plan suggested steps to accomplish the vision that comprised the following facets: economic dynamism, high quality of life, strong national identity and global city. It pushed beyond the quantitatively oriented approach for economic progress into one that also considered a qualitatively based development path.

Amongst various strategic thrusts, one was to create a conducive climate for innovation. Innovation was, in fact, explicitly recognised as an underpinning that prevails in all aspects of the economy, covering all functions and sectors of Singapore. This was a somewhat broader perspective that views innovation as a foundation for other direct input factors of competitiveness.

Facing the Future Through a New Technology Plan

In 1996, a new technology plan was unveiled. Extending beyond mere technology, the initiative produced a National Science and Technology Plan (NSTB, 1996). Building on the foundation laid out in earlier efforts, the new plan envisioned that Singapore would build a world class science and technology base in selected fields that match the country's competitive strengths and that would spur the growth of new high value-added industries. The attainment of this vision would accordingly inject economic dynamism such that Singapore could be groomed into an advanced economy in the next century.

It was envisaged that the vision would require 10 to 15 years to be realised. On a more immediate basis, by 2000, the Plan called for the fostering of industry clusters where Singapore could realistically attain leadership or near leadership due to the existence of ongoing competitive and technological edge.

A three-tiered approach towards technology development was used. The first tier comprised R&D involving near term technologies, under which industry would be extensively involved. As the major focus of R&D in the next 10-15 years, this tier would engage some 70% of the total GERD made available through various government agencies. To deepen technological capabilities, the next two tiers of technology development would deal with medium and longer term technologies that are economically relevant. Under these tiers, core strengths in strategic areas of research would be fostered to support the next generation of products and services. The approach recognises that investment in science and technology should be in line with the stage of economic development.

The Plan highlighted four major challenges that continued to be critical for success of Singapore's technology development, namely: (1) meeting the demand for manpower through education of local RSEs and attraction of foreign RSEs; (2) making it conducive for industry to undertake R&D through government support and incentives; (3) strengthening technological capability through the forging of a strong technology infrastructure such as R&D institutions; and (4) fostering technology innovation and commercialisation through a favourable climate for entrepreneurship.

A national framework for technology planning and responsibility allocation was proposed, under which various government agencies were identified to assume key driving roles to spearhead R&D for industry clusters within and across the multinational corporations (MNCs), promising local enterprises (PLEs) and small and medium enterprises (SMEs). In terms of funding, a significant budget of S$4 billion was proposed for the second phase of R&D fund for 1996–2000; this was twice the amount in the first phase from 1991–1995. Under realistic GDP growth assumptions of 8% from 1996 to 2000 and 6% from 2001 to 2005, it was projected that the GERD/GDP ratio would reach 1.6% in 2000 and 2.0% in 2005.

4. Issues In Technology Policy For Singapore

It has been readily noted that Singapore has consciously and systematically crafted and fostered a comprehensive technology policy consistent with its broader economic and national objectives. In this section, an assessment of Singapore's technology policy is attempted. The issues and challenges are cast within a framework of technology policy along three dimensions as follows:

(1) *Input Dimension*: This deals with the development of technological capability in terms of human and capital resources;
(2) *Throughput Dimension*: This covers policy thinking and initiatives in relation to the diffusion and adoption of technology throughout the economy;
(3) *Output Dimension*: This considers the outcome and impact of technology policy on the economy and society.

In positioning technology policy *vis-à-vis* competitiveness, the entire process spectrum — input, throughput and output — has to be contemplated. Further, as competitiveness is a relative notion, where appropriate, individual country and aggregated grouping benchmarks should be used for contrast purposes. Although this comparison is by no means judgmental or prescriptive, a norm-based evaluation provides policy analysts with a reality check and descriptive sense of the state of affairs in competing nations.

Selected Issues in the Input Dimension

(a) *State of Technology Development in Singapore*

Table 1 shows the key statistics for technology inputs. Starting from a GERD of S$81 million in 1981, a level of S$1,792 million was achieved by 1996, which represented a 22-fold increase over 15 years. Further, the GERD/GDP ratio was 0.26% in 1981, whereas it was 1.35% in 1996. In terms of R&D human resources, there was a mere total of 1,193 RSEs in 1981. This increased to 10,153 in 1996, thus attaining a nearly nine-fold increase over the period. More significantly, the ratio of RSE per 10,000 of the labour force took off from 10.6 in 1981 to 56.3 in 1996. The R&D expenditure per RSE also surged impressively from S$67,900 in 1981 to S$176,530 in 1996.

Singapore's progress in technology development over the years has been somewhat impressive as far as inputs are concerned. As the country is still in the relatively early stage of technology buildup, the policy focus on input oriented goals is apt and logical. The results based on the key policy indicators have pointed to a commendable level of success that will place the nation ready for the next stage of technology development to attain maximum impact in the future.

(b) *Sectoral Distribution of R&D Human Capital*

Table 2 shows the spread of RSEs in 1993 according to the three major sectors: business enterprise (i.e. private sector), government (including public research institutes and centres) and higher education. Nearly half of the RSEs are in business enterprise sector compared to 79% for the US, 70% for Japan and an average of 65% for the entire OECD.

Likewise, in terms of research expenditure, the private sector of Singapore accounts for 62%, compared with 71% for the US as well as for Japan and 67% for OECD (see Table 3). The figures are somewhat closer to the benchmarks than in the earlier case of RSEs. It is apparent that while the business enterprises in Singapore employ relatively fewer RSEs, they account for a proportionately higher level of R&D spending.

The locus of R&D is an interesting and important policy concern. As Singapore matures into a developed economy with a more vibrant business sector, it may move the emphasis of R&D increasingly into the private sector, where the incentives for innovation are more efficiently aligned with performance and growth. In fact, over the years, this shift is already apparent and on

Table 1 Gross Expenditure on R&D and Research Scientists & Engineers

Year	GERD (S$m)	GDP (S$m)	GERD/GDP Ratio (%)	RSEs	Labour Force ('000)	RSE per 10,000 Labour Force	R&D Expenditure Per RSE (S$'000)
1981	81.00	31,004.70	0.26	1,193	1,128.0	10.6	67.90
1984	214.30	40,048.00	0.54	2,401	1,304.4	18.4	89.25
1987	374.70	43,415.00	0.86	3,361	1,329.3	25.3	111.48
1990	571.70	67,878.90	0.84	4,329	1,562.8	27.7	132.06
1991	756.80	75,320.90	1.00	5,218	1,554.3	33.6	145.04
1992	949.50	80,997.50	1.17	6,454	1,619.6	39.8	147.12
1993	998.20	94,258.70	1.06	6,629	1,635.7	40.5	150.58
1994	1,174.98	108,224.00	1.09	7,086	1,693.1	41.9	165.82
1995	1,366.55	120,628.80	1.13	8,340	1,748.2	47.7	163.85
1996	1,792.14	132,629.30	1.35	10,153	1,801.9	56.3	176.53

Source: Compiled from NSTB (1996)

track (see Figure 1). However, the danger may be a hollowing out of pure and strategic basic research, which is not usually engaged in by business enterprises, a pattern which is clearly evident in Figure 2.

(c) *Organisational Distribution of R&D Human Capital*

Singapore is an economy that is, right from its post-independent economic takeoff, characterised by a high involvement of foreign

Table 2 Research Scientists & Engineers by Sector of Employment for 1993

Country	Business Enterprise	Government	Higher Education
Singapore	*49.0*	*21.4*	*29.6*
Australia	26.9	17.9	54.1
Denmark	43.0	22.0	33.8
Finland	35.8	22.8	40.0
Greece	16.6	23.7	59.3
Iceland	25.1	40.4	31.7
Ireland	40.4	9.1	46.7
Italy	38.3	17.6	44.1
Japan	69.8	5.7	21.8
Netherlands	37.7	24.1	35.3
Norway	48.4	19.5	32.1
Portugal	6.3	14.0	67.6
Spain	27.8	18.4	53.2
Switzerland	50.6	3.4	45.9
Turkey	11.9	13.0	75.1
United Kingdom	61.4	10.0	22.9
United States	79.4	6.2	13.3
North America	76.7	6.5	15.7
Total OECD	65.3	9.6	24.7

Note: The government sector includes the public research institutes & centres
Source: Compiled from OECD (1996c), NSTB (1996)

Table 3 Distribution of R&D by Sector for 1993

Country	Business Enterprise	Government	Higher Education
Singapore	*62.0*	*22.2*	*15.8*
Australia	44.7	27.4	26.6
Canada	54.4	17.9	26.4
Denmark	58.3	17.8	22.8
Finland	58.4	20.5	20.5
France	61.7	21.2	15.7
Germany	66.9	14.8	18.1
Greece	26.8	32.0	40.7
Iceland	22.0	43.4	30.6
Ireland	68.7	10.5	19.9
Italy	58.0	21.5	20.5
Japan	71.1	10.0	14.0
Mexico	8.0	50.3	41.7
Netherlands	53.0	19.4	24.9
Norway	53.5	19.2	27.3
Portugal	21.7	22.1	43.0
Spain	48.6	20.8	29.9
Sweden	71.1	4.0	24.7
Switzerland	70.1	3.7	25.0
Turkey	22.9	9.9	67.2
United Kingdom	65.9	13.8	16.5
United States	71.2	10.2	15.2
EU-15	62.6	16.6	19.4
North America	69.7	11.0	16.0
Total OECD	67.0	12.9	17.3

Note: The government sector includes the public research institutes & centres
Source: Compiled from OECD (1996c), NSTB (1996)

Figure 1 Research Scientists & Engineers by Sector in Singapore

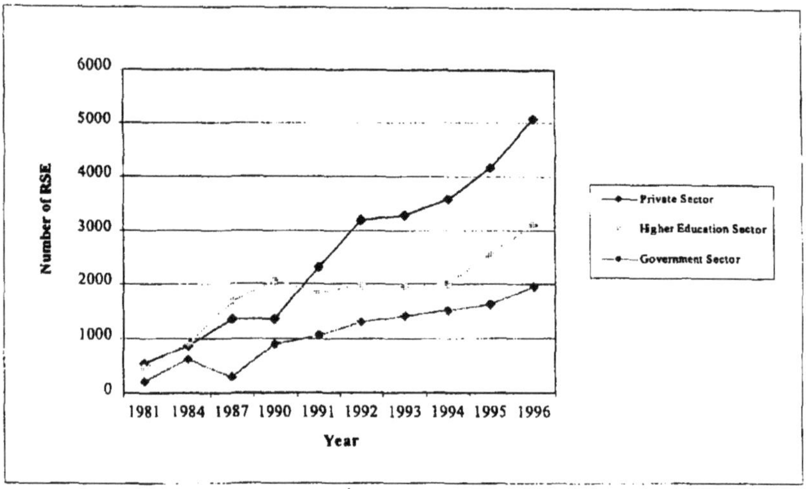

Source: Compiled from NSTB (1996)

Figure 2 R&D Expenditure by Strategic Focus for 1996

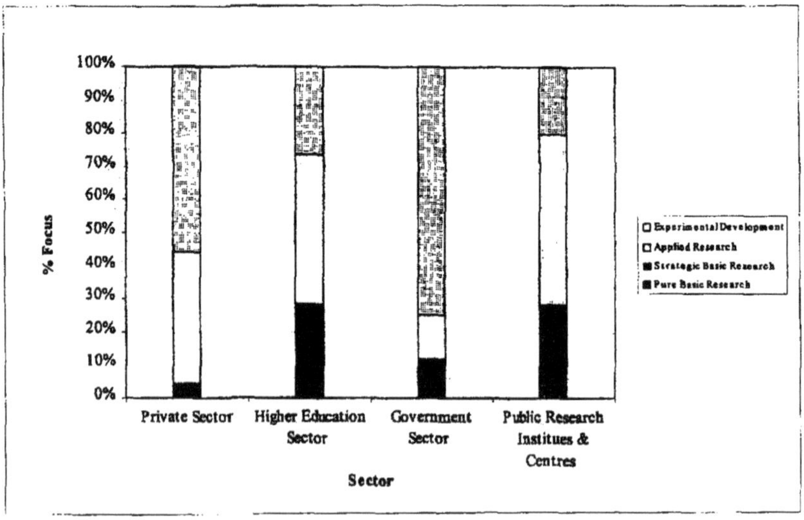

Source: NSTB (1996)

firms, especially MNCs. In fact, of the total local sales turnover of S$88.36 billion accounted for by the set of all firms performing R&D in Singapore, some S$66.31 billion or 75% are accounted for by the foreign firms (see NSTB, 1996).

Of the 5,085 RSEs in the private sector, a total of 3,095 or 61% are in the foreign firms (see Table 4). In the manufacturing sector, this proportion is 64%. Appendix A provides more details on the role of foreign firms in private sector R&D. It is noted that within the research area of engineering itself, 67% of the RSEs are working for foreign firms (see Table A1) while in that of computer and related sciences, the percentage is a lower 47%. On a related note, it is interesting to compare the participation of RSEs in foreign firms with the number of these firms and their corresponding R&D expenditures. The number of foreign firms performing R&D is, in fact, only 47% of the total pool in the private sector (see Table A2) although these firms account for 67% of the total GERD within the sector (see Table A3).

The pattern of organisation distribution of RSEs is perhaps reflective of the composition of the business economy in Singapore. However, from the angle of technology policy, the pattern suggests that indigenous technological capability amongst local firms needs strengthening. Further, many foreign firms may have incentives to perform R&D for reasons based purely on a need to be close to the market (see discussion later in the paper). A favourable observation is that the percentage of RSEs working in foreign firms has declined over the last decade (see Figure 3). In a way, this suggests that RSEs have shifted their contributions more towards local firms over time, a trend that perhaps reflects the better working agenda and conditions in these firms.

Selected Issues in the Throughput Dimension

(a) *Fostering R&D Through Foreign Firms in Singapore*

As discussed earlier, the percentage of RSEs working in foreign firms is somewhat high, although it has been declining. The concern arises when the criteria used by these firms in setting up R&D functions are understood. According to a study by Wong, Loh and Roberts (1994), the most important reason for foreign firms to

Table 4 Research Scientists & Engineers by Ownership, Type of Firm and Industry Group for 1996

Industry Group	Local Firms		Total RSEs in Local Firms	RSEs in Foreign Firms	Total RSEs	% RSEs in Foreign Firms
	RSEs in SMEs	RSEs in PLEs & Large Enterprises				
Manufacturing	**687**	**878**	**1565**	**2767**	**4332**	**63.9**
Electronics	305	578	883	1897	2780	68.2
Chemicals	88	24	112	323	435	74.3
Engineering	217	249	466	429	895	47.9
Life Sciences	52	16	68	113	181	62.4
Light Industries/Other Manufacturing	25	11	36	5	41	12.2
Services	**376**	**49**	**425**	**328**	**753**	**43.6**
IT and Communications	317	38	355	259	614	42.2
Finance and Business	17	6	23	57	80	71.3
Other Services	42	5	47	12	59	20.3
All Industry Group	**1063**	**927**	**1990**	**3095**	**5085**	**60.9**

Note: SMEs – Small and Medium Enterprises; PLEs – Promising Local Enterprises
Local firms — 30% or greater locally-owned; Foreign firms — less than 30% locally-owned
Source: Compiled from NSTB (1996)

Figure 3 Research Scientists & Engineers in Foreign Firms

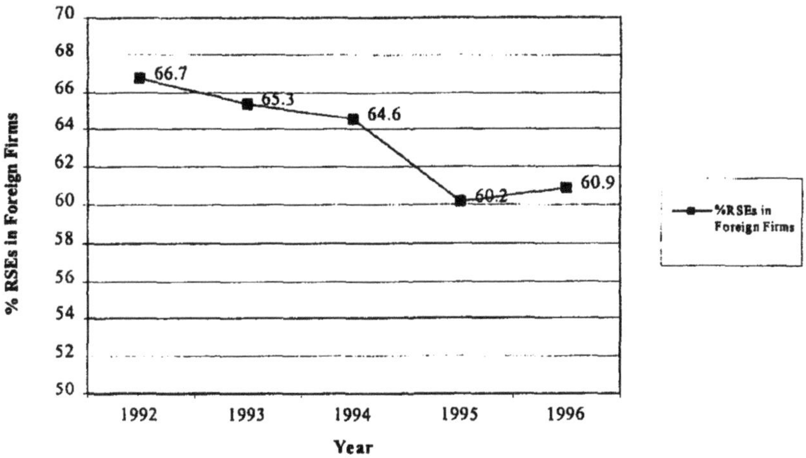

Source: Compiled from NSTB (1992-1996)

perform R&D in Singapore is to develop or adapt products to local or regional markets (see Table 5). In other words, the focus is on tailoring technological innovation for local conditions and preferences, rather than on radical creation or major breakthrough. In fact, the next reason of being close to lead users or customers is even more market oriented. The motivation to enhance local manufacturing capabilities or to establish centres of excellence in the Asia-Pacific is somewhat subordinated to more immediate demand-based considerations.

The consequence of a high degree of participation in foreign firms may be to sway technological capabilities to be centred around the market. More possibly, the diffusion of technological know-how to indigenous companies may not happen if research occurs more in foreign MNCs. In the same study by Wong *et al.* (1994), the top companies doing R&D identified by a survey of all types of firms were interestingly all foreign MNCs and not any local firms (see Table 6). Interestingly, of the 234 foreign firms performing R&D in Singapore as of 1996, 92 (or 39%) were from the US alone while 60 (26%) were from Japan (NSTB, 1996). In other words, there is a strong reliance on these two countries in terms of technology development, especially within the private sector.

Table 5 Criteria Used by Foreign Firms for Establishing R&D Function

Significance of Criteria for Establishing R&D Function in Singapore
1. To develop/adapt products to local or regional markets
2. To be close to lead users/customers
3. To enhance local manufacturing capabilities
4. To establish a "centre of excellence" in the Asia-Pacific region
5. To take advantage of excellent infrastructure support
6. To take advantage of government incentives for R&D activities
7. To tap local R&D manpower resources
8. To take advantage of technological capabilities of local organisations

Source: Wong, Loh and Roberts (1994)

Table 6 Top R&D Companies Cited

Companies
1. Motorola
2. AT&T/AT&T Bell Labs
3. Hewlett Packard/HP
4. Intel
5. Microsoft
6. IBM
7. NEC
8. Matsushita
9. Mitsubishi/Mitsubishi Electric
10. Rohm & Haas/Rohm GMBH
11. Sony

Source: Wong, Loh and Roberts (1994)

(b) *Mechanisms for Technology Transfer and Diffusion*

Wong *et al.* (1994) found that local firms have a greater tendency to rely on external mechanisms to obtain technology, compared to foreign firms. These mechanisms include licensing, incorporation of suppliers' technology and joint ventures or alliances. In fact, local firms view themselves as technology followers while foreign firms perceive themselves more as leaders.

From these specific findings and also in integration with the earlier observations, the priority for technology policy may be to provide closer attention to local firms. It is without doubt that MNCs had played a pivotal role in laying an expedient foundation for Singapore's economic progress in the past three decades. The reliance on these firms has considerably shortened the cycle time to assimilate and exploit cutting-edge technologies. It is, however, timely to groom indigenous corporations into world class leaders. These corporations will be the core of Singapore's long term competitiveness.

Selected Issues in the Output Dimension

(a) *GDP and Technology Factors*

The relationship between economic growth and technology factor inputs has received much scholarly debate, as discussed earlier. A clear direction of cause and effect is difficult to justify, based on data gathered. In the first place, some may wonder whether there is any causality at all. Figures 4 and 5 depict the plots of real GDP growth versus GERD/GDP ratio and RSE per 10,000 labour force respectively for selected countries. It is interesting to note that a definitive relationship is not immediately obvious. What is, however, illuminating is the observation that Singapore has attained remarkable GDP growth despite its relatively lower levels of technology inputs. In other words, even without a conjecture on the relationship of input and performance, it is easy to conclude that perhaps technology factors may have been more effectively transformed for the desired outcome in the case of Singapore.

Figure 4 Real GDP by GERD/GDP for 1993

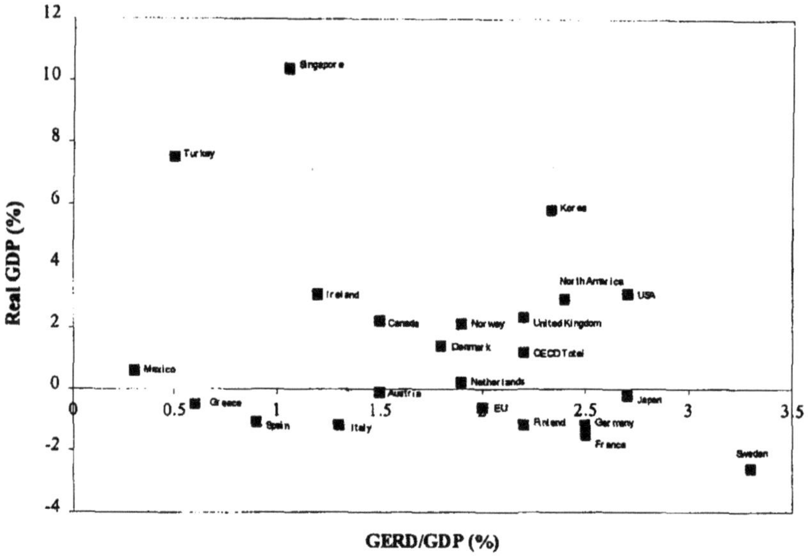

Source: OECD (1996c), NSTB (1996)

Figure 5 Real GDP by Research Scientists & Engineers/ 10,000 Labour Force for 1993

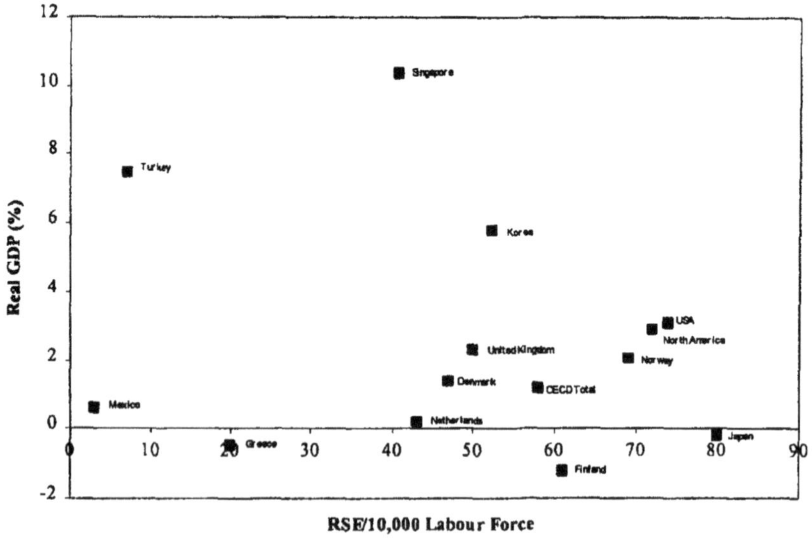

Source: OECD (1996c), NSTB (1996)

(b) *Overall Competitiveness and Technology Factors*

Figures 6 and 7 show the relationships between overall competitiveness rankings and technology rankings as resulted from the authoritative IMD and WEF studies. It is clear that a certain relationship does exist in the two rankings as technology is a constituent factor of the broader competitiveness. It is instructional to observe that Singapore's position is below an imaginary 45-degree diagonal line in the plots, thus suggesting that the country has been able to attain excellent overall performance in spite of relatively lower performance in technology development. The detailed rankings of the overall competitiveness and those for technology are displayed in Tables B1 and B2 of Appendix B.

(c) *Technology Results and Impact*

The measurement of R&D output has never been an easy or straightforward task. If patents are anything to indicate the effectiveness of R&D in any country, it is informative to compare the

Figure 6 Overall Competitiveness Ranking by Science &Technology Ranking for 1996 (IMD)

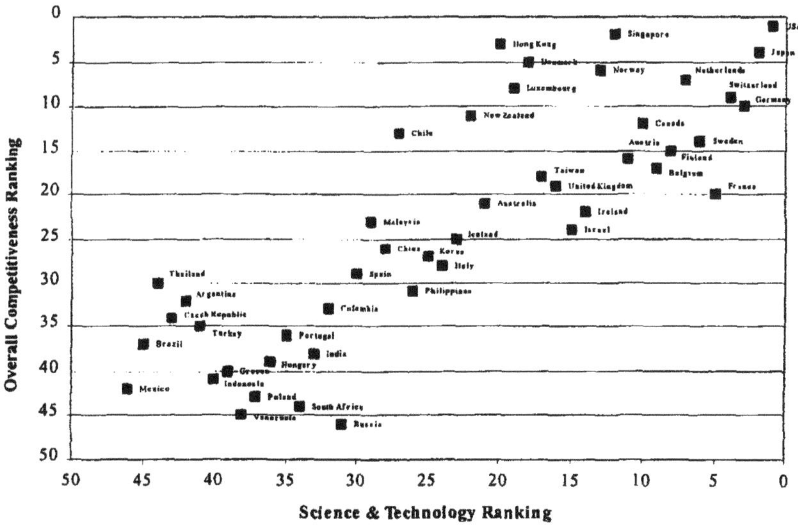

Source: IMD (1996)

Figure 7 Overall Competitiveness Ranking by Technology Ranking for 1996 (WEF)

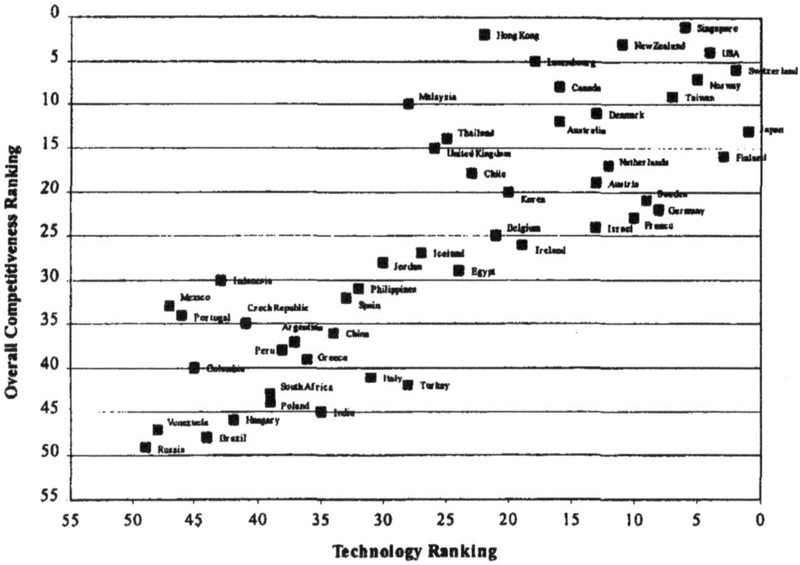

Source: WEF (1996)

flow and stock of patents across various countries (Table 7). The global leaders, by far, are the US and Japan with Germany, France and the UK in the next tier. Singapore is visibly lagging, compared even to Korea and Taiwan. This may be because of the hitherto underdeveloped local patent infrastructure and climate in the country.

However, there were remarkable developments recently with the new legislation, the Patent Act 1994, being instituted, under which any person in Singapore can lodge an application for a patent directly at the Registry of Trade Marks and Patents instead of having to rely on patenting mechanisms overseas. Singapore has also acceded to the Paris Convention for the Protection of Industrial Property, the Patent Co-operation Treaty and the Budapest Treaty (National University of Singapore, 1995). Under the Paris Convention, patents filed in Singapore will have the same priority date in countries that are parties to the Convention if the patents are subsequently filed in such countries within one year, provided the applications are first made in Singapore.

Table 7 Number of Patents by Country

Country	1990	1991	1992	1993	1994	Total 1990-1994
Singapore	*12*	*15*	*32*	*38*	*51*	*148*
Australia	432	463	410	378	467	2,150
Austria	393	359	370	313	289	1,724
Belgium	313	324	324	350	351	1,662
Canada	1,861	2,035	1,964	1,944	2,008	9,812
China	47	52	41	53	48	241
Denmark	158	210	193	197	207	965
Finland	304	331	360	293	312	1,600
France	2,866	3,030	3,029	2,908	2,779	14,612
Germany	7,610	7,680	7,311	6,891	6,731	36,223
Hong Kong	52	50	60	60	57	279
India	23	22	24	30	27	126
Indonesia	3	2	8	4	9	26
Israel	299	305	335	314	350	1,603
Italy	1,260	1,209	1,271	1,286	1,215	6,241

(cont'd overleaf)

Table 7 Number of Patents by Country *(Cont'd)*

Country	1990	1991	1992	1993	1994	Total 1990-1994
Japan	19,524	21,027	21,925	22,292	22,384	107,152
Luxembourg	17	27	26	28	22	120
Malaysia	3	12	5	13	10	43
Netherlands	958	992	854	801	853	4,458
New Zealand	52	41	44	39	37	213
Norway	112	111	108	117	126	574
Philippines	4	5	7	4	1	21
South Korea	225	404	538	779	943	2,889
Sweden	768	716	627	635	706	3,452
Switzerland	1,284	1,335	1,196	1,126	1,169	6,110
Taiwan	732	904	1,000	1,189	1,443	5,268
Thailand	2	2	1	5	5	15
United Kingdom	2,788	2,799	2,424	2,294	2,234	12,539
United States	47,393	51,183	52,253	53,235	56,066	260,130

Source: IMD/WEF (1992–1995)

5. Facing the Future for Technology Policy and Beyond

The above assessment, while acknowledging an overall effectiveness of technology policy in Singapore, highlighted several issues for further consideration. This section poses additional challenges for technology policy as the country moves into the new era of total development as an advanced economy.

Beyond Economic Upgrading as Overarching Goal

The approach of the first National Technology Plan in Singapore has been anchored strongly within a core philosophy of economic relevance and upgrading. It has had considerable success and has significantly uplifted Singapore's economic competitiveness and performance. By almost all appropriate indicators, marvellous results have been achieved through a systematic and conscious effort in technology planning and development. The accomplishments also appeared to be unparalleled in most parts of the world.

As clearly evident from the earlier discussion on the historical evolution of technology policy in Singapore, the central guiding philosophy is invariably founded on an imperative for economic development, that is, to contribute to wealth creation for national prosperity. This intent is not bad *per se*. With the unambiguous principle, there is a coordinated convergence and unity of purpose for the wide spectrum of state agencies and educational institutions involved in technology policy formulation and implementation.

As Singapore enters into the new phase of development, it is inevitable that a fresh perspective be adopted to root the sustenance of progress. The current National Science and Technology Plan constitutes a remarkable continuation of the foundation laid out in the earlier plan and has sharpened various concepts and initiatives in technology promotion. At some juncture in time, it may be appropriate to link technology more directly to quality of life. This linkage will be a more holistic perspective that stresses on the total well being of a country and its populace. Economic competitiveness is not a goal by itself; it is instrumental to a better standard of living and hence a better quality of life. Some countries, such as Korea (see Hillebrand, 1996; OECD, 1996b), at the verge of being a fully developed country, are already pursuing initiatives to drive technology from a broader array of objectives.

Beyond Technology to Encompass Science

Although the new plan in 1996 included the "science" component in the title beyond just "technology" as in the earlier case, there is a need to further strengthen the "science" part. Justifiably, during Singapore's earlier phases of economic development, the thrust of technology policies has to be on downstream R&D, where the linkage to economic upgrading is more obvious. However, the nation has reached a stage where a larger emphasis, especially on the basic sciences, which are more upstream, is a next logical step. Such a move will not only consolidate competence building in the fundamental sciences, but more importantly, it will contribute to a general climate of creativity and thinking in Singapore.

To build long term competitiveness, a fundamental review has to be conducted in the agenda and manner in which science research is being carried out in Singapore. Science and technology should begin to shed their support role and must assume a front-line posture in pushing the total development of Singapore. While not advocating a movement towards science for science's sake, it is a requisite that in order to develop national capabilities in the sciences, the surest strategy is to inculcate an indigenous foundation based on self-reliance (see also Charmarik and Goonatilake, 1994). The fastest way to attain long term competitiveness is often not necessarily through taking the shortest route. Indeed, it is timely to broaden the national paradigm in the way R&D, at least the part coordinated by public policies, is being administered to strengthen the significance of the sciences.

Beyond the Current Institutional Setup

The present institutional infrastructure to promote and spearhead technology development, viz. the NSTB which reports to the Ministry of Trade and Industry, and the National Science and Technology Council, is adequate for the current intent of technology policy. It has, in many ways, been efficient and effective and has served the country very well over the past decade. It has helped lead the country towards an initial quest for technological capability with commendable success. It has also facilitated all sectors in focusing on and engaging in well defined relevant R&D.

However, a more extended time horizon for technology policy is essential to attain sustainable total competitiveness. As the need to address the more fundamental sciences increases, and as the linkage towards more comprehensive development strengthens, there is a requirement for a purpose dedicated and elaborate setup. Such an institution may not necessarily subordinate its institutional and policy objectives directly in line with immediate economic development. It can, for instance, be a broader but reconfigured state agency or even a Ministry in its own right. As long-term competitiveness is predicated on elementary sciences, Singapore needs to move towards an even stronger focus on the fundamentals. The enlarged institutional setup can be a carefully conceived establishment with a broader mission and line responsibility in order to spearhead and coordinate national policies in science and technology, including the more basic scientific studies.

At the same time, Singapore can consider setting up an outfit similar to the National Science Foundation in the US, which is an autonomous establishment that funds researcher initiated investigations. Singapore can also contemplate fostering institutions like those in Germany, such as the Max Planck Society which has some 60 institutes and are funded equally by the Federal Government and the states. These institutes focus on basic research in the natural sciences and are closely linked to universities. They play a crucial role in postgraduate education. Further, the German innovation framework also has the institutes of the Fraunhofer Society, which is a large organisation that conducts contract research in various applied fields and provides strong links between universities and industry. There is, however, already a similar focus amongst many of the public research institutes and centres in Singapore which, being funded by NSTB, mostly deal with economically relevant research. Thus, the present public research institutes and centres in Singapore should continue in their research posture although new ones may concentrate on the basic sciences.

6. Conclusion

Far from being a buzzword or a fad and despite influential criticisms, competitiveness appears to be a deeply entrenched component of many a national policy. With the escalating criticality of technology in the global economy, technology policy has been put as a central underpinning of competitiveness.

The Asian economies have often been recognised as successful models of competitiveness and public policies (see for example, World Bank, 1993), although some of these economies are presently undergoing difficult economic and financial episodes (Montes, 1998). Singapore, in particular, has adopted an enlightened approach towards crafting of competitiveness policies, especially pertaining to the development of technological capabilities in support of a higher order economic imperative. Through the past three decades, deliberate technology policy thinking has co-evolved with economic policy in an unceasing quest for greater economic growth.

The use of competitiveness as a platform to launch various functional policies has provided a comparative barometer to propel Singapore into a higher level of achievement. Although global competition is definitely not a zero-sum game, norm-based benchmarking yardsticks enable business investors to make decisions in allocating scarce resources amongst alternative locations. To have a high position on the competitiveness ladder is surely a boost to attracting more investments.

While Singapore's performance in overall competitive performance is more than outstanding, as is readily evident in the annual report cards released by WEF and IMD, the country is still in the stage of improvement for science and technology. With the implementation of national technology initiatives, it is expected that Singapore's quest for global excellence in selected science and technology areas can be significantly expedited. However, to realise long term competitiveness, it is crucial to foster an indigenous foundation for technological capabilities that is physically anchored into Singapore as intellectual capital embodied in both human and organisational assets.

A broader perspective on the intent and philosophy of technology policy may be maintained to accomplish more than direct economic upgrading alone but also a holistic quest for a better quality of life for all. A stronger rooting in the sciences has to be considered to ensure a longer horizon in national capability development and to forge a general climate of thinking and creativity. To these ends, a review of the current national institutional setup for science and technology policy development may be timely in order to prepare Singapore for the key challenges of the near and distant future.

Acknowledgements

The assistance of Miss Ong Yee Shyuan from the Faculty of Business Administration, National University of Singapore in compiling the data is gratefully acknowledged.

References

Barro, R. and Sala-I-Martin X. (1995) *Economic Growth*, New York: McGraw-Hill.

Chamarik, S. and Goonatilake, S. (eds.) (1994) *Technological Independence: The Asian Experience*, Tokyo: United Nations University Press.

Clark, C. and Lam, D. (1995) "The Competitiveness Debate: Recognising and Transforming the Institutional Context of National Economic Behavior", *Business & the Contemporary World*, No. 2, pp. 12–27.

Dahlman, C.J. (1991) "The Role of Government: Education Policy, Technical Change, R&D, and Competitive Advantage", in Haque, I. (ed.), *International Competitiveness: Interaction of the Public and the Private Sectors*, Washington, D.C.: The World Bank.

Dahlman, C.J. (1994) "Technology Strategy in East Asian Developing Economics", *Journal of Asian Economics*, Vol. 5 No. 4, pp. 541–572.

Englander, A.S., Evanson, R. and Hanazaki, M. (1994) "R&D, Innovation and the Total Factor Productivity Slowdown", *OECD Economic Studies*, No. 22, Spring, pp. 8–42.

Englander, A.S. and Gurney, A. (1994) "Medium-Term Determinants of OECD Productivity", *OECD Economic Studies*, No. 22, Spring, pp. 49–109.

Government of Singapore (1991) *Singapore: The Next Lap*, Singapore: Times Editions Pte Ltd.

Haque, I. (1995) "Technology and Competitiveness", in Haque, I. (ed.), *Trade, Technology, and International Competitiveness*, Washington, D.C.: The World Bank.

Hillebrand, W. (1996) *Shaping Competitive Advantages: Conceptual Framework and the Korean Approach*, London: Frank Cass.

Howells, J. (1997) "The Globalisation of Research and Technological Innovation: A New Agenda?" in Howells, J. and Michie, J., *Technology, Innovation and Competitiveness*, Cheltenham, UK: Edward Elgar.

International Institute for Management Development (1996–1997), *The World Competitiveness Yearbook*, Laussane, Switzerland.

International Institute for Management Development/World Economic Forum (1992–1995), *The World Competitiveness Report*, Laussane/Geneva, Switzerland.

Inman, B.R. and Burton, Jr D.F. (1990) "Technology and Competitiveness: The New Policy Frontier", *Foreign Affairs*, Vol. 69, Spring, pp. 116–134.

Kotler, P., Jatusripitak, S. and Maesincee, S. (1997) *The Marketing of Nations: A Strategic Approach to Building National Wealth*, New York: Free Press.

Krugman, P.R. (1994) "Competitiveness: A Dangerous Obsession", *Foreign Affairs*, Vol. 73, No. 2, pp. 28–44.

March, J.G. and Olsen, J.P. (1989) *Rediscovering Institutions: The Organisational Basis of Politics*, New York: Free Press.

Ministry of Trade and Industry (1986) *The Singapore Economy: New Directions*, Singapore.

Ministry of Trade and Industry (1991) *The Strategic Economic Plan: Towards a Developed Nation*, Singapore: SNP Publishers Pte Ltd.

Montes, M.F. (1998) *The Currency Crisis in Southeast Asia*, Singapore: Institute of Southeast Asian Studies.

National Science and Technology Board (1991) *Science and Technology Windows of Opportunities: National Technology Plan 1991*, Singapore: SNP Publishers Pte Ltd.

National Science and Technology Board (1992–1996) *National Survey of R&D in Singapore*, Singapore.

National Science and Technology Board (1996) *National Science and Technology Plan... Towards 2000 and Beyond*, Singapore.

National University of Singapore (1995) *So, You Think You Have an Invention: Protecting and Transferring Intellectual Property Developed at the National University of Singapore*, Singapore.

Nelson, R.R. (ed.) (1993) *National Innovation Systems: A Comparative Analysis*, New York: Oxford University Press.

Organisation for Economic Co-operation and Development (1996a) *Industrial Competitiveness*, Paris, France.

Organisation for Economic Co-operation and Development (1996b) *Reviews of National Science and Technology Policy: Republic of Korea*, Paris, France.

Organisation for Economic Co-operation and Development (1996c) *Science, Technology and Industry Outlook 1996*, Paris, France.

Porter, M. (1990) *The Competitive Advantage of Nations*, New York: Free Press.

Simon, D.F. (1993) "The International Technology Market: Globalisation, Regionalisation and the Pacific Rim", *Business & the Contemporary World*, Spring, pp. 50–66.

Wong, P.K., Loh, L. and Roberts, E.B. (1994) *Global Benchmarking Study on the Strategic Management of Technology: The Case of Singapore*, Singapore: National University of Singapore, National Science and Technology Board, Cambridge, MA: Massachusetts Institute of Technology.

World Bank (1993) *The East Asian Miracle: Economic Growth and Public Policy*, New York: Oxford University Press.

World Economic Forum (1996) *The Global Competitiveness Report 1996*, Geneva, Switzerland.

Zysman, J., Tyson, L., Dosi, G. and Chen, S. (1990) "Trade, Technology and National Competition" in Deiaco, E., Hornell, E. and Vickery, G., *Trade and Investment: Crucial Issues for the 1990s*, London: Pinter Publishers.

APPENDIX A

Table A1 Research Scientists & Engineers by Ownership, Type of Firm and Area of Research for 1996

Area of Research	Local Firms		Total RSEs in Local Firms	RSEs in Foreign Firms	Total RSEs	% RSEs in Foreign Firms
	RSEs in SMEs	RSEs in PLEs & Large Enterprises				
Agricultural Sciences	7	3	10	12	22	54.5
Computer & Related Sciences	415	243	658	584	1242	47.0
Engineering	480	503	983	1986	2969	66.9
Biomedical Sciences	13	0	13	13	26	50.0
Natural Sciences	99	17	116	237	353	67.1
Other Areas	49	161	210	263	473	55.6
Total R&D Manpower	**1063**	**927**	**1990**	**3095**	**5085**	**60.9**

Note: SMEs – Small and Medium Enterprises
PLEs – Promising Local Enterprises
Source: Compiled from NSTB (1996)

Table A2 Private Sector Firms by Ownership & Type of Firm for 1996

Industry Group	Local Firms		Foreign Firms	Total	% Foreign Firms
	SMEs	PLEs & Large Enterprise			
Manufacturing	**146**	**50**	**199**	**395**	**50.4**
Electronics	28	17	59	104	56.7
Chemicals	31	6	62	99	62.6
Engineering	55	21	53	129	41.1
Life Sciences	20	3	22	45	48.9
Light Industries/Other Manufacturing	12	3	3	18	16.7
Services	**61**	**5**	**35**	**101**	**34.7**
IT and Communications	49	2	28	79	35.4
Finance and Business	3	2	5	10	50.0
Other Services	9	1	2	12	16.7
All Industry Group	**207**	**55**	**234**	**496**	**47.2**

Note: SMEs – Small and Medium Enterprises
PLEs – Promising Local Enterprises
Source: Compiled from NSTB (1996)

Table A3 Private Sector R&D Expenditure by Ownership and Type of Firm for 1996

Industry Group	Local Firms		Total Local R&D Expenditure (S$m)	Foreign R&D Expenditure (S$m)	Total R&D Expenditure (S$m)	% R&D Expenditure in in Foreign Firms
	SMEs R&D Expenditure (S$m)	PLEs & Large Enterprises R&D Expenditure (S$m)				
Manufacturing	**115.44**	**193.96**	**309.40**	**690.82**	**1000.22**	**69.1**
Electronics	52.46	135.96	188.42	414.73	603.15	68.8
Chemicals	12.53	3.54	16.07	160.96	177.03	90.9
Engineering	37.46	44.99	82.45	86.31	168.76	51.1
Life Sciences	6.86	3.89	10.75	27.11	37.86	71.6
Light Industries / Other Manufacturing	6.13	5.58	11.71	1.71	13.42	12.7
Services	**42.34**	**21.85**	**64.19**	**69.00**	**133.19**	**51.8**
IT and Communications	27.21	19.85	47.06	56.76	103.82	54.7
Finance and Business	4.14	0.71	4.85	9.87	14.72	67.1
Other Services	10.99	1.29	12.28	2.37	14.65	16.2
All Industry Group	**157.78**	**215.81**	**373.59**	**759.82**	**1133.41**	**67.0**

Note: SMEs – Small and Medium Enterprises PLEs – Promising Local Enterprises

Source: Compiled from NSTB (1996)

APPENDIX B

Table B1 Ranking of Overall Competitiveness vs. Ranking of Science & Technology for 1996 (IMD)

Country	Overall Competitiveness Ranking	Science & Technology Ranking
USA	1	1
Singapore	2	12
Hong Kong	3	20
Japan	4	2
Denmark	5	18
Norway	6	13
Netherlands	7	7
Luxembourg	8	19
Switzerland	9	4
Germany	10	3
New Zealand	11	22
Canada	12	10
Chile	13	27
Sweden	14	6
Finland	15	8
Austria	16	11
Belgium	17	9
Taiwan	18	17
United Kingdom	19	16
France	20	5
Australia	21	21
Ireland	22	14
Malaysia	23	29

(cont'd overleaf)

Table B1 Ranking of Overall Competitiveness vs. Ranking of Science & Technology for 1996 (IMD) *(Cont'd)*

Country	**Overall Competitiveness Ranking**	**Science & Technology Ranking**
Israel	24	15
Iceland	25	23
China	26	28
Korea	27	25
Italy	28	24
Spain	29	30
Thailand	30	44
Philippines	31	26
Argentina	32	42
Colombia	33	32
Czech Republic	34	43
Turkey	35	41
Portugal	36	35
Brazil	37	45
India	38	33
Hungary	39	36
Greece	40	39
Indonesia	41	40
Mexico	42	46
Poland	43	37
South Africa	44	34
Venezuela	45	38
Russia	46	31

Source: IMD (1996)

Table B2 Ranking of Overall Competitiveness vs. Ranking of Technology for 1996 (WEF)

Country	Overall Competitiveness Ranking	Technology Ranking
Singapore	1	6
Hong Kong	2	22
New Zealand	3	11
USA	4	4
Luxembourg	5	18
Switzerland	6	2
Norway	7	5
Canada	8	16
Taiwan	9	7
Malaysia	10	28
Denmark	11	13
Australia	12	16
Japan	13	1
Thailand	14	25
United Kingdom	15	26
Finland	16	3
Netherlands	17	12
Chile	18	23
Austria	19	13
Korea	20	20
Sweden	21	9
Germany	22	8
France	23	10
Israel	24	13
Belgium	25	21

(cont'd overleaf)

Table B2 Ranking of Overall Competitiveness vs. Ranking of Technology for 1996 (WEF) *(Cont'd)*

Country	Overall Competitiveness Ranking	Technology Ranking
Ireland	26	19
Iceland	27	27
Jordan	28	30
Egypt	29	24
Indonesia	30	43
Philippines	31	32
Spain	32	33
Mexico	33	47
Portugal	34	46
Czech Republic	35	41
China	36	34
Argentina	37	37
Peru	38	38
Greece	39	36
Colombia	40	45
Italy	41	31
Turkey	42	28
South Africa	43	39
Poland	44	39
India	45	35
Hungary	46	42
Venezuela	47	48
Brazil	48	44
Russia	49	49

Source: WEF (1996)

PART II

SECTORAL CONCERNS

3
Maintaining Singapore as a Major Shipping and Air Transport Hub

Anthony Chin and Jose Tongzon

1. Introduction

One area where Singapore's international competitiveness is increasingly under threat from its regional neighbours is in transport, particularly in the area of sea and air transport. As its neighbouring countries are in the process of improving their infrastructure and pursuing policies to promote themselves as alternative hubs for sea and air traffic in the region, the relative position of Singapore as a regional and international hub is increasingly challenged. This chapter attempts to evaluate Singapore's strengths and weaknesses relative to its neighbours in the area of sea and air transport and then draw some policy recommendations for Singapore to maintain and promote its position as the region's transport hub. Section 2 of this chapter is devoted to an exposition of Singapore's relative position in air transport and Section 3 looks at its relative position in the area of sea transport.

2. Air Transport

Globalisation and the liberalisation of international trade remain the prime motivating forces behind the tremendous change which is taking place in the air transport industry. Singapore Airlines is one of the main proponents of liberalisation and greater deregulation of air services while Changi Airport has remained a major hub and the best airport for many years. However, one cannot assume that this comparative advantage will remain, in the light of intense competition between airlines and the development of competing airports within ASEAN. Financing constraints and the currency crisis aside, several fundamental factors will determine Singapore's competitiveness as a major provider of airline and hub services. These are the presence of a competitive environment, strong airport infrastructure development, the development of strategic alliances between airlines, cost and pricing strategies of the airport and SIA, and the employment of management systems and technology in airport operations. The next section will briefly survey the present state of the air transport sector in Singapore. This is followed by an identification of potential strategies in the light of recent developments.

The World Travel and Tourism Council estimates that between 1997 and 2005, travel and tourism is expected to create (directly and indirectly) 125 million jobs worldwide or one new job every 2.5 seconds. Singapore receives more than 7 million visitors, generating approximately S$12 billion in tourist receipts a year. Employment arising from this sector accounts for one in every eleven jobs (STPB 1997).

Changi Airport handled 23 million passengers in 1996 and is expected to reach 25 million and 41 million in 1997 and 2006 respectively. Transit passengers made up less than 6% of the total in 1996. About a third of the passengers and more than half of cargo handled originated from and are destined for East and South East Asia (See Table 1). North America accounts for only 1% of total passengers and 8% of total cargo in 1996. A breakdown of East and South East Asian visitor arrivals shows that the main sources of visitor arrivals are Malaysia, Indonesia, Thailand, Indonesia, Thailand, Hong Kong and Japan (See Table 2). However, the US, the UK and Australia remain potential sources for visitors who stay on for more than one day (See Table 3). Total tourism receipts of US$9.4 billion were recorded for 1996, placing it as the 11th highest top tourism earner and accounting for a third of tourism earnings in Southeast Asia. Thailand was a close second with US$8.6 billion. However, since 1995, the Middle East has replaced East Asia/Pacific as the top tourism earner. The World Tourism Organisation has cited funding constraints in tourist and transport infrastructure development as some of the factors which have led to the slowdown (*The Straits Times* 1997). Singapore has a large travel market, given increasing incomes and the impact of its regionalisation drive.

Table 1 Summary of Air Traffic Statistics for Changi Airport 1994–1996

MOVEMENTS (Number)	1994	1995	1996
Number of Scheduled Commercial Flights	145,334	156,334	166,749
Number Scheduled Passengers (Pax)	21,644,677	23,196,240	24,514,248
Number of Transit Pax.	1,420,478	1,447,369	1,383,430
Cargo Carried (Tonnes) Transit	1,009,764 140,266	1,105,772 155,272	1,190,457 14,114
Total Number of Pax (TNP): All Regions	10,134,100	10,919,739	11,587,394
TNP: South East Asia (SEA)	4,614,467	4,943,776	5,210,633
TNP: North East Asia (NEA)	2,470,735	2,761,149	2,955,554
TNP: South Asia (SA)	516,968	602,262	644,344
TNP: West Asia (WA)	122,917	125,787	127,970
TNP: Western Europe (WE)	994,804	1,050,980	1,147,828
TNP: Eastern Europe (EE)	37,894	24,126	24,452
TNP: Oceania (O)	1,028,544	1,055,949	1,086,847
TNP: North America (NA)	245,856	240,690	264,420
TNP: Other Regions (OR)	101,915	115,020	125,364
Total Cargo Carried (TCC)	529,244	577,748	622,019
TCC: SEA	134,259	136,794	154,068
TCC: NEA	162,282	183,040	196,745
TCC: SA	31,165	32,450	37,665
TCC: WA	10,263	9,608	8,259
TCC: WE	85,633	96,014	101,709
TCC: EE	405	417	408
TCC: O	65,680	67,521	69,155
TCC: NA	36,441	47,945	49,779
TCC: OR	3,116	3,959	4,23

Source: Civil Aviation Authority of Singapore 1994, 1995, 1996

Table 2 Breakdown of Visitors to Singapore from South and Northeast Asia

Year	**1994**	**1995**	**1996**
Southeast Asia: Passenger			
Brunei	129,047	132,593	140,391
Indonesia	1,264,796	1,400,259	1,583,190
Philippines	229,293	206,871	278,749
Malaysia	1,827,623	1,929,505	1,832,542
Thailand	1,004,300	1,073,784	1,133,831
Vietnam	99,649	118,977	126,692
Others	59,759	81,787	115,238
Northeast Asia: Passenger			
Hong Kong	732,518	794,636	886,809
Japan	961,416	1,045,260	1,104,059
Taiwan	433,283	466,863	445,291
South Korea	130,060	184,325	213,346
China	n.a.	n.a.	298,375
Others	213,457	270,065	7,674

Source: Civil Aviation Authority of Singapore 1994, 1995, 1996

Investments in neighbouring ASEAN countries have increased tremendously. In 1996, 3.3 million Singaporeans and permanent residents travelled abroad. The total population of Singapore is approximately 3 million! (See Table 4).

Secondly, the region's share of worldwide scheduled passenger traffic will make up 51% of travel in 2010 (See Table 5). This phenomenal increase in international passenger air traffic within the past ten years can be attributed to high disposable incomes with equally high economic growth, political stability, concerted and effective marketing of tourism, economic and ethnic links, relaxation of travel restrictions in Korea and Taiwan, proliferation of frequent but shorter trips and the genesis of liberalisation between some countries. Liberalisation is expected to gather momentum and new airports are scheduled to be nearing completion soon. Intra-Asia Pacific trade and disposable incomes are expected to grow, albeit at

Table 3 Twelve Largest Visitor Generating Markets to Singapore 1996

(Average length of stay of more than one day)

Market	Number	%*	ALS+
1. Japan	1,171,899	−0.6	2.46
2. Indonesia	1,063,298	+1.2	3.60
3. Malaysia	700,748	+2.9	3.81
4. Taiwan	528,485	−6.2	2.08
5. S. Korea	384,509	9.5	1.69
6. USA	374,056	8.2	3.48
7. Australia	351,587	1.4	3.30
8. UK	312,516	8.3	3.77
9. Hong Kong	288,560	3.1	3.19
10. Thailand	252,572	−1.8	3.72
11. China	226,685	12.2	4.06
12. India	204,174	8.3	6.40

Notes: *Percentage increase (+) or decrease (-)
+Average length of stay (January to December 1996).
Source: Singapore Tourist Promotion Board 1996

a lower rate. Increased traffic is envisaged between China and Taiwan, as well as from transitional economies.

Challenges and Impediments to a Liberalised Air Transport Sector

The turmoil in the currency and equity markets in Asia will slow down the progress of liberalisation in the air transport sector. Prior to the economic crisis, we witnessed remarkable progress in the opening of markets within the ASEAN countries, with the opening up of multiple points of entry. Previously closed routes were opened up and competition encouraged.[1] Established national carriers now

[1]Indonesia joined Thailand and the Philippines in opening 16 airports to international services. Foreign carriers will be allowed 5th freedom rights, subject to reciprocity for Indonesian carriers. Limited cabotage rights will be allowed on domestic routes when code sharing agreements are established with Indonesian carriers (AAAP 1996).

Table 4 Outbound Travel by Singapore Residents (Nationals and Permanent Residents)

91	92	93	94	95	96
BY AIR & SEA					
1,607,162	1,863,190	2,156,236	2,446,519	2,867,242	3,304,714
BY AIR					
1,168,671	1,376,395	1,587,416	1,740,030	1,979,378	2,204,125
BY SEA					
437,889	486,495	568,820	706,489	887,864	1,100,589
GDP per capita in S$ (US$1:S$1.41)					
26,373	27,462	29,742	32,101	34,254	39,615

Source: Singapore Tourist Promotion Board 1996

Table 5 Scheduled Traffic of Commercial Airlines

(Pax-Km Performed by Region in Millions)

ICAO Statistical Region of Carrier Regn.	**1986**	**1995**
Europe	438,760	549,270
Africa	34,580	5,100
Middle East	42,900	66,960
Asia Pacific	237,040	549,690
North America	623,820	902,680
Latin America & Carribean	74,950	107,940
TOTAL	1,452,060	2,227,530

Source: ICAO 1997a

face competition from second tier Asian airlines.[2] However, in most markets free entry is not extended to foreign carriers and these are generally not allowed to carry purely domestic traffic (cabotage). Severe restrictions are in place on investment by foreign nationals or foreign controlled enterprises in national airlines. Nevertheless, as deregulation in domestic markets increases the efficiency and competitiveness of carriers under the force of competition, it will provide a powerful incentive for those carriers to expand their services abroad and thus create pressures toward international liberalisation. Progress in this field ultimately depends on the willingness of governments to accept a higher degree of international competition and a certain multinationalisation of corporate structures in air transport, away from a strict policy of protecting national flag carriers (OECD 1988).

In April 1997, Singapore signed an open skies agreement with the United States and has since concluded similar agreements with Brunei, New Zealand and Taipei.[3] Negotiations are underway with

---

[2]The introduction of second tier airlines such as SilkAir, Eva Airways, Japan Asia Airways, All Nippon Airways, Asiana, Sempati and DragonAir has injected competition with established national carriers. Limited or partial open skies initiated by Thailand, the Philippines and Indonesia indicate the awareness by governments of the benefits air travel contributes to travel and tourism, foreign investment and international trade. In addition, established carriers such as Philippines Airlines, Thai Airways, Qantas and Gulf Air have been privatised. However, one of the biggest obstacles to the expansion of air travel remains the lack of airport and supporting infrastructure.

[3]Key Points of the Agreement

1. The termination of restrictions on pricing, capacity, type of airlines, number of flights and routes.
2. Liberal charters.
3. The right to fly between any point in the US and any point in the other nation and beyond to third nations.
4. Open code-sharing.
5. Prompt conversion and remission of hard currency.
6. Self-handling provisions for carriers to perform or control airport activities which support their operations.
7. Non-discriminatory operation and access to computer reservation systems.
8. Fair competition in commercial activities such trucking and airport charges.
9. Membership of international conventions on safety and security.

The Sunday Times, 1997.

Malaysia and South Korea. From the perspective of the US, the treaty sets the tone and pace for its determined push into the high potential Asia Pacific market. Since early 1997, it has been working aggressively with countries in the region to remove restrictions on routing, frequency and capacity for passenger and cargo flights, and pricing. This translates into lower prices, better services and more choices for the consumer, i.e. the businessman, tourist and shipper.

Air Traffic Control Congestion

Almost 20 years of deregulation in the US has resulted in leaner and meaner airlines equipped with the comparative advantage in marketing strategies and control of unit costs.[4] Of greater concern is the effect liberalisation, privatisation, occurrence of take holders, development of mega carriers, and the hub and spoke system will have on the already limited airport capacity in Asia. In the absence of regulatory changes, the demand for air transport in the Asia Pacific is expected to grow by an average of 8.6% per annum between 1993 and 2000 and 7.1% between 2000 and 2010 (ATAG 1995). Air travel grew by 10.3% per annum between 1985 and 1993 and by 2010 the region share of worldwide scheduled passenger traffic is expected to reach 50.5%. Liberalisation will thus increase demand and exert tremendous pressure on already congested airports. Airlines and consumers are concerned about issues such as air safety, delays, sharing of air space, investment in airports and the development of hubs.

Hub Traffic Scheduling and Pricing

Few airports are endowed with the comparative advantage of location or geography in relation to major traffic flows so as to be in the best position to optimise sixth freedom rights. Sixth freedom

[4]Air transportation in the US is one of the most successful and fundamental sectors in the economy and plays a vital role in major economic activities. Airfares within the US have fallen by 30% in real terms and consumer benefits have been estimated at US$18 billion a year. The US-Netherlands open skies pact has increased traffic by 225% and the weekly flight frequencies have risen by 100%.

refers to the ability to pick up or let down passengers and goods between two points via a point in which the air carrier is registered. To maximise an airline's load factor it has to fly through a hub located along a major hub which provides regional linkages. Thus, in addition to ATC delays, the presence of curfews and a growing number of non-stop flights will combine to exacerbate congestion during peak hours at most major airports in the region. Air space congestion has been observed on the following routes:

1. Europe-Southeast Asia over India;
2. Bangkok-Hong Kong;
3. South China Sea;
4. Northeast Asia-Southeast Asia;
5. Japan-North America;
6. Europe-Japan/Korea.

Changi Airport's flight activities are concentrated between 1700–2300 with some delay. Singapore's national carrier, SIA, takes advantage of a 2–3 hour window to allow most of its flights from Europe to link up with services to New Zealand and Australia. Flights from Australasia arrive in the evening to facilitate connecting journeys to Europe just before midnight — operating an hourglass hub pattern for its long haul European-Australasia services. Passengers find the evening departures and early morning arrivals very convenient. However, an important consideration is to build into the schedule the curfew hours of spoke airports. Similar strategies have been developed for the North Atlantic flights. Other Asian airlines such as Cathay Pacific, Malaysian Airlines, Philippine Airlines, Thai International and Garuda have adopted similar strategies.

Traffic of the region's most congested routes will continue to grow with the number of movements expected to double over the next ten years. There are two levels in the development of airports. First, the identification of the primary gateway and secondly, the development of second or third gateways. Because of the size and the massive use of resources, comprehensive cost benefit evaluation must be carried out. Airlines are now exerting pressure that charges for infrastructure reflect the true cost of providing airport services. Asian airports are one of the most expensive places to land (see Chin

1997, Tae and Yu, 1997). Airport investments involve big risks which are relatively unknown to investment managers. As such, investments in airports must be made equally attractive, with security and rates of returns which are comparable to that in any other sector. Herein lies the dilemma in charging for the use of airports. It is a question of cost recovery versus the principal of relating to the cost of using the facilities and services.

Maintaining the Premier Hub Status in the Asia-Pacific

Japan will continue to be the dominant market, followed by Hong Kong, Singapore, Hawaii, Thailand, Taiwan and Australia. While long haul travel will remain dominant, short haul traffic is expected to increase more than long haul traffic i.e. traffic within the region will increase faster than between the region and other parts of the world. By 2010, air traffic between Europe and Asia Pacific is expected to quadruple 1990 figures. The US-Asia market will continue to be dominated by Northeast Asia-US (26–46%). Table 6 shows that 13 out of the top 25 city pairs with the highest passenger traffic are between Asian cities. In the absence of liberalisation, the ability of airlines to respond by increasing load factors, seat densities and aircraft size will be limited. Meeting the demands for travel must come from increasing the number of flights, new routes and increased frequencies.

Creating a Liberalised and Competitive Environment

The Singapore-US agreement allows for access to all gateways in the US and beyond, greater flexibility in code sharing and the freedom to create a wide variety of commercial relationships with US and third party carriers. US-Southeast Asian trade is forecast to grow at 7%. Many US and EU carriers are already exercising Fifth Freedom rights on many Asian routes. Yet Asian carriers are denied cabotage rights on US domestic and intra-EU sectors. There will be no immediate benefit to the US. Singapore is located too far south for some airlines such as Northwest to contemplate initiating services. The size of the market will only increase when a larger network has been enlarged for US carriers to take advantage of beyond rights and

Table 6 City Pairs with the Highest Passenger Traffic ('000) O–D

City pairs	A—>B	A<—B	<——>
1. HK-Taipei	**2055**	**2045**	**4100**
2. Lon-Paris	1711	1842	3553
3. Lon-NY	1322	1311	2633
4. Dublin-Lon	1268	1269	2537
5. KL-Sin	**1196**	**1119**	**2315**
6. Hon-Tokyo	**1157**	**1137**	**2294**
7. Amsterdam-Lon	1107	1101	2208
8. Seoul-Tokyo	1089	1081	2170
9. Bangkok-HK	993	910	1903
10. HK-Tokyo	940	937	1877
11. Jakarta-Sin	800	832	1632
12. Taipei-Tokyo	**794**	**789**	**1584**
13. Bkk-Sin	727	738	1465
14. HK-Sin	703	715	1418
15. Frankfurt-Lon	698	714	1412
16. Brussels-Lon	603	588	1191
17. NY-Paris	572	580	1161
18. HK-Manila	559	561	1120
19. Sin-Tokyo	559	545	1104
20. LA-Tokyo	515	532	1047
21. Lon-LA	523	507	1030
22. HK-Seoul	**502**	**504**	**1006**
23. Frankfurt-NY	500	497	997
24. Lon-Tokyo	**481**	**488**	**969**
25. Chicago-Toronto	480	481	961

Source: ICAO 1997b

code sharing agreements. Until borderless travel is achieved, travelling from Los Angeles to Jakarta via Seoul, Kuala Lumpur and Singapore will remain a distant possibility. Thus the open skies pact should be viewed more as a psychological strategy in setting the pace towards changing the mindset of bureaucrats who may still cling on to the old style protectionist regulatory approach to aviation policy. Full liberalisation in Asia will take a while longer, as countries such as China, Japan, Australia, Vietnam and Thailand are wary of US initiatives, whose domestic market alone accounts for 29% of world air travel.[5]

Cooperate to Compete

Unlike the European and North American continents, there is no large land mass in the Asia Pacific except for China. Concentrations of economic activity, population and locations of growth potential

[5]The experience within the US has shown that many airlines have been forced out of business and in half of the large airports, each dominant airline had captured 57% to 87% of market share. The fear of US airlines dominating the Asian market through predatory pricing and capacity dumping is a threat even to the most efficient of Asian airlines. One other concern is the failure of airport infrastructure in keeping up with the already booming economies of East Asia. High and sustained economic development has exerted considerable pressures on limited aviation infrastructure. Two important observations must be noted. First, deregulation in the US created a travel boom. Between 1971 and 1987 the number of passengers who had flown commercial airlines increased from 49% to 70%. Passengers taking advantage of discounted fares grew from 26.9% in 1977 to 91.3% in 1987. The increase in passenger and aircraft movements created a strain on the capacity of airport infrastructure and airways. The cost of air traffic control (ATC) delays have been estimated at $3 billion a year as air traffic demand outpaced traffic handling capacity (USDOT 1988). In Europe, 15.4% of flights experienced ATC delays of 16.7 minutes (ECU 2.5 billion or 5% of total airline costs) while the average delay in the US for domestic departures was 7.2 minutes in 1995. The cost of congestion to airlines and consumers is estimated at US$3 billion annually. These base estimates do not take into account losses to commerce and industry through higher prices and increased distribution costs. The extra fuel required for the aircraft because of congestion on routes between Europe and South East Asia is between 1.5 to 2.5 additional tonnes per trip (IATA 1996). There is an urgent need to invest and improve on aviation infrastructure to reduce the cost of congestion. Appendix 1 summarises the costs and indirect benefits of inadequate infrastructure.

are thousands of kilometres apart, separated by oceans. This is particularly true for insular Southeast Asia. Coordinated development of airport investments and tourist infrastructure will ensure that tourist flows are well coordinated between key origins and destinations. Europe s Airports Bureau facilitates and harmonises competition between London's Heathrow, Paris' Charles de Gaulle and Amsterdam's Schipol. Singapore must cautiously work with the ASEAN Committee on Transport and Communications (COTAC) in formulating a proactive air policy constantly reviewing future industry growth, infrastructure needs and developing a regional blueprint for coordinated development which allows technology to play an active role. For example, airport operations, in order to function efficiently, demand a fast, flexible, centralised information network with continuous updating about the status of the airport, its aircraft and passengers. Open system computer technologies are able to provide comprehensive and integrated information networks. Similar systems are employed at Amsterdam's Schipol, Washington DC, Dallas and LA. Changi's Terminal 2, Chek Lap Kok and KL Sepang will be similarly equipped. Singapore may have to put in more in the beginning.

Major airport investments are currently being undertaken in Hong Kong, Malaysia, Thailand and Singapore. While analysts predict that demand will outstrip supply, the close proximity of some of these major airports may be a cause for concern if each plans to be a major hub and gateway to Southeast Asia. This proximity is apparent from travel times between ASEAN capitals, which range from between 45 minutes to 2.5 hours (Chin 1997). Unlike London-Paris-Amsterdam, which are gateways to a large hinterland and great concentration of population and activities, insular Southeast Asia is definitely not Asia's gateway from a geographical and geopolitical perspective. Bangkok could geographically compete with Tokyo if not for the lack of supporting infrastructure such as good rail and road communications. The major Asian hubs for European and US traffic are Tokyo, Singapore, Bangkok and Hong Kong. Together with Seoul, Osaka and Taipei, the seven hubs share of total scheduled seats between European and Asia Pacific routes was more than 60% in 1990. They accounted for more than 85% seats on trans-Pacific routes (excluding Hawaii). Competition between regional airports will lead to some deliberately influencing passenger movements so as to capture a larger market share.[6] Success will depend on a number of factors.[7]

Consumer Sovereignty and Airline Alliances

Passengers increasingly exercise the option of which airline to fly and to which airport. Tourists and business travellers look beyond speed of processing, check-in, customs, and at factors like quality of shopping, comfort of the waiting area (positioned away from busy areas), contingency plans in view of severe congestion (including transit passengers, hotel facilities, lounges etc.). To the end point traveller, supporting services such as getting to hotels, getting to and around tourist sites, quality of hotels, banking and business services are essential in attracting the discerning traveller. Increasing airport capacity either through increasing the capacity of an existing runway or construction of a new one does not necessarily lead to optimal utilisation unless it is operating within a monopoly environment.

Increasing Airline Capacity

There are several schemes SIA could adopt to enhance its position in

[6]This is inevitable, considering the huge investments on airports. For example, the new KL airport city built on a 10,000 ha. site, 50 km south-west of KL (S$4.68 billion) in three phases, consists of a total of two terminals and two runways. Phase 1 is scheduled to be completed by early 1998, with a passenger handling capacity of 25 m per year and 1 million tonnes of cargo. Phases 2 and 3 will increase capacity to 35 million by 2008 and 45 million by 2012. When fully operational, it is expected to handle 100 million passengers. Highways and railways will link the airport to the city. Malaysian Airlines city check enables a passenger to arrive half an hour before a flight. Competition will increase with Bangkok and Singapore. Subang currently ranks third in Southeast Asia. The airport will be operated by Malaysia Airports Berhad, a private entity.

[7]There are a few factors which lead to the development of a hub. First, a strong domestic market that can command a certain level of air services. Secondly, geographical location. Thirdly, the absence of ground and air capacity constraints. Fourthly, a high standard of service. Fifthly, a liberal air environment where changing airline alliances will redirect traffic flows between airport hubs.

the air market. These are increasing load factors, seating densities, the number of flights and destinations, and using larger aircraft. Of the five, increasing the number of flights and destinations is perhaps the most plausible. It entails not replacing multi-stop flights by non-stop flights, increasing frequencies on existing routes and serving new markets. As such, alliances, code sharing agreements and moving towards a more open and competitive environment would contribute to the growth of the industry.

SIA should also attempt to strive to improve its cost competitiveness, which depends to a large extent on efficiency and input prices. Cost differentials between airlines are also influenced by network effects and output attributes such as stage length and product mix. Australasian airlines (except JAL and ANA) are generally more competitive than major US and European carriers. Among the Asian airlines which have been observed to have higher cost competitiveness relative to American Airlines are SIA, Cathay Pacific, Korean and Thai (16%, 4%, 23% and 9% respectively).

Increasing Hub Activity

Asian hubs will play a greater role in relieving the pressure off peak travel and flights during limited periods of the day. Some hub consolidation and rationalisation will have to be developed and strengthened because of the following implications as hubs develop. These are:

a. Coordination of days and departure times as a result of increased frequencies;
b. Monitoring of competitive fare and safety levels due to the employment of larger aircraft and hence reduced unit cost;
c. Optimisation of aircraft load for scheduled flights;
d. More direct and indirect revenues for the airport and its implications on pricing and investment strategies.

3. Port of Singapore as a Regional Hub

With the trend towards globalisation and market liberalisation, nations and industries are becoming more exposed to the pressures of international competition. As a consequence, there is a growing realisation that services supplied to these exposed industries must be provided on an internationally competitive basis. Ports in particular are increasingly under pressure from shippers for lower port and shipping charges. Needless to say, ports form a vital link in the overall trading chain and consequently, their level of efficiency determines to a large extent a nation's international competitiveness.

On the other hand, recent developments in operational strategies and technologies of shipping lines, due to highly competitive shipping markets, have put more pressure on ports to adjust to these developments and intensified interport competition. The traditional concept of the hinterland is losing its significance, due to significant improvements in efficiency in land transport and cargo handling. Containerisation in particular has facilitated the physical movement of freight in many transport modes. Ports can no longer ensure that cargoes generated domestically will be handled at their terminals. Nor can a port expect to attract shipping lines just because it serves as a natural gateway to its hinterland. Shipping lines are now major agents of change in oceanic transportation, possessing a more varied choice of ports of call than ever before.

A growing proportion of containerised trade is being handled on a door to door basis, from a point of production to the point of consumption (Haynes *et al.*, 1997:97). Most of this business is controlled by shipping lines that have turned into organisations engaged in logistic operations on a global scale. In light of these developments, ports are becoming increasingly marginal in the routing of container flows. In view of growing interport competition, port authorities have to develop competitive strategies to survive and remain relevant to port users.

The Port of Singapore is considered to be one of the busiest ports in the world. For sometime now, the port has managed to maintain its status as one of the world's busiest ports in terms of container throughput. In 1996, the port of Singapore generated 12.94 million TEUs, second only to the port of Hong Kong. In terms of shipping tonnages the port of Singapore still ranks as the world's busiest port. However, a large component of these traffic flows are transshipments, that is, cargoes originating from Singapore's neighbouring countries or destined for countries outside of

Singapore. It has been reported that about 50% of Malaysian sea cargo goes via the port of Singapore.[8] In 1990, approximately 70% of its four million TEUs was accounted for by containers transshipped from neighbouring ports (Airriess, 1993:34). Currently, more than two-thirds of Singapore's container traffic is transshipped. Large ships do not have to call at every port within the region, but only call at the port of Singapore to unload into or load cargoes from feeder ships. This will enable the shipping lines not only to cut their costs but also to provide a high frequency of service, maximise the utilisation of slots of the mother vessels and to have a broad choice of feeders. From the viewpoint of shippers, this system allows them a wider choice of shipping lines and times, at more competitive rates.

The port of Singapore has not been spared from the competitive pressures discussed above. Other ports in the region are now accelerating the process of indigenous port development with large injections of capital. For instance, in Malaysia an investment of S$2.6 billion on port development is committed for the next five years[9] and Tanjung Pelapas in Johor Baru is currently under construction, apart from Malaysian government's drive to promote the port of Klang in the region. Indonesia has planned to develop its port in Batam[10]. There are other infrastructure development plans in the region which challenge the port of Singapore as a regional hub.

What strategies should the port of Singapore adopt to maintain its role as the region's hub port? To address this question, we need to first establish how the port of Singapore compares with the region's other ports in terms of the determinants of hub port choice. Thus, this paper is organised as follows: section 1 outlines the determinants of hub port choice and assesses the port of Singapore as a regional hub port based on these determinants; section 2 further explores the external opportunities and threats, and section 3 discusses the strategies the port of Singapore should adopt in the context of growing interport competition.

---

[8]*Business Times*, October 16, 1997.

[9]*Straits Times*, June 26, 1996.

[10]*Straits Times*, July 10, 1996.

Determinants of Hub Port Choice and the Port of Singapore

To gain some insight into whether or not the port of Singapore can maintain its role as the region's hub port, it is useful to identify the various factors that determine hub port choice decisions and how the port of Singapore has fared in these areas.

1. *Volume of cargo throughput.* The ability of a port to attract mother and feeder ships under the hub-spoke system is largely dependent on the volume of cargo it can generate. Ports with large throughput are more attractive for ships to call at than smaller ports, because the former makes it easier for ships to maximise usage of their slots and thus minimise per unit shipping costs. It should, however, be pointed out that there is a two-way causation here. Shippers prefer to choose a port with a higher frequency of ship visits because it implies greater choice and flexibility for shippers, *ceteris paribus.* It is difficult to say which comes first.

Based on this determinant, the port of Singapore is clearly way ahead of its regional competitors. The only port that can match the port of Singapore's container throughput is the port of Hong Kong, but the port of Hong Kong does not directly compete with Singapore in terms of hubbing in the Southeast Asian region. It is currently servicing as a gateway to the big Chinese market. It is of course possible that main shipping lines could decide to use the port of Hong Kong as a hub port for the Southeast Asian region as well.

2. *Geographical location and features.* The location of a port, whether it is along existing shipping routes, or whether it is close to specific centres of cargo traffic, or to potential service customers, is another factor which influences hub port choice. Willingale (1984) and Murphy, Daley and Dalenberg (1991) have found in their respective surveys that in most cases location is low in importance due to significant improvements in domestic transportation systems, but have acknowledged that in some cases location is a very important factor. The biggest ports in terms of cargo throughput are located along heavy

shipping routes and have benefited from the growth of their neighbouring countries or regions. The port of Singapore is located along the Straits of Malacca, which is the main shipping route between East and West. It was estimated by the Oil Companies International Marine Forum that over 600 ships transit the straits every day.[11] The importance of this shipping route has not diminished over time with the introduction of new technology and improvements in air travel.

In terms of geographical features, the port of Singapore is fortunate to enjoy natural deep waters and harbours, which have allowed it to service ships with deeper draughts without necessarily resorting to extensive and expensive dredging operations. The waterways serving as entrants to Singapore allow even the largest ships to use them. Singapore does not have typhoons and other natural calamities, which make port operations and freight movements safe and reliable.

Singapore is located close to some of the world's dynamic economies. Even before rapid economic development of these economies started, the port of Singapore already played the role as an entrepot port servicing as a gateway to Singapore's regional hinterland. The recent remarkable economic development and growing trade orientation of its close Southeast Asian neighbours have only heightened its role as an entrepot port. However, recently these neighbouring economies have tried to reduce their reliance on the port of Singapore for nationalistic reasons. So far, however, we have not seen any significant effect on overall cargo traffic through the port of Singapore.

3. *Port efficiency*. Considered to be the most important determinant of port choice amongst the port of Singapore users,[12] port efficiency can be measured in many ways, depending on which aspects of port operations are being evaluated. It can also be viewed from different perspectives, as

---

[11]*Business Times*, October 16, 1997.

[12]Port efficiency was ranked as the most important determinant of port choice by a sample of shipping lines and freight forwarders using the port of Singapore in a survey conducted by Chia Yew Loon (1996).

> there are a number of port users with their different and at times conflicting objectives. For instance, a port may be efficient to shipowners, but may at the same time, be judged inadequate to cargo interests. Thus, port efficiency cannot be measured based on one criterion alone. A meaningful evaluation of a port's efficiency will require a set of indicators relating to the various aspects of port operations. These efficiency indicators can be classified into operational efficiency measures and customer oriented measures. The first category is concerned with the utilisation of the port's productive assets such as cranes, berths, terminal area, labour and tugs. The second category is concerned with how these operational efficiencies are translated into port users' benefits and satisfaction such as in terms of lower port charges, shorter ship turnaround, shorter cargo dwelling time and reliability.

Before any port comparison in terms of these efficiency measures is made, it should be pointed out, however, that there is a danger of making unfair international comparisons unless ports compared have similar characteristics in relation to cargo throughput, infrastructure and port operations. In light of this, Tongzon and Genesalingam (1994) have proposed a procedure to classify ports based on an optimisation technique cluster analysis. Another method suggested by Tongzon (1995b) is based on the principal component analysis. The advantage of principal component analysis over other methods (for example, cluster analysis) is that it allows us not only to classify ports but also to compare ports using the estimated principal component. Using these two methods, both studies have classified the port of Singapore in the same league as the ports of Rotterdam, Hong Kong and Kaohsiung. From this "like for like" comparison, it is clear that the port of Singapore does outshine all other similar ports in the area of ship turnaround time, labour efficiency, crane efficiency and in the utilisation of other assets. Moreover, the analysis has shown that as far as efficiency, timeliness and reliability go, the port of Singapore is way ahead of its regional counterparts.

Apart from the issue of port classification for "like for like" comparison, there is a need to come up with an aggregate or overall index of port efficiency. To show the overall ranking of the port of

Singapore in terms of efficiency, Tongzon and Poitras (1997) used a mathematical programming technique called Data Envelopment Analysis (DEA) to measure the port of Singapore's overall level of efficiency compared to other major ports in the world. The findings of this study have confirmed the port of Singapore's high level of efficiency relative to all other ports in the sample. In all cases, the port of Singapore is ranked as efficient and has appeared in all facets for port efficiency comparisons.[13] Table 7 below shows the relative efficiency rankings using the CCR DEA model.

4. *Quantity and quality of support infrastructure.* Port infrastructure refers not only to the number of container berths,

Table 7 Relative Efficiency Rankings Using the CCR DEA Model

Ports	CCR	Ports	CCR
1. Melbourne	0.5778	12. Auckland	0.8079
2. Sydney	1.0000	13. Le Havre	0.3015
3. Brisbane	1.0000	14. Hong Kong	1.0000
4. Fremantle	0.1820	15. Kaohsiung	1.0000
5. Adelaide	0.3244	16. Felixstowe	1.0000
6. Rotterdam	0.8833	17. Puerto Rico	0.9780
7. Tacoma	1.0000	18. Jakarta	0.6422
8. Zeebrugge	0.9713	19. Manila	0.2546
9. Wellington	0.2652	20. Klang	1.0000
10. Montreal	0.3911	21. Singapore	1.0000
11. Baltimore	0.3810	22. Bangkok	1.0000

Note: CCR is the Charnes, Cooper and Rhodes (1978) DEA method. A score of 1.000 indicates the port is efficient.

[13]For an inefficient decision-making unit (DMU), a facet is a combination of efficient DMUs which are used to determine the relative inefficiency. The CCR model is based on the assumption of constant returns to scale. Under a variable returns to scale assumption, the port of Singapore is also found to be efficient with the score of 1.0000.

> gantry cranes and adequate storage facilities, but also to the quality of the cranes, the quality and effectiveness of the port/interport information systems, the approach channel provided, the preparedness/unpreparedness of port management and a wide range of port related and ship related services offered in the port. To be a regional hub requires in particular an adequate number of berths and other required port facilities to deal with significant volumes of cargo traffic, high frequencies of ship visits and very large ships. It also requires an excellent information network to handle the high level of coordination required as a hub port. The port of Singapore has ensured that its port facilities are adequate to handle future increases in cargo traffic and ship visits in the region by investing in port expansion and upgrading. The almost completed development of the Pasir Panjang terminal, which is scheduled to open in 1998, will give extra handling capacity of 18 million TEUs. In addition, the port's terminals are supported by a number of district parks, providing over half a million square meters of warehousing. A district park is a large covered warehouse which provides automated storage facilities. Customers can process their documents, pack and unpack, mark, label and assemble their goods for distribution to other distribution centres.

The port of Singapore is fully equipped to handle almost all types of vessels, ranging from 80 TEU barges to third generation vessels of 4000 TEU capacity. It is one of the most automated ports in the world and uses the latest information technology in every aspect of administration, planning and operations services. Its electronic data interchange system is used to plan berth allocation, ship towage and yard management. All containers relayed through Singapore are systematically sorted out for distribution to the second carriers. Advanced cargo handling equipment, such as fourth generation quay cranes, double trolley cranes and double stack trailers, are used. In addition, the management is further upgrading its cargo handling technology by almost entirely automating its terminal operations. In the new Pasir Panjang terminal mentioned earlier, containers will be handled and transported by computer controlled machines. The port management is currently testing automatic guided vehicles (AGV) capable of navigating autonomously and stacking containers by remote controlled bridge cranes. The port of Singapore has been one of the world's top bunkering ports. Some 17 million tonnes of bunkers were lifted by vessels in 1994.

5. *Direct port charges.* There are different types of direct port charges, which vary between ports in terms of levels and structures. They are all levied on the basis of port visits. Direct port charges comprise ship based types (such as port navigation fees, berthage, berth hire, harbour dues and tonnage) and cargo based types (such as wharfage and area hire). Berth hire and berthage are levied either on the basis of net registered tonnes (NRT) or against gross registered tonnes (GRT). Wharfage and area hire are levied on cargoes with different rates for different cargoes. Direct port charges are eventually reflected in the freight rates shippers have to pay. Other types of costs which shippers eventually pay include ancillary charges such as costs of pilotage, towage, lines, mooring/unmooring, electricity, water and garbage disposal.

Studies by Foster (1978) and Murphy, Daley and Dalenberg (1991, 1992) have found port charges as an important determinant of port choice, but its importance must be seen in the context of overall costs. Apart from these direct charges, there are also indirect costs associated with delays, loss of markets/market share, loss of consumer confidence and opportunities foregone due to inefficient service. Indirect costs include the length of time a ship spends in a port (ships turnaround time) and cargo dwelling time (the time taken to move cargo into or out of the cargo handling area). In some cases port charges account for a considerable proportion of total transportation cost (such as in low valued primary goods) and in other cases they account for an extremely small portion of the total transportation cost (such as in high valued manufactures).

In terms of direct port charges, the port of Singapore does not fare well against other ports in the region. For instance, compared to its closest rival, port of Klang, its port direct charges, as reflected by container handling charges, are higher by 35% to 75%, as shown in

Table 8 below. In addition, its subsidiary costs are also considerably higher.

Despite the past year's decision to lower charges for a wide range of services, increase the free storage period up to nine days from seven and reduce port dues for container ships by 20%, Singapore's direct port charges are still much higher.[14] An increase in direct port charges is expected to occur as the port of Singapore is preparing itself for privatisation, since as a private entity it will then be liable to a higher corporate income tax of 26%.

Analysts have argued that the port of Singapore's future as a regional hub will depend mainly on how well it can deal with the twin challenges of escalating costs and diminishing productivity.[15]

Table 8 Container Handling Charges Per Container (1997)

	Port Klang (RM)		**Port of Singapore**	
	20 ft	40 ft	20 ft	40 ft
Full container load (FCL)	190	285	150	215
	(US$76)	(US$114)	(US$107)	(US$154)
Less container load (LCL)	330	495	325	452
	(US$132)	(US$198)	(US$232)	(US$322)
Transshipment container	140	210	115	175
	(US$56)	(US$84)	(US$82)	(US$125)

Note: Exchange rates used are US$1=RM3.5 and US$1= S$1.4.

Source: Fairplay Port Guide (1997)

[14]This decision was in response to the lobbying efforts made by major international shipowners to reverse the port of Singapore's move to raise tariffs by an average of 9.7% and reduce the free storage period for transshipment containers from 14 to seven days from January 1996. Some carriers claimed that the increase in tariffs have resulted in a 30% increase in their total costs (*Lloyd's List*, 4 January 1996). Hence, the port of Singapore responded to the discontent by cutting charges and extending the free storage period, a few months after the implementation of the pricing policy. The Maritime and Port Authority also reduced port dues for container ships by 20% from May 1996 (*The Straits Times*, 24 April 1996).

[15]*Investor's Digest*, August 1996.

Due to rising labour and land costs resulting from labour and land limitations, and appreciation of the Singapore dollar against other regional currencies, port direct charges have been under pressure.

Further port expansion may not be possible without incurring higher costs of land reclamation and development, due to the scarcity of land in Singapore. Thus, it may be said that there is a short limit to a continued port expansion in Singapore compared to its regional neighbours, as the land area of Singapore is small. The port of Singapore could probably increase its capacity up to three times its current level up to about 40 million TEUs.[16]

Labour costs and shortages of quality blue collar labour have caused many labour intensive industries to relocate to other low labour cost countries in the region, which results in logistics hub being established closer to the manufacturing sites. The use of foreign labour helps relieve this problem but does not substantially lower the costs, due to the existence of foreign workers levies and other on-costs, that may be incurred as these foreign workers are not eligible for housing subsidies.

On the other hand, Singapore's regional neighbours are constantly trying to develop their ports in order to attract more cargo and shipping lines, and are actively promoting their ports as logistics and transport hubs. Malaysia, in particular, has been trying to reduce the volume of cargo transshipped through the port of Singapore by lowering its port charges, improving infrastructure and efficiency and using other measures, including the imposition of additional levies for cargoes coming out of and entering into Singapore. In 1994, none of the cargo from Penang was shipped through the port of Klang. In the first nine months of 1996, 60,000 TEUs from Penang was already shipped through the port of Klang, reducing the cargo shipped through the port of Singapore to 57%.[17] The Thai Transport Ministry has also announced plans to cut dependency on transshipments through Singapore in light of its high port tariffs. One proposal being considered is for master vessels to be offered lower handling charges in return for loading their cargoes directly at Laem Chabang in

[16]*Straits Times*, March 5, 1996.

[17]*Business Times*, October 24, 1996.

eastern Thailand.[18] The Philippines has been seriously marketing the locational and good infrastructure and natural harbours of Subic Bay as a regional port hub since the expiry of the lease agreement between US and the Philippines. Although these ports are currently way behind Singapore in terms of throughput and infrastructure, they are also well geographically located to service Asia, and with adequate investments in technology and infrastructure it is just a matter of time before they can become a real threat to Singapore as a regional port hub.

External Opportunities and Threats

The above analysis of the port of Singapore's strengths and weaknesses relative to its regional port competitors has shown that it has enjoyed a number of competitive advantages. These internal strengths are further complemented by recent developments in the external environment. One recent development is the trend among shipping lines to use very large ships and to call at few ports. The deployment of larger ships to call at only few large ports is part of their strategy to lower costs and to deal with the increasingly competitive shipping market. This trend will favour larger ports, where the economies of scope can occur. The trend towards intermodalism, which requires a complete logistical and distribution package to meet Just-In-Time functions (such as the need to offer warehousing and storage space, processing facilities and efficient intermodal transfer and sophisticated information services), fits in with the port of Singapore's current orientation as a comprehensive provider of port services and as a logistics centre.

Another external development which augurs well for Singapore is the anticipated regional expansion in container trade. As more and more countries in the region are shifting away from low value added to high value added production in the process of economic development, an increasing proportion of manufactures will be traded, resulting in a greater demand for container usage and

[18]Lloyd's List Maritime Asia, January 1996.

deployment of container ships.[19] Continued industrialisation, economic dynamism and growing trade orientation of the countries in the region will provide ample business opportunities for the port of Singapore, which has been playing an entrepot role and the region's transshipment point.[20] The port of Singapore is in a better position to take advantage of this external opportunity, because of the economies of scale and scope it has enjoyed in containerised cargo operations, its high level of efficiency and excellent infrastructure relative to other ports in the region in container port management, as discussed above.

There are, however, external sources of threat for the port of Singapore as a regional hub. Aggressive policies by Singapore's competitors to promote their ports and attract mother vessels by offering incentives and other measures to discourage port users to use the port of Singapore, and the massive investments made to improve their infrastructure and technology have posed, and will continue to pose, a major challenge.

Development of round-the-world shipping services, which pick up trade on two or three of the major shipping routes, has increased competition with traditional end-to-end operators and widened the scope for feedering from hub ports to the smaller trade areas. There is a trend towards joint service operations and amalgamation in order to take advantage of the economies of scale in the current highly competitive environment. These trends have reduced the bargaining power of ports, including the port of Singapore.

[19]One of the major impacts of containerisation is the load centre concept. With containerisation, port time has been greatly reduced because of the increased costs of the new vessels and the goods they carry. The new ships call at but one or two ports on a range and for much shorter periods of time — hours rather than days. These ports have become the foci of international shipping on those ranges, and goods are moved by land (truck and rail) and water (barge) from/to inland centres and feeder ports to/from these global hubs.

[20]Container shipping is concentrated in the Asian region. Seven of the first ten world maritime enterprises are Asian, and together they account for more than 50% of total goods movement (Comtois, 1994:197).

Recommended Strategies to Deal with Increasing Regional Interport Competition

The strategies that the port of Singapore needs to adopt to maintain its status as a regional port hub may consist of the following:

- The port of Singapore needs to capitalise on its competitive advantages and continually invest to improve port efficiency, provide adequate and state-of-the-art infrastructure and technology, maintain a well motivated workforce and become more customer oriented. Although port charges must be lowered as much as possible, they should not be done at the cost of quality of port services. It has been pointed out previously that the total cost to port users includes not just direct port charges but also indirect costs associated with port delay and so on. The ideal situation, therefore, is to provide a high quality of services at minimum costs so that port users can get the best value for their money;
- At the same time, the port of Singapore should continue to be directly involved in developing and managing other ports in order to build more port linkages with other countries in a hub-spoke network. The port of Singapore has already adopted this strategy through various strategic alliances and investments in the logistics business and port terminal development in other countries. It is currently involved in projects in China, India, Indonesia, Vietnam, South Korea, Hong Kong, Yemen and Italy. This is an effective way to ensure that there will be cargo transshipped through the port of Singapore by having greater influence on the supply lines of transshipment cargo from other ports in the region;
- Given the changing technology of maritime transport and cargo handling, reorganisation of overall transport systems by intermodalism and the changing trends in shipping markets, the port of Singapore should consolidate its distribution role by consolidating its district parks and gateway functions, offering warehousing and storage space, processing facilities and efficient intermodal transfer with advanced and sophisticated information services;

- Finally, the port of Singapore should find ways of working more closely with its Asian neighbours to adopt a unified approach in dealing with greater interport competition. All ports will benefit if there is some unity in taking advantage of the rising opportunities in port business; if the whole ASEAN region can act as one unified group of ports, it can increase the group's bargaining position against the shipping lines and deal with competition from other ports outside the ASEAN region. In this case, every port will benefit and interport competition will become a positive sum game for the port of Singapore and other ports in the region.

4. Conclusion

The economic and travel boom, together with the gradual move towards liberalisation of air travel and privatisation/corporatisation of airports, will exert tremendous pressure on already crowded skies and airport infrastructure. Singapore is not only a major proponent of airline liberalisation but is way ahead in its infrastructure development of airport infrastructure. However, much of its success is still closely linked to the state of health of the economies in the region. Singapore and regional governments should map out a concerted and coordinated approach to competition between airports and development of the tourist and travel industries. Secondly, steps must be taken to effectively tap private sector capital in the development of airports, bearing in mind that not all airports guarantee a quick and high rate of return, such as in power and other non-infrastructure investments. Airports serving as secondary gateways may not be able to attract and sustain high traffic volumes within a short period to justify private enterprise involvement. Initiatives must be made to attract capital perhaps with the help of innovative regulations, priority approvals, guarantees and deregulation of financial markets. Airport investment should be made at par with any other business investment.

Based on the determinants of hub port choice, the port of Singapore has fared much better than its regional counterparts in most of the criteria used. Its strength is mainly grounded on its locational and historical advantage. Starting early as the region's transshipment port (reflecting the nation's historical reliance on entrepot trade due to its location), the port of Singapore has one major advantage which other ports in the region have great difficulty in catching up with — the size and volume of traffic which is consistent with the trend towards load centreing and intermodalism. However, this does not warrant complacency, since the other countries in the region are deliberately attempting to divert existing cargo from the port of Singapore and promote their ports as transshipment ports through various incentives. Further, in terms of port charges and labour costs, the port of Singapore does not fare well when compared with other regional ports. Thus, maintaining the port of Singapore's position as the region's hub largely depends on how well it can deal with the challenges of high port charges and escalating operating costs, and how well it can maintain its high level of efficiency and reliability. Further, if port charges and operating costs in Singapore remain high relative to its rivals, it is crucial for port users to see that the benefits of port efficiency, reliability and safety are far more important than the direct costs of port services.

References

Airport Analyst Asia Pacific (AAAP, 1996) December Edition, Sydney Australia.

Air Transport Action Group (ATAG, 1995) *Asia/Pacific Air Traffic Growth and Constraints*, 36 pp., Geneva, Switzerland.

Airriess, C. (1993) "Export-oriented Manufacturing and Container Transport", *Geography*, 78 (1), pp. 31–42.

Charnes, A., Cooper, W.W. and Rhodes, E. (1978) "Measuring the Efficiency of Decision-making Units", *European Journal of Operational Research*, pp. 429–444.

Chia Yew Loon (1996) "Determinants of Port Choice", *Honours Thesis*, Department of Economics and Statistics, National University of Singapore, p. 50.

Chin, A.T.H. (1997) "Implications of Liberalisation on Airport Infrastructure Development in the Asia Pacific", Paper presented in *Conference of the Air Transport Research Group of the World Conference on Transportation Research Society*, 25–27 June 1997.

Civil Aviation Authority of Singapore (CAAS, 1994, 1995, 1996) *Annual Airport Statistics*, Singapore.

Comtois, C. (1994) "The Evolution of Containerisation in East Asia", *Maritime Policy and Management*, 21 (3), pp. 195–205.

Fairplay Port Guide (1997) London: Fairplay International.

Haynes, K.E., *et al.* (1997) "Regional Port Dynamics in the Global Economy: The Case of Kaohsiung, Taiwan", *Maritime Policy and Management*, 24 (1), pp. 93–113.

Heaver, T. (1995) "The Implications of Increased Competition among Ports for Port Policy and Management", *Maritime Policy and Management*, 22 (2), pp. 125–133.

International Air Transport Association (IATA) Airport Monitor (1996), 78 pp., Montreal, Canada.

ICAO (1997a) *Civil Aviation Statistics of the World 1995*, Doc 9180/21, 102 pp., Montreal Canada.

ICAO (1997b) *On-Flight Origin and Destination*, Digest of Statistics No. 441, 146 pp., Montreal, Canada.

Investors Digest "Singapore's Port Under Siege", Economic Development Board, August 1996, p. 10.

Lloyd's List Maritime Asia "Regional Update", 4 January 1996.

Murphy, P., Daley, J. and Dalenberg, D. (1991) "Selecting Links and Nodes in International Transportation: An Intermediary's Perspective", *Transportation Journal*, 31 (2), pp. 33–40.

Murphy, P., Daley, J. and Dalenberg, D. (1992) "Port Selection Criteria: An Application of a Transport Research Framework", *Logistics and Transportation Review*, 28 (3), pp. 237–255.

Organisation of Economic Cooperation and Development (OECD, 1988) *Deregulation and Airline Competition*, Paris, France.

Singapore Tourist Promotion Board (1996, 1997) *Singapore Monthly Report on Tourism Statistics*.

Tae, H.O. and Yu, C. (1997) "Cost Competitiveness of Major Airlines: An International Comparison," Paper presented in *Conference of the Air Transport Research Group of he World Conference on Transportation Research Society*, 25–27 June 1997.

The Straits Times, 1997.

Tongzon, J. and Ganesalingam, S. (1994) "Evaluation of ASEAN Port Performance and Efficiency", *Asian Economic Journal*, 8 (3), pp. 317–330.

Tongzon, J. (1995a) "Determinants of Port Performance and Efficiency", *Transportation Research*, 29A (3), pp. 245–252.

Tongzon, J. (1995b) "Systematising International Benchmarking for Ports", *Maritime Policy and Management*, 22 (2), pp. 171–177.

Tongzon, J. and Poitras, G. (1997) "Measuring Port Efficiency: An Application of Data Envelopment Analysis" (mimeo).

United States Department of Transport (1988) "A Slot Allocation Model for High-density Airports", Federal Aviation Administration, Washington D.C., USA.

Willingale, M. C. (1984) "Ship-operator Port-routing Behavior and the Development Process", in Hoyle, B.S. and Hilling, D. (eds), *Seaport Systems and Spatial Change*, New York: John Wiley & Sons, pp. 43–59.

APPENDIX 1

The Costs and Indirect Benefits of Inadequate Infrastructure

Sectors	Nature of Cost	Costs Incurred	Economic Benefits (To Others)
1. Airlines	Growth curtailed, delays	Higher operating costs, Loss of revenues, profit and employment	Gains by substitute modes such as high speed train.
2. Airports	Growth curtailed	Lower revenues	Traffic diversion to competing airport ... increased revenues.
3. Air travellers	Delays	Fall in business productivity, Higher cost passed by airlines	
4. Tourism	Growth curtailed, loss of revenue	Loss in tourist arrivals	Increased revenues by other destinations
5. Employment	Less jobs	Income loss, increase social disruptions	
6. Business and industry	Higher operating costs, revenue loss	Lower profits for business	Businesses relocate thus benefiting other economies
7. Governments	Fall in tax and fee revenues	Revenue loss	
8. Aircraft manufacturers	Lower demand	Lower production, lower revenues	Some aircraft may be needed to offset moderate congestion

Adapted from IATA 1996b

4

Upgrading Singapore's Manufacturing Industry

Wong Poh Kam

1. Brief Overview of Manufacturing Growth in Singapore

Overall Manufacturing Growth

Singapore's manufacturing sector grew at an average annual rate of 9.9% in real terms over 1960–96, faster than the 8.4% GDP growth rate (see Table 1 and Annex Table 1). Manufacturing grew particularly rapidly over the first two decades (1960–80), but slowed to less than 2% per annum in 1980–85 due to the recession in 1985, which hit manufacturing particularly hard. However, the sector bounced back strongly, averaging 12.5% growth in the next five years. The growth rate moderated to 7.3% in 1990–95/96, slightly lower than the GDP growth of 8.3%. Despite the strong growth of Singapore's service industries in the late 1980s, manufacturing remains the single most important sector of the economy, consistently accounting for over a quarter of GDP since the late 1980s (see Annex Table 2).

Productivity Growth

The rapid expansion of Singapore's manufacturing sector has been accompanied by a reasonably high rate of productivity improvement and technological upgrading. As evidenced in Table 2, over 1960–95, value-added per worker in the manufacturing sector grew at 4.1% on average in real terms, while capital per worker had also increased at the comparable rate of 3.8% per year. Productivity growth was slowest in the 1960s, as industry was still highly dependent on

Table 1 Performance of Singapore's Manufacturing Sector, 1960–1995/96

Year	Manufacturing Sector Output Growth Rate (%p.a.)	Total GDP Growth Rate (%p.a.)
1960–70	13.7	9.1
1970–80	10.9	9.0
1980–85	1.6	6.2
1985–90	12.5	8.1
1990–96	7.3	8.3
1960–96	9.9	8.4

Source: Department of Statistics, Singapore Yearbook of Statistics, *various years.*

expansion of labour-intensive industries. Labour productivity increased in subsequent decades as manufacturing activities in Singapore increasingly shifted from labour-intensive production to skill-intensive to technology-intensive industries over the years.

The changing technology-intensities of Singapore's manufacturing industry is reflected in the changing sectoral composition by major industry groups. As can be seen from Table 3, the share of the more labour-intensive industries, such as food and beverage, textile and apparel and wood-based industries, declined from 45% of manufacturing output in the early 1960s to less than 15% by 1980, and just over 5% by 1995. On the other hand, the chemicals/petroleum sector increased its output share significantly from 18% in 1960 to over 41% in 1980, driven primarily by the growth of petroleum refining in the late 1960s and early 1970s. The sector that has grown the fastest, particularly since the late 1970s, has been the electronics industry. From a less than 4% share of manufacturing output in the early 1960s, it more than quadrupled to 17% by 1980, and further increased to 39% by the end of 1990. By the mid-1990s, electronics accounted for more than half of total manufacturing output.

Dependence on Foreign MNCs

Unlike Korea and Taiwan, Singapore's manufacturing growth has until recently been largely driven by MNCs (Low *et al.*, 1993). The

Table 2 Growth of Labour Productivity and Capital Intensity in Singapore's Manufacturing Sector

Year	Real Value Added Per Worker in Manufacturing ($'000 – in 1985 constant price)	Capital/Labour Ratio ($'000) (1985 constant price)
1960	17816	16973[1]
1970	23574	23090
1980	34738	30414
1990	55000	43784
1995	72690	55086
Average Growth % p.a.		
1960–70	2.8	4.6[2]
1970–80	4.0	2.8
1980–90	4.7	3.7
1990–95	5.7	4.7
1960–95	4.1	3.8[3]

Notes: [1]1963 figure; [2]Figure for 1963–70; [3]Figure for 1963–95

Source: Department of Statistics and Economic Development Board, Report on the Census of Industrial Production, *various years.*

overall high dependence of Singapore's manufacturing sector on foreign direct investment can be seen in Table 4. Except for the recession period of 1985–86, the share of local firms in total manufacturing output has been consistently less than 30% since the mid-1970s, and closer to 25% in recent years. In terms of share of new capital investment among the bigger manufacturing establishments, as monitored by EDB, the share of local equity capital has generally been even lower (see Table 5), although there have been greater variations from year to year. Overall, the stock of foreign equity capital accounted for close to 70% of total manufacturing equity capital in the late 1980s, although it has since declined to about 60% by 1993 (see Table 6). This is significantly higher than the one-third share of total equity capital in the entire economy. The rise in local equity capital in manufacturing in the 1990s has been due mainly to the large increase in the number of

Table 3 Sectoral Output Composition of Singapore's Manufacturing Sector (%)

Sector	1960	1970	1980	1990	1995
31-Food & Beverage	33.0	18.4	6.6	4.0	3.2
32-Textile & apparel	3.3	5.2	4.5	3.1	1.2
33-Timber & furniture	8.5	5.4	3.1	1.2	0.3
34-Printing & paper products	10.3	3.5	2.6	3.6	3.3
35-Chemicals/petroleum	17.6	36.6	41.4	25.0	17.7
36-Non-metallic mineral products	3.7	2.3	2.0	1.4	1.8
37-Basic metals	1.1	1.9	1.7	1.1	0.6
38-Metal products/ machinery	20.6	23.6	36.6	59.0	70.6
384-Electronic products	3.7[1]	7.3[1]	16.9	39.1	51.1
39-Other mfg industries	2.0	3.1	1.5	1.5	1.3
Total Manufacturing	100	100	100	100	100

Note: [1]Includes electrical products
Source: Same as Table 2.

local manufacturing firms that expanded their capital base by listing on the local stock exchange.

As expected, foreign majority controlled firms were on average significantly bigger in size than local firms. As can be seen from Table 4, the average output per firm among foreign firms was about 10 times higher than that for local firms. The share of local firms in Singapore's manufacturing sector varies significantly across different sectors, with the more labour intensive industries such as textile and garment, food and beverage, wood, rubber and plastic products generally having high local capital participation, while the technologically more advanced sectors like industrial chemicals, petroleum refining, electrical/electronics and precision equipment tend to have very low local participation. The basic metal industries and transport equipment (mainly ship repair and maintenance) had relatively high local capital participation due to heavy involvement of Government Linked Companies(GLCs).

Table 4 Composition of Manufacturing Output by Foreign and Locally Controlled Firms, 1976–95

Year	Number of Firms		Output $m			Average Output/ Firm $m	
	Local	Foreign	Local	Foreign	% Local	Local	Foreign
1976	1955	550	4121.27	11196.17	26.9	2.11	20.36
1977	2036	602	4665.91	12852.34	26.6	2.29	21.35
1978	2306	640	5597.72	14068.97	28.5	2.43	21.98
1979	2376	746	6639.06	18657.55	26.2	2.79	25.01
1980	2521	834	8328.71	23329.19	26.3	3.30	27.97
1981	2540	899	8824.97	27962.13	24.0	3.47	31.10
1982	2674	912	9581.93	26885.51	26.3	3.58	29.48
1983	2855	761	10601.37	26620.15	28.5	3.71	34.98
1984	2883	765	11968.62	29109.25	29.1	4.15	38.05
1985	2767	737	11422.65	27081.85	29.7	4.13	36.75
1986	2748	701	11443.91	25814.80	30.7	4.16	36.83
1987	2725	788	11522.13	34420.42	25.1	4.23	43.68
1988	2806	818	14105.56	42364.46	25.0	5.03	51.79
1989	2767	843	15110.71	48772.35	23.7	5.46	57.86
1990	2837	866	17215.62	54117.61	24.1	6.07	62.49
1991	2921	864	18435.15	56139.88	24.7	6.31	64.98
1992	3062	855	19936.15	57339.75	25.8	6.51	67.06
1993	3135	858	21810.31	65828.74	24.9	6.96	76.72
1994	3150	863	24697.32	75924.78	24.5	7.84	87.98
1995	3178	858	26733.99	86624.04	23.6	8.41	100.96
	Number of Firms		Output $m				
% Growth	Local	Foreign	Local	Foreign			
1980–90	1.2	0.4	7.5	8.8			
1990–95	2.3	−0.2	9.2	9.9			

Note: No corresponding data available for 1975 and earlier

Source: Same as Table 2.

Table 5 Foreign Share of Equity Investment in Singapore, 1984–93

%	1984	1987	1990	1993
Manufacturing	65.0	70.8	69.4	60.2
Total Economy	na	39.6	37.2	33.2

Source: Department of Statistics, Singapore Yearbook of Statistics 1995

Development of Indigenous Firms

Despite the continuing dominance of foreign MNCs in Singapore's manufacturing industry, there are signs that the indigenous sector is growing more rapidly in recent years. We can discern three distinct groups among these indigenous firms (Wong *et al.*, 1997).

The first, and by far the largest, consists of firms that are primarily contract manufacturers or precision engineering firms providing parts, components, automation equipment and process engineering services primarily to the electronics industry. Most of these firms first emerged as local suppliers to electronics MNCs operating in Singapore, and later succeeded in upgrading their technological capability in response to their customers' increasingly sophisticated demands. Since the late 1980s, many have also been able to internationalise their operations by moving to lower cost overseas locations like Malaysia, Indonesia and China. These overseas operations typically supply not only their original MNC customers in Singapore, but also increasingly MNC manufacturing plants that are rapidly expanding into these sites as well. The most successful examples of companies in this group are Venture Manufacturing and Flextronics (in PCBA), Amtek Engineering (in metal stamping) and MMI (hard disk drive baseplate machining). Indeed, a company like MMI has completely hollowed out its manufacturing operations to Malaysia, with its Singapore headquarters undertaking only product development and process engineering activities.

The second group consists of indigenous companies that have achieved some degree of success in own brand manufacturing (OBM). In contrast to the first group of companies, which developed their competitive advantages in manufacturing process technology and operational capability, this second group of firms were able to develop their own product technology and commercialisation/ marketing capability, rather than as component suppliers or contract manufacturers. The most successful among this group of companies is Creative Technology, the global market and technological leader in PC audio cards. Although Creative had pursued an OBM strategy from the start, a more typical route is for successful contract manufacturers to forward integrate into own product innovation; Goldtron (GSM phones) and Flextech (semiconductor packaging) provide interesting examples of this strategy.

While the first two groups comprise indigenous private enterprises, the third group consists of state owned enterprises that have been explicitly directed to enter targeted industrial sectors perceived as strategic to Singapore, including defence related sectors where government control is considered critical, or capital intensive sectors like semiconductor wafer fabrication where the entry barriers are high and MNCs on their own might not be willing to invest in Singapore. The strategic intent to develop indigenous technological capabilities in sectors seen as critical to future national competitiveness may also have been an important motivation of the government. The Singapore Technologies (ST) Group represents the most prominent and biggest of such state enterprises targeted at a wide-range of high-tech industries including aerospace, electronics systems integration, computer software and semiconductors.

International Competitiveness of Singapore's Manufacturing Industry

The World Competitiveness Report[1] has generally rated Singapore highly in terms of infrastructure, human resources, political and macroeconomic stability and pro-business environment, all of which obviously matter a great deal in making Singapore a competitive location for manufacturing investment. Nonetheless, a closer examination of Singapore's manufacturing competitiveness using several international benchmark indicators suggests that Singapore is still somewhat behind the leading industrial nations.[2]

---

[1] See IMD (various years).

[2] For a discussion on indicators and national innovation systems. See Nelson (1993), OECD (1994, 1997b, 1997c).

Table 6 compares the aggregate labour productivity of Singapore's manufacturing sector vs. the OECD countries, the other three Asian NIEs and Malaysia as of 1994. As can be seen, while Singapore's average labour productivity is comparable to the average of the OECD countries and comfortably ahead of the other Asian NIEs, there are 13 OECD countries which have a higher level than Singapore. A more disaggregated benchmarking of Singapore's labour productivities in the five more technology intensive three-digit SIC industry groups shows Singapore's average labour productivity to be biased upward by the highly capital intensive petro-chemicals subgroup (UNIDO,1996), and that Singapore still lags substantially in most other high-tech sectors.

It is also interesting to observe that Singapore, due to its small size, has a much more highly concentrated industrial structure compared to most other countries (Table 6). Indeed, as can be seen from Table 3 earlier, more than half of Singapore's manufacturing output in 1996 was accounted for by electronics alone. Despite its small size, Singapore was already the fourth largest producer of electronics goods in the world in 1994 (OECD,1997a).

While labour productivity can be said to measure the current level of competitiveness, future competitiveness will depend more on technological and innovative capabilities. As can be seen from Table 7, Singapore still trails significantly behind the leading industrial nations as well as Korea and Taiwan in terms of R&D intensities as measured by gross R&D spending/GDP ratio and the number of research scientists and engineers per 10,000 of the labour force. Singapore also lags behind these countries in terms of patent (see Table 8) and publication intensities.

Through continuous upgrading, Singapore's manufacturing sector has been able to maintain fairly high average profitability (as measured by return on equity in Table 9). Indeed, manufacturing has achieved consistently higher profitability than other sectors in the economy since the 1980s. Nonetheless, the above competitive benchmark assessment suggests that Singapore needs to continue the process of manufacturing upgrading to catch up with the more advanced industrial countries and to stave off competition in the region.

Table 6 Labour Productivity of Singapore Manufacturing vs. OECD and NIEs

Country	Value Added/Labour of Total Manufacturing (US$)		Structural indices for degree of specialisation	
	1980	1994	1980	1994
OECD:				
Australia	25280	70383	11.1	12.1
Austria	22681	61797	9.7	10.5
Belgium	30556	61596	12.5	13
Luxembourg	28479	53895	38.2	13.6
Canada	32187	58465	10.3	12.4
Denmark	31187	54677	14.8	15.6
Finland	26845	61365	13.3	15.2
France	30101	65118	10.4	11.4
Germany	36739	88680	12.1	15
Greece	16204	33368	11.8	12.4
Iceland	18864	38630	26.5	34.6
Ireland	25118	32017	14.9	23.6
Italy	28784	46871	10	12
Japan	30912	117764	11.8	15
Netherlands	29285	69616	15	14.5
New Zealand	16711	32618	14.6	16.4
Norway	19129	45828	12.2	14.5
Portugal	8087	14917	11.2	9.3
Spain	20475	43162	8.4	11.1
Sweden	36206	58602	15.4	17
Switzerland	40009	66570	11.6	15
Turkey	13617	25991	14.3	13.3
UK	25117	57635	11.1	12.5
US	40078	93199	11.9	12.8
Average of OECD	**26360**	**56365**	**13.88**	**14.70**
Singapore	**13942**	**56329**	**19.9**	**28.2**
Other NIEs:				
Hong Kong	7840	26436	24.2	19.5
South Korea	9545	52760	9.1	11.2
Taiwan	7470	33766	9.5	12.5
Average of other NIEs	**8285**	**37654**	**14.27**	**14.40**
Malaysia	**8060**	**15317**	**15.5**	**18.5**

Source: UNIDO(1997)

Table 7 International Comparisons of R&D Intensity

Country/ Year	GERD/GDP (%)	RSE/10,000 Labour Force
Japan (1994)	2.84	98.78
Korea (1995)	2.70	71.09
Switzerland (1992)	2.51	69.89
USA (1996)	2.43	68.90
Germany (1996)	2.26	61.70
UK (1995)	2.05	57.97
Taiwan (1995)	1.81	56.34
Singapore (1996)	1.35	56.14
Singapore (1995)	1.13	47.71

Sources: National Science and Technology Board, *National Survey of R&D*, various years.

Figure 1 Generic Routes to Upgrading of Manufacturing Industry

Industry Upgrading in Product Space

- Diversification/shifting of horizontal scope
  - shift from lower value-added to higher value-added products
  - shift from lower value-added to higher value-added industries
- Migration in terms of Product life cycle stage
  - shift from mature, commodity models to new, high end models
  - shift from late follower to fast follower to new product innovator

Industry Upgrading in Process Space

- Diversification/shifting of Vertical Value Chain scope
  - shift from lower value-adding stages to higher value-adding stages
  - shift to specialised components or flexible assembly
- Improvement in Process Capability
  - operation improvement (shift from within to on the production frontier)
  - process technology development/innovation (shift to new production frontier)

Table 8 Total Patents by Country (1974–1994)

State/Country	1974–94	1988–94
OECD:		
US	908,178	350,811
Australia	7,028	3,069
Austria	6,417	2,460
Belgium	5,940	2,323
Canada	30,045	13,260
Denmark	3,521	1,337
Finland	4,039	2,062
France	51,531	20,413
Germany	137,145	51,929
Italy	19,947	8,614
Japan	266,722	143,478
Luxembourg	488	178
Netherlands	15,984	6,324
New Zealand	886	326
Norway	2,089	821
Sweden	16,453	5,066
Switzerland	26,465	8,718
UK	53,560	18,212
Singapore	229	172
Other NIEs:		
Hong Kong	656	368
South Korea	3,462	3,145
Taiwan	7,608	6,316
Others:		
China	412	340
Indonesia	54	32
Israel	3,967	2,167
Malaysia	75	47
Philippines	108	32
Thailand	38	21
India	322	154

Source: Calculated from US Patent Data, Micro-Patent Database CDROM

Table 9 Return on Equity (ROE) in Singapore's Manufacturing Industry, 1987–94

Year	Electronics manufacturing (%)	All manufacturing (%)	All economic sectors (%)
1987	31.5	18.7	8.9
1988	24.7	21.8	11.7
1989	19.7	17.2	14.2
1990	20.8	18.3	12.6
1991	22.4	17.8	11.3
1992	21.3	16.9	10.4
1993	31.0	19.7	14.3
1994	19.7	16.2	12.9

Note: ROE is calculated by the Department of Statistics as the ratio of current year's earnings to the average of the stock of equity capital invested in the current & preceding year.

Source: Department of Statistics (1995), Singapore.

2. Generic Routes to Upgrading of Manufacturing Industry: Analytical Framework

Figure 1 provides a useful analytical framework to identify the possible routes to enhancing the competitiveness of Singapore's manufacturing industry in the future. In essence, the framework identifies two generic dimensions to enhancing competitiveness of a nation's manufacturing sector: "horizontal" upgrading by shifting to higher value-added products or industries in the "product space", and "vertical" upgrading by shifting to higher value-added activities along the process value chain of existing industries. Different combination of emphases along these two dimensions result in different generic routes to improving competitiveness.

A common upgrading route that has been pursued by many MNCs in Singapore in the past is to bring in higher end products while redistributing lower end products to other countries in the region, such as Malaysia or China. Another is to redistribute less automated, lower capability process lines, while upgrading the Singapore production plant to handle more advanced, sophisticated process equipment and systems. A third is to bring in either more upstream, technology intensive value-chain activities such as product R&D (e.g. product customisation to the region), or more value-adding downstream activities such as technical support, regional procurement and supply chain management.

For many indigenous manufacturing firms, a common generic route that has been successfully pursued (e.g. by Taiwnese companies like ACER) is that of moving from contract manufacturing (OEM) to original design manufacturing (ODM) to own brand manufacturing (OBM). Rather than seeking to diversify away from the existing industry, the firms seek to move upstream in terms of developing one's own product design and product technological capabilities, and downstream in terms of developing one's own brand and distribution channels (Lall, 1992).

An alternative route that has been successfully pursued by many indigenous contract manufacturing companies in East Asia is to stay focused on being a contract manufacturer by investing aggressively in developing one's process capabilities. By having the most efficient and/or highest quality manufacturing process, these firms seek to become the preferred manufacturers for other product developers.

From the perspective of the firms concerned, the specific route selected to enhancing competitiveness in Singapore is in principle derived from the firms' broader generic competitive strategy, of which the leveraging of Singapore as an operating base is only one component consideration. For example, some firms may choose to hollow out manufacturing operations entirely from Singapore, and concentrate instead on using Singapore as their operational headquarters and centre for product and/or process R&D activities.

From the perspective of the government, however, the focus of concerns is not only that the firms must be competitive globally, but that they should locate more of their higher value adding activities in Singapore. As such, it is the competitiveness of their Singapore based operations that is of central concern. Hence, in applying the framework to identify specific policies and programmes to enhancing the competitiveness of Singapore's manufacturing industry in the future, we need to take into account the various environmental factors specific to Singapore that facilitate the private firms' investment in enhancing the competitiveness of their Singapore operations. These factors include the extent of economies of scope and transferability of brand and distribution channels (for horizontal shift); the economies of vertical integration and learning by transacting (for vertical value chain shift); the transferability of skills and learning acquired in earlier industries; the extent to which the new industries or value chain activities stimulate the development of common shared supporting industries and infrastructure, or other sources of agglomeration economies; the ease with which existing operations can be easily regionalised; and the extent to which common ownership may make the shifting in product or process space easier.

3. Manufacturing Upgrading Strategies: Lessons from Other East Asian NIEs

Historically, the Asian NIEs shared a common characteristic with many other developing countries in that they were all rather late industrialising countries in the global economy (Hikino and Amsden,1994). These countries face two common problems in terms of developing high-tech industrial capability: firstly, they were typically distant from the lead user markets in North America, Europe and Japan; secondly, they were also far away from and disconnected to the leading sources of innovation in advanced countries. Despite these disadvantages, however, the Asian NIEs managed to achieve significantly faster high-tech industrial growth over the last three decades than all other developing countries. Moreover, their manufacturing sector upgrading strategies have been distinctively different from one another (Hobday,1994). The simple analytical framework above can be used to derive insights on how Taiwan, Korea and Hong Kong have successfully upgraded their manufacturing sectors through distinctly different generic routes.

The first generic technological upgrading strategy can be best characterised as one involving technology assimilation/transfer and cooperative R&D promotion through public research institutes (PRIs). Among the NIEs, Taiwan has been most successful in using PRI to promote the diffusion of industrially relevant technologies.

For example, the Industrial Technology Research Institute (ITRI) has been widely credited with helping to create an advanced semiconductor industry cluster in Taiwan through a well thought out and well executed strategy of assimilating foreign technology and transferring them to local enterprises through spinoffs [see e.g. Mathews (1995), Lin (1994), NRI (1995)]. The successful execution of this strategy depended on a number of factors, including careful long term technology development planning and vision at the top ("Electronics Industry Development Project (EIDP)"), competent leadership at the helm of ITRI (Dr. Morris Chang), an abundant supply of well trained engineers, and significant presence of, and strong linkage with, competitive local electronics industries which provided significant markets and customer feedback.

Besides such successful spinoffs as UMC and TSMC from PRIs, there are also many examples of PRI-orchestrated R&D consortia in Taiwan. These have been promoted in the belief that the many small and medium enterprises in Taiwan would underinvest in new technology development if left on their own. Over the last 15 years, it has been estimated that over 60 such R&D consortia had been established in various industrial sectors in Taiwan. Although the records of these R&D consortia in terms of eventual market commercialisation are mixed, it is undeniable that there has been much faster diffusion of product technological capabilities among the participating firms as a result of these consortium programs (e.g. the successful development of the notebook PC industry in Taiwan owes much to the ITRI-orchestrated development consortium). In particular, the significant inroads that Taiwanese firms have made into ODM in recent years are partly facilitated by these R&D consortia.

The second generic route to manufacturing upgrading can be characterised as one involving the deliberate promotion of high-tech conglomerate enterprises of sufficiently large scale. This has been the classic Korean *chaebol* model of expansion through horizontal diversification in product space and vertical integration in process space. In the early stage of development of "strategic" industries in Korea, the Korean government deliberately encouraged the growth of large scale *chaebols* as an instrument to bring about the economy of scale in capital intensive industries that were deemed "strategic".

A variety of policy tools were used [see e.g. Kim (1993)], including subsidised financing, protection of domestic market, incentives for technological learning through capital goods import or turnkey projects vs. DFI, and turning over failing state enterprises to the *chaebols*. Although there were notable failures in this heavy industry strategy, several of the big *chaebols* like Samsung, LG, Hyundai and Daewoo did develop significant technological capabilities in a wide range of export oriented, capital intensive industries as a result. Where Korea differs from other developing countries in promoting big businesses was in the discipline that the state exercised over these *chaebols* by penalising poor performances and rewarding only good ones. This "contest"-based approach (Amsden,1989) enabled a number of high performing *chaebols* to quickly establish large scale production, marketing/distribution or R&D economies to compete successfully in several global industries like shipbuilding, automobile, consumer electronics, telecommunications equipment, and semiconductors. The large size of these *chaebols* enabled them to build global brand and distribution channels, and hence move quickly into OBM in a wide range of consumer products. Deep pockets have also enabled the *chaebols* to acquire technology capabilities quickly by buying up established companies (recent examples include Maxtor, NCR microelectronics, AST). However, the large size of the *chaebols* appear to be a source of disadvantage when it comes to competing in technologically dynamic industries like PCs, software, biotechnology and specialty chemicals where scale economies are not important or less critical. Furthermore, indiscriminate and unrelated diversification had often led to over-extension and loss of strategic focus. This conglomeration trend had also become increasingly questioned as a result of political democratisation in recent years.

The excessive development of big businesses in Korea had become evident in the light of the recent debt crisis faced by Korea, which exposed the vulnerability of this high financial gearing approach to industrial growth. Nevertheless, the basic idea of "contest-based" resource allocation and the need to achieve sufficient scale economy remain valid policy concerns for late industrialising economies seeking to enter a wide range of capital intensive high-tech industries now dominated by advanced industrialised countries.

The third generic route to manufacturing upgrading, typified by Hong Kong, can be characterised as one of staying within relatively mature industries and product groups, but migrating along the vertical value chain towards marketing, logistics and technical support downstream and product innovation upstream. With little government support for R&D and technological development, Hong Kong manufacturing firms opted not to enter technologically advanced sectors or products involving the early stage of new technology life cycles. Instead, they sought to achieve cost competitive advantage in relatively mature, less capital-intensive sectors (e.g. textile and garment, watches, electronic toys and games) by redistributing manufacturing operations to China (particularly Shenzhen) and other low cost regions in Southeast Asia. At the same time, the Hong Kong base is turned increasingly into the headquarters for product design, marketing, logistics management, technical support and accounting/administration. By focusing on niche markets involving fast fashion changes or short product runs and leveraging on the excellent communications and transport infrastructure of Hong Kong, many Hong Kong manufacturers developed core competencies in managing fast response, dispersed production networks. For example, in textile and garment making, Hong Kong firms have developed sophisticated CAD/CAM design and electronic data interchange capabilities that allow them to quickly turn buyer requirements into design specifications, which are then partitioned into job assignments to different subcontractors, often outside Hong Kong. In reality, this generic route involves substantial deindustrialisation of Hong Kong itself, which retains largely the services value added stages of the manufacturing value chain.

Last, but not least, the industrial development strategy of Singapore can be best characterised as one emphasising government facilitation of MNC induced technological learning [Wong (1994, 1995a, 1995c)]. Through the Economic Development Board (EDB), the Singapore Government has encouraged MNCs to bring in success waves of new technologies to their subsidiary operations in Singapore. Although some have criticised this MNC led approach as stunting the growth of local firms, research evidence has shown that these MNC operations have spawned a large supporting industry in Singapore and induced substantial technological capability development among many local subcontracting and contract assembly firms (Wong, 1992, 1995b). Moreover, active innovative public assistance programmes such as the Local Industry Upgrading Programme (LIUP), programmes to promote the adoption of new information and automation technology by SMEs, advanced technical manpower training programmes like INTECH, and the early promotion of the ISO9000 certification infrastructure have been shown to have facilitated the technological and management learning process of these supporting industries. Many of these local supporting firms have pursued the process specialist route, and most have since internationalised their operations to the near NIEs like Malaysia and China, not only following the redistribution of their customers to these countries, but diversifying into new buyer markets as well. Regionalisation incentives provided by the government have facilitated these overseas ventures. Moreover, new innovative R&D incentives like Research Incentives Scheme for Companies (RISC) has been introduced by the government to fund integrative process technology capability development efforts in these companies, even though such efforts cannot be neatly packaged into specific R&D projects. A smaller, but increasing, number of companies have also pursued the reverse product life cycle strategy, moving into new product R&D while leveraging their traditional strengths in low cost, high quality manufacturing.

The generic routes described above serve to highlight the dominant route taken by Taiwan, Korea, Hong Kong and Singapore to upgrading industrial capability development. In reality, it should be recognised, of course, that none of these countries pursue only one route exclusively. For example, the Singapore Government has in recent years also started to stress the need to develop high-tech firms of sufficient scale by setting up a government controlled group, Singapore Technology Group, to spearhead entry into various high-tech industries (e.g. semiconductor wafer fabrication, chip design, aerospace repair and maintenence, systems software) where local entrepreneurs had been found wanting. Many Singapore firms have also adopted the generic upgrading route of Hong Kong by redistributing their manufacturing operations overseas and leveraging Singapore as their regional headquarter hub for product/process development, marketing, logistics and technical support.

The use of a public research institute to promote technology diffusion has also been used in Korea, particularly in the early years, as in the case of semiconductor technology acquisition through a public research institute like KIET (which was later merged into ETRI) (Mathews, 1995). The considerably larger resources of the big *chaebols* meant that further direct government involvement in technology transfer was deemed unnecessary once the basic 4M DRAM technology was diffused among Samsung, LG and Hyundai. More recently, the Singapore Government has also started to promote R&D consortia as a means to hasten technological capability development of local firms. Involvement with foreign firms or R&D institutions are particularly emphasised to facilitate technology transfer from advanced sources. Examples include the Digital Media Consortium (involving three local firms, three PRIs, and MIT Media Lab) and cooperative R&D programmes in aerospace, data storage and marine technologies.

In highlighting the differences among the East Asian NIEs, we do not intend to belittle the various common state facilitating roles as emphasised by the "East Asian Miracles" (World Bank,1993), such as high investment in education (especially technical education) and infrastructures, export orientation, and macroeconomic stability, etc. Indeed, in some sense, these fundamental policies represent the preconditions for the success of the more specific industrial policies adopted in the different countries.

In summary, our analysis of the manufacturing development strategies of the four Asian NIEs suggests that there had been several generic routes to manufacturing industry upgrading rather than a single common route. While Singapore has been rather successful in emphasising one particular route in the past (attracting MNC investments of increasingly higher value add contents), the country will need to consider selectively incorporating the best elements of other successful routes pursued by other NIEs in the future. Indeed, as evident in our earlier review, this process has already started. At the same time, the existing strategy of upgrading through MNC investments and technology transfer needs to be further refined.

4. Specific Recommendations for Singapore

Based on the current stage of development of Singapore's manufacturing industry and taking into account emergent development in advanced industrialised countries, we suggest the following areas of high value added opportunities for intensified promotion.

Intensification of the Agglomeration of Key Industrial Clusters

Singapore has already developed several clusters of highly competitive industries such as computer and peripherals, semiconductors and petrochemicals. The strengths of these clusters derives largely from the high degree of agglomeration of manufacturing operations as well as their supporting and complementary industries. While such high concentration has been a source of concern in terms of increasing the volatility and vulnerability of the economy as a whole to industry downturns, it must be recognised that it is often easier to leverage growth through related agglomeration rather than to promote entirely "green field" investments. In this regard, Singapore must in the future continue to leverage the benefits of agglomeration economies in the key industries she has built up over the years by attracting high value-adding related industries that will further expand and strengthen these clusters. For example, the attraction of disk media companies and the related diversification into other data storage technologies represent good ways to leverage the hard disk drive assembly industry, while the recent big push towards enlarging the industrial chemicals and petrochemicals cluster represents another good strategic move. Other potential electronics related diversifications include automotive electronics, industrial automation electronics equipment, and medical and scientific instrument.

World/Regional Product Charter

The recent push by the government to significantly increase R&D activities in Singapore in general under the National Technology Plan (1991–95) and the National Science and Technology Plan

(1996–2000) (NSTB, 1996) is certainly correct to enable more manufacturing firms in Singapore to shift towards new product and process innovation as their future source of competitive advantage. A key part of this R&D-push strategy is for Singapore to attract more world class MNCs to pursue the complete cycle of "idea-to-market" activities in Singapore, where Singaporeans have the chance to learn how to plan, develop and commercialise new products, manufacture them, and distribute them to markets. It is only through such complete product mandate that product innovation capability can be most easily indigenised, and from which new high-tech ventures in new product innovation can be most easily spawn. A key factor in the dynamism of new high-tech startups in the Silicon Valley in California (and on a smaller scale, Hsinchu in Taiwan) is the critical mass of experienced technical people who have acquired experience (and confidence) in launching new products in larger organisations; these experienced people constitute the main sources of new high-tech entrepreneurs, or the key managers of these new ventures.

Singapore has indeed achieved the status of being the regional/world wide charter for selected products by a small number of MNCs, e.g. the Asian printer and portable computing device charter for HP, the Asian pager product charter for Motorola, and selected audio electronics products by Philips. In the future, Singapore needs to become the home base for more such worldwide/region-wide product charters by leading global MNCs.

Lead Manufacturing Plant and Process Transfer Station

A number of leading MNCs like WD, Seagate in the hard disk drive (HDD) industry and Glaxo in the pharmaceutical industry have chosen to locate their most advanced manufacturing operations, or their *lead manufacturing plants*, in Singapore. Some have also used their manufacturing plants in Singapore as the "process transfer stations" for the region: the plants in Singapore are tasked with developing the manufacturing process to handle new products, but once the processes are stabilised they are then transferred to a lower cost location in the region. Singapore needs to attract more MNCs to use Singapore as their lead manufacturing/process transfer stations.

Regional Contract Design-Manufacture-Precision Engineering Hub

Over the last decade, Singapore has emerged as a major contract manufacturing hub in the world. For example, three of the top ten contract manufacturers in the world are Singaporean firms (Venture, Flextronics, and Natsteel Electronics), and most of the leading contract manufacturers in the world (e.g. SCI from the US, MKE from Japan) have operations in Singapore. Singapore has also developed a large and diverse cluster of precision engineering and other supporting industries (printed circuit boards, precision machining, metal stamping, surface treatment, plastic injection moulding, tool and die making, automation services, clean room design services, etc.) that are necessary to support fast ramp up, agile manufacturing. However, due to rising cost and labour shortage, many of these industries are redistributing to cheaper locations overseas. To maintain Singapore as a leading contract manufacturing hub in the world in the future, we need to upgrade to higher precision engineering services. At the same time, Singapore needs to quickly improve our original design manufacturing (ODM) capability, including in particular the development of industrial design and rapid prototyping capabilities.

Regional Supply Chain Integrator

Capitalising on the excellent transport and communications infrastructure, an increasing number of MNCs have used Singapore as their logistics management hub in the region, e.g. Sony and Matsushita from Japan, and Compaq and HP from the US. With product life cycle becoming increasingly shorter in most high-tech products in the future, supply chain management will become an increasingly important source of value addition. Consequently, Singapore needs to further strengthen her role as the regional supply-chain integrator, even as much of the goods are being manufactured outside of Singapore. In this regard, Singapore needs to strengthen not only her traditional transport and logistics infrastructure, but also to rapidly deploy new information infrastructure such as internet based electronic data interchange (EDI), secure electronic commerce transactions technology, and new legal framework or commercial codes to support electronic procurement.

Proactive Public R&D Push in Selected Emerging High-Tech Sectors

While the above largely build upon the established electronics, chemicals and industrial machinery manufacturing clusters where Singapore has been strong, global trends suggest that Singapore needs to open up new high-tech industrial clusters such as pharmaceuticals, biotechnology and advanced materials. The successful development of such clusters typically requires the prior existence of a large pool of upstream R&D expertise and facilities. Hence, there is a need for the government to proactively seed the growth of these industries through the establishment of public research institutes and strategic R&D programmes, and to attract local firms and MNCs to collaborate with these institutes. In this regard, the Taiwanese experience in public research institute led R&D consortia should be studied more carefully for adaptation to the Singapore environment (Wong, 1998).

Venture Capital Industry Development

To shift from commodity products manufacturing to the manufacturing of new generations of new, technically advanced products, Singapore needs to be able to draw upon a continuous streams of new product innovations. While the corporate headquarters of global MNCs had in the past been an important source of these products, and will continue to be so, these need to be supplemented by new sources of product innovation and commercialisation activities based in Singapore, even if the original technical invention may not have originated in Singapore. Singapore based companies must also improve their capability in prospecting for new technologies emanating in Silicon Valley and other innovation hubs of the world (e.g. like the way Flextech has invested in a new semiconductor packaging technology firm to obtain rights to manufacture using the technology). In either case, there is an urgent need for Singapore to develop a more sophisticated venture capital industry. In addition to incentives to lure global venture capital firms to set up operation in Singapore, existing domestic financial institutions need to be encouraged to become more active in this area. Besides independent venture capital firms, other high-tech venture facilitation mechanisms also need to be promoted, e.g. the development of a community of "business angels", the enabling of public research institutes and tertiary institutes to take on a more active technology spinoff and commercialisation role, and the strengthening of other supporting services such as "technopreneur" incubators, technology brokers, and IPR lawyers.

The development of a more sophisticated venture capital industry will also enable Singapore to position herself as the regional prospecting hub for new technologies emerging from within the region. For example, China and India have a large number of public research institutes, but most of their activities are divorced from industries, and many of these institutes have no capabilities to assess market potentials or to package technology for commercialisation. Singapore based public research institutes and venture capital firms can thus play a potential intermediary role of prospecting and packaging technology from these and other countries in the region for commercialisation by Singapore based manufacturing firms.

Green Manufacturing Strategy

With growing environmental concerns in the advanced industrial countries, we can expect increasingly stringent demand, both through regulatory requirements (e.g. Green Labeling and Emission Restrictions) as well as customer pressures, for manufactured products and manufacturing processes to be more environment friendly. Just as Singapore has led the region in terms of diffusion of ISO9000 quality certification, Singapore should similarly push for early widespread diffusion of ISO14000 in the manufacturing sector. At the same time, the growing environmental problems in the region and the relative backwardness of the East Asian region in terms of environmental technology adoption suggest tremendous scope for value adding activities in the form of environmental engineering services and technical consulting on "green" manufacturing practices. The early adoption of green manufacturing would thus put

Singapore in a good position not only to compete in markets where demand for "green" manufacturing certification will become an important differentiating factor, but also to capitalise on the early learning advantage to become the green manufacturing technology service provider to the region. A green manufacturing strategy can also leverage upon the already high reputation of Singapore as an environmentally friendly and progressive city.

3. Conclusion

In summary, while Singapore has achieved remarkable progress in developing her manufacturing sector in the past, more needs to be done in the future to sustain and further enhance Singapore's manufacturing competitiveness as the country increasingly needs to compete against the advanced industrialised countries. This paper has identified a number of priority opportunity areas for enhancing competitiveness of Singapore's manufacturing sector. In proposing these areas, however, we recognise that the government's "three-legged" strategy of attracting MNCs, promoting local enterprises and selective involvement of GLCs has served the country well in the past, and will continue to do so provided that the proper balance between the three is continuously adapted to the changing internationally competitive environment. In the future, we see the need for a greater emphasis on enhancing the technological capabilities of local enterprises. Similarly, the formula of proactive infrastructure investment, human resource development and pro-business environment that has made Singapore competitive in the past is fundamentally sound and hence should continue to form the basis for the new policy initiatives.

References

Amsden, A. (1989) *Korea: Asia's Next Giant*, N.Y.: Oxford University Press.

Department of Statistics, Singapore, Yearbook of Statistics, various years, Singapore.

Department of Statistics (1995) *The Extent and Pattern of Foreign Investment Activities in Singapore*, Singapore: Occasional paper on economic statistics, Department of Statistics.

Economic Development Board, Singapore, *Report on the Census for Industrial Production*, various years, Singapore.

Hikino, T. and Amsden, A.H. (1994) "Staying Behind, Stumbling Back, Sneaking Up, Soaring Ahead: Late Industrialisation in Historical Perspective", in Baumol, W.J., Nelson, R.R. and Wolff, E.N. (eds.) *Convergence of Productivity: Cross National Studies and Historical Evidence*, New York: Oxford University Press.

Hobday, M. (1995), *Innovation in East Asia: The Challengeto Japan*, E.Elgar.

Hou, C.M. and Gee, S. (1993) "National Systems Supporting Technical Advance in Industry: The Case of Taiwan", in Nelson, R.R. (ed.) (1993) *National Innovation Systems: A Comparative Analysis*, New York: Oxford University Press, pp. 384–413.

IMD (various years), *World Competitiveness Report*, Geneva, Switzerland

Kim, L.S. (1993) "National System of Industrial Innovation: Dynamics of Capability Building in Korea", in Nelson, R.R. (ed.) (1993) *National Innovation Systems: A Comparative Analysis*, New York: Oxford University Press, pp. 357–383.

Lall, S. (1992) "Technological Capabilities and Industrialisation", *World Development*, 20(2): pp. 165–186.

Lin, O.C.C. (1994) "Development and Transfer of Industrial Technology in Taiwan, R.O.C.", in Lin, O.C.C. *et al.* (eds.) *Development and Transfer of Industrial Technology*, Elsevier, pp. 1–30.

Low, L., Toh, M.H., Soon, T.W., Tan, K.Y. and Hughes, H. (1993) *Challenge and Response: Thirty Years of the Economic Development Board*, Times Academic Press, Singapore.

Mathews, J.A. (1995) *High Technology Industrialisation in East Asia: The Case of the Semiconductor Industry in Taiwan and Korea*, Taipei: Chung-Hua Institution for Economic Research.

National Science & Technology Board [NSTB] (1991) *National Technology Plan*, Singapore.

National Science & Technology Board [NSTB], *National Survey of R & D*, various years, Singapore.

National Science & Technology Board [NSTB], Singapore (1996) *National Science and Technology Plan: Towards 2000 and Beyond*, Singapore: NSTB.

Nelson, R.R. (ed.) (1993) *National Innovation Systems: A Comparative Analysis*, New York: Oxford University Press.

OECD (1994) *Manufacturing Performance: A scoreboard of indicators*, Paris: OECD.

OECD (1997a) *Information Technology Outlook 1997*, Paris: OECD.

OECD (1997b) *Industrial Competitiveness: Benchmarking Business Environment in the Global Economy*, Paris: OECD.

OECD (1997c) *Science, technology and Industry Scoreboard of Indicators*, Paris: OECD.

UNIDO (1997) *Industrial Development Global Report 1996*, Oxford University Press.

Wong, P.K. (1992) "Technological Development Through Subcontracting Linkages: Evidence from Singapore," *Scandinavian International Business Review*, 1(3): pp. 28–40.

Wong, P.K. (1994) "Singapore's Technology Strategy," in D.F. Simon (ed.), *The Emerging Technological Trajectory of the Pacific Rim*. N.Y.: M.E. Sharpe, pp. 103–131.

Wong, P.K. (1995a) "Competing in the Global Electronics Industry: A Comparative Study of the Innovation Networks of Singapore and Taiwan," *Journal of Industry Studies*, Vol 2, No. 2, pp. 35–61.

Wong, P.K. (1995b) "Technology Transfer and Development Inducement by Foreign MNCs: The Experience of Singapore", in Jeong, K.Y. and Kwack, M.H. (eds.) *Industrial Strategy for Global Competitiveness of Korean Industries*, Seoul: Korea Economic Research Institute, pp. 130–159.

Wong, P.K. (1995c) *National Innovation System: The Case of Singapore*, Seoul: Science and Technology Policy Institute (STEPI).

Wong, P.K. (1998) "Technology Acquisition Pattern of High-tech Firms in Singapore", *Singapore Management Review* (forthcoming).

Wong, P.K., Phang, S.Y. *et al.* (1997) *Development of Internationally Competitive Indigenous Manufacturing Firms in Singapore*, Tokyo: Foundation for Advanced Studies of International Development (FASID), November 1997.

World Bank (1993) *The East Asian Miracles*, Oxford: Oxford University Press.

Annex Table 1 Sectoral Performance of Singapore's Economy, 1960–96

Sector	% per annum				
	1960–70	**1970–80**	**1980–85**	**1985–90**	**1990–96**
Manufacturing	13.7	10.9	1.6	12.5	7.3
Construction	15.8	6.0	15.2	-6.1	15.8
Commerce	8.0	7.4	4.0	9.2	7.6
Transport & Communications	7.1	14.6	8.7	9.3	8.9
Finance & Business Services	11.3	11.1	12.5	7.0	9.0
Others	6.3	6.3	6.1	5.5	7.3
Total GDP	9.1	9.0	6.2	8.1	8.3

Source: Department of Statistics, Singapore Yearbook of Statistics (various years)

Annex Table 2 Sectoral Structure of Singapore's Economy, 1960–96

% Composition							
Sector	**1960**	**1970**	**1980**	**1985**	**1990**	**1995**	**1996**
Manufacturing	16.5	26.3	29.5	22.2	27.2	26.4	24.4
Construction	5.2	9.5	7.1	10.5	5.2	7.0	7.4
Commerce	24.5	22.0	18.9	16.9	17.9	17.3	17.4
Transport & communications	8.7	7.3	12.0	11.5	12.2	12.4	10.4
Finance & Business Services	14.0	17.0	20.5	25.6	25.0	25.3	28.6
Others	25.0	19.3	14.9	13.4	12.4	11.6	11.7
Total GDP	100	100	100	100	100	100	100

Source: Department of Statistics, Singapore Yearbook of Statistics (various years)

5

The Construction Industry: Restructuring for Competitiveness

Toh Mun Heng

1. Introduction

Construction influences all sectors of economic activity and private life. It includes civil engineering, commercial building, housing, and repair and maintenance. Just before the recession in 1985, the construction sector's share of GDP recorded a peak of 13.2% in Singapore. It has since reduced substantially to 8.2% in 1996, which is about a third of those by the manufacturing sector (26.9%) and the finance and business services sector (27.2%). (Table 1) Nevertheless, the sector has been enjoying robust growth in recent years and contracts awarded rose from $10.6 billion in 1993 to $19.6 billion in 1996. The figure is expected to exceed $20 billion in 1997.

Construction is also a major sector of employment in Singapore. As of 1996, it employs more than 115,000 people, which constitutes 6.6% of all employment. It is a sector that is intensive in professional workers. In 1996, almost 24.7% of the workers in the construction sector were professionals, including legislators, administrators and managers. This is about 8.3% of the professional workforce. Nonetheless, it is also highly dependent on low-skilled production workers and hence an increasing need for further automation and upgrading of the industrial structure and diversification of products of the sector.

The construction sector is the only sector that appears twice in the national accounts of most countries. As alluded above, the construction sector, together with other sectors like manufacturing and financial services, contributes to the national GDP. By measuring the national product as an aggregate of final demand, the expenditure

Table 1 Value Added by Industrial Origin

	(At 1990 Prices)			S$m / %	
	1980	**1985**	**1990**	**1995**	**1996**
GDP	33581.6	45344.9	67878.9	102652.4	109787.1
Manufacturing	9967.7	10768.6	19393.1	28528.6	29485.5
Construction	**2517.1**	**5112.8**	**3724.0**	**7585.5**	**8982.8**
Commerce	6737.2	8208.7	12764.2	18713.5	19834.9
Tpt & Comms	3683.2	5590.6	8715.6	13413.5	14500.7
Finance & Biz	6880.9	12381.6	17835.1	27633.8	29905.2
Others	3795.5	3282.6	5446.9	6777.5	7078.0
% Distribution					
GDP	100.0	100.0	100.0	100.0	100.0
Manufacturing	29.7	23.7	28.6	27.8	26.9
Construction	**7.5**	**11.3**	**5.5**	**7.4**	**8.2**
Commerce	20.1	18.1	18.8	18.2	18.1
Tpt & Comms	11.0	12.3	12.8	13.1	13.2
Finance & Biz	20.5	27.3	26.3	26.9	27.2
Others	11.3	7.2	8.0	6.6	6.4

Source: *Yearbook of Statistics, 1996,* published by the Department of Statistics, Ministry of Trade and Industry, Singapore.

on construction sector products often constitutes a substantial portion of the national expenditure on capital formation. The products of the construction sector are, in general, investment goods. These goods, together with the additional machinery and equipment acquired, add to the physical capital stock of the country. The national stock of capital, which includes both physical and human capital, reflects the productive capacity of the economy and hence the wealth creating potential of the country.

As indicated in Table 3, gross domestic capital formation (GDCF) accounts for 35.2% of the GDP in 1995. This amounts to S$36 billion at 1990 prices, of which about half were expenditures on construction related investment goods. The public sector

Table 2 Employment by Industry ('000)

	1980	1985	1990	1995	1996
Total	1077.1	1234.6	1537.0	1702.1	1748.1
Manufacturing	324.1	314.2	447.4	412.7	406.3
Construction	**72.3**	**110.0**	**122.1**	**113.9**	**115.0**
Commerce	229.8	290.0	337.5	347.8	405.9
Tpt & Comms	119.9	125.1	146.6	182.8	195.3
Finance & Biz	79.4	107.7	167.2	248.2	246.0
Others	251.6	287.6	316.2	396.7	379.7
% Distribution					
Total	100.0	100.0	100.0	100.0	100.0
Manufacturing	30.1	25.4	29.1	24.2	23.2
Construction	**6.7**	**8.9**	**7.9**	**6.7**	**6.6**
Commerce	21.3	23.5	22.0	20.4	23.2
Tpt & Comms	11.1	10.1	9.5	10.7	11.2
Finance & Biz	7.4	8.7	10.9	14.6	14.1
Others	23.4	23.3	20.6	23.3	21.7

Source: Same as Table 1.

continues to be an important purchaser of construction investment goods in the form of residential housing and civil constructions.

However, with the completion of major public infrastructure projects, such as housing and road works, the share of the public sector's investment in construction has been declining since the recession in 1985. In 1985, about half of the GDCF in construction was attributed to the public sector, but by 1995, the public sector's capital formation only constituted about a third of the total capital formation in construction. (Table 4)

In view of the upgrading and expansion in construction related activities, the standard coverage of the construction sector in the national accounts is incomplete and inadequate. Traditionally, only the bulk of the activities of building and contracting firms are covered. Quite often, the activities of consulting engineers,

Table 3 Percentage Distribution of GDP by Expenditure

	1980	1985	1990	1995	1996
GDP	100.0	100.0	100.0	100.0	100.0
Pte Consumption	50.9	44.7	45.3	41.8	42.2
Public Consumption	10.5	13.3	10.0	9.0	10.0
GDCF	**37.7**	**41.3**	**31.8**	**35.4**	**38.5**
Increase in Stock	6.0	0.9	4.1	−0.2	−1.7
Net Exports	−1.6	0.4	8.8	15.4	12.4
SDR	−3.7	−0.6	0.0	−1.5	−1.3

*GDCF = Gross Domestic Capital Formation
Source: Same as Table 1

Table 4 Components of Gross Domestic Capital Formation

	(At 1990 Prices)			S$m / %	
	1980	**1985**	**1990**	**1995**	**1996**
GDCF	12673.2	18721.9	21577.8	36371.3	42230.4
Non-Construction	7146.7	6671.3	13113.4	18423.1	20998.5
Public Construction	**2756.7**	**5818.2**	**3107.4**	**5856.9**	**6760.9**
Private Construction	2769.8	6232.4	5357.0	12091.3	4471.0
% Distribution					
GDCF	100.0	100.0	100.0	100.0	100.0
Non-Construction	56.4	35.6	60.8	50.7	49.7
Public Construction	**21.8**	**31.1**	**14.4**	**16.1**	**16.0**
Private Construction	21.9	33.3	24.8	33.2	34.3

Source: Ministry of Trade and Industry, *Annual Economic Survey of Singapore*, various years.

architects, interior designers and other construction related technical expertise are treated separately as business services. These activities are becoming increasingly important as our economy internationalises and firms expand their businesses abroad. An attempt is made to include these activities in the assessment of the overall contribution of the construction sector to the economy. In Table 5, the value added contribution of real estate developers, as well as architectural, consulting, engineering and technical services are included to provide a more comprehensive assessment of the augmented construction sector. In 1988, the augmented construction sector contributed 10.3% of the GDP, compared to 5.4% (if only the traditional construction activities are accounted for). More recent estimates indicate that the augmented construction sector contributed 12% or more of the GDP for the period 1992 to 1996.

Obviously, this new definition will enhance the importance of the construction industry in the economy in terms of value-added and employment. More importantly, it provides a better perspective of the career opportunities and scope for job enhancement and enrichment for workers who are trained in technology related disciplines. The vision of a more technology oriented workforce to cope with increasing international competition cannot materialise without the availability of job opportunities for such workers.[1]

Another cogent rationale for the restructuring of the construction industry is in response to the increased project complexity and technical sophistication exercised by consumers and competitors in the international economic environment. In a land scarce and labour deficit economy like Singapore, rising wage costs and rentals exert immense pressure on the construction industry to restructure and upgrade. In this chapter, we survey the major issues faced by the construction industry. These include the introduction of new management techniques, the problem of productivity improvement, the role of technology, the constraints posed by labour scarcity and the need for regionalisation and bidding for international contracts.[2]

---

[1] The government has adopted measures, such as the provision of more scholarships, research career induction camps, and preferential adjustment of tuition fees, to encourage more students to enrol in engineering and science related fields of study at the universities.

[2] In this paper, we refrain from providing a historical overview of the development of the construction sector in Singapore, as this is already succinctly discussed by writers, such as Ofori G. (1993) and Low S.P. (1996).

Table 5 Estimated Share of Construction Sector in the Overall Economy GDP At Current Market Prices/S$m

	GDP	Constrn	% of GDP	Real Est Develop	Arch/Engr Services	Augmented Constrn	% of GDP
1988	51,642	2,772	5.4	2,289	252	5,313	10.3
1989	59,344	3,227	5.4	2,526	377	6,131	10.3
1990	67,879	3,724	5.5	2,891	522	7,137	10.5
1991	75,321	4,799	6.4	3,300	579	8,678	11.5
1992	80,998	6,212	7.7	3,418	643	10,274	12.7
1993	94,259	6,772	7.2	3,877	754	11,403	12.1
1994	108,224	7,976	7.4	4,717	1,105	13,797	12.7
1995	121,081	8,581	7.1	4,656	1,167	14,404	11.9
1996	132,629	10,431	7.9	5,251	1,316	16,998	12.8

Notes: 1988 figures are from IO Table. For other years, information are from the *Singapore System of National Accounts, 1996* and *Yearbook of Statistics, 1996.*

Figures for Real Estate Developers and Architect/Engineering Services are obtained from the Survey/Census of Services for years 1990 to 1995. 1996 figures are extrapolated using ratio to financial and business during the previous years.

2. New Management Strategies

The construction industry is undergoing a process of restructuring, arising from changes in the market, and from new competitive pressures. Prior to the recession in 1985, construction activity in Singapore was split quite evenly between the public and private sectors. However, with the decline of public sector work, combined with increasing competition from foreign companies operating in Singapore, firms have to look for new ways of sustaining their workload and profitability. One outcome of this is the shedding of directly employed labour to reduce overheads. This leads to an increased use of subcontractors, self-employed labour and foreign workers, possibly accompanied by a reduction in training. Another important outcome is the greater willingness and impetus to seek business opportunities in overseas markets.

In the industrialised economies, a number of conditions have provided the stimuli for change in the techniques used to manage engineering and construction projects. The dwindling volume of domestic and overseas construction projects (especially in the Middle East) in the 1980s, without commensurate reduction in the number of firms bidding for such contracts, has created a "buyers' market". Clients have begun to demand buildings of increasing complexity. The widespread diffusion of Information Technology (IT) and the need for greater environmental control have led to increased sophistication in building services (Gann, 1989). Private sector clients are demanding better performance by imposing more stringent contract conditions.

Large penalties have been imposed on contracts which failed to be completed on time, creating a highly competitive environment. Increased project complexity and fragmentation due to the rise of subcontracting, together with greater technical sophistication, have led to the growth in the number of specialist trades in developed countries (Bennett and Ferry, 1988). The sourcing of building materials, components and equipment from a growing international market has added to the complexity of managing many large projects.

There are two inter-related ways in which construction firms have adapted their competitive strategies to respond to these conditions. First, they have sought to extend their markets by offering different services — of particular interest here is the shift into professional construction management and consultancy. Second, they have attempted to reduce their costs. There are four principal mechanisms by which cost reduction can be achieved. They are:

1. To adjust labour inputs through organisational changes.
2. To adopt new materials and components.
3. To shift production off site by the use of prefabrication.
4. To utilise more capital equipment.

The move away from traditional methods of contracting has had a profound impact on skills and employment, but leading edge firms have also attempted to innovate through the use of new technologies. We shall consider the linkages between organisational and technical changes later.

The need to restructure the construction industry is felt not only in Singapore. The industrialised economies in Europe and North

America have also encountered similar difficulties. In some sense, the problems of the construction sector have "globalised". While cutting costs and exploring new markets are rational responses, new management strategies have to be devised in order for the construction sector to deal with demand volatility and uncertainties in order to remain competitive.

After the Second World War, the Fordist production paradigm was widely adopted and geared towards the production of single products for mass markets using highly specialised, single purpose machinery. However, the Fordist production technique is unsuitable for the construction industry, as each product is unique and producers have to be flexible in response to customer demand. There is a perceptible trend towards embracing greater flexibility in the engagement and deployment of labour in the construction industry. This appears to be part of the modernisation strategy of the industry as a whole and an outcome of the restructuring process. This has sometimes been referred to as "flexible specialisation" (Piore and Sabel, 1984). The concept of flexible specialisation has been used to denote new methods of organising the labour process in mass production industries.

Compared to the manufacturing sector, the construction production process is characterised by three main features:

1. A lengthy production cycle divided into many distinct stages, each of which is undertaken by different economic actors with different and often conflicting interests.
2. A complex system of relationships between the various interventions, which is traditionally organised around a "vertical" and hierarchical (from planning to construction) set of relationships.
3. A discontinuous production process, which is particularly illustrated by the marked separation between the product conception stage and the realisation stage.

Each of these aspects is currently the object of profound transformations: the hierarchical and discontinuous pattern of traditional project management no longer seems adapted to the economic constraints being experienced within the construction sector. Since the beginning of the 1980s, there is evidence of actors developing new strategies aimed at ensuring the control of a more integrated management of the production cycle. This is very much facilitated by the advancement in information and computer technologies.

Three major ways of reorganising production processes in the construction industry can be identified (Rainbird and Syben, 1991):

1. Productivity can be gained not only from mechanisation of the construction process, but also through changes in work organisation. Rationalisation is achieved by speeding up processes and removing interruptions in the continuous flow of work. "Just-in-time" management as employed in manufacturing can be adapted for use in construction (Lim and Loh, 1991).
2. Firms have been restructured so as to reduce costs of maintaining workers and equipment when they are idle. In this way, some of the factors of production that are normally owned by the companies are simply hired when they are needed. As a result, there has been a growth in the numbers of plant-hire companies and specialist subcontracting businesses. In some instances, large corporations have set up plant-hire companies as separate operating units within their overall business structure.
3. Patterns of cooperation between firms have been restructured. Overall subcontracting has increased. Some of this represents an increased reliance on specialist techniques and materials. In many instances, however, it represents a strategy of passing economic risks to smaller companies and the construction workers themselves.

These general processes of restructuring in the construction industry occur in varying forms as the economy grows and develops. The specific characteristics of the construction industry arise from the central problem of mastering *variability* in the production process. This refers to the uncertain nature of the workload in an industry which does not produce for an undifferentiated market, but has to meet special demands as well as uncertainties which arise from the physical variability of site conditions, and in the production process itself. Firms respond to these uncertainties using two types of strategies: the *externalisation of variability,* whereby risk is passed on to other firms and workers through subcontracting, and the *internalisation of variability,* whereby firms increase their internal domination of the factors of production and attempt to make them more adaptable to market uncertainties.

The traditional method of contracting is slowly giving way to a number of alternative forms of contract. The most distinctive point about traditional contracting is the division between the design and construction stages. This separation often leads to long project times and has been a major factor in the shift to alternative forms of contracting. It may also lead to the design of unbuildable details, a problem that often hinders the construction process. New methods of contracting include management contract, management fee, construction management, project management, and design/build contract. These have been adopted by innovative firms at the "leading edge" of change in the industry. Each involves the contractor in a slightly different role in relation to planning, pricing and managing the construction project. This proliferation of new forms is an indicator of the industry's state of flux.

Worthy of mention is fast-tracking — a management technique as opposed to a contractual form. It aims at cutting costs by speeding up the construction process, giving a faster capital turnover rate, thus reducing the time that the clients' capital is tied up in production. This method of construction is, in some respects, similar to the Japanese "just-in-time" techniques used to speed up manufacturing output. It is often used in management contracting in attempts to link and overlap design and construction. Operation research methods, such as critical path analysis (CPA) and programme evaluation review techniques (PERTS), which are taught in colleges and widely practised in other industries, are also being adopted in the construction sector with increasing vigour.

Fast-track owes its origin to techniques developed by US project management teams. Fast-tracking in American construction has become a way of thinking about construction, and therefore, a method for instilling performance into the workforce. In Britain, fast-track means something more specific. It is a method of overlapping design and construction into concurrent processes. The work is divided into work packages and enables working drawings to be prepared just before they are required, rather than a long time in advance.

Work is usually carried out in phases: phasing permits construction to begin before design is completed, thus reducing total project time. It also permits partial occupation before the whole development is complete, thus providing clients with earlier returns on investment. The potential time savings due to concurrent design and construction are significant. In fast-track, the main contractor is usually employed as a management contractor. The management contractor acts as a project manager, and is brought in by the client at an early stage, well before the design is completed. Whilst requiring higher levels of skill and coordination amongst professionals, the overall effect is a reduction of labour requirements on site, with greater emphasis on specialist skills on the one hand, and 'limited skills' for assembly type work on the other. Many large commercial developments in the city of London, such as the Canary Wharf, London Docklands and King's Cross redevelopment projects have used the fast-track techniques.

While fast-track is essentially an operational management technique, it is closely linked with changes in technology. Management teams aim to reduce on-site labour to a minimum in order to achieve faster construction times. The recent shortage of skilled labour in the UK has provided additional incentives for reducing reliance upon site operatives. This has been achieved through the use of prefabrication, wherever possible. A wide variety of prefabricated, components are now being used, from toilet pods, plant rooms, lifts, cladding panels, to steel work, ductwork and new pipe joints. This reduces the content of labour on site primarily to tasks of clipping components together.

3. Technological Strategies

Using Technologies to Increase Productivity

The popular characterisation of the construction industry as technologically less advanced is correct only if technological progress is equated with automation of production processes.

Automation is rarely found in the construction industry itself, though it may be found in the building materials sector, especially in prefabrication. Likewise, new technologies based on electronic data processing are only being introduced slowly in certain parts of the production process, and their full potential has yet to be realised.

Specific features of the construction industry have influenced this. In particular, we would emphasise two important points of difference with the manufacturing industry in general. Firstly, each product of the construction industry is in fact fixed to the particular location where it is being built. Transportation of the product is practically impossible. As a consequence, plant and equipment must be mobile. There is a technological barrier to technical progress in as much as it is more important that the machinery is robust than that it is capable of performing sophisticated functions. These conditions of production have consequences for the labour process itself. Whilst in other industries the problem of efficient production is one of organising the flow of materials through the factory to optimise the use of machinery, the problem in construction is to optimise the flow of inputs in the form of materials, equipment and labour around the product as it is being constructed. Therefore it is appropriate to have machinery and tools which can be adapted to perform a variety of tasks rather than for specialised functions. This normally requires skilled labour with a high level of knowledge about handling materials and tools. In addition, variations in physical conditions mean that the workforce must have sufficient knowledge of the labour process as a whole in order to react to unforeseen problems. In this respect, relatively high levels of worker autonomy are needed.

The second major feature distinguishing construction from manufacturing is that production is not normally for a generalised market but has to meet the needs of a specific client. As a result, production is organised in such a way so as to produce a high level of variability in the product, normally referred to as "one off" production. So the standard means of rationalisation applied to production processes in other industries, such as the standardisation of goods, use of assembly lines, single purpose machinery and the subdivision of tasks, have very limited applicability. There is also an economic barrier to technical progress in so far as there are few economies of scale to be gained. The concentration of capital, which is normally considered to be a precondition for the development and implementation of technological progress, does not confer any special advantages in production techniques. Because there are few economies of scale affecting production processes, firm size does not influence the technical level of the construction process to the same extent as in the manufacturing industry. Firm size has a greater bearing than technology employed on the types of construction projects the firm is engaged in. In other words, economic power and technical know-how affect the segments of the construction market in which firms operate. In broad terms, the biggest firms work on large projects for which considerable amount of capital and technical know-how are required, whereas smaller firms work on lesser projects, such as house building, domestic repair and maintenance, which can be produced with less equipment and do not burden them with heavy overhead costs.

Technological strategies can be identified where technical solutions are developed for assembly type operations despite economic and technological barriers. Within this, there are three starting points: (1) planning and design; (2) construction equipment and (3) the use of prefabricated parts.

In the planning and design phase, attempts can be made to standardise components and design buildings in such a way that they do not require more expensive production processes. There are two obstacles to achieving this: designers may oppose changes which undermine their conception of professional standards, and clients have individual requirements. These obstacles are significant if buildings made from prefabricated components do not produce profits. In many countries, prefabricated units are only popular in industrial construction which amounts to 35% of construction investment.

Singapore and other countries in the region are at the takeoff stage in adopting precast concrete design and construction technology. Many firms are seen incorporating precast concepts in their design in order to remain competitive. In the long run, precast construction should attract greater interest in Southeast Asia, particularly in countries where there are increasing demands to develop a skilled work force and improve construction productivity.

Already, a number of large civil engineering projects are using precast components, and precast technology is widely used in many civil engineering projects in the region. Some common examples are flyover sections, underground tunnel linings, paving blocks, road culverts, curbs and sewers.

The increase in demand for precast has prompted manufacturers to source for technologically advanced equipment in order to increase their production capacities and help meet the high quality standards set by their clients. Upgrading projects of precasting facilities usually range from small scale investments, such as installation of gantry cranes and conversion of conventional tables to battery moulds, to large scale investments, such as setting up of fully automated precast factories. The government has planned to set aside more land for the precast industry as part of a concerted push to encourage the use of prefabricated products in building projects. New locations at Tuas and Changi, in addition to the existing areas at Sungei Kadut and Kranji, are targeted for development to house landing facilities for sand and granite aggregates, ready mixed concrete batching plants and precast concrete plants.[3] Established local companies can play an effective role in leading the campaign for using more prefabricated products in construction. Lee Kim Tah, a local construction firm which has won many public housing projects, is one that specialises in the precast construction process. Another local construction firm, the Singapore Technologies Group, has successfully utilised the "top-down" and the "precast columns" technique to cut down the construction time of buildings.

Technical solutions would have to involve the development of machines which equal or exceed human abilities in a number of aspects. These include chronological and spatial coordination in directing materials and tools; the ability to change direction and enlarge motions; the ability to control the radius of operation; precision and reliability. Speed of work and ability to react to environmental conditions are also important characteristics. The machinery must also continue to operate, regardless of variations in temperature, vibration, dust and humidity. It would be extremely useful to develop robots which are usable in building sites and face special problems which are not comparable to those in the fixed

[3] *Business Times*, November 18, 1997

production processes found inside factories. Japan has been the prime mover behind the development and use of construction robotics. However, it has not yielded significant market advantages, as more attention has being given to expert system development. Rather than automating individual tasks, the new approach aims to turn job sites into prefabricated-component factories and optimise the mix of computer control, automation, mechanical innovation and manual labour.[4]

Computerisation Strategies

During the last few years, faced with increasing market variability, there has been no evidence of any particular technological revolution within the building sector; this is particularly true of the execution phase of production. However, the sector has been affected by the development of information technology (IT) and its application to the conception, organisation and control of the production cycle. Thus, the development of new technologies, centred on computerisation, has primarily affected the rationalisation of the whole production process, from conception to realisation, rather than the strictly defined execution tasks, particularly those that take place on-site.

Nevertheless, some important developments have made their mark on the labour process. However, these would seem to depend more on organisational changes linked to the industrial strategies of firms, especially those of large firms, than on the actual development of techniques to be used on-site. Despite the limited nature of the spread of IT within the construction industry, as compared with other industrial sectors, there can be no doubt that computerisation is at the heart of the major organisational and social developments that have accompanied firms' strategies to adapt to market developments.

Recent research[5] indicates that IT plays an important role in the emergence of new forms of rationalisation. IT facilitates the search for a more integrated management of the whole production cycle, from conception to construction. The restructuring of the organisational phase of production, dictated by the search for greater

---

[4] *Engineering News Record,* Vol 230, No 9, March 1, 1993, page 22.

[5] See for instance Campac (1991).

flexibility in production structures, allows specific constraints of site based production to be taken into account.

The increase in financial risk attached to the launch of property development operations has led clients to make new demands on the contractors in order to ensure control over the conception to realisation cycle. Many clients, especially large ones, have equipped themselves with computer software capable of helping them to exert some control over the economic and financial parameters of development projects. From this development stem new demands that are placed particularly on the contractor to include the integration, with the aid of reliable estimates, of the economic and financial repercussions of various technical and architectural choices made at different stages of the project. They also include the systematic development of analysis in terms of "global cost" (investment, operating and maintenance costs) and the optimisation of the economic returns of the project.

This means that new channels of information have to be developed and managed in order to ensure coherence between the diverse stages of production, to guarantee information feedback from each site and to service the need of the clients.

Computer Aided Design and Drawing (CADD) technology is available worldwide. CAD has become so widespread that it is now a *sin qua non* of business. This technology is used in a variety of ways, including: proposal writing, pre-construction planning, site logistics, obtaining/issuance of permits, communicating with clients, subcontractors and regulatory agencies, materials takeoff specifications, project scheduling, cost estimating, and preparing shop drawings. It is also changing the nature of the relationships between design/engineering and construction firms.

The various advantages offered by CAD have helped construction and engineering companies to enhance competitiveness and win more contracts. CAD has helped to lower costs of preparing proposals, enable more options for teaming and more flexibility when weighing alternatives for preparing a bid. CAD is an enabling technology critical to the efficient production of reliable and high quality products. This increases production efficiency by minimising materials, energy and time in making products. Because of CAD, the design and production phases in engineering and construction are also becoming more integrated and often virtually concurrent. Furthermore, there are savings in labour attributable to CAD. Estimates of the ratio of manual workers to CAD users required to complete a single design vary. At one extreme, the United Nations Industrial Development Organisation (UNIDO) estimates that it is 1 to 50 for a developing country. Another source puts the savings in a developed country at "about 20% on the cost of drawings", or about 5 to 1 compared to manual methods.

The construction industry lags behind the engineering industry in the adoption of CAD. However, firms involved in design and subsequent construction that use CAD derive additional benefits from adopting this technology. First, design data is almost instantly usable, thus saving the contractor hours of work in putting data. Second, CAD can help to save on actual construction costs by reducing errors in buildings which require reworking. Rework due to various interferences (for example, in the installation of piping and concealed wiring) has been cut from 5% of costs to 1%, according to information from Bechtel (United Nations, 1993).

The ability of firms to work together on design is greatly improved with CAD. CAD system data can be shared among the various partners on a bid, therefore reducing duplication of efforts. An indirect advantage from the adoption of CAD is the development of more uniform industry standards. A CAD system offers dimensionality, scale and ease of change. Obviously, it is also easier to communicate when developing overall designs. This flexibility is especially important for small firms because it allows more of them to join together and bid for large projects. This may result in a tremendous change in the structure of the industry. After all, most international design contracts are awarded to larger firms, although, in fact, most engineering firms are small. Hence, CAD may open the market to a host of new players that represent the bulk of the firms in the industry. It becomes apparent that firms, especially those aspiring to tap the international market, would see a reduced level of competitiveness if they do not adopt the required technology.

Thus, the introduction of CAD has been accompanied by profound transformations of the system of contract management. In the developed countries, it is now possible for a tripartite group of owners, architects and trades people to work from one CAD system, follow work in progress, and plan their next steps. Recently, firms have moved from 2-D to 3-D CAD, and engineering firms have been ahead of construction firms in doing so. The use of software capable of estimating future costs has enabled both clients and contractors to gain better financial control of their projects. Along with traditional methods of price fixing, new methods of estimating future costs at the preliminary stages of a project have been developed which are capable of calculating, on the basis of ratios, the economic repercussions of the project at each stage of its development.

The Construction Industry Development Board (CIDB) of Singapore is well aware of the importance of technological competence for the industry to prosper. It has set up a Technology Development Division to help firms keep abreast with development in construction techniques, materials and equipment in industrialised countries. It administers various schemes (such as the Investment Allowance Scheme, Accelerated Depreciation Scheme) which offer financial assistance, and initiates and collaborates with national institutions of higher learning (the polytechnics and universities) in several R&D projects.

In the area of information technology, CIDB has collaborated with other agencies, such the National Computer Board (NCB), to promote and encourage construction professionals to use IT as a productivity tool. CIDB has also made an effort in compiling a "Construction Industry Software Directory" in 1991, which provides the industry with valuable information on software applications, the type of hardware and operating systems that the software supports, where to get it and how much it costs. According to industry analysts, the use of information technology is relatively common among construction firms in Singapore. However, intensive and effective use of high-end IT such as CAD/CAM is only prevalent among large companies with higher turnovers and big projects. Furthermore, IT has yet to become a common tool for communication and information exchange in the construction industry. Apparently more effort is needed to encourage the use of IT intensively and effectively for gaining a competitive edge. Obstacles to construction technology development in Singapore still exist. While the government has acted vehemently, the response from the private sector is mild. The reason could be a structural one: both the small size of firms and scale of contracts may make R&D look redundant, and the use of high-tech equipment and techniques cost ineffective.

4. New Ways of Dealing with Labour Force Constraints

Construction firms are confronted with a two-fold problem, that of labour force rejuvenation and the content of qualification and training. The incumbent indigenous workforce is evidently ageing, while its regeneration is made more difficult by the fact that young people going into the labour market have negative impressions of the construction trades. Reliance on foreign workers is no permanent remedy to the problem.

Table 6 Comparative Statistics on Labour Characteristics (Average for the period 1991–1996)

	Total (across all sectors)	Manufacturing	Construction
Average productivity growth (%)	3.7	6.6	1.3
Average monthly earnings (S$)	2,007	1,921	1,757
% change in monthly earnings	7.2	8.5	7.1
Average hours worked per week	46.9	49.1	50.9
Average % of foreign workers*	31.2	30.5	46.6

Note: *Estimated by the proportion of workers not contributing CPF.
Source: Department of Statistics, Singapore Yearbook of Statistics 1996.

Some comparative statistics may highlight the unfavourable image as perceived by young people. From Table 6, it can be seen that, compared to the average monthly earnings across all sectors ($2,007) for the periods 1991 to 1996, construction workers only earn a monthly average of $1,757. In addition, the average number of hours worked per week is as high as 50.9 which is much higher than the national average of 46.9 hours. The average percentage of foreign workers is at least 15% higher than that in the manufacturing sector and the national average.

Construction firms have to attempt to find ways of dealing with production flexibility. Thus, labour force adaptability and operational flexibility are at the forefront of the preoccupation of firms that have gained an awareness of the implications of the revival of the personnel management function.

Economic control over the entire production cycle, from conception to execution, requires a redefinition of the conditions and factors of productivity in a highly variable market situation. In this sense, the strategies of large firms have undergone an important transformation and the solutions adopted have important implications for working conditions.

Researchers have characterised the labour constraints typically encountered by the construction industry as external and internal variability.[6] *External variability* is linked to the heterogeneous nature of products (qualitative variability) and the variability in the size of operations (quantitative variability). In contrast, *internal variability* is linked to the variation in the quantity of labour required at different stages in the production process, which implies specific constraints as far as the overlap of tasks and the distribution of workload over the duration of the project are concerned. Thus the site represents the "nodal point of variability" within the production cycle.

What today's firms are looking for in worker competence combines factors based on the personal qualities of the worker (aptitude, familial and professional career, practical and moral relationship to work) with the recognition of levels of education, qualification and status. A new form of professionalism is being created here based on professional relationships that are no longer connected to specific job descriptions. Basically, the firm needs workers who are *multiskilled,* to counter the variability of tasks and operations encountered in the production process.

---

[6] The concept of variability as applied to the products of the construction sector is considered in Section 2.

The strategy of internalisation of labour constraints can be exercised in two main ways. Firstly, firms can attempt to exercise control over uncertainty by adopting technical solutions and by placing the responsibility for some of the uncertainty of production with manufacturers at the very beginning of the production process. New divisions within continuous production sites are organised around the fitting of components of the finishing trades (technical pipe lagging, toilet plumbing, electric hoist) that call traditional trades and qualifications into question. Of course, workers are required to undertake extra tasks, but these are simplified and limited to the fitting of fabricated products: a new form of "multiskilling" is put into operation; the reconstruction of qualification takes place around the profile of the "multiskilled assembler/fitter". This strategy does not stop firms from externalising more technical tasks that require craft skills.

Secondly, firms can attempt to meet the requirements of flexibility and quality control by undertaking a detailed revision of qualifications. The objective here is no longer for the firm to make decisions about internalisation of tasks according to the capacities of the labour force at its disposal. Rather, it attempts to broaden labour force qualification and modify its content so as to make it possible to adapt the existing labour force to new technical and organisational conditions. A new profile of manual qualifications is thus sought by the firm, which attempts to achieve this by training or replacing a proportion of its manual labour force, not only to widen its operational field, but also to equip it with "new competencies". In this instance, different characteristics directed towards the self-organisation of work, management of task boundaries and taking responsibility are emphasised. It is another form of multiskilling that surpasses the "multiskilled assembler/fitter", whose activities are limited to the adoption of a few related and simplified tasks. The new approach implies a shift in emphasis from labour management strategies linked to the control and discipline of the workforce to those aimed at providing greater autonomy to the workers, establishing a higher level of trust and the identification of the worker with the firm.

Multiskilling represents a great variety of concrete situations and covers a range of competencies which vary according to markets, stages of production, types of firms and personnel management policies. It ranges from straightforward *job enlargement* through the widening of operations to several related fields, the aim of which is usually limited to getting skilled manual workers to make better use of slack periods, to a situation where it can also enable true *job enrichment* through the addition of tasks of a totally different kind to those that define the traditional trade speciality.

Lately, the more technical workforce (electricians, plumbers, brick and tile layers) who have to confront technological developments to a greater extent than those of main trades, reckon that they can no longer limit the training of their manual labour force to specialised technical know-how. Faced with changes in the conditions of production, firms value flexibility and the need for workers to adapt to new demands and to develop and acquire new types of knowledge.

Singapore has been relying heavily on foreign workers to man a variety of jobs in the construction sector. With a large unskilled foreign construction workforce, the productivity of the sector is low. The relatively low wages coupled with the perceived harsh working conditions have made the sector an unattractive career option for local entrants into the labour market.

The Construction Industry Development Board (CIDB) has recently launched a comprehensive ten year plan to raise productivity and skill levels of construction workers in Singapore. It will screen foreign workers in their home countries and raise their skill levels at training centres established there by private companies with help from CIDB and other Singapore government agencies. The plan targets to train and certify 100,000 skilled workers so as to raise the number of skilled workers in the construction workforce to 30%. Compared to developed countries such as Japan and Germany, where the proportion of skilled workers in the construction workforce exceeds 60%, Singapore's figure is a small 12%.

Furthermore, the plan envisages training 30,000 workers and 15,000 supervisors over the next ten years. This will help to strengthen the supervisory and technical management skills of workers. Currently, the industry has a 26% shortfall of foremen and clerk of work. Of the 7,300 positions available, 1,900 remain vacant. The aim is to improve the ratio from one supervisor to 30 workers at present to one supervisor to every 20 workers.

As part of a concerted effort to upgrade the skill profile of the sector, the Singapore Government has recently raised the levy for unskilled foreign construction workers to wean Singaporean firms from their high dependence on unskilled foreign labour. Concurrently, the levy for skilled foreign workers is reduced. Moreover, the government has announced two measures to help the industry become more productive and rely less on foreign labour. Firstly, a law will be passed to push the industry to build time and labour saving designs by using standard precast and prefabricated building components. Building plans for construction projects will not be approved if they do not meet the minimum standards for buildable designs, which will be raised gradually. The Government, has been promoting buildable designs for the last five years, but with meagre results. The average score on an index of how buildable designs[7] for private projects in the previous year was 53 to 63 points, compared to 68 to 71 points for public projects. There is much room for improvement and the Ministry of National Development (MND) is now studying how this might be done. It is believed that a minimum buildable score requirement would also enhance product quality.

For a more rational utilisation of foreign labour, a new system for allocating work permits will be implemented from 1998. Entitlements to hire foreign construction workers will only be allocated to main contractors, based on their total project workload. Each main contractor will manage his entitlement. He can employ foreigners himself or give some of his entitlement to his subcontractors. Only subcontractors with such entitlements can apply for work permits. The current ratio of five foreigners to one Singaporean will apply to both main and subcontractors. The new allocation system gives main contractors better control over manpower input and deployment. It can foster long term relationships between main and subcontractors and enhance joint efforts to upgrade and make the industry's workforce more productive.

---

[7] The Construction Industry Development Board (CIDB) has developed a *Buildable Design Appraisal System (BDAS)* which provides a measure of the potential impact of a design on the usage of site labour. The system results in a "buildable score" in which a higher score means a more efficient labour usage in construction and therefore higher site labour productivity. CIDB (1996).

An area in which the government or the contractor association can intensify their effort is to further promote computer literacy among firms and workers in the construction sector. It is noted that in some cases, the adoption of information technology, such as the CAD system, can accelerate skill acquisition and the time it takes to train employees. Today, high school graduates with relatively little specialised training can use the turnkey CAD systems available from numerous vendors. Furthermore, it takes less training to become a capable CAD operator than to become a competent drafter. This often requires no more than vocational school training and most training is actually acquired on-the-job. Work can also be completed more quickly with CAD, which can cut the time for architectural rendering, electrical piping, plumbing layouts and highway routings to 10 or 20%.

5. Regionalisation and International Contracting

As the growth in domestic construction activities dwindles, construction firms have to look to regional and international markets for business and sustainability.[8] Furthermore, competition among construction firms is getting tougher. There is a steady deterioration in the profit margins of most construction projects. This is exacerbated by the increase in the number of construction firms that are able to handle jobs of larger contract values. The increase in the pool of qualified firms comes from multinational engineering firms and local firms that have managed to upgrade themselves through the years. By 1996, there were more than 200 contractors who could handle projects that cost more than $30 million. As shown in Table 7, this indicates an increase of more than seven times the number recorded in 1990.

The regionalisation of the construction industry will provide a very wide scope for local construction companies to expand their businesses (Yong, 1996). By spreading the "second economic wing", the local construction industry would have a better prospect, not only

[8] For an excellent exposition of the theory and practice of construction export marketing, see Low S. P. (1996).

Table 7 Total Number of Registered Contractors

Project Tendering Capacity (Financial) Limit					
Year	**$ 3 m**	**$ 5 m**	**$10 m**	**$30 m**	**Above $30 m**
1990	55	47	54	51	34
1993*	111	86	70	77	94
1996	244	187	204	111	214

Note: *Year of re-classification of contractors. From July 1999, all contractors registered for handling projects worth S$30 million and above must possess an approved ISO 9000 certificate. Currently, there are about 4,000 contractors and suppliers in the register.

Source: CIDB, *Directory of Registered Contractors, Singapore.*

for the firms themselves, but also for the Singapore economy as a whole.

Several factors favour the campaign for Singapore's construction companies to venture and expand their businesses abroad. The Asia-Pacific region is considered to be the growth region for the next century. There are many developing countries, new NIEs and emerging economies poised to take off. As such, they would offer a tremendous amount of business opportunities in infrastructural developments and construction in particular. The concurrent rise in demand for construction goods and services follows the course of national integration, industrialisation and urbanisation. It may in part reflect that construction resources, in addition to satisfying demand for investment in productive facilities, are also required for the satisfaction of one of the most basic human needs — shelter; and in this respect, there may be a huge backlog of suppressed demand to be accommodated. Thus the expansion of construction output in middle income countries would seem to be due to a rapid increase in both "growth initiating" and "growth dependent" construction. International agencies such as the World Bank and the Asian Development Bank have estimated that the buoyant growth in Asia would need infrastructural development expenditures of US$300 to 500 billion for the next five to ten years. In Asia alone, development expenditures would amount to US$20 to 30 billion per year.

After more than 35 years of nationhood and development, local firms have mastered sufficient track records to bid for international construction and engineering projects. Though they may be disadvantaged by the size and financial manoeuvrability of the established companies of the developed countries, they can still capitalise on their local knowledge and cultural familiarity with the regional economies to establish joint ventures or partnerships with foreign enterprises.

Singapore's successful public housing projects and urban town planning[9] experience has helped to nurture several local companies, such as Four Seas Construction Company, Lee Kim Tah Pte Ltd, Hock Chuan Ann Construction Pte Ltd and Ho Lee Construction Pte Ltd, which will be able to market their expertise in housing construction services to the regional countries. In particular, companies such as Lee Kim Tah which have specialised skills in designing and constructing precast panels for modern HDB flats, will be able to make significant inroads into the regional market. Singapore's contractors and builders have also gathered much experience in the construction of many tall commercial buildings and shopping complexes that dominate the country's landscape. Though many of the big projects are being executed by international construction firms, the fact that such projects are being carried out in Singapore has given valuable opportunities for local engineers and management staff to gain the know-how of complex building construction management. Lum Chang, one of the biggest construction firms in Singapore, has successfully completed several prestigious projects, such as the UOB Plazas, Bugis Square, and Suntec City, both alone or in partnerships with other companies. These local construction firms should be able to export their services in the building sector to the regional markets.

Besides housing and commercial buildings, Singapore contractors and engineers also have opportunities to construct petrochemical processing plants, refineries, storage terminals, power stations and environmental control projects. Singapore, being a

[9] In fact, Tampines New Town, a local public housing estate has won the World Habitat Award from the Building and Social Housing Foundation of the United Kingdom in 1991.

regional oil refining centre as well as a nodal manufacturing base for multinational companies, has generated the need for such construction activities. All these should place Singaporean builders in good stead for bidding and competing for overseas construction projects.

The economic reform and deregulation of the Chinese economy has engendered tremendous investment opportunities for investors. China has opened its doors to foreign investors and will need massive investments in infrastructure, buildings, civil engineering, private and commercial projects to support its economic development initiatives. Singapore's investors are well positioned to benefit if they can capitalise on their comparative advantages in terms of language and technological and management expertise. Local construction and project management firms can certainly provide, at the very least, project management for China's projects. For large construction projects, there would be much purchasing to be done. The supplies, in most cases, would come from all over the world. In addition, the consultancy firms would usually have internationally renowned consultants. With the unique bilingual capabilities of most Singaporean professionals, local firms could act as bridging parties for the mainland Chinese.

Thus local construction and building companies will have to quicken their pace of upgrading their capabilities to tap the business opportunities which come with economic growth in the region. Singapore's efforts in enlarging its external economy are based on an intensive regionalisation programme. Singapore based enterprises, which include local companies and multinational enterprises (MNCs) could make use of the Economic Development Board's (EDB) incentive schemes to expand their business investment abroad. In 1995, EDB facilitated a total of 381 regional projects by 187 local enterprises and 123 MNCs. The number of companies setting up abroad grew from 3,540 in 1993 to 4,128 in 1994. The contribution of overseas operations to the value added of the Singapore economy amounted to 12%.

The information in Table 8 indicates that Singapore's investments abroad are predominantly in the manufacturing and financial sectors. Construction services only constitute a small percentage (1.1%) of the total investment abroad. Thus, there is still tremendous scope for expanding the investments abroad in areas related to construction and building, especially at a time when the need for infrastructural investments to support economic expansion in regional countries is expected to accelerate.

Table 8 Singapore Direct Investment Abroad in 1995

	S$M	%
Manufacturing	11397	24.6
Construction	505	1.1
Real Estate	3380	7.3
Commerce	4528	9.8
Financial	23172	50.1
Other	3258	7
Total	46240	100

Source: Department of Statistics, *Singapore Investment Abroad*, 1994–95, Singapore: Ministry of Trade and Industry.

International Contracting

While investing abroad is a way to broaden the scope and activities of the construction sector, it will have to increase its participation in international contracting activities. This is basically concerned with the export of construction expertise overseas. Such activities can be engaged in while the firms are still based in Singapore. International construction services can be divided into two main groups which are inter-related and equally important in bringing an investment project from conception to realisation, including operation and maintenance. They include consulting and engineering design (CED) services and physical construction services (PCS), which is sometimes also referred to as project implementation services.

Consulting and engineering design services are knowledge intensive services that are essential to optimising investment in all areas — choice, technical process of execution, and management. The designs and specifications that these services produce should be the least costly and the most productive solutions consistent with the social and economic constraints of individual markets. Many of these services are multidisciplinary in nature, requiring general and specialised engineering as well as other technical and economic skills to produce requisite outputs. The latter can take different forms, ranging from drawings to general and training reports and operating manuals.

Physical construction services pertain to investment projects of an infrastructural, industrial or agricultural type. They bring together labour, materials and equipment in order to translate the techno-economic specifications produced by the CED into concrete physical entities (e.g. industrial plants, hotels, and infrastructural projects). While construction services require general and specialised engineering and managerial skills, they also make use of abundant unskilled and semi-skilled labour.

CED services determine the technological dimension of investment projects and help to establish forward and backward linkages in the national economy. The linkages produced between these services, local R&D activities and the capital goods sector are of particular importance. Decisions regarding supply sources for these services also affect the procurement of construction implementation services and equipment. Mainly because of the externalities that they generate, these services have a strategic role to play in economic growth and development.

Apart from the linkages they produce within national economies, CED services are often used as a mechanism for the transfer of technology in all economic sectors. Through their international activities, consulting and engineering design organisations (CEDOs) have contributed to the transfer of technical knowledge among firms and countries at different levels of development.

The international design related billings of the top 200 international design firms totalled US$14.5 billion in 1996, up from US$8.8 billion in 1990.[10] The markets in Asia and Australia accounted for 31.2% of the total billing in 1996. The other major market was Europe, which accounted for 30.5% of the total billing.

[10]The information is obtained from the annual survey conducted by *Engineering News Record (ENR)*. The 1996 survey on design firms is published in the July 21, 1997 issue.

Among the top 20 international design firms for 1996, eight were from the United States, three from the United Kingdom, four from the Netherlands, and one each from Canada, Finland, Egypt, Italy and Japan. Each of the top 20 firms had a total billing exceeding US$200 million. These companies were of different types and provided engineering design services to a variety of investment projects and sectors. Worthy of note is the fact that there were firms from a few developing countries among the list of top 200 international design firms. Among the 13 firms listed, four were from South Korea, three from South Africa, and one each from Egypt, Yugoslavia, Brazil, Lebanon, Taiwan and the Republic of China. The value of international construction contracts for the top 225 international contractors was US$126.8 billion in 1996.[11] The bulk of the contracts (68.0%) were won by firms from the developed western countries. Japanese firms also had a sizeable share of 19.1%. The remaining 12.9% was shared by firms from the developing countries, with South Korea and China taking 5.0% and 3.2% respectively.

Assistance in various forms from the Singapore Government to encourage local construction companies to tap the international contracting market and export their services is not lacking. Back in the early 1970s, the authorities concerned had already seriously thought about exporting Singapore's construction expertise overseas. The Ministry of National Development Holdings, together with the Urban Redevelopment Authority (URA), set up Indeco Pte Ltd[12] in 1972 to avail countries in the region with expertise and know-how developed by Singaporean professionals in the areas of public housing, urban renewal, town and city planning, industrial estate, and other infrastructural development. Indeco was to act as a vehicle agency to spearhead the export drive and to farm out successful overseas contracts to various Singaporean subcontractors. In 1979, PSA set up SPECS[13] Consultants Pte Ltd as its consulting arm to sell its services abroad. SPECS has since undertaken numerous projects across Asia and the Middle East. The realisation that Singaporean

[11] The top 225 international contractors survey is conducted by *Engineering News Record (ENR)* and published in the August 25, 1997 issue.

[12] Indeco is the acronym for International Development and Consultancy.

[13] SPECS is the acronym for Singapore Engineering and Consultancy Services.

contractors may not be able to compete effectively with their foreign counterparts who can offer better technological skills and competencies in meeting clients' needs, has prompted the Singapore Government to set up its own construction company, CONTECH[14] Pte Ltd in November 1980 to compete for HDB contracts, and in the process take the lead in experimenting and promoting new technologies within the local industry. CONTECH has played a major role in exploring the use of new technologies in construction and the experiences gained are passed on to local contractors.

The Trade Development Board (TDB) set up the Market Development Assistance Scheme (MDAS) in 1985 to provide financial and other forms of assistance to companies producing goods and services for the export market. The scheme provides up to 50% of the cost incurred by companies, subject to a maximum sum of $25,000.

In early 1986, the TDB set up an on-line information retrieval service to provide crucial advanced information to local businessmen, and in the process help them in clinching deals. By assessing the "Scan-a-Bid" database, the TDB can furnish the latest information on consulting, contracting and supply opportunities for Third World country development projects long before tenders are called for. In December 1986, the TDB also introduced the International Bidding Scheme to encourage the participation of local engineering services companies in international tenders. In 1987, the Construction Industry Development Board (CIDB) introduced the Tenders Estimating Data Services (TEDS) to provide Singaporean tenderers with a means of gauging the prevailing wage levels and prices of important construction materials in other countries. TEDS enables companies to assess the quotation submitted by indigenous subcontractors or suppliers for particular overseas projects. Tender prices can then be computed and checked for pricing risks. As a co-ordinator, the CIDB also helps to promote the exchange of cost information between local construction companies. In conjunction with TDB, the CIDB has organised overseas missions for the

[14]CONTECH is the acronym for Construction Technology. This company has become a subsidiary of the Singapore Technologies Group and is renamed ST Construction.

construction industry in order to identify export opportunities in foreign countries.

The Singapore Government has also introduced several tax incentive schemes to encourage the promotion of the service sector. These include the Pioneer Service Incentive scheme in 1985, the Approved Headquarters Incentive Scheme in 1987, and the Export of Services Incentive Scheme in 1988. The Export of Services Incentive Scheme, under the provision of the Economic Expansion Incentive Act, has been extended by the Ministry of Finance to cover the export of selected services, including, among others, consultancy management, construction, technical and engineering services.

In fact, the private sector can, if it wishes, tap on the specialist resources available in the various government bodies which have accumulated and acquired wide-ranging experiences in numerous fields, including housing, town planning, airport and port design and operations, parks and recreation, industrial estate and land reclamation to win international contracts and market their services abroad. Launched in 1987, the APPECS (Attachment of Public Service Professionals for the Export of Construction Services) Scheme was designed to enable government employees and professionals to be attached to private firms so as to help them compete for and carry out overseas projects. This scheme has scored some success in the early years but it is seldom used nowadays, as private companies have accumulated enough experience, and government agencies are offering such services through their consulting subsidiaries, such as CESMA of HDB and JTC International of JTC. Corporatisation of public agencies has also fostered the formation of business units within the agencies to seek overseas contracts and business opportunities.

In the quest for further growth of the Singapore economy, the export of construction services can undoubtedly contribute to achieving this objective. There is a need for construction industries in Singapore to explore and expand abroad for more business opportunities. In this regard, efforts by the private sector, coordinated by a unified agency such as the Singapore Contractors Association, are very much needed for upgrading the capabilities of local construction firms. Mergers of small companies to form larger entities may be one option for pooling resources so as to face international competition more effectively. Most firms might already have attained the capability to offer PCS or contracting services both locally and abroad. However, to achieve the target of an advanced technology driven economy, construction firms need to develop capabilities in CED services. More efforts by the private and public sectors are required to help nurture firms to be ranked among the list of top international design firms and contractors.

The expanded role of international trade and foreign investments in the economy, as well as the quickened pace of technology transfer, have made rapid development and adoption of new technologies a critical determinant of a country's competitiveness in the global market. This is especially true in the consulting engineering and design (CED) industry.

6. Conclusions

The Singapore Construction Industry has developed over the last 35 years, but it has yet to mature fully. It has certainly contributed to the economic development and capital formation of the economy. For the industry to continue to grow and prosper, it would be required to undergo some strategic restructuring with respect to management methods, technological applications, human resources development and international contracting.

The industry has to be vigilant of new trends and demand of clients. In particular, there will be the desire to exert some control over cost fixing from the conception stage of the project. This leads large firms to invest to a greater extent than before in obtaining information concerning the constituent elements of costs within finishing trades (through a breakdown in terms of supplies, material and labour costs) and to integrate information concerning operations and site practices as rapidly as possible into their systems. Thus, the use of IT in general and CAD in particular is accompanied by the development and rationalisation of production is required, essentially in response to the need to identify and to exert some control over realisation costs. This rationalisation of production is also extended to the later stages in the production cycle, to the study of the site timetable, schedule and methods. Such an approach requires firms to multiply their collection of information directly from the site and to undertake frequent analysis of such data.

With the development of buyer markets i.e. with too many firms chasing too few contracts, contracting firms are obliged to arrange soft credit. Increasingly, contractors find that they have to arrange for financial packages to ensure greater chances of successful job bidding. In fact, the huge sums of money involved in the financing of construction projects have led many governments to back their contractors with export credit guarantees, aid packages and soft loans. The extent of home government support to contractors obviously varies. Japan and France have been singled out as having not only a high level of government support, but also a highly coordinated approach between government and contractors, including extensive help from the domestic banking sector. However, this use of "mixed credits" in support of overseas contracts is a practice which is highly controversial; it has been much criticised, in particular by the United States.

To be able to establish a foothold in the international contracting market, it may require the combined efforts of private firms (architects, engineers, surveyors and financial analysts) and the public sector. The government has already relaxed the legislation to allow architects and engineers to form consortiums. Private companies may have to review their management practices to allow greater utilisation of information technology to improve productivity. Training of workers should not be neglected but has to be strategically programmed such that the objective of a "multiskilled" workforce will evolve with the change in management methods required to meet new demands. It is the CED type of firms which Singapore firms should aspire to become. It is this type of firm which would yield high value-added and offer challenging jobs for the technologically oriented graduates emerging from polytechnics and universities.

References

Bennett, J. and Ferry, D. (1988) *Specialist Contractors*, Centre for Strategic Studies in Construction, University of Reading.

Campac, E. (1991) "Computerisation Strategies in Large French Firms and their Effects on Working Conditions", in Rainbird and Syben (ed.) *Restructuring A Traditional Industry.*

Construction Industry Development Board (1991) *Construction Industry Software Directory*, Singapore.

Construction Industry Development Board (1996) *The CIDB Buildable Design Appraisal System*, 3rd edition, Singapore.

Department of Statistics, *Yearbook of Statistics 1996*; Ministry of Trade and Industry, Singapore.

Department of Statistics, *Singapore System of National Accounts,1996*; Ministry of Trade and Industry, Singapore.

Department of Statistics, *Singapore Input-Output Tables, 1988*; Minstry of Trade and Industry, Singapore.

Department of Statistics, *Singapore Investment Abroad, 1994–95*; Ministry of Trade and Industry, Singapore.

Gann, D. (1989) *New Technology, Employment and Operative Skills in Building Services*, Science Policy Research Unit, University of Sussex.

Lim, L.Y. and Loh, S.P. (1991) *Just-In-Time Productivity for Construction*, Singapore: Singapore National Printers.

Low, S.P. (1996) *Theory and Practice of Construction Export Marketing*, Britain: Avebury, Ashgate Publishing Ltd.

Ministry of Trade and Industry, *Annual Economic Survey of Singapore*, annual publication, Singapore.

Ofori, G. (1993) *Managing Construction Industry Development*, Singapore: Singapore University Press.

Piore, M. and Sabel, C. (1984) *The Second Industrial Divide*, New York: Basic Books.

Rainbird, H. and Syben, G. (1991) (ed.) *Restructuring A Traditional Industry*, New York: Berg Publisher.

United Nations (1993) *Information Technology and International Competitiveness: The Case of the Construction Services Industry*, United Nations Conference on Trade and Development (UNCTAD), Geneva.

Yong, E.W. (1996) *Regionalisation of Local Construction Firms*, Advanced Study Project, Graduate School of Business, National University of Singapore, Singapore.

6

Maintaining Competitiveness in New Age Tourism

Wong Poh Poh

1. Introduction

Tourism is the world's largest industry in terms of gross output and jobs generated. In 1996, total international tourist arrivals numbered nearly 595 million, with a 5.5% increase over 1995. International tourism receipts were over US$425 billion and 400 million passengers were carried on international air services (WTO, 1997). Singapore was ranked 22nd in the world's top 50 tourism destinations and 15th in the world's top 50 tourism earners (WTO, 1997).

There are three objectives in this paper:

1. Examine "Tourism 21", Singapore's current National Tourism Plan.
2. Discuss the New Age Tourism, regional tourism and other issues relevant to Singapore's competitiveness.
3. Suggest some conceptual and methodological frameworks for increasing Singapore's competitiveness.

2. Tourism 21

From the early 1990s, Singapore faced a decreasing growth rate in tourist arrivals due to a combination of several factors — maturity as a tourist destination, a strong local currency and increasing competition from neighbouring destinations for tourist traffic. It was difficult to sustain the high growth rates of the late 1980s. This was compounded by the short length of stay (Figure 1).

Figure 1 Visitor Arrivals, Hotel Rooms and Average Length of Stay for Singapore, 1990–1996.

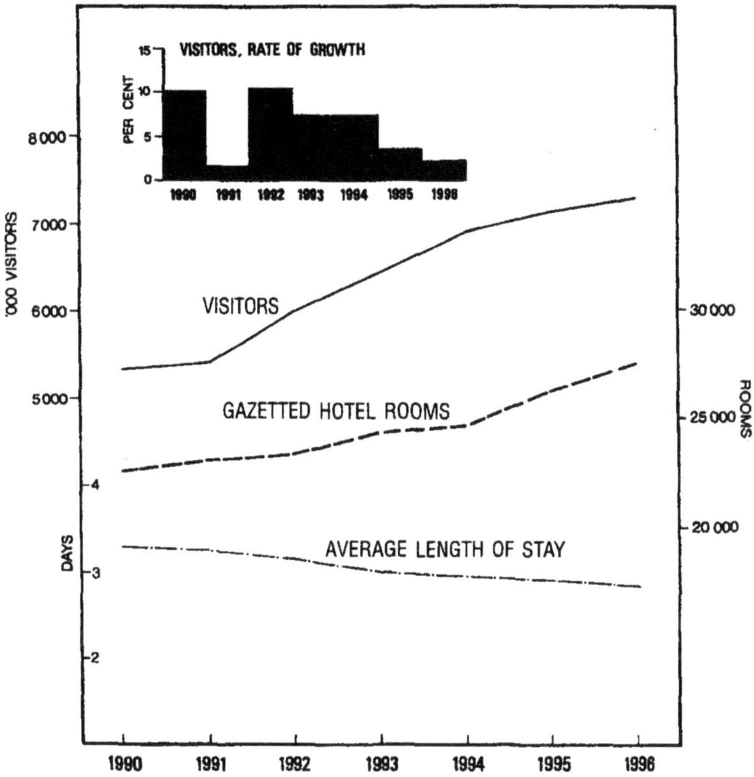

As a holiday destination, Singapore is comparable to Hong Kong as both are city based destinations. Both are in sharp contrast to the other countries in the Asia-Pacific region, which are multi-faceted holiday destinations (Table 1) (Edwards, 1995). As an island city-state destination, "Singapore faces the problems of developing a *mature* destination as a *world* destination and marketing it as a *complete* destination" (Wong, 1977, p. 265, italics in the original). A mature destination is one that has reached its height of development in the product cycle curve, a world destination is one that enjoys instant worldwide recognition, e.g. Disneyland, London, and a complete destination is one that fulfils the expectations of the tourists.

Table 1 Holiday Types of Selected Countries, 1993

('000 visitors)	Total	Beach & Other Resorts	City Based	Touring	Others
Singapore	3,275	0	3,275	0	0
Indonesia	2,250	1,825	n.a.	350	75*
Korea	3,300	1,975	700	400	200
Philippines	400	75	275	n.a.	50**
Thailand	4,925	1,850	1,550	800	700
Hong Kong	4,825	0	4,825	0	0
South Korea	1,900	325	1,275	300	0
Taiwan	725	50	650	0	25**

Notes: Breakdown of holidays by main types are normally rough estimates.
* Includes city visits.
**Includes touring.
Source: Edwards, 1995.

The results of the biennial surveys on overseas tourists give insights into these problems. For example, in the 1996 survey, pleasure/vacation was ranked as the main purpose of visit to Singapore (Table 2). For the Pleasure/Vacation, Honeymoon and Shopping respondents, the main reasons for the choice of Singapore as a destination were part of a package tour (31.1%) or breaking the journey (13.7%). Attractions or sightseeing (11.8%) or shopping (9.8%) were not important. However, this does not destract from the fact that shopping remained the most important component of tourist expenditure (57.1% in 1996) compared to accommodation (20.4%) and food and beverage (10.0%) (STPB, 1997).

"Tourism 21" was launched as the new National Tourism Plan on July 1996 to maximise Singapore's tourism potential (STPB, 1996; STPB Annual Report 1995/96). It envisages Singapore as a worldclass tourist destination, a premier tourism business centre and an ideal tourism gateway to, and a hub for, the Asia-Pacific region. The strategy as encapsulated in "Singapore *Un*limited" is a shift in

Table 2 Main Purpose of Visit to Singapore, 1996

Main Purpose	Percent	
	Survey (N = 10,002)	D/E Card*
Pleasure/Vacation	45.7	53.2
Business	14.3	14.6
Transit	11.9	9.4
Stopover	9.0	N.A.
Business/Pleasure	6.2	2.9
Visiting Friends/ Relatives	4.3	4.4
Shopping	2.1	N.A.
Conventions/Exhibitions	1.5	1.1
Honeymoon	1.3	N.A.
Medical/Dental Treatment	1.3	N.A.
Education/Training	0.7	0.4
Sports/Recreation	0.1	N.A.
Incentive Travel	0.1	N.A.
Others	1.5	3.9

Note: *Disembarkation/Embarkation Card.
Source: STPB, 1997.

paradigm from "smallness in Singapore" to "no real limits or constraints". It is intended to create new space for the tourism industry growth and to enhance Singapore's own attraction by "harnessing" the scenery of neighbouring countries (STPB, 1996).

Tourism 21 recognises and utilises specific opportunities which include the following (STPB, 1996; STPB Annual Report, 1995/96):

- the Internet to maximise the global awareness of Singapore as a premier destination and a tourism gateway to Asia;
- the importance of Asian travellers (particularly from China, South Korea and Taiwan) and business and transit visitors;
- the relationships with destinations such as Malaysia and Indonesia where natural attractions complement Singapore's tourism product;

- a shopping strategy to create memorable shopping experiences and encourage worldclass retailers to set up regional bases;
- active promotion for arts tourism;
- growth in other tourism segments such as cruises and conventions.
- enhancing service standards;
- establishing a new headquarters at Tourism Court as the focal point of Singapore tourism and restructuring the STPB as a multi-faceted organisation covering Tourism Marketing, Tourism Business, Regional Tourism and Corporate Services.

Tourism 21 marks an important change in the perception of the tourism industry in Singapore. It takes a multi-approach to the industry and recognises not only its importance but also the competition and the need to say ahead in the next century. Tourism 21 represents perhaps the single most important change in the paradigm of the local tourism industry in recent years.

3. New Age Tourism

From the mid-1990s, a number of factors heralded the emergence of a new tourism (Cleverdon, 1993):

- sociodemographic changes, such as the postwar birth bulge moving up the age groups, and women becoming an increasingly important travel segment;
- increasing use of electronic information and communication systems;
- more knowledgeable and demanding consumers, e.g. eco-tourists;
- deregulation, especially in the airline industry; and
- polarisation of travel and tourism operators between global business and "niche" players.

This was dubbed the New Age of Tourism (NAT), a term coined by Fayos-Sola in 1993. He noted that "the growing complexity of demand segmentation, market globalisation, the flexibility provided by new technologies and the search for synergy as a source of profitability through diagonal integration have led to the dramatic transformation of the tourism business paradigm" (Fayos-Sola, 1997, p.10). He emphasised that "the future of tourism businesses today depends on their achieving *competitiveness*, which means having the capacity to generate and maintain profits above those attained in the reference sector, even in changing circumstances". In short, "the business paradigm of mass or Fordian tourism is now giving way to new circumstances and professional rules of play which question the linearity (continuity) of the conditions governing supply and demand" (Ibid, p.119).

It is now evident that the new tourism has five driving forces (Poon, 1993):

- new consumers;
- new technologies;
- new production practices;
- new management techniques; and
- changes in the industry's frame conditions.

The new tourism has implications for destinations if they want to remain competitive or maintain their market share. First, a good understanding of the forces of new tourism is necessary. Sometimes, this requires a change in the mindset. Second, it is necessary to monitor the new changes in tourism. Some changes may occur outside the tourism sector and may not appear to be of immediate importance. Full understanding and monitoring would help in forming a better response to the changes in the tourism industry.

4. Regional Tourism

In New Age Tourism, the Asia-Pacific region has been increasing its importance. In 1996, the Asia-Pacific region generated a total of 94 million tourist arrivals (one million more than North America). For the last decade, it has been the fastest growing region in terms of tourist arrivals, achieving the highest regional growth in 1996, 9.6% compared to 5.5% for the world. For the period 1990–1996, its average annual rate was 8.6%, compared to 4.5% for the world (WTO, 1997).

There are some tourism trends in regional tourism with

implications for Singapore's tourism industry. First, Singapore faces growing competition from countries in Southeast Asia and, to a much smaller extent, from countries in Northeast Asia (Figure 2, Table 3). For example, Indonesia is developing a range of new resorts, Malaysia is a strong competitor, Thailand is developing new products to regain its position, Philippines is a fast growth destination with improved infrastructure and political stability and Vietnam has great potential (Waters, 1997).

Table 3 Average Hotel Occupancy Rate, Average Length of Stay and Per Capita Expenditure for Selected Countries, 1995

	Occupancy Rate (percent)	Average Length of Stay (days)	Per Capita Expenditure (US$)
Singapore	84.1	3.4	526
Indonesia	52.3	10.2	1,209
Malaysia	65.5	4.8**	486
Philippines	62.2	10.1**	1,520
Thailand	59.6	7.4	1,066***
Hong Kong	85.5	3.9	917
South Korea	68.0	5.3	1,491
Taiwan	61.5	7.4	—

Notes: * Metro Manila only.
** Reporting by nights.
*** Estimate.
Source: PATA 1995 Annual Statistical Report

Northeast Asia can be viewed more as a source of potential tourists for Singapore. Three quarters of the tourist arrivals in the Asia-Pacific region are within the region, with Northeast Asia recording the highest growth in intra-regional travel. Japan, Taiwan and South Korea are currently the major generators of tourists with increasing numbers from China (Table 4).

Significant differences can be noted in the outbound traffic from Northeast Asia. The Japanese outbound constitutes an increasingly sophisticated market with defined segments, e.g.

Figure 2 Tourist Arrivals of Selected Countries in Southeast Asia and Northeast Asia, 1991–1996.

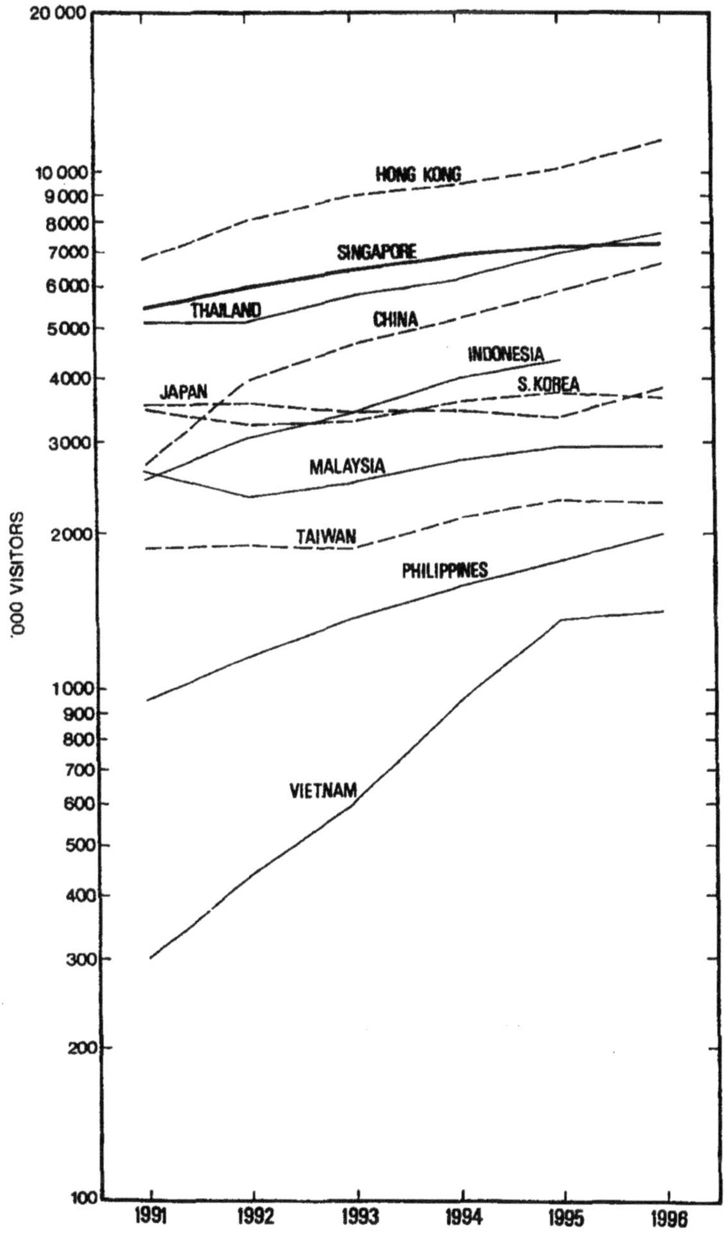

Table 4 Concentration Ratios for Selected Countries, 1996

	Concentration Ratio (top 3 countries, percent)
Singapore*	40.3 (Japan 16.1, Indonesia 14.6, Malaysia 9.6)
Indonesia**	47.2 (Singapore 24.2, Malaysia 11.8, Japan 11.2)
Malaysia*	41.0 (Thailand 19.0, Japan 11.5, Singapore 10.5)
Philippines	45.4 (USA 18.2, Japan 17.1, Taiwan 10.1)
Thailand	32.8 (Malaysia 13.9, Japan 12.3, Korea 6.6)
China***	42.2 (Japan 23.2, Korea 10.4, USA 8.6)
Hong Kong	55.7 (China 19.7, Japan 20.4, Taiwan 15.6)
Taiwan	73.7 (Japan 39.8, USA 12.5, Hong Kong 11.4)

Notes: * Excludes Malaysians and Singaporeans arriving by land to Singapore and Malaysia respectively.
** For 1995.
*** Arrivals by nationality, all other countries used arrivals by residence.
Source: PATA 1996 Annual Statistical Report.

honeymooners, an increasing number of experienced travellers that bypass the package tour market commonly identified with Japanese travel. Taiwan and South Korea are increasing significant generators, although curbs in South Korea are likely in the light of the recent economic crises. China is a sleeping giant with potential. With the growth in GDP and real private consumption and the liberalisation of travel abroad, it could become a dominant influence in the Asia-Pacific region's travel and tourism scene. In 1996, five million Chinese travelled abroad with one-third using travel agencies and the bulk visited neighbouring countries (WTO, 1997).

Another aspect of regional tourism is the long haul travel to the Asia-Pacific region, which continues to grow faster than intra-regional travel. The steady increase of European travel is due to a combination of factors: the economic importance of the Asia-Pacific region which encourages business travel, the effective promotion by airlines and tourist boards, good quality and varied tourism products, a high level of customers' satisfaction and reasonable air fares (WTO, 1997). With more nations committed to the General Agreement on Trade in

Services (GATS), the Asia-Pacific region is also an area for new opportunities for European tourism business in providing services, establishing commercial presence abroad, and supplying services.

It should be noted that certain actions taken by the European Union can have a direct impact on the outbound traffic to the Asia-Pacific region. These include the encouragement of quality-led tourism policies in third country partners, ensuring the protection of European tourists as consumers, and applying an "eco" label for tourist services (CEC, 1997). The impact of such measures will vary from country to country in the Asia-Pacific region and some can benefit more than others.

Singapore relies on both short and long haul markets (Table 5). Excluding Malaysians arriving by land, air traffic plays a paramount role for both intra-regional and long haul traffic. In recent years, Singapore's geographical position favoured its role as a gateway to Australia and has become a hub for Qantas Airlines to distribute its converging European traffic in Singapore to regional Australian airports. Singapore has also entered into air agreements with Indonesia with flights to regional airports in Indonesia, making it an alternative choice to Jakarta as a gateway to Indonesia. It has bilateral agreements with China which increase air frequencies to many points in China and is one of only a few Asian airlines to operate in both China and Taiwan (IATA, 1995).

Table 5 Visitor Arrivals by Residence, Singapore, 1990–1996

	ASEAN	Other Asia	Europe	Oceania	America	Others
1990	27.11	37.28	17.73	10.35	6.33	1.21
1991	31.03	36.99	16.59	8.81	6.04	1.05
1992	30.23	38.68	15.99	7.80	6.13	1.17
1993	30.20	39.37	15.87	6.97	6.06	1.53
1994	31.04	40.26	14.74	6.29	6.20	1.47
1995*	30.68	42.62	13.53	5.98	5.97	1.22
1996	30.94	42.00	13.75	5.91	6.30	1.09

Note: * From July 1995, arrivals from ASEAN include Vietnam arrivals.
Source: STPB Annual Statistical Report on Visitor Arrivals to Singapore.

The IATA (1995) air transport forecast for Singapore for the period from 1980–2010 is as follows. Southeast Asia will remain the most important region for Singapore, constituting 40% of its total air traffic in 2010, as compared with 46% in 1993. Australia will be the most important country of origin or destination, with 9.6 million passengers in 2010, increasing from 8.5% in 1993 to 16% in 2010. The number of visitor arrivals will increase at lower rates of growth than airline passenger traffic. This means that outbound Singaporeans and transfer passengers will contribute most to growth in airport traffic (IATA, 1995).

Within the Asia-Pacific region are a number of issues which will have implications for tourism development in the region (Muqbil, 1994, 1996; Dain Simpson Associates, 1996).

- The liberalisation in trade and services and the growth of regional trade blocs will mean more business meetings and conventions.
- As competition increases between countries, this means the need to maintain the share of growth and the search for "new" tourists.
- The use of new technology and telecommunication will see dramatic changes in travel, e.g. the smart card.
- Environmental degradation arising from unplanned tourism development, air traffic congestion and overcrowding at major attractions still exist. Tourism has a role in protecting the environment and measures need to be taken to reduce the problems.
- Manpower training in tourism and hospitality is inadequate and this has to be remedied.

In summary, some of the main regional tourism prospects for Singapore are as follows: the neighbouring countries constitute increasing competition; Northeast Asia and Europe can be tapped for more tourists but requires further study on market segmentation; measures from the EC affecting tourist flows to the Asia-Pacific region can be advantageous to Singapore; and a continual strong development in air traffic for short and long haul traffic is crucial.

5. Methodological and Conceptual Frameworks for Competitive Strategies

The strategy of Tourism *Un*limited has identified ongoing measures and those to be implemented over periods of one year, five years and ten years (STPB, 1996). Its six thrusts and major measures are reinterpreted and shown as a mind map (Figure 3). Mind maps are powerful thinking tools and serve many functions (Buzan and Buzan, 1993). Figure 3 has been useful in showing all the major strategic thrusts and measures of Tourism *Un*limited on a single diagram. It has also helped show the emphasis on regionalisation and new (interpreted also as innovative) measures. A mind map of a national tourism strategy helps in sharpening the overall view and provides a better understanding for the maintenance of competitiveness. It should be noted that Figure 3 remains a personal interpretation of Tourism *Un*limited and other mind maps can be made.

Figure 3 Mind map of Tourism *Un*limited.

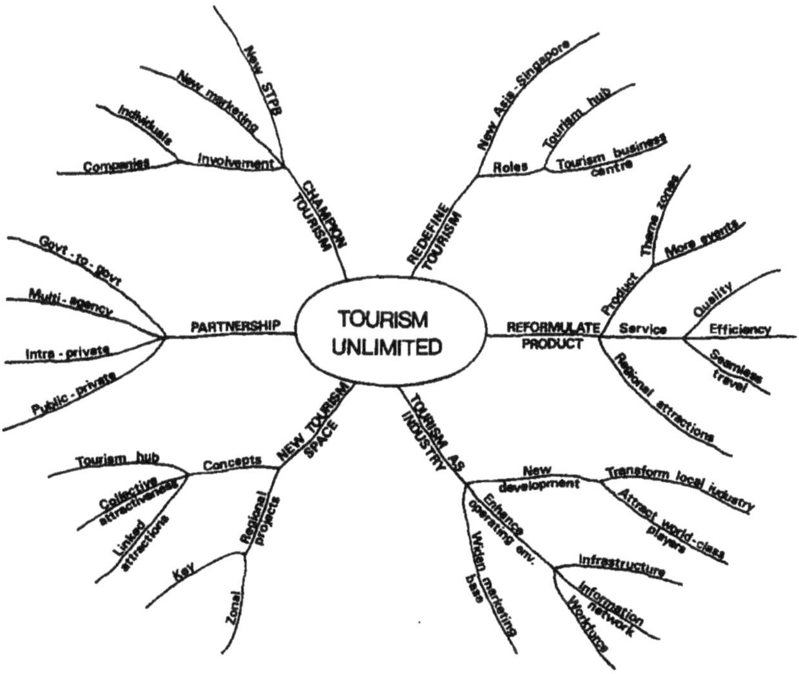

In her seminal book on new age tourism and technology, Poon (1993, pp. 291–336) recommended and discussed four competitive strategies for tourism destinations:

1. Put the environment first.
2. Make tourism a lead sector.
3. Strengthen distribution channels in the marketplace.
4. Build a dynamic private sector.

Basic to these strategies is the emphasis on "new" measures and the importance of "developing niches". This is obviously a call to be innovative in competitive strategies.

Poon's typology of competitive strategies serves as a starting point if strategies are not available, or for comparison if strategies are available. For Singapore, the typology serves as a useful comparison for Tourism 21. For Singapore, the environment is not included in its list of strategies. Emphasis is given to the region (tourism business hub, linked attractions, regional projects, etc). But what has been left out in the regional emphasis has been the environmental perspective. The environmental degradation in the region (sometimes arising from tourism development) as a factor in influencing Singapore's tourism has not been considered. For example, there is potential for Singapore to expand business in "green engineering" for tourism.

Innovations (i.e. new ideas, new methods) are important in strategies and measures to meet challenges of the New Age Tourism. As a starting point for innovations in tourism, the paper by Hjalager (1997) on the typology of innovations on sustainable tourism can be adapted for conceptualising competitive strategies and measures in the tourism industry. According to Hjalager, the following types of innovations can be identified: product, process, information, management and institutional.

For example, in applying the above typology to Tourism 21 (STPB, 1996), some of the major competitive strategies and measures (classified under six strategic thrusts) can be categorised as follows:

1. Product Innovations

- theme zones
- cultural tourism
- mega conventions

2. Process Innovations
- tourism hub
- tourism business centre
- regional investments
- regional marketing

3. Technology Innovations
- web site
- smart card

4. Management Innovations
- quality and skilled workforce
- standards
- automation

5. Institutional Innovations
- improved operating environment
- forging multi-links at all levels
- new STPB

The usefulness of the typology by Hjalager (1997) is its emphasis on innovations which are essential in a highly competitive industry such as tourism. Barras (1986) has noted that innovations tend to be implemented as follows: efficiency is improved first, then a shift to improve quality and finally the innovation to generate a new service. Barras' comments would be useful for evaluating the effectiveness of innovations. Poon, Hjalager and Barras have been quoted to show the usefulness of conceptual alternatives and possible evaluation modes for the various measures listed in Tourism 21.

Although emphasis is placed on innovations in the typology by Hjalager (1997), there are shortcomings. The tourism industry has a level of high volatility and sensitivity and is highly vulnerable to events completely outside the system which are not considered in any tourism strategic plan. Take, for example, the two recent events: The smoke haze affecting Southeast Asia (considered a small scale impact), and the current economic and currency crisis in the Asia-Pacific region (obviously a large scale impact that cannot be ignored).

While there is no immediate solution to such events, there are several methods of arriving at a better competitive position in the decision-making process. As tourism is an information based industry, the competitive intelligence analysis (Fuld, 1995) is recommended. Competitive intelligence analysis is the process of dealing with masses of information to develop intelligence that will support tactical and strategic decision-making (but does not include corporate spying). The basic framework of analysis has four stages: identify an action, identify the stakeholders as information sources, gather the information from the public sources, and analyse the action to be taken. Normally, 95% of the intelligence required is already available in the public domain. The importance of this methodology for the tourism industry was introduced to PATA members in a recent information workshop (PATA, 1996).

Competitive intelligence analysis can be illustrated by the following example:

1. Adoption of the smart card (action identified).
2. Government agencies, travel agencies, financial institutions, etc. (stakeholders identified).
3. Web pages, financial reports, trade journals, etc. (sources identified).
4. Details on expansion plans (intelligence revealed).

It should be noted that there are times when it is important to be aware of "conditions on the ground" and be able to adapt to the changing conditions. For example, lessons can be learnt from the growth of arrivals from Thailand, Malaysia, South Korea, Taiwan, China and other Asian countries. Such visitors have a preference for two-star hotels instead of the top-quality hotels preferred by Europeans, Americans and Japanese.

There is also much discussion and optimism on the use of Information Technology in the tourism industry. Tourism is an industry that is dependent on information and nearly every aspect of the industry has been affected by technology (Poon, 1993). This is best exemplified in the CRS (computer reservation system). However, this is a costly system and has not been fully exploited by all involved in the tourism industry. The Internet is now a less costly alternative for those that cannot afford the CRS. "Of the industries which have made best use of the vast potential that the Web has to offer is the tourism sector itself, in the endless production of documents by national tourist offices, hotels, tour operators, airlines and other sub-sectors and business niches" (Fayos-Sola, 1997, p.125). The potential of tourist cybermarkets is still limited to some developed countries. In Asia, only Japan, with its large outbound traffic, presents the most potential.

With the decline in tourism arising from the regional economic crises, it is suggested that some of the above conceptual and methodological frameworks can be used to focus on the following issues/measures:

- make Singapore cheaper (in the light of the currency and economic crisis)
- make tourists stay longer (a perennial problem)
- increase tourist numbers (made difficult by the currency and economic crisis)
- increase long haul traffic from Europe (good potential)
- expand business and business niche traffic (good potential)
- expand cruise industry (good potential)

Perhaps rethinking is required on proposed measures such as:

- offer industry-wide discounts
- develop B&B (bed and breakfast) as a flexible accommodation measure
- develop green environment services for tourism
- encourage diagonal integration
- introduce casinos for tourists

6. Conclusion

Tourism is a highly competitive and multifaceted industry. It is also an information-based industry and highly dependent on technology and telecommunications. While attractions such as beaches and cheap shopping can attract tourists, innovations will make a difference to a country's competitive edge. And to remain competitive in a highly competitive industry requires sound command and analysis of relevant information.

References

Barras, R. (1986) "New Technology and the New Services: Towards an Innovation Strategy for Europe", *Futures*, Vol. 18, pp. 748–772.

Buzan, T. and Buzan, B. (1993) *The Mind Map Book*, London: BBC Book.

Cleverdon, R. (1993) "Global Tourism Trends: Influences, Determinants and Directional Flows", *World Travel and Tourism Review*, Vol. 3, pp. 81–89.

Commission of European Communities (CEC) (1997) *Community Actions Affecting Tourism*, Brussels, Commission Staff Working Paper, SEC (97) 1419, 11.07.1997.

Dain Simpson Associates (1996) *Impediments to Tourism Growth in the APEC Region*, Singapore, APEC Secretariat.

Edwards, A. (1995) *Asia-Pacific Travel Forecasts to 2005*, London: The Economist Intelligence Unit.

Fayos-Sola, E. (1997 ed.) *An Introduction to TEDQUAL*, Madrid: World Tourism Organisation.

Fuld, L.M. (1995) *The New Competitor Intelligence: The Complete Resource for Finding, Analysing and Using Information about your Competitors*, New York: John Wiley.

Hjalager, A–M. (1997) "Innovation Patterns in Sustainable Tourism: An Analytical Typology", *Tourism Management*, Vol. 18, pp. 35–41.

International Air Transportation Association (IATA) (1995) *Asia-Pacific Air Transport Forecast, 1980–2010.*

Muqbil, I. (1994) "Review of Tourism Development in the ESCAP Region", *ESCAP Tourism Review*, No. 15.

Muqbil, I. (1996) "Issues Facing Tourism in Asia", *ESCAP Tourism Review*, No. 16, pp. 125–128.

Pacific Area Travel Association (PATA) (1995, 1996) *Annual Statistical Report*, San Francisco.

PATA (1996) *Developing Leading Edge Libraries and Information Centres for the Tourism and Hospitality Industry*, Workshop proceedings, Kuala Lumpur, Malaysia, March 5–6 1996.

Poon, A. (1993) *Tourism, Technology and Competitive Strategies*, Wallingford: CAB International.

Singapore Tourist Promotion Board (STPB) *Annual Report 1995/96*, Singapore.

STPB (1996) *Tourism 21: Vision of a Tourism Capital*, Singapore.

STPB (1997) *Survey of Overseas Visitors to Singapore 1996*, Singapore.

Waters, S.R. (1997) *Travel Industry World Survey: The Big Picture 1996–97*, New York: Child and Waters.

Wong, P.P. (1997) "Singapore: Tourism Development of an Island City-State", in D. G. Lockhart and D. Drakakis-Smith (eds.) *Island Tourism: Trends and Prospects*, London: Pinter, pp. 249–267.

World Tourism Organisation (WTO) (1997) *Tourism Market Trends: The World 1985–1996*, Madrid.

7
Strategies for Financial Sector Development

Lim Guan Hua

Fourth largest foreign exchange market in the world since 1992 with an average daily trading volume of US$128.6 billion in 1996. Fourth largest over-the-counter (OTC) market for derivative products in 1995 with an average daily turnover of US$79 billion, according to the Bank of International Settlements (BIS). International Financing Review (IFR) International Exchange of the Year in 1989, 1992, and 1993. IFR Derivative Exchange of the Year in 1993. These are some of the honours and accolades bestowed upon Singapore and signal our success in positioning the country as a world-class financial centre. While we are still not in the same league as New York or London, we are one of the major financial centres in the world. In Asia, we rank favourably alongside Tokyo and Hong Kong. Our banking system is rated the least risky in Asia by Standard & Poor's.[1] Our Big Three local banks are ranked in the world's 200 largest banks, and these same three banks consistently emerge among the top banks in terms of Tier 1 capital ratios as calculated by the BIS, making them some of the world's strongest banks.

We have arrived, but the challenges ahead are not going to be any easier to overcome. We need to take stock of our position, and improve upon our competitiveness in the years ahead. The benchmark is not the up-and-coming regional financial centres like Bangkok and Labuan Island in Malaysia. Neither is it simply Hong Kong, our traditional rival. Like everything else, our competitors at this stage of our economic growth are global in nature.

---

[1]*Straits Times*, November 26, 1996.

The development of Singapore as a world class financial centre is not an accident of history, nor is it spontaneous. Rather, it is the result of a set of deliberate policies and actions carefully planned and executed by the government. Starting in the late 1960s, the government recognised that banking and financial services could become a pillar of the island's economy. It now contributes 12% to our Gross Domestic Product (GDP) and employs some 10% (this is for the finance and business services) of the workforce. The goal then was (and still is) to develop Singapore into a world class financial centre in order to take advantage of the country's traditional role as the centre for trade and finance, its ideal location at the centre of Southeast Asia and the fact that it operates in a time zone that complements the European and American financial markets. It also seeks actively to become the management and distribution point for a wide range of financial services to the region.

The set of deliberate monetary and fiscal policies was aimed at liberalising the economy and making the country an ideal place for banks and other financial institutions from around the world to set up operations. In pursuit of this, Singapore modified and updated its financial laws and legal system, introduced various tax incentives, and invested heavily in good infrastructure and education. Foreign exchange controls were also removed and all foreign talents/ expertise needed to achieve the goal of transforming Singapore into a world class financial centre are welcome. So far, we have succeeded in making Singapore a premier financial centre as shown by the number (see Table 1 below) and diversity of financial institutions operating here.

1. Challenges Ahead

We are now on the verge of the third stage in the development of Singapore as a world class financial centre. We have succeeded (first stage: late 1960s to mid-1980s) in getting foreign financial institutions to set up and conduct financial operations in Singapore and have (second stage: since the mid-1980s) considerably broadened and deepened the financial structure since. It is now time

Table 1 Number of Key Financial Institutions in Singapore

Year	Commercial Banks*	Representative Offices**	Merchant Banks	Insurance Companies
1970	37	8	2	–
1975	70	38	21	69
1980	97	49	37	71
1985	129	50	55	82
1990	141	45	68	124
1995	140	57	77	141
1996	143	58	79	146
1997	152	65	80	154

Notes * Includes those with full, restricted and offshore licences.
** Offices of both banks and merchant banks.
Source: MAS Annual Reports

for consolidation. The Monetary Authority of Singapore (MAS) will have to change its orientation and focus to take Singapore forward into the next century. Even though it has a well earned reputation worldwide as a tough regulator, giving investors and market players confidence in Singapore's financial institutions and markets, some argue that it has retarded their creativity and growth. The emphasis from now on is to ensure that proper internal controls are in place in the financial institutions under its charge and that these controls are well executed. As Deputy Prime Minister BG Lee mentioned recently, MAS will emphasise supervision and not regulation. In order to meet the new challenges that will be thrown up from time to time by an increasingly competitive environment, closer cooperation between the market regulator and the players in the financial system is needed. Efforts should be directed towards the provision of a conducive environment which fosters creativity and product/service innovations. The market would also need clearer rules from MAS and the tax authorities (IRAS) to succeed in this aspect. The speed of MAS in approving new products/services, in which the financial institutions can assist by providing detailed product information and necessary risk assessment profiles, will be important as the financial services sector is deregulated.

WTO and Trends towards Deregulation of Regional Financial Markets

The recently concluded financial services agreement at the World Trade Organisation (WTO) has many implications. Admittedly, the recent currency and stock market crises have dampened the official mood among many Southeast Asian countries towards further opening and deregulation of the financial sector. Given these circumstances, many of these countries are simply not in any position, economically or politically, to further deregulate and open up their domestic financial sector and markets. This, however, does not mean that the WTO negotiations have come to nought. The adoption of the financial services agreement will, I believe, be at most delayed and countries may stretched out the implementation of the agreement over a sufficiently long period of time to make it politically acceptable. Hence, we have to prepare ourselves for the eventual pressure from the rest of the developed world, especially the USA, to open up our financial services sector and markets. Competition will only become more intense in the years ahead.

There is also a shift in government policies, especially among Southeast Asian countries, towards economic and financial nationalism. This will mean that in future, more countries will try to bring home some of the banking and financial services currently conducted overseas. In order to deal with this, Singapore needs to re-orient its foreign exchange (forex) market. We should aim towards becoming the market making centre and information clearing centre for the region, not for indigenous currencies but for cross-currency services. Growth here would most likely be determined in the short to medium term by the underlying growth in investments and trade flows rather than as a result of increased speculative forex activities.

As it is, we have been facing, for some years now, some indirect competition from Bangkok and Labuan Island. They are not direct competitors. In fact, we could say that they complement the offshore banking market in Singapore. Thailand's international banking facilities were created to support the country's economic and financial needs and to serve as a launch pad into Indochina while the international offshore financial centre in Labuan is part of the package designed to help develop Malaysia into an attractive investment centre. Admittedly, the current baht and ringgit crises will slow down the development of these two offshore financial centres. We cannot, however, discount them. The problems faced by Thailand and Malaysia will eventually be solved and the two countries will get their acts together.

In addition, Australia and the Philippines have both started to open their banking markets and to grant licences to a handful of foreign banks. The coming big bang planned for Tokyo and the expected deregulation of the financial sectors in Taiwan and South Korea will also bring forth added competition for Singapore's financial institutions and markets. The Hokkaido Takushoku Bank/ Yamaichi Securities failures in Japan and Seoul's need for a multi-billion dollar IMF bailout should be viewed as a temporary setback and should not affect the eventual deregulation of the financial sectors in these two countries.

The Euro and Its Impact on Financial Markets

The other major development is the planned unification of the currencies of Western Europe and their eventual replacement by the Euro. A common currency for the major economies of Western Europe will have many implications. Without the problems related to different currencies, we may see mergers of banks (the recent proposed merger of Union Bank of Switzerland and the Swiss Bank Corporation is an example) and other financial institutions all over Europe. This will result in fewer but financially stronger banks which will become much more prominent players in the world arena.

The Euro may also lead to an integration of the financial markets of Europe. What we may see is the creation of a huge stock market, based possibly in London, rivalling New York and Tokyo, with smaller regional bourses in other European cities like Paris, Amsterdam and Frankfurt, somewhat like the situation in the US. The Euro-denominated fixed income securities market may also become a force to be reckoned with, as it will probably be of a size comparable to the current US$ market. Already the battle for supremacy has begun. The battle is on for the key money market benchmark rivalling the US$ London Interbank Offer Rate or Libor

(London has just introduced the Euro Libor) and the German futures exchange, Deutsche Terminboerse (DTB), has embarked on an aggressive campaign to link up with its competitors in other European cities to try and become the major financial futures market for an eventual unified Europe. The Swiss Options and Financial Futures Exchange (SOFFEX) is its first partner in its overall plan to cut costs and increase exposure ahead of monetary union. The new joint platform, called Eurex, is due to start in mid-1998. DTB has also signed an agreement with SIMEX which allows the latter to trade its German Treasury products on its trading floor.

Without the different European currencies, a big portion of the forex market will become non-existent. There will no longer be currency pairs such as US$/DM, £/US$, ¥/DM, £/¥ to trade, price and arbitrage. These internationally important forex markets will be replaced by the Euro/US$ and Euro/¥ markets. All these developments will have an impact on Singapore's role as an offshore financial market and a major world foreign exchange trading centre, given the current importance of such currency pairs in its forex market.

Technological Advances

The latest advances in technology have made round-the-clock, round-the-world electronic trading easy. This reduces the advantage of Singapore's strategic position within the Asian time zone. With access to electronic trading systems, players in Europe and America will find it less vital to establish operations in Singapore in order to effectively manage their positions on a 24-hour basis.

The Internet poses yet another credible threat by changing the way banking is done. Virtual banking and high speed communication lines have the potential to reduce the need for physical bank branches. This would make the one-location restriction imposed by MAS on restricted licensed and offshore banks less onerous. The Internet may also change the way investors buy and sell shares and with that, the whole brokerage industry.

Pressures to Internationalise the Singapore Dollar

One of the principles underpinning our policies towards the development of Singapore as an international financial centre is the government's long and persistent stand against the internationalisation of the Singapore dollar. Under the MAS Notice to Banks #MAS621 dated November 1983, all banks have to consult the MAS before granting S$ credit facilities in excess of S$5 million to non-residents. This restriction also applies to S$ credit facilities to residents if the money is to be used outside Singapore. Furthermore, it also applies to syndicated loans, bond issues and other financial products.

While the policy of not internationalising the S$ ensures control over domestic money supply and allows the MAS to implement monetary policy with relative ease, it may be time to re-examine it. With the government's encouragement, many Singapore companies have gone regional. These companies need to fund their overseas ventures. Borrowing in the currency of the country of venture may not be feasible as the companies may not have achieved the required credit standing or clout in the overseas markets. There may also be a lack of Singapore-owned banks operating in many of these regional markets. Borrowing in US$ from the Asian dollar bond market may also not be an option for some small and medium enterprises, given their small size and funding needs. The alternative of establishing banking relationships in Singapore with a bank from the country of venture may be infeasible as the bank would most likely have only an offshore banking licence.

As more companies are given the permission to borrow in S$ to fund their overseas projects, the S$ will get internationalised. Further developments of the debt and financial futures markets would also lead to the same outcome. This appears to be inevitable and may not adversely affect our increasingly sophisticated and resilient economy. The government would have to find new ways of shielding the domestic market from external shocks and the MAS would have to be more creative in its regulatory and monetary policies. A paradigm shift towards more supervision rather than more regulations, as mentioned by Deputy Prime Minister BG Lee, may just be the answer.

2. Where Are We Today?

Separation of Domestic and Offshore Markets

While we seek to develop Singapore as a world class financial centre, we have given existing local financial institutions some form of protection. The government has always given differential treatment to the developments of domestic and offshore markets and has shielded the domestic market partially from foreign competition. This has given the financial sector in Singapore rather unique characteristics.

The most important and well known example of this separation of markets is the banking industry. No full banking licence has been issued since the last was given to Tat Lee Bank in 1974. In fact, full banking licences were given to all existing foreign banks in 1971 and new entrants were offered restricted (starting from 1971, with the last one awarded in 1984) and offshore (starting from 1973) banking licences. All newcomers since 1984 were given only the offshore or ACU licences. Their access to the S$ market is restricted. They get S$ funds mainly from the interbank market. Currently, the total loan amount to Singapore residents may not exceed S$200 million at any one time.

In addition, no new licence has been issued to finance companies since the early 1980s. Rather, there is a concerted effort to seek out the weaker ones and force them either to merge or to leave the industry. The number of finance companies has thus fallen steadily over the years, from a high of 35 in 1982/83 to only 19 in July 1997. Further consolidation among the remaining finance companies is expected.

Foreign access to the stock exchange was granted in the aftermath of the 1985 Pan-Electric Crisis. The SES Committee has set 49% as the maximum limit for foreign equity participation in locally incorporated brokerage firms. Access to the market is hence rather restrictive to foreign stock brokerages. New international members, all of whom were admitted in 1992, are restricted to the offshore and domestic wholesale segments of the market.

Vitality of Local Banks

The domestic banking market is closed not only to foreign players but also to local institutions. There is a further partitioning of the domestic market into the retail and corporate/wholesale markets. Only banks with full banking licences are allowed to serve the entire domestic market. Those with only a restricted licence are allotted one banking location and can only operate in the corporate sector. All six local banking groups have full banking licences.

Through their extensive branch networks, the six local banking groups command a huge share of the markets for S$ deposits and loans. The six local banking groups are Tat Lee Bank (TLB), Keppel Bank (KB), Overseas Union Bank Group (OUB, which also owns the International Bank of Singapore), United Overseas Bank Group (UOB, which includes Chung Khiaw Bank, Far Eastern Bank, and Industrial and Commercial Bank), Overseas-Chinese Banking Corporation (OCBC, which has in its stable the Bank of Singapore and Four Seas Bank), and DBS Bank (DBS). In terms of size, their average total assets ranged from S$9.13 billion to S$52.46 billion in 1996.

The local banking groups are not all of equal strength and market presence. DBS, OCBC and UOB are large and have the size to be respectable regional players. OUB, the other "Big Four" bank is smaller. OCBC, UOB, OUB and TLB are mainly family owned while DBS and KB are government-linked companies (or GLCs).

Singapore's banking system is the least risky, most highly capitalised, and one of the most profitable in Asia, according to a 1996 study by S&P. The rating agency assigned a Aapi rating to the big three local banks (OCBC, UOB and DBS) and Api ratings for OUB, TLB and KB. Since 1993, MAS has been trying to get the local banks to increase their market capitalisation — they were given five years to raise their shareholder's equity to S$800 million. In 1996, before this target is even reached, MAS ordered the banks to increase their shareholder's equity to S$1.5 billion by 2001. This has resulted in some consolidation in the industry. Chung Khiaw Bank tried (unsuccessfully) to take over Far Eastern Bank, while UOB completely absorbed the operations of its 100% subsidiary, Lee Wah Bank, giving up the latter's separate banking licence altogether. More restructuring is expected.

A total reorganisation of the industry is strongly recommended. It is, however, important to note that even if all the 12 local banks are merged, it will still not create a bank big enough to stand shoulder to shoulder with the global giants of the industry. On the other hand, it will lead to an unhealthy concentration of banking services in Singapore. Some degree of competition among the local banks is needed. They are currently the industry leaders in the S$ segment of the banking market. They set the trend for prime rate changes which are then followed by the other banks. Even then, the local players are not always at the forefront in terms of banking services and products. They face stiff competition from the foreign-owned full licensed banks, especially HongKong Bank, Standard Chartered, Citibank and Maybank.

With this in mind, we suggest that the three smaller banks (OUB, TLB and KB) should be encouraged and permitted by MAS to merge with the three bigger ones (DBS, OCBC and UOB). The existing banking subsidiaries should be merged into their parent banks as was the case with Lee Wah Bank and UOB. The advantage of having separate licences and brand names may not be there anymore, and may even be counter-productive. Furthermore, as a policy, no new bank should be created nor any of the existing banking licences transferred to a new set of players. Prominent entities like Sembawang Corporation and ST Capital could be roped in as shareholders in any of the existing banking groups to add managerial, marketing and technological expertise, and much needed capital funds and connections for regional expansion. Stripped of its development bank role, there is no need for the government to retain an equity stake in DBS. The government should divest its stake in DBS through a secondary offering of shares similar to that used to sell shares in Singapore Telecoms. Without the government as a substantial shareholder, DBS would find it easier to expand regionally.

At the moment, we require the local banks to have one of the highest capital reserve requirements in the world. They are required to have a ratio of 12%, compared to the BIS mandated 8% ratio for Tier One capital. While this gives Singapore banks a solid reputation, it may become a severe disadvantage when they are competing in the international arena. With such high capital requirements, their cost of capital is higher and hence, their ability to compete is reduced especially since the margins in the international markets are small. The other problem is the rather rudimentary asset-liability management regime that most Singapore banks currently employ. Currently they are building a lot of slack and safety margins into the system to overcome their inadequacy in risk management. While it is good enough for the local market, it will put them at a disadvantage when competing in the international markets. Banks in Singapore should urgently take up this matter and make appropriate changes before competition in the banking industry heats up.

Competitiveness of the Local Brokerages

Prior to the Pan-Electric crisis that forced the closure of the stock market for three days in December 1985, member companies of the Stock Exchange of Singapore (SES) were small (paid-up capital requirement for member companies which were incorporated as limited companies then was a mere S$2 million). The crisis brought forth much needed corporatisation of the stockbroking firms. In addition, the need to inject more capital and expertise into the industry led to numerous organisational changes. The local banks (DBS, UOB, OUB, OCBC, and TLB) were allowed to enter into the securities business together with two industrial corporations (Lum Chang and Keppel Corporation). The Big Four banks set up their own securities subsidiaries while TLB took over Lyall and Evatt's seat. A few of the weaker brokerages (Associated Asian Securities, City Securities, EG Tan & Co, and Lin Securities) were allowed to fail while the rest were given permission to take in local and/or foreign partners. Four brokerages (Kim Eng, Kay Hian, GK Goh, and Vickers Ballas) were subsequently publicly listed on the main board of the SES through very successful IPOs.

To further toughen up the brokerages, the minimum paid-up capital and adjusted net capital requirements were raised in 1993 to S$30 million and S$10 million respectively. Today, these stockbroking firms are financially much stronger. Adjusted net capital and shareholders' funds of all 33 SES member companies stood at S$656 million and S$791 million respectively in 1990. The corresponding numbers in 1996 were even more impressive at S$2,625 million and S$2,895 million. Furthermore, the total assets of the 33 member companies rose more than 275% from S$1,414 million to S$5,312 million over that six-year period.

Amendments were also made in 1992 to the Securities Industry Act to make it easier for SES member companies to participate in underwriting and trading in stocks. For example, their underwriting limits were raised to 100% (or 150%) of their adjusted net capital if it is below (above) S$50 million. Furthermore, bigger stockbroking firms (defined as those with ANC in excess of S$50 million) saw their investment limits raised to 300% of their ANC. In November 1997, SES gave the go-ahead to dealers and remisiers to sell unit trusts, an activity that promises fatter (up to 5%) commissions if they satisfy certain guidelines.

Financial strength is only one aspect affecting the competitiveness of local brokerages. To succeed in an increasingly competitive market, stock brokerages have to offer value-added services besides the mere execution of buy and sell orders. Research capabilities and regional and international linkages certainly help to provide an edge over competitors. In this regard, local stockbroking firms might want to form strategic alliances with foreign stock brokerages and research institutions. Further mergers and consolidations among the 26 regular member companies of the SES should be seriously contemplated.

Challenges to the local stockbroking companies not only come from the seven brokerages admitted under a newly created category of international membership but also from off-exchange trading facilities like the authorised trading centres (ATCs), ATMs, and in the near future, Internet stock trading. The introduction of the ATCs in 1993 following the successful introduction of SingTel Share Selling Centres took some businesses away from the brokerages. Small retail investors are now able to trade without having to open accounts with the brokerages. However, the impact of these additional trading facilities (located in both selected bank branches and in the offices of brokerages) on average daily trading volume is so far relatively low. The ATM, on the other hand, is used for IPO and rights applications and for the settlement of share transactions. What would make share trading easier is to have self-service ATCs and/or upgrades to the existing network of ATMs to allow for share trading. This would really open up a new trading avenue for small investors who are happy with market orders. The vast network of conveniently located ATMs make this very appealing to small investors even if, as a start, these only allow market buy and sell orders. To guarantee success of these trading facilities, the computerised trading system on SES should be able to handle the additional transaction volume that such share trading facilities would add to the market.

The feasibility and future of share trading on the Internet has also to be addressed. Phillip Securities recently launched an on-line electronic mart system called POEMS that allows 24-hour stock trading via the personal computer and telephone. It allows the user to place buy/sell orders on the SES and KLSE and to change or cancel any outstanding orders. This is a first step. Increasingly, Internet trading has taken root in the bigger stock markets elsewhere like those in the USA. On-line brokerages like ETrade Group Inc., Charles Schwab & Co., Fidelity Investments, Donaldson Lufkin & Jenrette Securities Inc., and Discover Brokerage are now part and parcel of the landscape. Despite some problems investors faced trying to connect to these on-line sites, these Internet brokerages have fared as well as the traditional ones. On October 27, 1997, both the NYSE and Nasdaq had their very first billion trades and the benchmark Dow Jones Industrial Average fell 554.26 points. The performance of these on-line brokerages on that day ensured that they will continue to command a place in the stockbroking industry and to expand in the years to come.

Internet share trading may change the brokerage industry as we know it in Singapore. The Internet is capable of allowing investors to either make market buy or sell orders with electronic trade settlements just like the ATCs. It also allows direct access to the trading system itself, that is, giving the public the ability to post limit orders. Whatever form it finally takes, the Singapore market will become even more open to foreign competition if Internet share trading takes off in the country. This will increase trading volumes and reduce the cost of brokerage activities across the board.

3. Openness to Foreign Market Players

Underlying Philosophy in the Development of the Financial Sector

In areas where we do not have the expertise, foreign institutions have right from the start been, and are still, welcome. Most of the 80 merchant banks here are foreign owned, controlled, and incorporated. We have welcomed the entry of large world known merchant and investment banks from USA, UK, Japan, and continental Europe. Similarly, most of the 154 insurance companies are non-indigenous. We have also admitted a whole range of fund management companies even as we try to encourage the development of a local fund management industry.

While foreign financial institutions are welcome, the MAS is known for its strict regulations and control of the financial sector. Stringent entry requirements are imposed and internationally well known names are not spared. For example, the entry of BCCI was repeatedly denied and Jardine Flemings was previously (in 1984) forced to give up its merchant banking licence. Our strict control has nevertheless paid off. We were not affected by the BCCI collapse. We also emerged unscathed from the 1995 financial futures crisis which brought down the Barings group. Both MAS and SIMEX came out of the crisis with their reputations intact. Our banks are more than adequately capitalised. Over the last three decades, we have seen neither any major market disaster (despite the Pan-Electric crises in 1985, and the October 19, 1987 world stock market meltdown) nor the collapse of public confidence in the financial system (Overseas Union Finance and Barings notwithstanding). All these give Singapore a sound reputation which we must maintain and continuously seek to enhance.

The S$ is strong, stable and regarded by some as a safe haven in times of currency crises despite the recent beatings it has to endure when the entire Southeast Asian region went under speculative currency attacks. We, as a nation, rank among the biggest savers in the world. The national savings rate is high (gross national savings as a percentage of gross national product (GNP) is almost 50% in 1995 and 1996) and the local banks are flushed with cash. The government runs persistent and large budget surpluses. Government borrowing is kept to a minimum and we have no external borrowings for 1995 and 1996. All these allow us to concentrate on developing the financial sector even though it may retard the development of our debt market given the lack of an appropriate risk-free benchmark that can be provided by Treasury bonds.

The Banking Industry

There are 24 foreign banks operating in Singapore with full banking licences. These are mainly banks from India (Bank of India, Indian Bank, Indian Overseas Bank, UCO Bank), Malaysia (Ban Hin Lee, Maybank, Sime Bank), USA (Bank of America, Chase Manhattan, Citibank), Hong Kong & China (Bank of China, Bank of East Asia, HSBC, Kwangtung Provincial Bank). Fourteen other banks, all of which are foreign-owned and with more than half of them from Europe, have restricted licences.

As such, we do have a fairly open banking system. The majority (24 to 12) of the full licensed banks are foreign owned. Including the 14 restricted licensed banks, the ratio of foreign to local banks in the domestic banking sector is even greater, at 34 to 12. However, in term of bank branches, the reverse is true. The local banks have a total of 273 as at the end of 1995, compared to only 104 by the foreign (full and restricted licensed) banks. The foreign banks have also not made much inroads into the local domestic market, as can be seen by their much smaller (83 versus 113) ATM networks[2] compared to the local banks. They are also excluded from the shared ATM network owned jointly by the six local banks.

The high foreign content of the banking market is, however, evident when we look at total assets, and at the size of the loan and deposit markets. In terms of total assets, the 12 domestic banks have 9.4% of the total market in 1995, compared to 16.7% and 11.3% by the 24 foreign full licensed banks and 14 restricted licensed banks respectively. Furthermore, while the local banks command a huge share of the S$ loans market, they have only 30% of the total loans market in 1995, compared to 14.2%, 9.8% and 46% for the foreign

[2] *Straits Times*, August 26, 1997.

full licensed, restricted licensed, and offshore banks respectively. In terms of deposits, the market shares that year were 23.6%, 15.8%, 8,8% and 51.8% respectively. Hence, the foreign components of our banking sector are not small. What is small is their access to the S$ deposit and loans market.

Stock Brokerage Industry

Many foreign institutions bought into local brokerages after the Pan-Electric crisis. The Kuwait Investment Office, for example, took an equity stake in JM Sassoon. Others who entered the industry include Morgan Grenfell (which bought into Su E-Min & Co., which has since been renamed Deutsche Morgan Grenfell & Partners), de Zopete & Bevan (BZW Pacific Union), Bankers Trust of New York (BT Brokerage & Associates), and Deak Morgan (SBCI & Associates). Of the 26 member companies, 16 are locally owned while the remaining 10 are joint ventures between local brokerages and foreign financial institutions. The local stockbroking industry is, however, not entirely open to foreign competition either, as all joint ventures have to be approved by the SES Committee.

In March 1992, SES introduced a new category of international membership and admitted seven big name foreign financial institutions as its members. They are Daiwa, Nikko, Normura, Yamaichi, Barings (now ING Baring), Credit Lyonnais, and Smith New Court (since taken over by Merrill Lynch). These are the equivalent of offshore banks. They are 100% foreign owned, and can trade without restrictions on behalf of foreign or non-resident clients. They are, however, barred from the domestic retail segment of the market. Dealings with a Singapore resident must be at least S$5 million per transaction. They are also not allowed to contest for seats on the SES Committee and hence, have only limited say in how the exchange is run.

The SES has also admitted a total of eight authorised foreign brokerages (ABN Amro Hoare Govett Securities, BOC Securities, Indosuez WI Carr Securities, Jardine Fleming International Securities, Peregrine Securities, Sanyo Merchant Bank, Schroder Securities, and UBS Securities) in a bid to enhance liquidity in foreign equities. These authorised foreign brokerages are not members of SES but are given direct access to the computerised CLOB trading system to deal in foreign currency denominated equities listed or quoted on SES without the need to put the trade through an SES member firm. They are allowed to deal directly with non-resident clients and with resident clients for trades above S$5 million.

The stockbroking industry also includes other broking firms which are neither member companies of the SES nor have direct access to the CLOB trading system. While they are not allowed to trade directly on the SES, they are well known brokerages from around the world, and form an important component of the brokerage industry here. The number of non-SES stockbroking members has increased steadily over the years from 31 in 1990 to 56 in March 1997.

International Nature of SIMEX

SIMEX started off with its doors wide open to foreign participation. Financial futures trading was new then to Singapore and we did not have the necessary expertise. To ensure the success of SIMEX, we even started off by tying up with the premier futures exchange in the world — the Chicago Mercantile Exchange (CME) and co-pioneering the mutual offset system (MOS) to allow futures positions opened on SIMEX to be offset in CME and vice versa. As such, most of the futures companies trading on SIMEX are foreign owned. Twenty-seven out of the 37 corporate clearing members as at September 1997 are non-indigenous. So are all the 27 corporate non-clearing members. Furthermore, some 86% of the trades on SIMEX in 1996 were by customers originated from outside Singapore, with Europe, USA and the Asia-Pacific region each contributing 28%.

All the futures and options on futures products traded on SIMEX are non-indigenous. All the products were introduced with the international market in mind. Hence, the contracts are not exclusive to SIMEX. Another indication of its international focus is that SIMEX is even open for trading on certain Singapore public holidays that are not public holidays in Japan, Europe or North America. This is welcomed by SIMEX's users as it leads to more efficient risk management.

4. Competitiveness is Multi-dimensional

Competitiveness of the financial sector is not simply a question of whether we give the best deal in terms of lowest taxes and greatest fiscal incentives. There is a catch. We do not want to end up being classified as a tax haven, as this would negate some of the valuable avoidance of double taxation treaties we have signed with our trading partners. We have provided generous tax incentives since the beginning. Most of the offshore operations are subject to corporate taxes at the concessionary rate of 10%, compared to regular corporate tax rate of 26%. These concessions have recently been extended and a concessionary tax rate of 5% now applies to certain higher value-added activities like fund management and securities trading. Offshore operations and transactions in the offshore markets are also not subjected to the 3% Goods and Services Tax (GST). Furthermore, there is no capital gains tax in Singapore and dividends are only taxed at the individual level under our tax imputation system.

Singapore will maintain its competitive edge and standing amongst other financial centres if we are able to provide a better overall package to the financial institutions. Tax incentives are but one component of this package. There are other factors. Financial institutions are worried about market transparency, stability in regulations, ease of bringing in needed talents and expertise, few if not no restrictions on capital flows, and the overall costs of doing business in Singapore. The latter includes the availability of office space, its cost, the availability and reliability of telecommunications facilities and air links, and political stability. Singapore's recent performance in the midst of the currency and stock market crises has strengthened our position as a world class financial centre.

So far, we are up to mark on most of these factors. There is an ample supply of good office space. We have regular air links to most of the major cities around the world and the region. Our Changi Airport is among the world's best airports and our telecommunications facilities are excellent. The market is fairly free from regulations. Employment passes are easily available for needed financial expertise. We are very receptive to foreign workers and the Prime Minister has just reiterated our policy of making foreign talents welcome in Singapore in his National Day rally speech in August 1997. In fact, the foreign worker dependency ceiling for the services sector, which includes the financial sector, has been raised to 30% from 25% since October 1, 1997.

The factors that we need to look into in order to determine our competitiveness are the following. One, the range and diversity of products and services our financial institutions and markets have to offer. This is covered in the next section under "Strategies for Success in the Future". Two, we have to ensure that the market microstructure, including rules and transaction costs of our markets, are in tandem with international standards. We must (see the section on "Fine Tuning") keep up with the latest developments in the financial markets so that we do not unnecessarily impose rules that would only frustrate international investors. These are in addition to how open our markets/industry are to foreign financial institutions and competition, and how ready (that is, whether our local financial institutions are strong enough to face international competition without assistance from MAS or the government) are we to open the financial services market.

5. Strategies for Success in the Future

Banking and Finance

Future of Restricted Licences

The distinction between domestic and offshore banking market should still be kept. What is more debatable is the need for full and restricted licences. Restricted licensed banks are barred from the retail market. They are not allowed to have more than one office, and cannot accept savings accounts and small (less than S$250,000) fixed deposits.

One way to rationalise the banking industry is to scrap restricted banking licences. Hong Kong neither discriminates between local and foreign banks nor between the domestic and offshore market. Despite the large number of banks in the territory, the banking industry there is still considered strong. In spite of intense competition, the local banks there are holding up surprisingly well. This is something we should seriously study and reflect upon.

We could encourage mergers within the industry. Some of the smaller banks, holding full or restricted licences, should be encouraged to merge by imposing upon them more stringent capital requirements in order for them to retain or get full licences. Those who do not wish to merge or invest more capital into the business should be given offshore licences instead. Such a measure would open up the domestic market to more but still manageable foreign competition. With the mergers among the local banks as mentioned earlier, the impact on local banking institutions would also not be too great.

Access to the S$ Market and New Branches

Foreign banks have often complained about their restricted access to the S$ market. While we have been increasing the S$ lending limits for offshore banks progressively over the years (it is now S$200 million), what these banks want is access to cheap retail S$ deposits and participation in the cashless shopping and payment service called Network for Electronic Transfers or NETS system. They would also like to have shares in a company providing ATM services for all banks. At the moment, POSB has the largest network of ATMs and the customers of the six local banks can use the ATMs of any of the six local banks. This is a big competitive advantage the local banks have over the foreign banks and one that the foreign banks wish to acquire.

Internet Banking

Internet banking was introduced, on a pilot basis, into the local market by DBS, UOB, OCBC, and POSB recently.

As a policy, Internet banking should be encouraged. The technology is out there. We can harness it and develop it further. Both UOB and POSB are using encryption technology imported from USA, while DBS is using security features developed in-house. The existing problems hindering the growth of Internet banking are security of on-line transactions and the authentication of the service providers. Third party accreditation (by Netrust for example) and encryption could solve the problem. Users also want some control over the Internet to prevent anyone from setting up sites similar (in terms of layout and domain name) to that of the real service provider in order to extract user name and password pairs. Legislation not only in Singapore but also worldwide may be required here. We need to coordinate the registration of domain names across countries. At the moment there is nothing to prevent someone from registering, say, dbs.com.xx and trying to pass itself off as dbs.com.sg.

As we wire up the entire country and Singapore One becomes more widely available and accessible to every household in Singapore, Internet banking should take off. The simple banking operations would then be done mainly electronically through the Internet, telephone, or at the ATM machines. Activities like the selling of unit trusts, third party fund transfers, loan applications, IPOs and rights applications, balance enquiries, account statements requests, GIRO applications, fixed deposit placements/renewals, cash top-ups for share margin trading accounts and stop payments on cheques requests can all be done over the Internet.

Widespread acceptance of Internet banking should also alleviate the long standing labour shortages in the banking industry and allow for more value-added work. It will also reduce the need for more physical branches. It might even allow banking services to be available on a 24-hour basis not only from the convenience of your home but from anywhere in the world. Studies done in the USA have found that Internet banking is much cheaper.[3] The cost is US$0.01 per transaction on the Internet compared to US$0.27 through the ATM. The cost through the telephone and over-the-counter are comparatively much higher at US$0.54 and US$1.07 respectively.

On-line banking services is another threat to the banking industry. Software vendors like Microsoft and Intuit have been pushing aggressively in this area. As technology accelerates and simplifies the distribution of information, banks are increasingly at risk of being a commodity. Internal transaction processing systems, at the moment, are the real stumbling blocks. The systems are antiquated and in need of a major overhaul. So far, such services,

[3] *Straits Times*, September 22, 1997, p.50.

which are in violation of the Banking Act, have not appeared in Singapore, but we cannot ignore them. They can drastically affect the entire world banking industry.

Role of Finance Companies in the Twenty-first Century

Besides the banks (and the ACUs) and POSB, the only other depository institutions in Singapore are the finance companies. We have to seriously consider the need for finance companies as part of our financial structure. They are now treated as second class banks and their range of permissible activities is very much restricted. As such, they are very vulnerable to changes in the regulatory environment. As it currently stands, they are too exposed to the property and car markets, making them vulnerable to a downturn in the property market and to changes in the COE/public transport policies. We do not want a replay of the S&L crises in the USA, nor problems with housing loans in Japan (the jusen crisis) and more recently, the crisis affecting finance companies in Thailand which has forced the government to shut down 56 finance companies.

The Finance Companies Act should simply be scrapped. The finance companies do not add much value to the financial system. They are too small and they duplicate services that are provided by the banks. They do not have the competitive advantage to take on the banks, neither in terms of scale of operations nor in terms of being more nimble and closer to the ground. The banks are increasingly eating into the traditional finance companies' territories. POSB does a much better job at reaching the small depositors such that the finance companies' traditional role in terms of pooling domestic savings has been upstaged. Thus, removing them would not cause too much disruption to the financial structure and loss of financial services to the public.

All the current bank owned finance companies can be easily absorbed into their respective parent banks. There is a precedent to this, Standard Chartered Finance was absorbed into Standard Chartered Bank in April 1996. Most of such finance companies are small and competing now with their parent banks anyway. They were first created way back in the 1970s to take advantage of the ability by finance companies to pay higher interest rates to depositors, something that the banks are prohibited from doing under the Banking Act. This interest rate ceiling is no longer in existence and hence the existence of bank owned finance companies should be re-examined.

As for the independently owned finance companies, they could be encouraged to merge, preferably with the banks. Most of them are very small and do not have huge branch networks. Companies like Far East Finance, Golden Castle Finance, Lian Huat Hang Finance, Nanyang Finance, and Public Finance do not have S$50 million in shareholder's equity and are unlikely to be able to raise the necessary capital on their own to keep their finance company licences. However, they could continue to operate as leasing companies. All of them, including the bigger ones like Sing Investments and Finance, and Singapura Building Society, who meet the new paid-up capital requirements, can be easily absorbed by any of the banks. For the two big independents, Hong Leong Finance and Singapore Finance, we suggest that they too be encouraged to merge with the local banks.

Broadening and Deepening the Stock Market

New Listings

While the number of IPOs over the last decade or so are encouraging, more companies should be encouraged to get public listings. The number of companies listed on SES rose steadily from 185 in 1990 to 294 in 1995 and 318 in 1996. Despite this, most companies still depend heavily on bank borrowings and internally generated funds. In order for these companies to venture overseas, wider and more reliable sources of funding are needed. That source is the equity market.

The decision to tender out part of the IPO through single or discriminatory price auctions has been used by listing aspirants to signal their "high quality" to the investing public (Allaudeen and Lim, 1995 and 1998). The combination fixed price-tender method was widely used in 1993 and 1994, but has since disappeared from the IPO market. We should not abandon it. They should be used by the government for privatisation issues, especially in the international portion of the public offering so as to ensure that we do not sell our national assets at below market prices.

One source of new IPOs is from the group of GLCs and corporatised statutory boards. More privatisation should be considered. PSA Corporation, JTC, Singapore Power, Tuas Power, MRTC, CISCO and a whole host of government bodies should be corporatised and sold to the investing public. This would add depth to the stock market. While this call for privatisation is not something new, regrettably, the rate of privatisation is still too slow. The government should also consider the development of a buoyant local capital market. Other GLCs like Raffles Hotel, Raffles City, Pidemco, Silk Air, SATS, and even the restructured hospitals could be considered for public listings on the stock exchanges.

SESDAQ was created to cater to the capital needs of small and medium enterprises (SMEs). More SMEs, especially those on the Enterprise 50 lists compiled annually by Business Times and EDB, should be encouraged to seek listings on either the Main Board of SES or SESDAQ. The top 10 companies on the 1995 and 1996 lists are potential candidates. Of these, only Serial System, Ossia International and Thakral Brothers (they listed Thakral Corporation) are listed. Others like power operator Salcon, entertainment company Europa Holdings, heavy equipment supplier Tat Hong Holdings, tools and metal components maker Singapore Shinei Sangyo, computer company GES Singapore (its parent is listed in Australia), trading firms Asiatic Enterprises, TT Importers and Exporters, SUTL Corporation and Windmill International, and companies like Batey Ads and Yongnam Engineering and Construction are still not publicly listed. Other potential companies for public listings would include the tour operators like Chan Brothers, Ken-Air, SA (UIC) Tours, Dynasty Tours, and Reliance, and even the S League teams, just as some of the well known football clubs in Britain are listed on the London Stock Exchange.

We have to encourage companies to rely less on bank loans and look to the equity market for additional funds. We also need to know why these companies are not seeking public listings. The disclosure requirements for SESDAQ companies can be relaxed if the need arises. Listing fees can be lowered and the admission criteria/process made less stringent and/or simplified. We could also create separate sectors for SESDAQ companies just like the SES Main Board (see Table 2). It is good that we are now seeing a wider variety of companies on SESDAQ other than manufacturing or electronics.

Apart from domestic companies, we should also try to entice more companies from the region to obtain a listing. We should try to get more European and American companies with regional exposure to raise capital in Singapore through a listing on SES. So far we have managed to get only a handful of such companies. These include

Table 2 Suggested Changes to Sector Classifications on the SES

Existing Sectors	**Recommended Classifications**	**Examples of Companies in each of the Recommended Classifications**
Industrial & Commercial	**I&C**	
	Manufacturing/ Marine	Amtek, Fu Yu, Jurong Shipyard, Jaya Hldgs, MCL
	Services	Robinson, Auric Pacific, Comfort, CWT, Eng Wah
	IT/Electronics	Acma, Creative Technology, Tri-M, Clipsal, Singatronics
	Construction/ Engineering	IPCO, Van Der Horst, L&M, Natsteel, United Engineers
	Trading	Burwill, C&C, Jack Chia-MPH, Stratis Trading, Intraco
Finance	Finance	Including the closed ended funds, BT-SRI fund, IFS, Transpac from the current I&C Sector plus open ended unit trusts
Hotel	Hotel	No change
Properties	Properties	No change
Plantations	Scrapped	The only company here should be transferred to I&C
SESDAQ	**SESDAQ**	
	Electronics/ Manufacturing	Aztech, Flextech, Gul Technology, Rotol, Vikay
	Services	Amara, Form Hldgs, RMG, Second Chance, Noel Gifts
Bonds, Loans & Warrants	Bonds, Loans & Warrants	Including preference shares and all the warrants and bonds

Norwegian telecommunications company Nera (SEA), Italian/ Australian external facades specialists Permasteelisa Pacific, Australian property company Australand and Australian insurance company FAI Insurance. It is interesting to note that none of the merchant banks, which are mostly locally incorporated, are listed on SES. Why?

We could also target the Singapore-based operations or the regional (SEA or Asia-Pacific) businesses of MNCs. Companies like Shell Eastern Petroleum, Asea Brown Boveri Holdings, BP Singapore, Exxon Chemical Singapore, Du Pont Singapore, Sharp Corporation, Sanyo Electronics, Carrier Singapore, and Caterpillar Asia are potential targets. The other targets are companies and joint ventures going to China but based in Singapore. To do this, we may have to re-examine the listing fees, requirements (such as the need to have US$2,000 or equivalent lot sizes) and be more liberal with the granting of S$ listing status. Companies can still be forced to raise equity funds through a non-S$ currency, but the quotation and trading of the shares in the secondary market can be in S$. This is not new. Shares in Malaysian companies are quoted and traded in S$ on CLOB International. That does not violate the non-internationalisation of the S$ policy. Furthermore, more foreign companies should be encouraged to get joint or secondary listings on SES.

Trading in a non-S$ currency need not be a disadvantage for companies listed on the SES. We are probably the only stock exchange in the world with this foreign currency quotation and trading requirement even as we actively encourage the listings of foreign companies. The fact that such stocks are now easier to trade with the introduction of the Foreign Currency Cheque Clearing System have made more investors interested in these counters. Nonetheless, more needs to be done. For a start, we need to expand the cheque clearing system beyond that of the US$. With the system, it now takes three days instead of two weeks to clear US$ cheques and drafts through the Automated Clearing House. It is also cheaper. Share financing for these counters is also available now and banks have been known to fix the exchange rate for IPOs which are quoted in a non-S$ currency during the offer period to reduce the foreign exchange risks to the potential investor.

The existing classifications on the Main Board are definitely outdated. The Industrial and Commercial (I&C) sector is too big and should be reclassified to create sub-sectors so that investors can better monitor the market (see Table 2 above for suggested changes). KLSE, for example, sub-classifies its Industrial and Commercial Sector into Consumer Products, Industrial Products, Construction, Trading/Services and Infrastructure. A good reference point would be the classifications used by the CBRD in its *Financial Highlights* and that used by the BT-SRI. Furthermore, some of the companies now in the I&C sector should be reclassified. For instance, closed ended funds like Harimau and OUS, unit trusts like the BT SRI, venture capitalist fund like Transpac, and mutual funds like the Asian Fund, China Fund should be reclassified more appropriately under the Finance Sector. The Plantation sector should also be scrapped and its only occupant moved to the I&C sector.

The Foreign Board

The Foreign Board was created to allow foreign companies and infrastructure projects that do not meet the stringent Main Board listing criteria to be listed on the SES. Right from the start, we have faced competition from KLSE and HKSE in the race to get infrastructure projects publicly listed. In this regard, KLSE is ahead at the moment with four listings (L Trans Kota Holdings, Powertek, Puncak Niaga Holdings, and YTL Power) and there are many potential candidates in Hong Kong, given that many companies there are heavily involved in infrastructure projects in China.

To date, only one company (CM Telecoms) was listed on the Foreign Board although others were reportedly given approval by SES and despite moves by SES to make it easier (cutting the minimum project value requirement by half to S$150 million) for companies to get a listing. With the recent promotion of CM Telecom to the Main Board, the Foreign Board is now empty. One possible solution to the lack of activity and interest in the Foreign Board would be to get the government to take the lead as it did with SESDAQ. Possible listing candidates would include the Suzhou Industrial Park and the projects it has in countries like India and Indonesia (if politically feasible). GLCs like Sembawang

Corporation should also be encouraged to list its power projects. These might just create the momentum to get the Foreign Board up and going.

Alternatively, we could scrap the Foreign Board and create a separate sector on either the Main Board or SESDAQ and call it, say, Infrastructure. As a separate sector on the Main Board, companies that do not have the requisite five-year track record for a listing on the Main Board and are not infrastructure related would be directed to SESDAQ. However, this may not be the best solution. China National Chemicals Import & Export Corporation (Sinochem) which was reported to have given SES a miss after it was referred to the Foreign Board, may not want a listing on SESDAQ either. Restructuring the Foreign Board, as part of SESDAQ ties in with SESDAQ's original goal of listing companies with good potential but without the requisite five-year track record. It is also in line with the government policy of opening up SESDAQ to foreign companies by allowing them to float their shares in a non-S$ currency. The two-year promotion rule that applies to SESDAQ compared to the shorter one-year promotion rule of the Foreign Board should not be of concern as most infrastructure related projects are unlikely to get promoted within a year in any case.

Whatever the decision may be, we should not abandon our objective of helping infrastructure projects get capital funding through a public listing. The region's need for highways, power and water plants, sea and airports would only increase in the years ahead. These projects need to be funded either through new equity or long term debt. It is a growth area and we should encourage the acquisition and development of project financing expertise. We might even want to allow infrastructure related companies to raise debt and then list such long term bonds on the SES. In this regard, the two financial guarantee insurance companies that have been established here so far fit well into the master plan to position Singapore as a centre for infrastructure financing.

Listings of Unit Trusts

Public listing of unit trusts would also solve the distribution problems faced by many international fund managers who do not have the extensive distribution networks like the six local bank owned asset management companies. The recent attempts by foreign fund managers to sign up brokerages to sell unit trusts have enlarged the existing third party unit trusts distribution network provided by Standard Chartered, Citibank and Maybank. However, this cannot be compared to the reach once these unit trusts are publicly listed on SES. The listing of the BT SRI Fund is the first step in the right direction. In addition, we should keep track of the trends towards exchange listings of open ended funds in Europe and see whether the same can be done in Singapore.

At the present moment, an investor has to go through a fairly lengthy process to transfer his units in the BT-SRI fund from the fund manager to his CDP accounts and *vice-versa* if he wants to sell his units on the SES or through the fund manager. This paperwork is unnecessary and something should be done to remove this. Otherwise, exchange listing of the BT-SRI fund with its attendant brokerage, clearing fees and stamp duties is of limited use to the investors. SES has made the right move in setting lower brokerages for listed unit trusts at 0.5% for trades up to S$250,000 and 0.3% otherwise subject to a minimum of $2 per trade.

Public listing of open-ended funds is still a relatively new concept. Some even argue that it is redundant given that the fund manager stands ready to sell additional units to and redeem existing units from the investing public at any time. These open-ended funds also post daily manager's prices. However, for many of these funds, especially those investing in Europe and North America, the prices quoted are often only indicative. This makes the redemption process risky as the investor is uncertain of the price at which he bought or sold his units. While we acknowledge that investments in unit trusts are for the medium to long term and that daily manager's prices do not change much from one day to another, we should nevertheless make transactions easier and less risky. Investors can now apply for additional units for some unit trusts through the ATMs. Selling unit trusts through the ATMs is however still not possible. The investor is still required to sign redemption forms. There is no reason why investors cannot sell units through the telephone, Internet or the ATMs and have the proceeds from such sales credited directly into pre-designated bank accounts.

Linkages to Other Bourses

SES is at the moment working on a possible link with the Taipei stock market which would allow for the listing of Taiwanese companies on the SES and Singapore companies on the Taiwanese bourse. The earlier link up with Nasdaq in 1988 was not too successful given the lack of local interest in the stocks available through the link. This was despite the fact that Singaporeans could trade, via the link, shares in such well known companies as Apple Computers, Intel, Ericsson, and Jaguar. While the Taipei link would increase the number of listed companies on SES, there is no guarantee that it will succeed or that the companies on the listing will appeal to Singapore investors.

New Strategic Directions in Futures Trading

Merger of SIMEX and Sicom

Organised futures trading is now conducted at two locations and regulated under two different set of laws and governed by two different regulatory bodies. SIMEX handles financial futures trading under the Futures Trading Act administered by MAS. On the other hand, the Ministry of Trade and Industry through the Trade Development Board (TDB), is responsible for the Commodity Futures Act and the regulation of rubber and coffee futures trading on Sicom. This may not be very efficient. The two exchanges also operate under two different trading systems. SIMEX uses the traditional but more widely used open outcry system with physical trading pits and is a recognised success. Sicom, on the other hand, trades using a screen based computerised order driven system and has seen dismal volumes in its rubber and coffee contracts.

Something has to be done before we lose our position as an important centre for commodity trading. Closer cooperation with the major rubber producing countries of Thailand, Malaysia and Indonesia may help. We might want to get them in as members of the exchange. Their governments and/or trade association representatives may even be offered seats on the board of directors and/or on the board of international advisors. We could use the computer based trading system and set up terminals in Jakarta, Kuala Lumpur and Bangkok to expand the reach of, and add liquidity to, Sicom.

A restructuring involving the merger of Sicom with SIMEX could be another alternative. Sicom could then become a separate division of SIMEX, just like IMM is a separate division of CBOT. Mergers and consolidation of futures trading is not new. New York Mercantile Exchange merged with Commodity Exchange Inc. in 1994 to create the largest commodity exchange in the world, and CSCE and the New York Cotton Exchange have recently agreed, in principle, to merge in 1998.

Given the track records of the two trading systems, a case can be made to scrap the computer based market making system used by Sicom. Sicom could operate on the open outcry system and deal exclusively with commodity futures. SIMEX could even transfer the gold and energy futures contracts over to Sicom. Additional contracts such as those on cocoa and cotton which Sicom was reported to be considering could then be added. We could also expand the products offered on Sicom to encompass those currently traded on the Singapore Chinese Produce Exchange (SCPE) in the long run. Futures contracts on products like coconut oil, copra, pepper, nutmeg and gambler can be added. The combined membership of Sicom and SIMEX would add liquidity and much needed futures trading expertise to the market. With SCPE, the market will become even more vibrant and should be in a much better position to withstand the challenge of regional futures market from Malaysia and Philippines.

Keeping Open Outcry While Preparing For Electronic Trading

The battle between open outcry and electronic trading is not new. At the moment, open outcry is the most popular system and commands a higher volume of futures trading than electronic systems. Nonetheless, the battle is far from over.

Sydney Futures Exchange has just recently decided to convert to a 24-hour screen trading system by early 1999. Electronic newcomer DTB has caused concern for the Chicago Board of Trade (CBOT) and the London International Financial Futures and Options Exchange (LIFFE), both of which use the open outcry system, by its gains in Bund futures trading and its aggressive expansion plans including the opening of an office with 24 terminals in Chicago. The Hong Kong Futures Exchange, on the other hand, chose to have electronic systems alongside their open outcry trading pits in order to extend their trading hours and to gain access to the Chinese market. LIFFE is reported to be now looking into a possible electronic link with SIMEX instead of the original open outcry link.

Part of the dilemma for open outcry exchanges, is that there is no impetus for change since the exchanges are flourishing and trading volumes are high. A move to electronic systems could threaten liquidity. Hybrid systems, with electronic trading cards and headsets gradually gaining acceptance, should help to pare the higher costs associated with open outcry — costs which could drive companies into the arms of the electronic exchanges, such as British bank Lloyds TSB which has closed its 42-strong LIFFE floor operations.

While some people may argue in favour of the liquidity and transparency of the open outcry system, others feel that electronic trading is the future. Although electronic trading systems have high setup costs, they are very easy to modify, making the introduction of new products very cheap. The record for open outcry versus electronic means so far has the former winning hands down. LIFFE trades 82% of the Italian government bond futures and 82% of the options, while Milan's electronic exchange garners a mere 15% of the futures and 5% of the options trade. SIMEX trades Eurodollars futures contracts in an open outcry forum and out trades the electronic Globex Eurodollar contract 8-1/2-to-one. The electronic exchanges have not taken this setback lying down. For example, DTB has fought back against LIFFE to increase its market share of Bund contracts to 35%, after increasing the number of members outside Germany who trade using the exchange's remote terminals. It is also extending its trading hours for Bund and Bobl futures and options (and Schatz and Euromark futures) to make it more convenient for exchange members in the US to trade on these futures contracts.

SIMEX has hedged itself. It has introduced the Automated Trading System or ATS to extend trading via electronic means for some of its contracts. The latest addition to the ATS is the MSCI

Taiwan stock index futures contracts. With this, a total of nine contracts are now listed on the ATS. These are the JGB, Euroyen, Euromark, Nikkei 225, Nikkei 300, Deferred Spot US$/DM, Deferred Spot US$/Yen and Gold futures contract in addition to the MSCI Taiwan futures contract mentioned earlier. Furthermore, starting next year, the gold futures and the two deferred spot contracts (which are all thinly traded) will be traded purely on the ATS, freeing up precious trading pits for other contracts. LIFFE, on the other hand, has the Automated Pit Trading System (APT). The APT allows the open outcry pit trading mechanism to be represented electronically. It is used to extend the trading day for major futures contracts as well as to provide a daytime trading environment for non-floor traded products (currently, only the JGB).

Beyond Offshore Futures Trading for SIMEX

While SIMEX has emerged as a global player of some importance, what is needed are indigenous and exclusive products. Malaysia, through its two financial futures exchanges (the Malaysia Monetary Exchange Berhad and the Kuala Lumpur Options and Financial Futures Exchange), has indigenous products like contracts on the KL Composite Index and on the three-month Malaysian Ringgit Klibor. SIMEX needs its own products. This need for more products and market innovations was reinforced by the Prime Minister on his recent visit to Chicago.

An example of a product that SIMEX needs would be a local stock index futures contract. The ongoing study on the possible use of the BT-SRI index as a basis for a stock index futures contract is a step in the right direction. However, given the relatively poor reception of the virgin index by the public and fund mangers, its success is by no means guaranteed. The most widely reported and followed index in Singapore is the Straits Times Industrial Index (STII). This is a price weighted index comprising 30 blue chip stocks from the industrial and commercial sector of SES. However, its structure is subject to manipulation. Instances of stock index ramping were widely reported in 1996 and if nothing is done to curb this, the STII would not be a good candidate on which we can design a derivative product. We need to study the recently launched trading of options and futures contracts on the Dow Jones Industrial Average (DJIA) in Chicago and what the US regulatory authorities are doing to prevent undue manipulations of the DJIA. Success with a local stock index futures could pave the way for the introduction of options on the stock index futures contract and individual stock futures *a la* the Hong Kong Futures Exchange.

We could also tie up with MSCI to trade futures contracts on some of their other indices besides the unpopular MSCI Hong Kong (now delisted) index which is a proxy for the widely followed Hang Seng Index. The MSCI Taiwan Index is currently in demand, but once the Taiwanese market opens up and the Taiwanese authorities introduce a contract based on a more popular and widely followed index, we may see falling volumes in the MSCI Taiwan Index. A possibly attractive contract could be the MSCI Far East Index. With fund managers moving their funds worldwide, futures contracts on indices like the MSCI World, MSCI Pacific, and MSCI European should also get their attention and fulfil their hedging and speculative needs. There should be a demand for such futures contracts and if we are the first to launch and trade such products, we might be able to capture a big slice of the eventual market. SIMEX could use its good working relationship with MSCI to create and launch such derivative products in the near future.

We could also start a three-month S$ Sibor interest rate futures contract. This would complement our current offerings of Eurodollar, Euroyen and Euromark contracts. Malaysia's Klibor contract has been a success and the Hong Kong Futures Exchange has just relaunched the three-month Hibor futures contract in September 1997. We might also want to look into the possible trading of interest rates futures contracts based on the recently announced Euro Libor rate once the Euro becomes a reality. The agreement with DTB which allows SIMEX to trade short, medium and long term German government debt instruments — the Schatz, Bobl and Bund, could become useful when trading in Euro-related futures contract starts.

Trading in regional currency futures or futures on a basket of regional currencies is another alternative. The New York Cotton Exchange has just cancelled its plans to trade futures contracts on the S$ after it failed to generate interest in its futures contracts on the Malaysian ringgit, the Thai baht and the Indonesian rupiah (it has since announced that trading in these three currencies will resume shortly). SIMEX terminated trading on its pound sterling, Deutschemark, and Japanese yen futures contracts some years ago when interest in them fell. Their replacement contracts (deferred spots on the yen and deutschemark) are also disappointing despite volatile DM and yen exchange rates. Hence, we need to think carefully before we launch a S$ futures contract, especially in the light of the government's non-internationalisation of the S$ policy. What is more promising would be to learn from the New Zealand Futures and Options Exchange's experience with their newly launched futures contract based on the nation's trade weighted index which is a measure of the domestic currency against the currencies of major trading partners. If this catches the investors' interest, SIMEX might want to seriously consider starting futures trading on, say, the OCBC Foreign Exchange Index. Such a contract would allow market players to hedge against adverse movements in the value of the S$. This index represents the trade weighted average of the S$ and is a good proxy of what the government likes to see as the value of the S$.

Strategic Repositioning of Option Trading

As far as options contracts are concerned, we do have a fairly active OTC market for forex options. In fact, we are ranked fourth largest in the world in this area.

SIMEX has also been trading options on futures contracts for quite some time. While it has not always been smooth sailing, these contracts do command respectable volumes on SIMEX. In addition, SES trades warrants and covered warrants. These derivative instruments have seen good trading volumes and attracted the attention of market novices and experts alike. Nonetheless, more needs to be done to stimulate the development of the options markets as the stock options market on the SES is as good as dead. The last trades were done in March 1996. Stock options trading was first introduced into the Singapore market in February 1977, making us the fourth country in the world, after the USA, Canada and Australia, to have organised call options trading on individual stocks. The market was initially a success with trading for the first few weeks as high as 10% to 15% of the total turnover of all securities. Sadly, this interest was not sustained and died out by 1980. In March 1993, SES revived the market by introducing put and call options trading on two stocks (SIA Foreign and Keppel Corporation). Options on another five stocks (City Developments, NatSteel, Creative Technology, DBS Foreign, and UOB Foreign) were later added. Once again, the market failed to sustain the early trading interest and volumes. Average daily trading volume was 68.90 lots in 1993 valued at some S$30,000. This fell to 17.98 lots worth less than S$4,000 in 1994 and 19.43 lots with a value of about S$5,000 in 1995. A total of seven lots were traded for the entire year of 1996.

Perhaps we should seriously consider transferring stock options trading to an expanded SIMEX. The restricted membership and derivatives trading expertise of SIMEX might just do the trick. More stocks should have options traded on them. The choice of stocks on which options are written should be left to the market. We could set criteria which a stock has to satisfy before options can be written on it. Controls could be imposed to prevent manipulation of thinly traded stock options.

It may be possible to transfer individual stock options to SIMEX and let it trade using the open outcry system. Equity options were originally traded on the London Stock Exchange (LSE) using the open outcry system. In March 1992, London International Financial Futures Exchange merged with the London Traded Options Market (LTOM) to create the London International Financial Futures and Options Exchange (LIFFE). Since then, all trading on equity options is done in the new entity and away from the stock market. Members of the LSE are entitled to carry out a number of activities including broking, market making and clearing on the new exchange. LIFFE operates on an open outcry system supplemented by APT, a system that replicates the open outcry method of trading on the computer screen and equity options are traded there in a competitive environment with at least three market makers.

Another example where open outcry trading of options is used is the world's leader in options trading, the Chicago Board of Options Exchange (CBOE). CBOE market makers combined with CBOE's state of the art technology has enabled the exchange to execute record numbers of contracts with unsurpassed levels of speed and efficiencies for customers, member firms and floor traders. Today, CBOE accounts for over 65% of all options trading and 44% of all equity options trading in the US.

In newly listed options, a modified trading system is used to enhance initial liquidity. In these markets, a designated primary market maker makes a market and fills customer orders. Only when the option's liquidity has reached an acceptable level would trading revert to the regular market maker system. Market makers provide liquidity in option trading and form the backbone of the CBOE's trading system. They take the opposite side of public orders by competing in an open outcry auction market. Retail customers are also well taken care of by the CBOE. Public customer market and marketable limit orders of up to 10 contracts are routed to the Retail Automatic Execution System (RAES) to be filled automatically at the prevailing bid or offer prices. Fill reports are made within seconds thereafter. We could learn from CBOE's experiences.

A Rethink of the Role of CPF in the Twenty-first Century

The monetary environment has developed a great deal since the early 1970s. There is now less need for the government to use CPF to mop up excess liquidity in the local market. Better tools are available to the MAS to manage money supply. With most of the major infrastructure projects (expressways, housing, utilities, and MRT) built, there is also less need for the government to use the CPF to obtain cheap financing.

There are enough local investible funds around. All we need is to amend the Central Provident Fund (CPF) Act. The CPF could remain as the dominant pension fund with control over the Special and Medisave accounts. At the moment, CPF is nothing more than a savings bank. The interest rate is low and equal to the average savings and one-year fixed deposit rates of the local banks. This is not good enough. Changes are required. Piecemeal liberalisation of the ways in which CPF moneys can be invested is too myopic. Bolder measures should be adopted. A complete rethinking of the role of CPF and how this role is to be fulfilled needs to be done.

CPF members can still use the balances in their ordinary accounts to buy properties but any remaining funds should be invested through proxies. CPF members should be allowed to assign their moneys to these designated fund managers who would invest some of the money in the local share market (see Table 3 for a list of potential fund managers). This not only releases huge amount of funds into the local bourse but might also help the development of the local fund management industry. CPF account holders may also get better returns which would motivate them to accumulate even more funds to meet future retirement needs. This is important with increasing life expectancies and an ageing population.

Table 3 List of Potential Fund Managers for the Management of CPF Account Holders' Funds*

Owned by Local Banks	Others
DBS Asset Management (12)	Singapore Unit Trusts (6)
Keppel Investment Management (4)**	Schroder Investment Management (6)
OCBC Asset Management (9)	Nicholas-Applegate Capital Mgt Asia (5)
OUB Asset Management (6)***	Templeton Investment Fund (7)
Tat Lee Asset Management (2)	Morgan Grenfell Investment Management (3)
UOB Asset Management (15)****	Rothschild Asset Management (3)

Notes: * Numbers in brackets refer to the total number of unit trusts managed by the company as at Dec 1997.
** Keppel Insurance has 3 unit trusts under its management.
*** OUB Manulife has an additional 3 unit trusts under its management.
**** The most aggressive asset management company. Another 4 funds are managed by UOB Life Assurance.

Investing through professional fund managers may also alleviate the fears of the government and the general public that CPF account holders might lose their old age pension money in unwise investments. This is especially so given the presently depressed state of the stock market. It would also change the nature of the stock market from one that is highly retail based to one dominated by more institutional investors. That may make the market less susceptible to rumours and improve the efficiency of the market. It may also reduce the market's exposure and vulnerability to short term foreign funds.

The added advantage of investing through professional fund managers is that these fund managers can be used to control/monitor the performance of companies.

Staking Our Claims on Future Growth Areas

Fund Management

The fund management industry has witnessed tremendous growth recently. Total funds managed as at the end of 1996 was S$125.0 billion, representing a growth of 45% over the previous year. These funds are managed by 161 (135 in 1995) institutions employing 712 fund managers, investment analysts and other related fund management professionals. They are all high calibre professionals, with requisite qualifications and experience. The recent formation of the Investment Management Association of Singapore should help to give the industry a higher profile and help in its development.

The latest development in this increasingly competitive industry here is to bring professional investment management services to the not so high net worth individuals. For example, with as little as S$50,000, DBSAM will structure an investment portfolio based on its locally authorised unit trusts to meet specific investment needs of the individual. This is at the low end of the spectrum. At the high end, we have companies like Schroder Investment Management's private client unit who caters to anyone with more than US$1 million to invest. Investors are given access to as many as 160 mutual funds and unit trusts globally.

Private Banking Hub: Switzerland of the East

Singapore is now establishing itself as the Asian hub for the growing private/premium banking market. Private/premium banking combines trust and fund management services with traditional banking services. It is no longer exclusive to the super rich as banks in the region start to cater to the not so well heeled but nonetheless high net worth individuals. This is because research findings have indicated that the fastest growing segments of the Asian wealth market are represented by private investors between the ages of 25 and 44. The Asia-Pacific region (excluding China), according to a recent Citibank study, is worth some US$2-3 trillion, with Indonesia alone worth some US$30 billion.

The objective here is to capture these potential super rich individuals early, hoping that they would remain as loyal customers. Private banking is still for the super rich (typical entry level is between S$1 million to S$5 million) while premium banking is for the growing numbers of nouveau riche. Entry level for premium banking could be as low as S$200,000. This service comes under various names today. It is known as Preferred Banking by Bank of America, CitiGold by Citibank, Asset Advantage by HongKong Bank, Priorty Banking by Standard Chartered Bank and Privilege Banking by UOB.

At the moment, the industry is dominated by foreign players as they have the reputation and global reach. These include the big-name private bankers like Coutts & Co., Pictet, Citibank Private Bank, ABN Amro, Credit Suisse, Indosuez, Swiss Bank Corporation, UBS, and Rabobank. Some of these (Pictet) hold only investment advisor licences from MAS while others are associated with banks.

The high growth potential of this industry has attracted new competitors and existing players have increasingly accorded this greater priority. The complexity of the market and the needs of clients have also resulted in clients being served not solely by a single relationship manager but assisted by a core team of product specialists. For example, DBS has recruited additional staff to add to their 15 relationship managers and five product specialists.

We should try to further enhance Singapore's edge in this area. Private/premium banking with its emphasis on long term relationship building seems ideally suited to the Asian market. Asians have long treasured relationships and *guanxi* in businesses, and are known to have agreed to contract terms with a simple handshake. Some of the factors that play a part in our attractiveness as a private/premium banking hub include a high degree of political stability and neutrality, well regarded banking secrecy laws, good infrastructure, and a strong currency. The wide diversity of products in the region's financial markets has also played a major role in channelling the funds back from Europe. We should try to keep it here in Singapore. Our lower costs of doing business *vis-à-vis* Hong Kong where the market's continuing concern about the status of "one-nation-two-system" gives us an advantage.

Risk Management

Increasingly, companies, financial institutions and regulators have come to recognise the importance of proper risk assessment and management. The Baring scandal coming after the many derivatives fiascos has only helped to heighten this awareness.

Singapore is well placed to play the role of risk management centre for the region. We have the world's fourth largest foreign exchange market and a very active OTC market for derivatives. We are also the hub for the Asian dollar and Asian bond market. The Finance and Treasury Centre scheme has also played an important part in furthering the growth of the risk management industry. About 30 MNCs with substantial operations in the region have established such centres in Singapore to manage their group treasury and funding needs in the region. This was identified as a growth area more than 10 years ago and it is still a growth area today.

Overcoming the Size Problem through Strategic Alliances

While we are a world class financial centre, none of our financial institutions is large enough or an important player in the world arena compared to the big American, European and Japanese institutions. Size will become important as the world financial services industry undergoes further consolidation and governments all over the world embark on deregulation.

We could employ strategic alliances as identified by Lee, Lim and Tan (1997) and Lee, Lim, Tan, and Wee (1998) as one of the three generic strategies for SMEs. Singapore financial institutions (such as banks, insurance companies, and stock brokerages) should try to seek strategic partners in the countries of ASEAN and beyond. They could hold strategic equity stakes in one another, not unlike the global airline alliances. These strategic alliances would not only have the size to compete effectively in the international markets but would also allow its members to offer customers better services and a broader range of products. It might even allow Singapore financial institutions to gain access to regional markets that are otherwise closed to foreign players. The Singapore Insurance group set up by 12 Singapore insurance companies to take on risks of between S$100–S$500 million is a step in the right direction.

6. Fine Tuning

SES: Keeping up with the Joneses

Transaction Costs

The SES should move immediately to a T+3 business days period settlement system. The current T+7 calendar days system is too long and out of line with the major world bourses. With computerisation and scripless trading, the need for a uniform board lot trading size has to be re-examined. Exceptions are so far given on an *ad hoc* basis. SingTel is allowed to trade in lots of 10 and 100. More transparency is needed. Other than possibly increasing the transaction volume, there is no other compelling reason why trading has to be in uniform lots.

I am not convinced that freeing up the existing brokerage structure is good. At the present moment, brokerages for trades above S$1.5 million are negotiable but subject to a minimum of 0.3%. The experience from other stock exchanges is that negotiable brokerages benefit only the larger investors while the smaller investors end up having to pay much higher brokerages than before. What we need to look into is whether the present brokerage (0.5% to 1% for trades below S$1.5 million) is excessive. We may need to cut rates across the board, rather than to abandon the system in a manner that would benefit only the big investors. Only when the market is more institutional investor based, would fully negotiable brokerages be good. Retail investors may then trade either through self-service ATC counters (like the ATMs we now have) or through the Internet. As the services of the broker is not required in these transactions, there could be a case for fixed (maybe even flat) but still affordable fees to cover the running and clearing costs for small (less than 10 lots, less than S$50,000) trades.

Brokerage is only one aspect of transaction costs. The stamp duty, which has been reduced to 50 cents per $1,000, can be cut further. We might even want to consider exempting small transactions done through self-service ATCs from stamp duty in line with the government plans to get Singaporeans to own shares. As a start, it can be scrapped for small trades in privatisation cases like SingTel. We might also need to look into the bid-ask spreads and the minimum tick size requirements to see whether further changes are needed.

Foreign Share Ownership Restriction and Separate Share Tranches

While it is true that most of the countries in the region have foreign ownership controls (Indonesia removed theirs, except for banks, in September 1997), we have to ask ourselves whether this is in fact necessary. Malaysia, Philippines and Thailand have foreign shareholding restrictions. Taiwan and South Korea similarly place restrictions on foreign ownership of certain companies listed on the stock exchanges.

Having separate listings of local and foreign shares may not be desirable in the long run. Scrapping it altogether today may not be feasible either. A short term solution may be needed and local controls kept until we are confident enough to let market forces replace it. As Dr Richard Hu mentioned in his recent (September 21, 1997) speech at the World Bank/International Monetary Fund seminar on investments in India, dual listings will be removed once the companies are no longer in the defence related and other strategic industries. Of the 35 companies that have foreign ownership restrictions, not all are stipulated by law. Banks are subjected to a 40% foreign shareholding limit by MAS while stock brokerages are subjected to a 49% limit mandated by the SES. The Singapore Technologies group of companies is deemed important enough to the security of Singapore to have a 49% limit.

That said, how do we ensure that control of the company will not fall into the hands of foreign shareholders? Some methods of doing so include:

- Having the golden or special share. The soon-to-be-formed Singapore Technology Engineering and Singapore Telecoms both have such shares held by the Minister of Finance (Incorporated).

- Making sure that one local shareholder or a group of local shareholders holds more than 50% of the company's shares. An example of this would be SIA.
- Depriving foreign shareholders the right to vote altogether.

Short of the above, none of the existing schemes will guarantee local control of the company. Not the separate listings of foreign and local shares. Not the scheme used by Malaysia's Public Bank which allows foreigners to buy local shares (minus the voting rights) in excess of the foreign shareholding limit. Not even regulatory control of substantial shareholders as it is with the banks and finance companies. They are subjected to such regulations under the Banking Act and Finance Companies Act respectively. What I am proposing below (which I will call separate voting blocs) would guarantee local control without depriving all shareholders of the right to vote.

As an interim measure, shares will be traded in one tranche and the local shareholders will always have the larger voice at general meetings. There is no restriction on the number of shares that foreign shareholders collectively can buy and hold even though the company has a foreign shareholding limit. Every shareholder here gets to vote but foreign and local shareholders vote separately with the final vote tally depending on the assigned foreign shareholding limit. The scheme does not require that there is a local shareholder with more than 50% of the votes or that all shareholders turn up to vote. The latter point is important as most of the foreign shares are in the hands of institutional investors meaning that it is very likely that a large percentage of these shares will be represented at the general meeting. Local shareholders are usually smaller and most of them do not attend AGMs or sign over proxies. To see how my proposal works, let us take a look at the following hypothetical example.

- The foreign shareholding limit is 40%.
- The company has 100 shares.
- Foreigners hold 45 of these shares. In a vote, 5 voted for the motion while 40 voted against the motion.
- 29 local shareholders are absent. 21 of the local votes are cast for the motion with the remaining 5 against.

The overall vote tally is 26 for and 40 against. Under the one share one vote system, the motion would have failed even though the vast majority of the local shareholders are in favour of the motion (21 versus 5). Control has passed to foreign hands. Under my proposal system, the vote tally is 5/45 for the motion amongst the foreigners and 21/26 amongst the local shareholders. Given that the foreign shareholding limit is 40%, the final vote tally is 0.4* (5/45) + 0.6* (21/26). This means that 52.9% of the votes are cast in favour of the motion. The motion has majority support and is passed. To prevent foreign shareholders from buying up proxies to gain control, we can require that local shares can be vested only with local proxies.

Notice that under this proposal, the local shareholders are guaranteed control, something which the current dual listing cannot provide. Local shareholders have control of the general meeting and do not have to depend on a larger turnout of local shareholders. All foreigners are also entitled to a vote even though collectively, they own 45 shares instead of 40 as would be implied by the foreign shareholding limit.

This proposal does not mean that foreigners have no say whatsoever in the management of the company. They just have to work harder to convince the local shareholders of the merits of their arguments. In the hypothetical example, if they managed to persuade two of the local shareholders to change their votes from yes to no, they would have defeated the motion. The final vote tally would then be 48.3% for (that is, 0.4* (5/45) + 0.6* (19/26)) and 51.7% against the motion.

Corporate Governance

In the longer term, we should rely more on the market for corporate control. For sensitive industries like banks, media and defence, we could extend the 5% individual holdings rule under the Banking Act and/or the special share held by the Minister of Finance (Incorporated) scheme. Other than this, there is no need to restrict foreign share ownership.

Using the market to discipline the company may not be possible at the moment. Most of the listed companies are either tightly controlled by the founding families or are GLCs. In the long run, we should aim for a greater spread of shareholders to loosen the control held by the founding family and/or controlling shareholders. Similarly, the government could divest more of its shareholdings in publicly listed companies. For most of the listed GLCs, there is no compelling reason why the government should continue to retain ownership control. Most are not strategically important or crucial to the defence of the nation. Divestment would free up more shares for trading, improve the free floats of the companies, boost liquidity in these stocks, and allow market forces to do a more efficient job of price discovery. More efficient pricing would lead to better allocation of scarce economic resources and attract more foreign funds into the country.

The US/UK or Anglo-Saxon model whereby the stock market is used to discipline the companies is very different from the German and Japanese models which use banks to make sure that companies operate in a manner beneficial to shareholders. Hostile takeovers are rare in Asia and even in continental Europe, including Germany. The German/Japanese model may not work as well in Singapore. Under the Banking Act, banks are restricted in their acquisition of shares in companies. As such, they cannot exert much pressure on management. In any case, the small number of local banks may make the German/Japanese route undesirable. The local banks would end up holding too much power and/or corporate power in a lot of companies could end up in the hands of foreign owned banks.

As such, we would have to develop the securities market so that they can play a more active role in corporate governance in the long run. This would only be possible when companies are less tightly held, Singaporeans become more sophisticated shareholders and retail investors and rumours do not dominate the market. In the meantime, we have to develop other corporate control mechanisms. The SES could ensure that companies are more transparent and engage in timely and fair disclosure of sensitive information. It can also make the board of directors play a more direct role in monitoring the company's management. In this regard, it might want to ensure that so-called independent directors do not have business or other relationships with the company. One way to do this is to adopt aspects of the German or Rhineland model by requiring companies to have directors representing employees and minority shareholders on their board.

The other reason this might be difficult at the moment is that small retail investors play a very significant role on the SES. The May Asia Market Intelligence Survey of seven cities in Asia[4] showed that Singaporeans have significant preferences for direct investing rather than investing through professionals (see Table 4). The long term plan should be to encourage Singaporeans to channel more of their investible funds to professional managers. This would make the market less retail based and less rumour driven. It would also allow for a liberalisation of brokerage fees and for the market to exercise greater control and be more effective in its oversight of the management of companies.

Table 4 Preferences over Different Forms of Investment Vehicles

Cities	Unit Trust/ Mutual Funds	Local Stocks/ Shares
Bangkok	17%	14%
Hong Kong	6	24
Jakarta	5	16
Kuala Lumpur	15	12
Manila	11	22
Singapore	5	39
Taipei	6	41

Other Market Microstructure Issues

The market has matured enough for us to go for strict dematerialisation instead of the current immobilisation of scrips. We have gone scripless for quite some time now and investors should by now have confidence in the scripless system. All transactions and trades are now book entry based. Most investors do not see the need for certificates. As such, we should do away with share scrips completely. This would free up the vaults of the Central Depository

[4] *Business Times*, September 19, 1997, p.3.

(CDP) and make clearing of transactions easier. We could start with IPOs and proceed to all the other existing companies in the same manner as we implement the scripless system.

The SES could also consider other changes to make the stock market more buoyant. As a start, short selling should be legalised and regulated. Regulated short selling is permitted in both the Hong Kong and Malaysian stock markets. Starting from January 1998, Thailand plans to allow regulated short selling for its biggest listed companies — those in the SET 50 index. At the moment, investors can short sell if they cover their positions within the day. The introduction of "when issued" trading allows investors to short sell shares in newly listed companies as long as these positions are covered at the end of the first day of ready trading. Of course, one can argue that, technically, investors can short sell albeit at great risks if they do not mind being "bought in" by the SES. What is needed is an organised form of share lending and short selling, not naked short selling. This would involve some changes to the share custodian business. It would also put SES on par with regional bourses.

SES/SIMEX may have to come up with some regulated form of short selling of shares if the stock options market is to succeed. There are some existing models which we can study and modify to fit our needs. We should not worry too much about what is happening in Malaysia with regard to share short selling. Our experience with the "when issued" trading facility during the first few days of trading for a new share counter showed that short selling would not be too disruptive. While regulated stock borrowing and lending are now no longer popular in Malaysia given the political climate, there is still demand for it. With proper regulations and safeguards, it has a useful role to play in hedging and speculative activities.

The SES should also look into allowing share buybacks by companies and be more forthcoming and transparent in its dealings with the listed companies. In particular, the industry would be better off if the SES could be more explicit in its rules allowing for share splits, bonus issues, and rights issues. It would make for a more efficient market if the SES could give detailed responses to companies when it rejects their applications for capital changes.

Options Trading

One of the major problems with options trading in Singapore has to do with transaction costs. The existing margin structure on SES is too high and discourages options trading. In addition to brokerage, clearing fees, and GST, the exchange requires margin for naked positions of 20% (revised downwards from the original 25%) of the market value of the underlying security plus or minus the amount in or out of the money. Settlement of premiums is T+1 and while trades are guaranteed by the Options Clearing Company, an investor can only close out a position with the same broker with whom he opened his position.

Debt Market

Despite a series of changes to the Singapore Government Securities Market (relaunched in 1987) and the SES (more information on the daily price quotation sheets and the setting up of the bond quotation system for dragon bonds and FRCDs), the fixed income securities market is still relatively under-developed in Singapore. Treasury notes (two, five and seven years tenure) issues are small and infrequent. They are also generally held to maturity, making the prices in the secondary market anything but truly representative. With the government having huge and persistent budget surpluses and able to tap CPF (S$51.62 billion in government stocks as at December 31, 1996) for cheap funds, it is unlikely to issue more Treasury notes in the near future. One way around this problem is to reduce the cash surpluses of the statutory boards and encourage them to borrow in the debt markets. Such bond instruments are as good as risk-free as Treasury notes and bonds.

The market could also do with more detailed price information than what is currently provided by the Business Times daily. Prices of all existing Treasury bills and notes should be listed as, for example, a seven-year note issued one year ago is now a six-year note and its price will give the market an indication of what the required yield is for a debt instrument that has a six-year tenure. It must be noted, however, that given the low yields of Treasury instruments, they are unlikely to attract the interest of the retail investors and hence making it available through ATCs or ATMs is unlikely to lead to an increase in trading volumes.

The corporate bond market is also relatively thin. Part of the reason for this is that Singapore companies are very conservative in their use of financial leverage. They tend to pay small dividends, retain most of their earnings and value internally generated funds heavily. The average dividend yield and D/E ratio for the 154 companies on the industrial and commercial sector of the SES in 1995, for example, was 0.044 and 0.265 respectively.

Much has been done to date to stimulate the development of the debt markets but without much noticeable impact. The market needs further fine tuning to the system. GLCs should take the lead by increasing their dividend payout ratios. This would hopefully have the impact of pressurising other companies to pay higher dividends. Higher dividends would then mean that the companies have to go into the market to raise capital through either debt or new equity. This would not only increase the supply of corporate debt instruments but also has the added advantage of subjecting companies to market discipline. The SES could help by requiring a much wider spread than the current minimum of 100 bondholders. This could be achieved through raising the minimum nominal sum requirement of S$750,000 and/or the relaxation of the 1,000 units lot size requirement for loan stocks. Corporate bonds which tend to be in large denominations (typically in the range of S$100,000 and S$250,000) could also be repackaged and listed just like what DBS Bank did to Teledata's five-year notes.

7. Conclusions

On the whole, our financial markets are fairly open and our financial institutions and intermediaries are strong enough to face the intense competition that will arise once the world's financial services sector is liberalised. Key strategies to enhance our financial sector competitiveness include the following. We should remove the distinction between full and restricted licence banks, scrap the Finance Companies Act, and actively encourage mergers among the local banks. Sicom should be merged into SIMEX, and SES should transfer the trading of stock options to an expanded SIMEX. SIMEX should also seek to go beyond offshore futures trading and develop some unique and indigenous products. A complete overhaul of the CPF scheme should also be seriously contemplated.

References

Allaudeen, Hameed and Guan Hua Lim (1995) "Fixed or Tender? An Empirical Study of the IPO Market in Singapore", *Paper presented at the Inaugural NUS Seminar On Finance,* August 11, 1995 (Marriott Hotel, Singapore).

Allaudeen, Hameed and Guan Hua Lim (1998) "Underpricing and Firm Quality in Initial Public Offerings: Evidence from Singapore", *Journal of Business Finance and Accounting,* 25 (3) & (4), pp. 455–468.

Lee, Khai S., Guan H. Lim, and Soo J. Tan (1997) "Dealing With Resource Disadvantage: Generic Strategies For SMEs", *Working Paper, NUS.*

Lee, Khai S., Guan H. Lim, Soo J. Tan, and Chow H. Wee (1998) "Generic Marketing Strategies For SMEs: Applications In Asia", *Working Paper, NUS.*

PART III

SOCIAL & CULTURAL PERSPECTIVES

8

Entrepreneurship and SMEs in the Singaporean Context

Björn Bjerke

1. The Importance of Entrepreneurship and of SMEs Today

In all national economies, a majority of business firms are small (or medium-sized). Take the US, for instance. Of the roughly 19 million businesses in that country, about 97% are in the small business sector — and the share of that sector is expected to grow (Holt, 1992, p. 69). Approximately 99% of businesses in the US employ fewer than 100 people (Hale, 1992, p. A10). The importance of small and medium-sized enterprises (SMEs) is also great in all national economies. Back to the US again, the small firms created the most net jobs in the economy from 1977 to 1990 (Kuratko & Hodgetts, 1995, p. 13). Small businesses account for approximately half of all US employment and created over 80% of all new jobs in the US between 1960 and 1985 (Hale, 1992, p. A10). Behind every small firm there is (or at least was) an entrepreneur, a founder of a new business venture. Well over 60% of the total of new jobs in the US between 1960 and 1985 were created by new business ventures (ibid).

Despite their more limited resources, small companies not only produce more jobs, but also more innovations than do large outfits ("Enterprise", 1993, p. 51). Research reveals that small firms in the US spend almost twice as much of their R&D dollars on fundamental research as do large firms. As a result, small companies in that country are responsible for a higher proportion of innovative products and services ("The State of Small Businesses: A Report to the President", 1987, p. 117). For example, new small firms in the US are producing 24 times more innovation per research dollar than do the larger Fortune 500 firms (Keats & Bracker, 1988, p. 43; Dougherty, 1992, p. 78). The National Science Foundation in the US estimates that 98% of "radical" product developments result from the research done in laboratories of small companies in that country (Castro *et al.*, 1988, p. 49). One reason small businesses are more innovative is that their key people stay closer to the customer, so they are more in tune with what is happening in the marketplace ("Enterprise", 1993, p. 53).

SMEs are defined differently from one country to another. For instance:

1. In the United States, a small business has less than US$20 million in annual sales and fewer than 500 employees (Wheelen & Hunger, 1995, p. 362);
2. In the United Kingdom, government statistics on SMEs are concentrated on those firms that employ fewer than 200 people (Carson *et al.*, 1995, p. 61);
3. In some Asian countries ("The APEC Survey on Small and Medium Enterprises", 1994, pp. 10–12):
   - Japan divides its SMEs into three groups, viz., mining, manufacturing, transportation and construction industries as one group; wholesalers as a second group; and retailers and service industries as a third. In the first group, an enterprise is counted as an SME if it has up to 300 employees, in wholesalers up to 100 employees, and in retailers up to 50. There are also (different) limits to capital to be invested in the three groups to be counted as a "small and medium-sized enterprise" in Japan;
   - Hong Kong limits the number of employees in SMEs to 100 in manufacturing and to 50 in non-manufacturing industries;
   - Malaysia restricts its public interest in SMEs to manufacturing only and prefers to talk about "small and medium-sized industries" (SMIs) to stress this fact;
   - Philippines divides enterprises below 200 employees into "medium" (with 100–199 employees), "small" (with 10–99 employees) and "cottage enterprises" (1–9 employees). If cottage enterprises have assets not exceeding 100,000 pesos, they are called "micro enterprises".

Although the contribution of SMEs varies widely between economies, in static terms they typically make up around 98% of enterprises, contribute over 50% of employment, about 50% of GDP, and over 35% of exports (Hall, 1995, pp. 2–5). Small enterprises are normally the most common form of enterprise or establishment in a nation regardless of industry, and most small businesses consist of a single establishment (Kuratko & Hodgetts, 1995, p. 13).

In Singapore, which is the focus of our interest here, an SME is defined as a company with at least 30% local ownership and with fixed assets of less than S$12m, if it is in the manufacturing sector. For a company in the service sector, the employment size is less than 100 ("Best Practices for Small and Medium Enterprises in APEC", 1995, p. 229). They constitute approximately 91% of the total number of establishments, 44% of employment, 24% of value added, and 16% of direct exports in the country in question (ibid, p. 229; "The APEC Survey on Small and Medium Enterprises", 1994, p. 13).

There are many different models for the relationship between entrepreneurship and the growth and development of an economy (Bjerke, 1989, pp. 75–78). No matter which one we use, it is clear that entrepreneurship has become a force driving both economy and society (Zimmerer & Scarborough, 1996, p. 2). Change and growth can be seen as a cause as well as a solution to our economic problems (Bjerke, 1989, p. 28). As an academic field, entrepreneurship has a long history (in Economics only until our century), and made headway in the US in the past few decades, but today it is hot everywhere. In minor or major ways (most of the time the first), creativity (if tangible) may lead to innovation, which in turn (if commercialisable) may lead to entrepreneurship, i.e., a start of a new business venture. This, in turn, may lead to an SME. Creative people tend to gravitate towards entrepreneurial environments that offer more independence and flexibility, say a small firm ("Enterprise", 1993, p. 53). Above all, entrepreneurs are gathering, directing and using resources in opportunities rather than allocating them to problems (Holt, 1992, p. 7). These people move a firm, an industry and a nation forward — the more of them, the better!

There seems to be a general understanding among researchers, politicians and commentators that our economies are increasingly moving in the direction of favouring smaller firms. A sign of this is that the employment share of small businesses is growing almost uniformly across the industrialised world ("Munchkin management", 1989, p. 91; Howard, 1990, pp. 118–119). There are many reasons why this is so:

1. An increasing number of work tasks have to do with managing information in some form or another, a decreasing number with managing physical objects. The industrial engine becomes more and more dependent on the carriers and processors of this information, i.e., individuals. (Bjerke, 1989, p. 71; Toffler, 1991, p. 238)
2. Many entry barriers are erased, and there are less natural economies of scale for most activities. It is a simpler economy to enter but also an economy in which it is easier to fail. (Bjerke, 1989, p. 49; "Enterprise", 1993, p. 52)
3. Advancing computer and telecommunication technology is "de-massifying" production and distribution. It is possible today to turn out, and to deliver, short runs of highly varied, even customised products at costs approaching those of mass production and distribution. ("Munchkin management", 1989, p. 91; Toffler, 1991, p. 238)
4. Flexibility is becoming increasingly important. Turbulence in the economy via factors like bouncing currencies can hurt any firm, big or small. Small firms, however, are inherently more flexible than larger firms and should be more resilient in riding the waves. Constant innovation and constant change has been part of the establishment. (Bjerke, 1989, p. 71; "Munchkin management", 1989, p. 91; Toffler, 1991, p. 239; Hall, 1995, pp. 2–5)
5. The move towards a service-based economy is a characteristic of all developed economies. Small firms are typically more prevalent in such economies. (Hall, 1995, pp. 2–5)
6. The removal of competition-crashing regulation has spawned shoals of minnows in industries like airlines and telecommunications. Those minnows are, on the other hand, often quickly eaten by bigger fish. ("Munchkin management", 1989, p. 91)
7. Technological changes and increasingly more open economies raise the level of international competition and globalisation.

Many business functions spill over national boundaries, integrating activities of small units in many nations into a network of a single productive effort. (Bjerke, 1989, p. 71; Toffler, 1991, pp. 239–240; Hall, 1995, pp. 2–5)

8. Consumer tastes are changing. Mass markets are breaking up. Consumers are increasingly put off by the idea of buying the same products as their neighbours. They will pay for unique and upmarket products. The result is a flood of small companies in various niche markets. ("Munchkin management", 1989, p. 91)
9. More women in the workforce have created an ample supply of the sorts of people who create and staff small firms. Well educated women with small children are today particularly likely to start their own businesses to balance home life with careers. ("Munchkin management", 1989, p. 91; Naisbitt, 1995, p. 188ff)

There are many commentators of business who assert that the most important *strategic* resource in an increasing number of industries and in all economies is no longer financial capital, but people with drive, energy and willingness to start new business ventures and rejuvenate old ones (Bjerke, 1989, p. 49; Toffler, 1991, p. 239). And if entrepreneurs and their endeavours, i.e., SMEs, are going to lead us into a new economic era, it is essential that we understand more about these people and what it is they do (Sexton & Bowman-Upton, 1991, p. 5).

To conclude on the importance of entrepreneurs and SMEs for an economy, we can say that they (Ushido, 1995, pp. 1–2):

1. Contribute to employment;
2. Play a role as the "innovators" of technology, commodities and services;
3. Play a role as exporters to world markets;
4. Expand the band of consumers' choice by responding to the change in market trends and offer more diversified, sophisticated and specialised products and services.

Up to a certain stage in the development of a nation and its economy, it is enough to rely on copying others, importing systems from more developed economies, letting the government run major and strategic sectors of the economy and opening the borders for foreign MNCs to establish themselves. But it becomes increasingly necessary, as the development of the economy is progressing, to rely more on the nation's own local entrepreneurs and SME sector. Singapore has come to that stage. There is a recognition that "while MNCs will continue to play an important role in the development of Singapore, that by itself is no longer sufficient — local, smaller enterprises must develop themselves at home and abroad to propel the country to new heights of economic sources" (Ghosh & Kwan, 1996, p. 220). It has also been acknowledged that the "promotion of local entrepreneurship has become increasingly important for Singapore's future economic development. It is the key component in the strategy to develop Singapore into a major node in global business and a total business center" ("Best Practices for Small and Medium Enterprises", 1995, p. 229). SMEs in Singapore are more and more recognised as "a significant source of employment creation, innovation and economic vitality. They are also the hothouses of many local entrepreneurs" (Department of Statistics, "Profile of Growing Small and Medium Enterprises in Singapore", 1997, p. 1).

Every country needs to learn how to encourage and develop entrepreneurs today. Every advanced country needs (Drucker & Nakauchi, 1997, pp. 77–79):

1. new independent entrepreneurs;
2. entrepreneurship within existing companies;
3. organising for entrepreneurship and innovation.

2. My Understanding of Entrepreneurship and of SMEs

There is no entrepreneurial licensing procedure and no evidence of entrepreneurs' professional status. An entrepreneur may operate in schools, in government as well as in corporations (Holt, 1992, p. 8). In this chapter, I limit my discussion of entrepreneurs to business only. Some authors make a distinction between entrepreneurial small firms and other small firms (for instance, Carland *et al.*, 1988) and some authors require of a business founder to go for growth in order to be called an entrepreneur (for instance, Sexton & Bowman-Upton, 1991). I make no such distinction or limitation. In my opinion, every start of a new business is an entrepreneurial effort. Some of them may grow and some may stop growing (sometimes deliberately). However, a company must not necessarily be non-entrepreneurial because it is or even stays small, but companies stop in qualitative as well as quantitative growth, no matter what size, when they stop to act entrepreneurially (Bjerke, 1997a, p. 5; Bjerke & Hultman, 1998, pp. 9–10). I would like to define entrepreneurship as the process of creating a new business venture. The entrepreneur can be an individual, a team and even, say, a government institution.

This definition requires two additional comments:

1. I have a liberal understanding of what is meant by "new". Most new business ventures are based on minor, even if creative, modifications or developments of business concepts which exist already. So, "new" here does not have to mean more than, say, a different design of an existing product or a more convenient access to a service.
2. It is normal today to include intracorporate entrepreneurs, called intrapreneurs (a term which was coined by Pinchot, 1985), among entrepreneurs, i.e., entrepreneurship going on within existing corporations, but staying there. For practical reasons I exclude these entrepreneurs from my discussion in this chapter, limiting myself to independent entrepreneurship only. It should be noted that independent entrepreneurship includes people who leave their existing job to strike out on their own, even if the idea (and some preparation) was generated where they worked before. This is, by the way, probably the most common way to start a new business venture today. We may call such people extrapreneurs (Bjerke, 1989, p. 529ff).

As far as SMEs are concerned, there is no reason, in this chapter, to restrict those to any specified upper limit in terms of local ownership, employment, investment or sales. Let me just say that I consider an enterprise as small or medium-sized as long as it has competitors and does not dominate the field in which it is operating.

The remainder of this chapter consists of three parts:

1. A summary of the existing picture of entrepreneurship and SMEs in literature and research. As we shall see, this is based on the industrialised Western world.

2. A discussion of how this picture needs to be modified to better fit the Asia-Pacific in general, and Singapore in particular.
3. A presentation of some ideas of how we can help and assist entrepreneurs in Singapore better. "Help and assist" means:
   - To generate more start-ups.
   - To improve the chances for start-ups to survive as SMEs or expand.

3. The Existing (Western) View of Entrepreneurship and of SMEs

What is an Entrepreneur?

Economists have been interested in entrepreneurs for several centuries. There is a long list of economists contributing to the definition and theory of entrepreneurs (such lists can be found, for instance, in Hisrich & Peters, 1992, p. 6 or Kao, 1995, p. 71). Two aspects from these contributions that have been taken over by business scholars are:

1. Entrepreneurs are risk takers. This idea was originally suggested by one of the founders of the theory of entrepreneurship, Richard Cantillon, a Frenchman, in the 18th century.
2. Entrepreneurs are innovators. This requirement came from the Austrian-American Joseph Schumpeter in the beginning of this century.

But business scholars, who have done serious research on entrepreneurship only for a few decades, have gone much further. To give three examples of the "definitions" of entrepreneurship:

- "Entrepreneurship is the dynamic process of creating incremental wealth. The wealth is created by individuals who assume the major risks in terms of equity, time, and/or career commitment or provide value for some product or service. The product or service may or may not be new or unique but value must somehow be infused by the entrepreneur by receiving and allocating the necessary skills and resources." (Ronstadt, 1984, p. 28)

- "Entrepreneurship is the ability to create and build a vision from practically nothing: fundamentally it is a human creative act. It is the application of energy to initiating and building an enterprise or organisation, rather than just watching and analyzing. This vision requires a willingness to take calculated risks — both personal and financial — and then to do everything possible to reduce the chances of failure. Entrepreneurship also includes the ability to build an entrepreneurial or venture team to complement your own skills and talents. It is the knack for sensing an opportunity where others see chaos, contradiction, and confusion. It is possessing the know-how to find, marshal, and control resources (often owned by others)." (Timmons, 1990, pp. 5–6)
- "Entrepreneurship is the process of creating something different with value by devoting the necessary time and effort, assuming the accompanying financial, psychic, and social risks, and receiving the resulting rewards of monetary and personal satisfaction." (Hisrich & Peters, 1992, p. 10)

Characteristics of Successful Entrepreneurs

Much research has been done on, and many lists have been suggested of, traits that characterise successful entrepreneurs. Let me summarise the major elements of such lists (McClelland, 1961, p. 16; Timmons, 1990, pp. 165–170; Kuratko & Hodgetts, 1995, pp. 41–47):

- Desire for responsibility
- Desire for immediate feedback
- High level of energy
- Future orientation
- Skill at organising
- Value of achievement over money
- Opportunity obsession
- Tolerance for risk, ambiguity, and uncertainty
- Self-confidence and optimism
- Creativity, flexibility and innovation
- Motivation to excel
- Willingness to learn from failure
- Leadership ability

- Commitment, determination and perseverance
- Initiative and responsibility
- Persistent problem solving
- Internal locus of control
- Integrity and reliability
- Vision
- Independence
- Team building

The Start of a New Business Venture

There are basically three reasons why people make the vocational choice of starting a business venture (Dubini, 1989, pp. 11–26):

1. desire for achievement combined with a sense of independence and autonomy;
2. desire for a change due to dissatisfaction with present working conditions; and
3. desire to follow traditional family role models.

To put it slightly differently, research has shown four triggering factors of importance to get the entrepreneurial process started (Bjerke, 1989, pp. 520–524):

1. Dissatisfaction with present work
2. Displacement (or redundancy)
3. Identification of a new venture opportunity
4. Encouragement and support

Entrepreneurs are inspired by the following factors (Zimmerer & Scarborough, 1996, pp. 3–4):

- Opportunity to gain control over one's destiny
- Opportunity to reach one's full potential
- Opportunity to benefit financially
- Opportunity to contribute to society and be recognised for one's effort

There are also potential drawbacks to becoming an entrepreneur (ibid, pp. 5–6):

- Uncertainty of income

- Risk of losing your entire invested capital
- Long hours and hard work
- Lower quality of life until the business gets established
- Complete responsibility

There are various attempts to classify small businesses into different types, based on different ambitions of the entrepreneur. For instance (Bjerke, 1989, pp. 652–653):

- marginal firms — "ordinary" new independent business ventures, often based on some kind of service orientation – the overwhelming majority of firms started;
- high-potential ventures — companies started with the intention that the venture will grow rapidly in sales and profits and become a large corporation (the entrepreneur's big dream);
- small, attractive companies — those that are not intended to become large corporations, but which might provide high salaries, perquisites and flexibility in lifestyle to the owner.

A similar classification is given below (Hisrich & Peters, 1992, pp. 13–14):

- lifestyle firms — usually achieves only modest growth due to the nature of the business, the objectives of the entrepreneur, and the limited money allocated for research and development;
- foundation companies — are created from research and development and lay the foundation for a new industry;
- high potential ventures — may start out like foundation companies, but grow far more rapidly, and therefore receive the greatest investment interest and publicity.

The Entrepreneurial Process and Managing an SME

Let us continue our overview of the existing picture of entrepreneurship and SMEs, a picture which is, as mentioned before, derived mainly by research done in the Western world, by looking at what is happening after the entrepreneur has decided to start a new business venture. Entrepreneurship is not a series of isolated activities or undertakings. It is a process by which individuals plan, implement, and control their entrepreneurial activities. The progress of an entrepreneurial undertaking (or an SME) is commonly placed in a growth model. One example (Holt, 1992, pp. 104–105):

1. Pre-start-up stage: The period during which entrepreneurs plan the venture and do the preliminary work of obtaining resources and getting organised prior to start-up. This includes the following activities: business concept definition, product-market study, financial planning, and pre-start-up implementation.
2. Start-up stage: The initial period of business when the entrepreneur must position the venture in a market and make necessary adjustments in order to ensure survival.
3. Early growth stage: A period of rapid development and growth when the venture may undergo major changes in markets, finances, and resource utilisation.
4. Later growth stage: The evolution of a venture into a large company with active competitors in an established industry when professional management may be more important than entrepreneurial verve.

Reasons why a small business fails could be external as well as internal. The literature is consistent in pointing out the qualities of the founder/entrepreneur/owner as a common fault factor (Hofer & Sandberg, 1987, p. 20; Holt, 1992, pp. 73–79; Scarborough & Zimmerer, 1996, pp. 37–41). Four behavioural factors associated with the business leader which are key to a new venture's success according to Hofer & Sandberg (1987, p. 22) are:

1. Identifying potential venture opportunities.
2. Sense of urgency (action orientation).
3. Detailed knowledge of the key factors.
4. Seek outside help.

Suggestions to avoid the pitfalls of small businesses are (Scarborough & Zimmerer, 1996, pp. 42–44):

- know your business in depth;
- prepare a business plan;
- manage financial resources;
- understand financial statements;
- learn to manage people effectively;
- keep in tune with yourself.

It is also a common suggestion in the literature to use strategic planning to survive in an SME (see, for instance, Scarborough & Zimmerer, 1996, p. 95). A strategic plan is supposed to give a competitive edge. It is natural for a strategic plan to be market focused and for the procedures involved in strategic planning in SMEs not to be too extensive; at a minimum, they should be based on the following tactics in a small business (ibid, p. 96):

- Use a relatively short planning horison — 2 years or less for most small companies.
- Be informal and not overly structured; a shirt-sleeved approach is ideal.
- Encourage the participation of employees and outside parties to improve the reliability and creativity of the resulting plan.
- Do not begin with setting objectives, as extensive objective-setting early on may interfere with the creative process of strategic management.
- Focus on strategic thinking, not just planning by linking long range goals to day-to-day operations.

Use of planning is highly recommended throughout the literature on SMEs.

Whichever power base is used, owner/managers are closely involved personally in the management process in an SME (Carson *et al.*, 1995, p. 71). Change, innovation and growth will depend very much on the aspiration, ability and managerial approach of the proprietor (Mintzberg, 1982, p. 466). In general the small business owner plays many roles (Holt, 1992, p. 71).

Nevertheless, the expertise, opinions and knowledge of employees is a crucial resource for the small firm and the owner is foolish to ignore them (Carson *et al.*, 1995, p. 70), especially if they want to grow (Scarborough & Zimmerer, 1996, p. 793). The problem is that most owners of small firms are reluctant to delegate (Goffer & Scase, 1985, p. 55). Delegation involves trust, and many business owners feel that undue trust in another can be dangerous. A tension may therefore exist between the desire of the owner to exert a strong influence on events and the need to empower personnel (Carson *et al.*, 1995, p. 70).

Employees in small firms are normally in a weaker position

than their counterparts in large firms, perhaps because they are employed only part-time or short-term. SMEs often also have difficulties in recruiting enough skilled workers (Storey, 1985, p. 243). Lack of specialised expertise and leverage can place the small firm at a disadvantage (Carson *et al.*, 1995, p. 64).

The power exercised by owners can impair organisational effectiveness. This happens when they do not share information, engage in one-way communication and resent any negative feedback from managers or employees (Osborne, 1991, p. 30). The owner/manager of an SME cannot manage through the organisation like managers in large companies can and he or she has to be more personalised (Hales, 1993). The ideal working arrangement in a small firm is that of an informal, flexible and problem-solving team. The organisational consequences of these realities are clear. Such small firms have non-sophisticated, flexible and organic organisational structures, which exhibit few bureaucratic characteristics (Carson *et al.*, 1995, p. 67).

Finance is a challenge for SMEs. They are normally shackled by a general lack of financial reserves (ibid, p. 81). SMEs can therefore not ignore financial planning. In particular, the name of the game is cash management (Maturi, 1989, p. 100). Out of cash, out of business!

Somehow the money is often there, but creativity counts on the SME owner and manager side (Berton, 1994, p. B2). Many sources of funding will probably have to be used (Gupta, 1990, p. B2).

SMEs may have different orientations in their business (Geursen, 1996, p. 10), i.e.:

- A customer orientation.
- A competitor orientation.
- An interfunctional coordination orientation.

They should never forget, however, that the primary function of a business is to create and keep a customer. The rest, given reasonable good sense, will take care of itself (Shaw, 1987, p. 28).

Carson *et al.* (1995, pp. 87–88) summarise the marketing advantages of SMEs in terms of:

- Loyalty (among workers)
- SME/customer interface (closeness to the customer)

- Flexibility (in response to customer inquiries)
- Speed of response (quicker)
- Opportunity-focused (propensity to seek and exploit opportunities)
- Easy access to market information (in a constant, informal and face-to-face manner)

Such marketing advantages allow the SME to be insulated against direct competition from large organisations by focusing on (ibid, p. 88):

- Exploiting market niches.
- Reducing the cost gap between themselves and larger competition (possibly even operating at lower cost).
- Persuading customers that only they produce the right quality, provide the right service and operate at the right cost/price level.

But all this requires to staying very close to the environment (in spite of no ability to influence it) and reacting quickly to it. Many SMEs are probably weak in this respect. The understanding of marketing concepts and theory by small businesses is generally limited:

- Scanning of the environment is often rudimentary (Wheelen & Hunger, 1995, p. 368).
- Marketing is often limited to selling or a simple orientation level (Kenny & Dyson, 1989; Romano & Ratnatunga, 1995).
- When it is done, marketing planning, decision-making and implementation is best characterised as informal, intuitive, loose and unstructured (Carson *et al.*, 1995, pp. 89–90).

The content of SME marketing is probably dependent on the development stage of the firm. The more developed the firm is, the more sophisticated is its marketing function.

An Analysis of the Existing View

An analysis of the above view on entrepreneurship which, as mentioned before, is developed through research made in the Western industrial world (mainly the US), will give us the following results:

1. These "definitions", concepts and theories are very action specific, often normative, i.e., they specify what issues to explore, what questions to answer, and what route and phases to follow in order to succeed as an entrepreneur. I have suggested elsewhere (Bjerke, 1997a, pp. 6–7; Bjerke & Hultman, 1998, p. 9) that, in order to avoid such specificity and normativity (and cultural bias; next point in our analysis) and in order to gain a more generalised understanding of what entrepreneurship is and what it can be, an alternative definition of entrepreneurship could be:

Entrepreneurship = The co-creation and co-maintenance of a new business venture by various economic actors.

2. Above all (not unrelated to the first point), the whole picture is very culturally biased (sometimes implicitly, often unconsciously, so). Several aspects of the American culture can clearly be seen in there (Compare Bjerke, 1998, Ch. 4):
   - The need for progress: Americans foster a cult of progress (Samovar *et al.*, 1981, pp. 71–72). Their belief in progress involves change and the idea that change can be controlled, mainly by technological means. This American orientation is based on an economy of abundance, stemming from the immense physical and natural resources of an entire continent (McMillan, 1985, p. 20). In business, American managers not only value change relatively highly but also value caution lower (Davis & Rasool, 1988, p. 17). Growth is seen as a vital need in the US in its own right (Peters, 1989, p. 13; Humes, 1993, p. 112).
   - The importance of innovation: One aspect closely associated with American progress and growth is that they live in a society where youthfulness is appreciated (Ferraro, 1994, p. 109). Americans tend to emphasise what is new and innovative by keeping up with new trends (creating many of them themselves!), conforming to standards that are contemporarily current and up-to-date, rather than old fashioned (Samovar *et al.*, 1981, p. 79). On the business scene, American managers endorse "modern" management ideas (Hofstede, 1984, p. 174).

- Individualism: If we should choose the hallmark of American culture, this should probably be the value of the individual (Hofstede, 1984, p. 158; Humes, 1993, p. 113; Ferraro, 1994, p. 109), i.e., reliance on individual initiative, self-assertion, personal achievement and responsibility. The ideal of the individual is deeply rooted in the American social, political, and economic institutions. The "success story" and the respect accorded to the self-made person is distinctly American (Samovar *et al.*, 1981, p. 77).
- Action orientation: The American way is an almost perfect example of a culture that stresses activity and work. A foreign visitor in the US quickly gains an impression of life lived at a fast pace and of people constantly active (Samovar *et al.*, 1981, p. 69). Throughout its history as a nation, the US has been known for its high levels of human energy, its aversion to idleness, and its preference for the person of action over the person of ideas (Ferraro, 1994, p. 95). The failure of an individual means that he or she did not try hard enough, is lazy, or even worthless. Promotion and pay should be based on performance, not seniority (Schwind & Peterson, 1985, p. 71), and people should be removed, or even fired, if they cannot perform (Hodgetts & Luthans, 1991, p. 41).
- The prominence of efficiency, logic and "science": Efficiency is a primary value in the West in general (Sitaram & Cogdell, 1976, p. 191). "Efficient" is a word of high praise in the US, having long emphasised adaptability, technological innovation, economic expansion, mass production, standardisation, up-to-dateness, practicality, expediency, and "getting things done" (Samovar *et al.*, 1981, p. 70). We may even say that American problem-solving is scientific instead of traditional. Logic and scientific methods have been internalised as the means of solving new problems, and solutions are perceived as progress or improvements. American corporations have developed a disposition for sophisticated structures and systems (Humes, 1993, p. 114). Marketing is a very

American skill. The American culture has also been characterised as "cybernetic" (Trompenaars, 1995, p. 156), appreciating the use of planning and quantitative techniques, looking for feedback and considering mistakes as moments of learning rather than failures.

- Informality and equality: Informality seems to be a theme that runs through the US value system, assuming, among other things, that informality is a prerequisite for sincerity (Ferraro, 1994, p. 101). It has been suggested that frankness is a primary value in the American type of culture (Sitaram & Cogdell, 1976, p. 191) and that, therefore, company information should be available to anyone who needs it within the organisation (Hodgetts & Luthans, 1991, p. 41). There are also no generally recognised social classes in the US, income and achievement act as the main differentiators, and the American culture emphasises equality in social relationships. The value of basic human equality and democracy is so ingrained among Americans that many of them become shocked and even frightened when they perceive that a nation undermines such a value in substance and pretends otherwise in form. Increasingly popular in the American business society (which corresponds well to the calls for informality, to the democratic norms prevalent there, and to its increasingly better educated workforce) is to use task forces, integrating managers, and project structure.

Much of the above picture does not fit the Asian (Singaporean) business society and culture well. We need another picture to understand the Asian business society and to do well in assisting the Singaporean entrepreneurs and SMEs. There is an important difference between explaining and understanding entrepreneurs, i.e., to place an entrepreneur in the context of the economic development of a society and explaining such a person by opportunities, technology and markets, as compared to really understanding such a person by getting to the roots of his or her norms, values and assumptions, i.e., to the essence of culture (for a discussion about differences between culture as norms, values and assumptions as compared to cultural manifestations such as behaviour, organisations and other institutions in a society, see Bjerke & Al-Meer, 1994). Before we turn to developing a picture of the Singaporean entrepreneur, etc., there are a few aspects of culture which are important to the reader to keep in mind:

- Most nations are very complex and subculturally heterogeneous. Even if reasonably homogeneous, there are many potential cultural dimensions to consider. Therefore, when we study nations from a cultural point of view, we can only meaningfully do so with a limited group and a limited aspect of life in mind! The discussion in this chapter is limited to business.
- When we compare national cultures, we do not compare single individuals! In all nations, there are huge variations around any norm. Many individuals do not even fit this picture at all. But in every nation, as well as in every social group, experiences "are joined together" intersubjectively, somehow, and there are feelings of belonging and non-belonging among the inhabitants in a nation. A culture should be seen only as tendencies which are ingrained in people due to their birth, upbringing and socialisation. These tendencies may or may not externalise themselves in individual cases and situations.

One conclusion from this is that much of the picture of American entrepreneurship and SMEs above (as well as of Chinese business culture, and Singaporean entrepreneurship and SMEs later) is *not* a statistically *average* picture, *not* even a *typical* one (most common among, say, Americans as individual entrepreneurs), but a *typified* picture, i.e., a natural and consistent outcome in terms of actions and behaviour, *if* a person would, in most or all aspects, follow his or her cultural norms, values, and assumptions (which they never do in full in practice), in the American case, *if* the entrepreneur and/or manager of an SME could be "completely" progressive, innovative, individualistic, action oriented, efficient, logical, "scientific", informal, and egalitarian. (For a more detailed discussion of differences between "average", "typical" and "typified", see Arbnor & Bjerke, 1997, p. 61.)

4. The Chinese Business Culture

The purpose of this section is to present aspects of the Chinese business culture as a contrast to the Western (American) business culture discussed earlier, and to explore how the former might manifest itself in entrepreneurship and in the management of SMEs. I will use the Chinese business culture as an approximation of the Singaporean business culture in the next section. The body politic of Singapore owes much of its basic ideology to Chinese traditions, with the population being over 70% ethnic Chinese, and Confucianism is taught at schools here. Even if Singapore is not a totally Chinese city-state, it is overwhelmingly so (Redding, 1993, p. 24).

My intention is not, of course, to discriminate against or to belittle Singaporean Indians and Malays. Also, remember that my discussion is limited to business aspects of culture and that Indian and Malay business cultures are, most likely, closer to that of the Chinese than to the American.

I would like to discuss Chinese business culture in the following sections (compare Bjerke, 1997b and Bjerke, 1998, Ch. 6):

- Power and autocracy;
- Familism;
- *Guanxi*;
- Face and prestige;
- Flexibility and endurance.

Power and Autocracy

It is an interesting fact that the Chinese business organisation has so strongly retained its original basic character in spite of very open economies where the overseas Chinese are in place, and in spite of potential influences by outside connections, in the case of Singapore, by deliberately courting Western technology since its independence (Redding, 1993, p. 116). Some say that the typified Chinese organisation structure is informal (for instance, Jansson, 1987, p. 28; Lasserre & Schütte, 1995, p. 105). "Informal" is probably not the right word here, at least not in the sense of "unconventional" and "unconstrained". But nor is the organisation formal in the sense of "planned" and "impersonal". The proper word for a Chinese business organisation is rather personalised or personified. There are conventions as well as constraints, which are not planned or impersonal, and these are given by the person at the centre of the organisation (the owner or his representative).

Another related conceptual phenomenon is that Chinese organisations are not personnel bureaucracies (where people, but not their procedures, are controlled). Nor are they workflow bureaucracies (i.e., procedures, but not people, are controlled), as is claimed by Redding (1993, p. 176)! Personnel as well as workflow are controlled in a typified Chinese organisation, but not as rigidly, consistently and impersonally as in Weber's original model. In line with the above, personalised bureaucracy would be a better term to characterise a Chinese organisation and management style.

Chinese management is even in modern times a top run, one man show by an autocratic boss assuming responsibility for all management functions (Chee, 1992, p. 44). The Chinese manager is very "boss-centred" (Sheh, 1995, pp. 27–28), but also self-reliant (Naisbitt, 1995, p. 73). We could also say that the Chinese culture is a very power-centred culture. The Chinese-dominated countries in the Asia-Pacific score high in power distance (Hofstede, 1984, p. 77). Power distance connotes the differences in values and role models between higher status and lower status individuals in a given culture. If these differences are substantial — if they call for materially different behaviour — the power distance is long. The more stratified a society, the greater are the feelings of inequality and the lesser are social interactions between people in different strata.

Hofstede (1984, pp. 94, 107) characterises a high power distance culture (like the Chinese), among other things, as follows:

- Power is a basic fact of society which antedates good or evil. Its legitimacy is irrelevant.
- Hierarchy means existential inequality.
- There should be an order of inequality in this world in which everyone has his or her rightful place; high and low are protected by this order.
- A few should be independent; most should be dependent.

- Other people are a potential threat to one's power and can rarely be trusted.
- Low qualifications of lower strata.
- Large wage differentials.
- White collar jobs valued more than blue collar jobs.

The very idea of class is an ingrained part of Chinese life (Chu, 1991, pp. 185–186). Dependence on "class" and importance of power is shown in many different ways among Chinese. One is a general lack of communication across positions, particularly in a vertical downward direction (ibid, p. 194). Withholding information to gain or maintain power is acceptable among Chinese (Hodgetts & Luthans, 1991, p. 41). Openness is, in fact, often considered to be a sign of weakness in the Chinese culture (Samovar *et al.*, 1981, p. 41).

In a Chinese type of culture, achievement is defined in terms of recognition and wealth (Hofstede, 1984, p. 200).

Autonomy, to become a boss, is the dominant driving force in Chinese entrepreneurship. But this driving force seems to be more vigorous and widespread in, say, Hong Kong than in Singapore (Wong, 1995, pp. 145–146). The former is fostering what may be called entrepreneurial capitalism, while the latter is championing managerial capitalism (Pang, 1988, p. 230).

Familism

Asian tradition puts the rights of the group ahead of those of any individual (Seagrave, 1996, p. 237). In Asian cultures, individuals have a very deep attachment and sense of belonging to social groups (Hoon-Halbauer, 1994, p. 85; Lasserre & Schütte, 1995, p. 270). Asian countries score very low on individualism (Hofstede, 1984, p. 158). Singapore is a clearly collectivistic society as well (Redding, 1993, p. 62).

At the same time, if we try to put together a coherent picture of Chinese culture in terms of harmony, conflicts and cooperation, it may seem somewhat heterogeneous. On one hand, we can read that a top Asian societal value is harmony (Naisbitt, 1995, p. 73). A Chinese is to be in harmony with nature (Harris & Moran, 1979, p. 313) and "the Chinese have never been warlike" (Chu, 1991, p. 188).

There is a doctrine in Chinese culture stressing tradition, continuity and links with the past. Avoiding conflicts is one Chinese way to keep the social harmony (Jansson, 1987, p. 27; Lasserre & Schütte, 1995, pp. 272–273). The Confucian tradition has emphasised cooperation. According to some reports, the Chinese is a fair person (Harris & Moran, 1979, p. 311) and a top Asian personal value is honesty (Naisbitt, 1995, p. 73).

We can also read that Chinese are suspicious and do not trust others (Jansson, 1987, p. 14). Chinese are inclined to avoid involvement (Chu, 1991, pp. 191–192), especially with "government and its nuisances" (Rohwer, 1995, p. 231).

An answer to these contradictions is possible if we keep two things in mind:

- Harmony and tradition are aspects of Confucian teachings. Confucian ideas are supported in the Asia-Pacific, having been stressed by government and the élite to foster the ideal of conformity (Redding, 1993, p. 84). It is officially sponsored and reinforced in Singapore (Tu, 1984). However, it is not to be taken for granted that these values are honoured in all social classes or at the grassroots level.
- The societal unit in Chinese culture is the family. Individuals are born into extended families or clans which protect them in exchange for loyalty (Hofstede, 1984, p. 17). An individual in Asia is not an individual in the Western sense of an isolated person, but includes his or her relations as well (Jansson, 1987, p. 8). Chinese values are based more on personal obligations than individual rights. Confidence is important to the Chinese, but it stays within the family.

The importance of the family and strong family ties among Asians in general and maybe particularly so for the Chinese is certified by many commentators (Harris & Moran, 1979, p. 311; Chau, 1991, p. 161; Chu, 1991, pp. 200–201; Hoon-Halbauer, 1994, p. 89; Lasserre & Schütte, 1995, pp. 271–272).

One reason why the Chinese family system is so important is that it provides security in an insecure world (Jansson, 1987, p. 27). For the Chinese who left their homeland (often forced out) and tried to settle abroad, environments were not always easy. Except for

Singapore, the society was often outright hostile (excluding Hong Kong and Taiwan, of course, where the people are not strictly overseas Chinese). As a consequence, family self-interest is rampant in many of these societies and, perhaps not surprisingly, it is only in Singapore that strong declarations have emerged about the social responsibility of the businessman (Redding, 1993, p. 188).

Families are not only the bedrock of the Chinese society, they are also the bedrock of Chinese business ("Fissiparous Fortunes and Family Feuds", 1996, p. 69). A Chinese firm is almost always a family firm (Jansson, 1987, p. 27). This is especially so in the overseas Chinese business system (Chen, 1995, p. 84; Rohwer, 1995, p. 232). Peter Drucker has expressed it such that "the secret of Japan consists in Japan's ability to make a family out of a modern corporation. The secret of Chinese management may well consist in the ability of the Chinese to make the family into a modern corporation" (Drucker & Nakauchi, 1997, p. 7). Comparing Japanese and Chinese managements, we can also say that Japanese style management may be described as "head office oriented", while Chinese style management may be characterised as "family oriented" (Tanaka *et al.*, 1992, p. 18). But, a "family" may here include the same ethnic background and even birthplace. Kinship terms (like "uncle" and "aunt") are widely used in social interaction, even if not genealogically related (Wong, 1995, p. 141). Overseas Chinese have built up their strength, among other factors, on an unusual ethnic solidarity (Seagrave, 1996, p. 17).

The implicit model of the Chinese organisation and management is also the family. This statement is supported by several researchers (Hofstede, 1984, pp. 215–217; Jansson, 1987, p. 8; Lasserre & Schütte, 1995, pp. 129–131). The senior manager/owner has a patriarchal relation to his subordinates and decisions are made in the best interest of "the family" (Jansson, 1987, p. 27). Characteristics of Chinese firms are (Hofstede, 1984, pp. 166–167, 171, 173–174; Trompenaars, 1995, pp. 85–86; Lasserre & Schütte, 1995, pp. 135–136):

- Managers rate having security in their position more important;
- Managers aspire for conformity and orderliness;
- Managers endorse "traditional" points of view, not supporting employee initiative and group activity;

- Promotion from inside and on seniority;
- Expertise, order, duty, security provided by organisation or clan, in China even housing (not in Singapore, except for guest workers);
- Business logic is reliant on personal commitment in organic business entities;
- More importance attached to training and use of skills in jobs, not to individual self-fulfilment.

Family businesses dominate in the economies of many countries, of course (Braadbaart, 1995, pp. 179–180). Boswell found that the boards of nearly two out of three medium sized British manufacturing enterprises (25–500 employees) were family dominated (Boswell, 1973, p. 248). According to one estimate, 80 to 90% of all Dutch businesses are family owned (*Social Economische Raad*, 1990). Pollack reports that "family farm products accounted for 67.6% of the value of farm products sold in the U.S. in 1974" (Pollack, 1985, p. 591). Comparable findings have been reported for rural agricultural and industrial enterprises in India (Upadhya, 1988, pp. 1,376–382, 433–442). However, the "family" in a Chinese "family firm" is something deeper than in most other cases. There is, for instance, a much stricter borderline between family and non-family members both in attitude and behaviour. Also, growth in Chinese business is commonly done not by expanding the same firm too far (then possibly losing the family control), but by mushrooming another family unit, run by a relative.

Guanxi

The Asian business environment can be best described as a series of interlocked networks (Lasserre & Schütte, 1995, p. 124). It is a key element of Chinese business (Hoon-Halbauer, 1994, p. 85). The distinctive feature of the Overseas Chinese model has never been the individual firm, but a network of them (Rohwer, 1995, pp. 240–241). In Chinese, this is called *guanxi*, which can be translated as "relationships" or "connections".

Everywhere in the business world you need contacts. But you must magnify its importance many times to understand *guanxi* (Chu,

1991, p. 199). Hundreds of books have been written about *guanxi*, but it takes a lifetime to master. Every society in Asia is built around relationships and it is more than a matter of degree compared with the West. In the West, there is business first, then starts the networking; in Asia, there is networking first, then starts the business ("And never the twain shall meet", 1997, p. 73).

Guanxi is based on mutual obligations. In an extended family, members are mutually obligated to help one another, for instance, a wealthy member helps a poor one. Also, in business organisations, it is rather common for members of a family to use their family connections to try to obtain jobs or other benefits (Hoon-Halbauer, 1994, p. 88).

But *guanxi*, which tends to be more utilitarian than emotional, goes beyond the extended family. It is also relevant to other ties, such as clan, shared surname, home village, region, education or other shared experiences. Good *guanxi* both inside and outside the firm is a guarantee of success at the personal as well as at the professional level (ibid, pp. 88–89).

The overseas Chinese found that dialect, kinship or common origin in a clan or a village gave a more sure footing of trust to a business deal conducted even at a great distance (Rohwer, 1995, p. 233). In fact, the Overseas Chinese power rests on an underground network. Regional identity is important to a Chinese everywhere in the world, including Singapore (Hsieh, 1978). Same-native-place ties can play a crucial role (Seagrave, 1996, pp. 173–174).

For Chinese, networking is a natural thing to do (ibid, p. 341). It is a natural tendency for a Chinese manager to focus on the person who can best resolve the particular problem or clinch the deal (Lasserre & Schütte, 1995, p. 124). Business with Chinese over and above simple buying and selling is to a large extent based on trust. Chinese business boils down to contacts. Trust does not, however, exist naturally between people for the Chinese and it may take a long time to establish, if commonality does not exist in, say, dialect or birthplace. Trust is intimately associated with obligation and duty for the Chinese. "A common business interest" is itself not enough for him to trust somebody else.

The importance of influential contacts is characteristic of all Asian societies (Chu, 1991, p. 200), but more so in some societies than in others. *Guanxi* is more important in China, the Philippines and Indonesia than in Hong Kong and Singapore (Lasserre & Schütte, 1995, p. 127). The Chinese society is neither individual based nor society based, but rather relation based (Liang, 1974, p. 95).

Face and Prestige

An important aspect of Chinese culture is "face" (Hoon-Halbauer, 1994, p. 85). This concept has two meanings (Hofstede, 1984, p. 151; Jansson, 1987, pp. 9–10; Hoon-Halbauer, 1994, p. 87). One (*li-an*) concerns a person's moral character and honour, the other (*mian-zi*) connotes reputation and prestige. Both are important in social interactions, considering the importance of recognition by others in Chinese culture. They are often mixed when the Chinese interact with each other to protect, save, add, give, exchange or even borrow "face". *Mian-zi*, however, "enters more into everyday transactions as a form of social currency" (Redding & Ng, 1982, p. 207).

The fear of losing face is nothing more than the fear of having one's ego and prestige deflated. It can be caused by a broad range of things: having an expected promotion fall through, one's child failing an examination, one's daughter marrying a poor man, one's brother working in a lowly position, receiving an inexpensive gift. The list goes on and on (Chu, 1991, p. 197). In general, a person will lose his/her face if he/she is found to be unable, or unwilling, to satisfy the claims imposed upon him/her by his/her friends or subordinates (Sherriff, 1989, p. 27).

The logical counterpart to "losing" face is to "gain" face. The prestige of a Chinese may be inflated by working in a large company, surrounding him- or herself with influential "friends", showing off materially, etc.

Asian cultures stress "shame" and Western cultures stress "guilt". Shame is associated with public disgrace and loss of prestige, guilt carries a sense of individual responsibility and conscience (Lasserre & Schütte, 1995, p. 273). The importance of shame for a Chinese makes it hard for him to admit a mistake (Jansson, 1987, p. 17; Yang, 1991, p. 14) or to ask for help (Lasserre

& Schütte, 1995, p. 273). Also, he or she is not happy to be told how to do things, especially in public (Jansson, 1987, p. 17).

The importance of face in the Chinese society is well captured in Singapore by the Hokkien term *kiasu*, which can be translated as "afraid to lose out". This is used to describe the Singaporean fear of being left behind or out, which to Westerners sometimes can give the impression that a Singaporean does not want to miss any opportunity which someone else is offered or taking (even if none of them gains anything). Singaporeans attach tremendous stigma to failure; the idea of learning from mistakes is practically unknown ("Enterprise Singapore style", 1993, p. 46).

Face is important in business as well, of course (Jansson, 1987, pp. 19–20):

- Gaining "face" leads to strong feelings of satisfaction, pride and confidence. Losing "face" brings negative feelings, which are equally strong.
- "Face" is justified primarily for pragmatic reasons, and it is instrumental to reach several goals and has many effects. It is difficult to understand this complex of "facial effects"; it requires conscious measures as well as instinct.
- "Face" is mutual. What is given should be returned; it becomes a delicate social balancing act.
- "Face" is of relevance mainly in social relations between colleagues, but also in business relations in, say, purchasing, banking and personal sales. In relations with public institutions, it is of less importance, probably because these contacts are more official and bureaucratic.
- If "face" is important in hierarchic vertical relations within companies, it is more important in horisontal social relations.
- Status is important when gaining "face".

Flexibility and Endurance

Chinese enterprises may often appear impressive in terms of market capitalisation and growth. But looking under the hood, management may look like a mess in Western eyes (Hoon-Halbauer, 1994, p. 298; "Fissiparous Fortunes and Family Feuds", 1996, p. 345). There is often no formalised personnel management to speak of (Hoon-

Halbauer, 1994, p. 298) and constant supervision of staff is common. And employees expect it. Chinese SME leaders also often have a narrow perception of the marketing function (James, 1988, p.15) and do not believe in advertising and promotion. There are few standard trademarks in Chinese business, less standardised displays, almost no sales policy, little market research and less organising of distribution (Redding, 1993, p. 171). The promotional method of choice is personal selling and free samples (James, 1988, p. 10). One reason for this limited management orientation could be that Chinese business managers often have a trading background and remain traders at heart.

One thing Chinese are good at, however, is financial management. Chinese entrepreneurs "have an excellent mastery of financial levers" (Lasserre & Schütte, 1995, p. 106). In their daily business dealings, they pay close attention to cash. Chinese do not apply formal long term planning very often (Sheh, 1995, p. 31) and they are even resistant to formal planning in general (Redding, 1993, p. 173). The common belief that Chinese are good strategic thinkers, and that modern Chinese business strategies can be seen as updated versions of old Chinese texts on military strategy (see, for instance, Chu, 1991, p. 12), is probably a myth! Another story is that Chinese businessmen can be long term in the sense of having the "ability to persevere on the basis of a steady accumulation of small return" (Pan, 1991, p. 241), being extremely hard working and disciplined, and that they see the business as something their children (particularly sons) will ultimately inherit (Sheh, 1995, pp. 31–32).

Chinese replace strategic thinking in business with flexibility. Whether this could be called strategy is a matter of taste. I prefer to say that Chinese business people are very good tacticians. Chinese business leaders are highly adaptive and pragmatic (Jansson, 1987, p. 28; Seagrave, 1996, p. 17), especially when it can lead to a business advantage. Modern Asia has a passion for change and for the future (Rohwer, 1995, p. 78). Willingness to learn and to change should not, however, generally be taken as creativity and innovation here (Chu, 1991, p. 190). Chinese business leaders are cautious about accepting risk (Redding, 1993, p. 171). To cushion themselves against failure, many of them seek support in religion or, more often, in superstition (Wong, 1995, p. 144).

5. The Singaporean Entrepreneur and SME?

Let us summarise some possible differences between Western entrepreneurship and entrepreneurship in Singapore in order to get a proper perspective for understanding the rest of this chapter:

Entrepreneurial Characteristics

In the West	In Singapore
• Moderate, calculative risktaker	• No difference
• Creative and innovative	• Less of an innovator, more of an adaptor of business concepts already existing elsewhere
• Self-confident and optimistic	• Even more so, once willing to take the plunge
• Seeking feedback and learning from mistakes	• Very flexible and willing to learn from what others have done, but look at own mistakes as loss of face
• Committed, persevering and hardworking	• Even more so
• Obsessed by opportunities	• (no difference)
• Motivated by personal achievement	• Motivated by social status and prestige of family

Reasons to Start a New Business Venture

In the West	In Singapore
• To become autonomous and independent	• The same but more in financial terms
• Dissatisfied with present situation at work	• More tolerant of present work position, even if bad
• Following role models and given support	• An even stronger motivator, especially within the own family

Necessary SME Management Skills

In the West	In Singapore
• Be a good planner	• Planning is more informal
• Manage finances	• (where the Singaporeans excel)
• Have a customer focus (where the Americans excel)	• A more limited view of marketing
• Be informal, involve employees in problem, get to know management skills	• Much more autocratic and using a more personalised approach
• Using contacts to get initial capital and to supplement lack of skills and resources	• Networking throughout (as a way of life)

Much of what is said above (especially on the Singaporean side) is speculation. Much more is needed as far as knowledge of Singaporean entrepreneurship and SMEs is concerned, especially at the level of understanding instead of the level of explanation.

ADVICE 1: DO MORE RESEARCH ON THE SPECIFICS OF SINGAPOREAN ENTREPRENEURSHIP AND SME – ESPECIALLY AT THE LEVEL OF UNDERSTANDING

We should be very careful when trying to transplant what knowledge we have about entrepreneurship and SMEs in the West into the Singaporean society.

ADVICE 2: BE CAREFUL WHEN ADOPTING THE WESTERN STYLE OF ENTREPRENEURSHIP AND SME KNOWLEDGE AND USING AMERICAN TEXTBOOKS ON ENTREPRENEURSHIP AND SME MANAGEMENT. PRODUCE MORE SPECIFICALLY SINGAPOREAN TEXTBOOKS IN ENTREPRENEURSHIP AND SME MANAGEMENT.

6. The Entrepreneurial Engine

The entrepreneurial engine works by (Hall, 1995, pp. 2–13):

- entrepreneurs pursuing opportunities. They do this by setting up new start-ups; and
- they force unsuccessful or unpromising ventures to close down ("creative destruction").

To work effectively, however, the size and change of the entrepreneurial engine should reach a critical mass. And this differs depending on the stage of development of the economy.

1. For every million people in developed economies there will be about 50,000 non-agricultural SMEs (ibid, pp. 2–7).

The approximate number of firms per million people in some economies are: (sources: Country statistics)

Economy	**Population (in millions)**	**SMEs ('000s)**	**SMEs per million people**
USA	260	15,000	57.7
Japan	125	7,000	56
Australia	17	900	52.9
Singapore	3	95	31.7
Hong Kong	6	90	48.3
Taiwan	21	900	42.9
Indonesia	200	13,000	65

Care should be taken in interpreting these figures. The statistical definition of an SME varies widely as to the purpose of the statistic and to the size and the degree of formality of the SME. For example, the US figure above includes all firms registered for tax purposes, while the Indonesian one is an estimate including many informal and unregistered SMEs. One conclusion is clear, however: Singapore has very few SMEs!

2. For every 50,000 firms in an economy each year, about 5,000 new SMEs will start up (ibid, pp. 2–7).

Start-up rates in some economies are (in very rough figures; some sources as previously):

Economy	Start-up rate (%)	Economy	Start-up rate (%)
USA	15	Belgium	13
Japan	7	Germany	17
Australia	12		

According to the Registry of Companies and Businesses in Singapore, between 7,000 and 9,500 new companies have been started each year during the 1990s. This is approximately 7–10%, which is on the low side.

3. Among start-up firms in an economy,
20% to 30% will survive more than 8 years,
50% will survive about 5 years,
70% will survive 3 years, and
85% will survive the first year (ibid, pp. 2–7).

Survival rates in some economies after five years (in rough figures from the same sources):

Economy	Survival rate (%)	Economy	Survival rate (%)
USA	38	France	48
Australia	17	Germany	63

In a study by the Department of Statistics in Singapore, out of total SMEs in 1984 of 65,852 firms, 46% were still operating after 10 years ("Profile of Growing Small and Medium Enterprises in Singapore", 1997, pp. 2–5). This is, in fact, quite a high number, compared to the "norm". Also, the turnover of number of companies in an economy should be seen more as a sign of vitality and change than a sign of economic decay (Bjerke, 1989, p. 25). Could it be that Singaporeans are selecting their start-ups more carefully and, therefore, giving them a higher chance of survival?

4. Among SMEs in an economy,
5% are high growth firms,
20% are growth oriented survivors, and
75% are low growth SMEs (Hall, 1995, pp. 2–6).

In the 1984 cohort of Singapore SMEs mentioned above, 29% were found to be growth oriented ten years later (Department of Statistics, "Profile of Growing Small and Medium Enterprises in Singapore", 1997, pp. 2–5).

Singapore needs to get more new businesses up and going. To start more business ventures is not to change the direction of the economy, but to make it stronger and more vital by opening more economic fronts and options. There are several reasons given in the literature for the small stock of SMEs in Singapore and the slow growth of this stock:

- SMEs are "crowded out" by the huge multinational corporations and state-sponsored enterprises (Wong, 1995, p. 138);
- Too much order, too little chaos for the entrepreneurial flair to prosper (Rohwer, 1995, pp. 81–82);
- Few Singaporeans have much appetite for risk — they are much more likely to seek a job with a foreign multinational or quasi-state firm ("Enterprise Singapore Style", 1993, p. 46; Wong, 1995, p. 146).

7. Getting More Business Ventures Started in Singapore

Singapore must activate its entrepreneurial pool and at the same time acknowledge that entrepreneurs always face some genuine uncertainty and therefore always make some mistakes on their way to success. There are several aspects to this:

1. Mistakes as part of the learning process suggests that if the basic talents are there the beneficial lessons of mistakes should be emphasised rather than the loss of credibility or venture investment.

ADVICE 3: *CONTACT THOSE WHO HAVE FAILED IN THEIR ENTREPRENEURIAL EFFORTS AND GIVE, AT LEAST SOME OF THEM, A SECOND CHANCE, SOMEHOW. THIS WILL SERVE THE DUAL PURPOSE OF BRINGING SOME PEOPLE FORWARD WHO HAVE, ON THE AVERAGE, MORE ENTREPRENEURIAL TALENT THAN THE AVERAGE CITIZEN AS WELL AS GIVING STATUS TO MISTAKES.*

2. A huge entrepreneurial group on its way in all industrialised nations consists of women. So also in Singapore, where women entrepreneurs were put at 22% of the total in mid-1996 ("They're minding their own business", 1997, p. 19).

ADVICE 4: *GIVE MORE RECOGNITION TO WOMEN ENTREPRENEURS, EVEN THOUGH THEY MAY LACK TRACK RECORDS.*

3. Role models have always played an important part in triggering new entrepreneurs. There are many of these in Singapore, e.g., Sim Wong Hoo (Creative Technology), Han Keen Juan (Old Chang Kee), Y Y Wong (Wywy Group) and Jannie Tay (Hour Glass).

ADVICE 5: *PUBLISH MORE STORIES OF ROLE MODELS.*

4. When presenting business "heroes", there is a tendency to stress what they have done well, neglecting mistakes they made. There is more for others to learn from the latter than from the former.

ADVICE 6: *TELL TRUE REAL-LIFE ENTREPRENEURIAL STORIES.*

Entrepreneurial talents are likely to show themselves in school, at college, or in the early stages of employment. With some honourable exceptions, the institutions involved act generally to suppress or inhibit them, since they are seen to be either disruptive or anti-cultural (Robinson, 1990, p. 107). Peter Drucker says: "Unless you start to innovate in your twenties or, at the latest, in your early thirties, you will never do it" (Drucker & Nakauchi, 1997, p. 79).

ADVICE 7: *TEACH ENTREPRENEURSHIP AT SCHOOLS AND ENCOURAGE THOSE WHO REALLY WANT TO TRY IT OUT.*

In an entrepreneurial society, individuals are facing a big challenge, a challenge which they need to take as a possibility: the need for continuous learning and relearning. One consequence of this is that individuals more and more have to take responsibility for their own learning and for their own careers. If entrepreneurship is given a high status in a society, trying it out becomes a definite option (Bjerke, 1989, p. 659).

ADVICE 8: *WHY NOT START A SINGAPORE INSTITUTE OF ENTREPRENEURSHIP (SIE) WITH THE STATUS OF A TERTIARY EDUCATIONAL, TRAINING AND RESEARCH CENTRE?*

I am convinced that, if we really put our minds to it, we can teach entrepreneurship, just as we teach other professions where the same kind of argument (that "you have to be born with it") exist, e.g., teaching, sales or management.

Subsidies are one of the least significant means to promote entrepreneurship. Still, the subsidies offered in various countries are numerous, come in various shapes and forms, and seek a variety of objectives (Bjerke, 1989, p. 676).

ADVICE 9: *DO NOT TRUST SUBSIDIES AS A MAJOR TOOL FOR PROMOTING ENTREPRENEURSHIP.*

One exception to this issue of subsidies, however, is using the tax system to assist entrepreneurs. There are several advantages with this (ibid, p. 677):

- companies are used to it; they know what it is,
- there are mechanisms to handle it;
- it leads to few problems of responsibility, insight, and judgement.

ADVICE 10: *USE THE TAX SYSTEM TO ASSIST ENTREPRENEURS, BUT NOT SELECTIVELY.*

As important as taxation policy is to encourage entrepreneurship, or at least not to punish it, it is also to protect the new venture from the growing burden of government regulation, restrictions, reports, and paper exercise. If government does not do anything else, at least it can remove obstacles.

ADVICE 11: *REVIEW BUSINESS REGULATIONS ON ENTREPRENEUR'S TERMS SO THAT POLICIES THAT ARE RESTRICTIVE AND UNFAVOURABLE FOR PRIVATE BUSINESS ARE MODIFIED AND, IF NEED BE, DISCARDED.*

The most significant way in which the state affects entrepreneurship is, of course, through its direct assumption of the entrepreneurial role, i.e., by starting public companies. Also, governments in most countries have the ability to influence collective research efforts. However, a distinction has to be made between research and entrepreneurship. Research has to do with generating new knowledge, while entrepreneurship is to apply new knowledge in new business ventures. The difference between the two lies primarily in the person who pursues the latter, i.e. the entrepreneur.

ADVICE 12: *IF NEW BUSINESS VENTURES ARE STARTED BASED ON PUBLIC RESEARCH, DON'T APPOINT THE ENTREPRENEUR. LET PEOPLE APPLY FOR THIS POSITION. APPOINTED ENTREPRENEURS OFTEN BECOME DISAPPOINTED ENTREPRENEURS.*

An innovative society is characterised by the following pattern (Bjerke, 1989, pp. 658–659):

- an action orientation without too much analysis;
- many role models to follow;
- doing business having a high profile and status;
- an informal network, even across competitive lines;
- strong engagement in social and political issues;
- access to technical knowledge, e.g., universities.

One important message from an area like Silicon Valley is the role of a critical mass of experiments, champions and skunkworks. With a critical mass, networks arise and a near-perpetual-motion machine is possible. Without a critical mass, the possibility of continuing innovation collapses in a society.

ADVICE 13: *ENCOURAGE ENTREPRENEURIAL NETWORKS OF ALL KINDS.*

Singapore has several programmes in play to promote entrepreneurship, e.g., giving pioneer status to some entrepreneurs, conducting public research and exempting firms below a certain sales volume from GST. However, there seems to be a tendency to steer them into publicly favoured industries, mainly high tech ones, and to try to handpick those having high growth potential. Entrepreneurs are facing genuine uncertainty. It is not generally possible to say at an early stage who will be the winner. "Golden eggs" cannot be identified in advance, because there are so many ingredients and so many recipes that make an agreeable "omelette". There is no general and foolproof method to evaluate and handle ideas, and to choose only the successful ones. Therefore, it is important that systems and methods — in society as well as in companies — are characterised by multiplicity and flexibility.

ADVICE 14: *MAKE SURE PUBLIC PROGRAMMES FOR PROMOTING ENTREPRENEURSHIP ARE MULTI-FACETED AND FLEXIBLE. ENTREPRENEURSHIP IS A PLAY WITH NUMBERS. IT IS THE QUANTITY THAT COUNTS.*

8. Assisting Singapore SMEs

There are four main areas where governments can assist SMEs (Hall, 1995, p. 2–1):

- Investing in HRD;
- Improving access to cash and finance;
- Improving the business environment;
- Increasing access to markets and information.

Apart from this general comment, I intend in this section only to raise a few specific points, often discussed in the context of small and medium-sized enterprises:

1. Venture Capital

Venture capital is a very American affair and nobody is doing it better than the Americans, even if many other countries have tried to copy it. One main factor associated with the success of venture capital in the US is probably not only that they do not stigmatise failure, sometimes they even admire it! Venture capitalists actually like to see a little failure in the résumés of the entrepreneurs (Peters, 1994, pp. 54–55).

> ***ADVICE 15:*** *ENCOURAGE AMERICANS TO COME TO SINGAPORE TO RUN VENTURE CAPITAL BUSINESSES.*

2. Procurement

The use of government demand through procurement policies has the effect of reducing risk and uncertainty for the innovative firm, and as such constitutes an effective tool for stimulating technological change in most industrialised countries (Bjerke, 1989, p. 674).

> ***ADVICE 16:*** *USE GOVERNMENT PROCUREMENT POLICIES FOR ALL KINDS OF ENTREPRENEURSHIP AND SME SUPPORT.*

3. Mobility

Innovation is associated with uncertainty and risk and it requires, almost by definition, reallocation of resources, especially personnel, knowledge, and capital. Innovation policy must therefore stimulate mobility. This may be accomplished by means of policies to encourage labour mobility from non-industrial to industrial activities, and immigration in cases where labour supply is limited, by assisting SMEs to acquire proper resources and by encouraging SMEs to provide programmes that train workers in necessary skills.

> ***ADVICE 17:*** *ENCOURAGE MOBILITY OF RESOURCES AND PRODUCTION FACTORS IN ALL WAYS.*

Singapore has many different programmes in place to assist SMEs. There is neither time nor reason in this chapter to bring them up. The interested reader can find out about these programmes elsewhere (for example, "The APEC Survey...", 1994, pp. 35, 221–227; "Best Practices for Small and Medium Enterprises in APEC", 1995, pp. 25–27, 43–44, 229–245; Hall, 1995, pp. 2–24; Singapore Chinese Chamber of Commerce & Industry, "Roadmap for SMEs", 1997).

However, it is important to separate SMEs into different groups in order to provide adequate and focused support to them. Two classifications that might be important are:

- growth oriented and non-growth SMEs (This is not the same as picking "golden eggs" from the entrepreneurial start!)
- SMEs based on adoption and modification of existing business concepts and SMEs based on radically new concepts

The point is, however, not to favour any of the groups. They are all important!

***ADVICE 18**: CLASSIFY SMEs IN DIFFERENT GROUPS TO PROVIDE FOCUSED ASSISTANCE. HOWEVER, REMEMBER THAT ALL GROUPS ARE IMPORTANT!*

9. Conclusion

Singapore has come to the stage of development where assistance to entrepreneurship and SMEs is of utmost importance. This article has provided some advice on how to handle this difficult problem. However, as long as it maintains its discipline and focus, Singapore will no doubt continue to surprise the world by adapting to new conditions and finding solutions to this problem as well.

References

"And never the twain shall meet ..." (1997) *The Economist*, March 29, pp. 73–74.

Arbnor, Ingeman & Bjerke, Björn (1997) *Methodology for Creating Business Knowledge* (Second Edition), Thousand Oaks, California: Sage Publications, Inc.

Berton, Lee (1994) "Small Companies Try Avant-Garde Methods for Funds", *The Wall Street Journal*, May 20, p. B2.

"Best Practices for Small and Medium Enterprises (SMEs) in APEC" (1995) *Asia-Pacific Economic Cooperation.*

Bjerke, Björn (1989) *Att skapa nya affärer* ("Creating new business ventures"), Lund, Sweden: Studentlitteratur.

Bjerke, Björn (1997a) "Managing entrepreneurship — on whose terms", paper presented at *UIC/AMA Research Symposium on Marketing and Entrepreneurship*, Chicago, July 31–August 3.

Bjerke, Björn (1997b) "SMEs and Marketing. A Cross-cultural Study (The Overseas Chinese version), report to the *AMA/UIC/SFSBR Project on Cross-Cultural Studies on SMEs and Marketing*.

Bjerke, Björn (1998) *Business Leadership in Five Different Cultures*, Singapore: Prentice Hall (forthcoming).

Bjerke, Björn & Al-Meer, Abdul Rahman (1994) "A Behavioral Consciousness View of Corporate Culture", *The Association of Management 12th Annual International Conference*, Dallas, Texas: Proceedings of the Organisational Studies Group. Vol. 12, No. 1, pp. 174–179.

Bjerke, Björn & Hultman, Claes (1998) "Marketing and Entrepreneurship. A Conceptual Discussion", *Marketing Education Review*, Special Issue on the Marketing/Entrepreneurship Interface.

Boswell, Jonathan (1973) *The Rise and Decline of Small Firms*, London: George, Allen & Unwin.

Braadbaart, Okke (1995) "A Comparison of Chinese and *Pribumi*-managed Engineering Firms in Indonesia", in Brown, R.A. *Chinese Business Enterprises in Asia*, London: Routledge, pp. 177–196.

Carland, J.W., Carland, J.C., Hoy, F. & Boulton, W.R. (1988) "Distinctions Between Entrepreneurial and Small Business Ventures", *International Journal of Management*, March, pp. 98–103.

Carson, D., Cromie, S., McGowan, P. & Hill, .J (1995) *Marketing and Entrepreneurship in SMEs. An Innovative Approach*, Hertfordshire: Prentice Hall International (UK) Limited.

Castro, J., McDowell, J. & McWhirter, W. (1988) "Big vs. Small", *Time*, September 5, p. 49.

Chau, Theodora Ting (1991) "Approaches to Succession in East Asian Business Organisations", *Family Business Review*, Vol. IV, No. 2, Summer, pp. 161–179.

Chee, Peng Lin (1992) "Potential and Problems of SMI", in Kim Seung Jin & Suh, Jang-Won (eds.) *Co-operation in Small and Medium-scale Industries in ASEAN*, Kuala Lumpur: Asian and Pacific Development Centre, pp. 29–51.

Chen, Min (1995) *Asian Management Systems*, London: Routledge.

Chu, Chin-Ning (1991) *The Asian Mind Game*, New York: Macmillan Publishing Company.

Davis, H.J. & Rasool, S.A. (1988) "Values Research and Managerial Behavior: Implications for Devising Culturally Consistent Managerial Styles", *Management International Review*, Vol. 28, 1988/3, pp. 11–20.

Department of Statistics (1997 June) "Profile of Growing Small & Medium Enterprises in Singapore" Singapore, *Ministry of Trade and Industry*.

Dougherty, D. (1992) "A Practice-Centered Model of Organisational Renewal Through Product Innovation", *Strategic Management Journal*, Summer, pp. 77–92.

Drucker, Peter & Nakauchi, Isao (1997) *Drucker on Asia*, Oxford, MA: Butterworth-Heinemann.

Dubini, P. (1989) "The Influence of Motivators and Environment on Business Start-Up: Some Hints for Public Policies", *Journal of Business Venturing*, Vol. 4, No. 1, January, pp. 11–26.

"Enterprise" (1993) *Business Week*, Issue pp. 50–53.

"Enterprise Singapore Style" (1993) *Newsweek*, Jan. 4, p. 46.

Ferraro, Gary P. (1994) *The Cultural Dimension of International Business* (Second Edition). Englewood Cliffs, New Jersey: Prentice-Hall.

"Fissiparous Fortunes and Family Feuds" (1996) *The Economist*, November 30, pp. 69–70.

Geursen, Gus A. (1996) "Marketing Theory: Its Importance and Relevance to Entrepreneurs and Small Business", paper presented at *UIC/AMA Research Symposium on Marketing and Entrepreneurship*, Stockholm, Sweden, June 14–15.

Ghosh, B.C. & Kwan, Wayne (1996) "An Analysis of Key Success Factors of SMEs: A Comparative Study of Singapore/Malaysia and Australia/New Zealand", paper presented at *ICSB 41st World Conference*, Stockholm, Sweden, June 17–19.

Goffer, R. & Scase, R. (1985) "Proprietary control in Family Firms: Some Functions of Quasi-organic Management", *Journal of Management Studies*, 22, pp. 53–68.

Gupta, Uayan (1990) "Venture Capital Dims for Start-Ups but Not to Worry", *The Wall Street Journal*, January 24, p. B2.

Hale, D. (1992) "For New Jobs, Help Small Business", *The Wall Street Journal*, August 10, p. A10.

Hales, C. (1993) *Managing Through Organisation*, London: Routledge.

Hall, Chris (1995) "Investing In Intangibles: Improving the Effectiveness of Government SME Advisory Services in the APEC Region", keynote speech at *1995 APEC Symposium on HRD for SMEs*, Taipei, November 8–10.

Harris, Philip R. & Moran, Robert I. (1979) *Managing Cultural Differences*, Houston, Texas: Gulf Publishing Company.

Hisrich, Robert D. & Peters, Michael P. (1992) *Entrepreneurship* (Second Edition), Homewood, IL: Irwin.

Hodgetts, R.M. & Luthans, F. (1991) *International Management*, Singapore: McGraw-Hill.

Hofer, C.W. & Sandberg, W.R. (1987) "Improving New Venture Performance: Some Guidelines for Success", *American Journal of Small Business*, Summer, pp. 19–24.

Hofstede, Geert (1984) *Culture's Consequences* (Second edition). Beverly Hills, California: Sage Publications.

Holt, David H. (1992) *Entrepreneurship: New Venture Creation*, New Jersey: Prentice-Hall.

Hoon-Halbauer, Sing Keow (1994) *Management of Sino-Foreign Joint Ventures*, Lund, Sweden: Lund University Press.

Howard, Robert (1990) "Can Small Business Help Countries Compete?", in "Entrepreneurship. Creativity at Work", *Harvard Business Review* paperback No. 90076, pp. 117–125.

Hsieh, Jiann (1978) "The Chinese Community in Singapore: The Internal Structure and its Basic Constituents", in Chen, P J S & Evers, H-D (eds.) *Studies in ASEAN Sociology*, Singapore: Chopmen Enterprises, pp. 78–98.

Humes, Samuel (1993) *Managing the Multinational*, Hertfordshire, England: Prentice-Hall.

James, Kenneth (1988) "Marketing Factors Affecting Small and Medium Businesses in the ASEAN region", in James, Kenneth & Akrasane, Narongchai (eds.) *Small and Medium Business Improvement in the ASEAN Region: Marketing Factors*. Singapore: ASEAN Economic Research Unit, Institute of Southeast Asia Studies. Field Report Series No. 20, pp. 1–18.

Jansson, Hans (1987) *Affärskulturer och relationer i Sydöstasien* ("Business cultures and Relations in Southeast Asia"), Stockholm, Sweden: Marknadstekniskt Centrum, No. 29.

Kao, Raymond W.Y. (1995) *Entrepreneurship: A Wealth-creation and Value-adding Process*, Singapore: Simon & Schuster (Asia) Pte Ltd.

Keats, B. & Bracker, J. (1988) "Toward a Theory of Small Firm Performance: A Conceptual Model", *American Journal of Small Business*, Spring, pp. 41–58

Kenny, Brian & Dyson, Karen (1989) *Marketing in Small Business*, London: Routledge.

Kuratko, Donald F. & Hodgetts, Richard M. (1995) *Entrepreneurship. A Contemporary Approach* (Third Edition), Orlando, FL: The Dryden Press.

Lasserre, Philippe & Schütte, Hellmut (1995) *Strategies for Asia Pacific*, London: Macmillan Press Ltd.

Liang, Su-ming (1974) *The Basics of Chinese Culture*, Hong Kong: Zhicheng Books.

Maturi, Richard J. (1989) "Staying Afloat", *Entrepreneur*, January, pp. 100–102.

McClelland, David (1961) *The Achieving Society*, Princeton, N J: Van Nostrand

McMillan, C.J. (1985) *The Japanese Industrial System* (Second Revised Edition), New York: Walter de Gruyter.

Mintzberg, Henry (1982) "Tracking Strategy in the Entrepreneurial Firm", *Academy of Management Journal*, Vol. 7, pp. 465–499.

"Munchkin management" (1989) *The Economist*, October 14, pp. 91–92.

Naisbitt, John (1995) *Megatrends Asia*, London: Nicholas Brealey Publishing.

Osborne, R.L. (1991) "The Dark Side of Entrepreneurship", *Long Range Planning*, Vol. 24, pp. 26–31.

Pan, Lynn (1991) *Sons of the Yellow Emperor*, London: Mandarin Paperbacks.

Pang Eng Fong (1988) "The Distinctive Features of Two City-states' Development: Hong Kong and Singapore", in Berger, Peter L. & Hsiao, Hsian-Huang Michael (eds.) *In Search of an East Asian Development Model*, New Brunswick and Oxford: Transaction Books, pp. 227–239.

Peters, Tom (1989) *Thriving on Chaos*, London: Pan Books Ltd.

Peters, Tom (1994) *The Tom Peters Seminar*, London: Pan Books.

Pinchot, Gifford (1985) *Intrapreneuring*, New York: Harper & Row.

Pollack, Robert A. (1985) "A Transaction Cost Approach to Families and Households", *Journal of Economic Literature*, Vol. 23, pp. 590–598.

Redding, S. Gordon (1993) *The Spirit of Chinese Capitalism*, Berlin: Walter de Gruyter.

Redding, S. Gordon & Ng, Michael (1982) "The Role of 'Face' in the Organisational Perceptions of Chinese Managers", *Organisational Studies*, Vol. 3, No. 3, pp. 201–219.

Robinson, David (1990) *What Is an Entrepreneur?* Holbrook, Massachusetts: Bob Adams, Inc.

Rohwer, Jim (1995) *Asia Rising*, Singapore: Butterworth:Heinemann Asia.

Romano, Cladio C. & Ratnatunga, Jenak (1995) "The Role of Marketing: Its Impact on Small Business Research", *European Journal of Marketing*, Vol. 29, No. 7, pp. 11–24.

Ronstadt, Robert C. (1984) *Entrepreneurship*, Dover, MA: Lord Publishing Co.

Samovar, L.A., Porter, R.E. & Jain, Nemi C. (1981) *Understanding Intercultural Communication*, Belmont, California: Wadsworth Publishing Company.

Scarborough, Norman M. & Zimmerer, Thomas W. (1996) *Effective Small Business Management* (Fifth Edition), Upper Saddle River, NJ: Prentice Hall, Inc.

Schwind, Hermann F. & Peterson, Richard B. (1985) "Shifting Personal Values in the Japanese Management System", *International Studies of Management & Organisation*, Summer, pp. 60–74.

Seagrave, Sterling (1996) *Lords of the Rim*, London: Corgi Books.

Sexton, Donald L & Bowman-Upton, Nancy B (1991) *Entrepreneurship. Creativity and Growth*, New York: Macmillan Publishing Company.

Shaw, Howard Dana (1987) "Customer Care Checklist", *In Business*, September/October, pp. 28–31.

Sheh Seow Wah (1995) *Chinese Management*, Selangor, Malaysia: MPH Distributors Sdn. Bhd.

Sherriff, T.K. Luk (1989) "Culture, Manipulative Power and Channel Management: The Chinese Experience", paper presented at *The 2nd International Conference on Comparative Management*, National Sun Yat-sen University, Taiwan, June 4–6.

Sitaram, K.S. & Cogdell, Roy T. (1976) *Foundations of Intercultural Communication*, Columbus, Ohio: Charles E. Merrill.

Singapore Chinese Chamber of Commerce & Industry (1997) *Roadmap for SMEs*.

Sociaal Economische Raad, Upvolging in Familjebedrijven ("Social Economic Council: Controlling Family Firms") (1990) The Hague, Holland.

Storey, D.J. (1985). "The Problems Facing New Firms", *Journal of Management Studies*, Vol. 22, pp. 237–245.

Tanaka, Yozo, Mori, Minako & Mori, Yoko (1992) "Overseas Chinese Business Community in Asia: Present Conditions and Future Prospects", *Pacific Business and Industries*, Vol. II, pp. 2–24.

"The APEC Survey on Small and Medium Enterprises" (1994) *APEC Committee on Trade and Investment*, APEC Secretariat.

"The State of Small Business: A Report to the President" (1987) *US Government Printing Office*, Washington, D.C.

"They're Minding Their Own Business" (1997) *Business Week*, April 7, pp. 19–20.

Timmons, Jeffrey A. (1990) *New Venture Creation* (3rd ed.). Homewood, IL: Irwin.

Toffler, Alvin (1991) *Power Shift*, London: Bantam Books.

Trompenaars, Fons (1995) *Riding the Waves of Culture*, London: Nicholas Brealey Publishing.

Tu, Wei-ming (1984) *Confucian Ethic Today — The Singapore Challenge*, Singapore: Federal Publications.

Upadhya, Carol B. (1988) "The Farmer Capitalists and Coastal Andhra Pradesh", *Political and Economic Review*, Vol. 23, pp. 1,376–442.

Ushido, Yoshio (1995) "Small and Medium Enterprises and Government Policy", paper presented at *1995 APEC Symposium on HRD for SMEs*, Taipei, November 8–10.

Wheelen, Thomas L. & Hunger, J. David (1995) *Strategic Management and Business Policy* (Fifth Edition), Reading, Massachusetts: Addison-Wesley Publishing Company, Inc.

Wong, Kevin & Edwards, Ron (1996) "Singapore", in Edwards, Ron & Skully, Michael T (eds.) *ASEAN Business Trade & Development*, Australia: Butterworth-Heinemann Asia, pp. 131–154.

Wong, Siu-lun (1995) "Business Networks, Cultural Values and the State in Hong Kong and Singapore", in Brown, R.A. (ed.) *Chinese Business Enterprise in Asia*, London and NY: Routledge, pp. 139–151.

Yang, Bo (1991) *The Ugly Chinaman and the Crisis of Chinese Culture*, St. Leonards, Australia: Allen & Unwin.

Zimmerer, Thomas W. & Scarborough, Norman M. (1996) *Entrepreneurship and New Venture Formation*, NJ: Prentice-Hall.

9

Globalisation and the Social Fabric of Competitiveness*

Ho Kong Chong

1. Introduction: The Social Fabric of Competitiveness

The phrase "social fabric of competitiveness" is an attempt to recognise that economic competitiveness — the ability to respond successfully to global forces — has a social dimension. The social fabric, the relationships between different groups in society, has important effects on competitiveness. While economists may talk about the competitiveness of nations and of economies, the agency which drives this competitiveness resides in individuals and organisations. To be competitive in the face of changes requires an intelligence function (the ability to recognise that new solutions are needed, and the ability to come up with new solution) and an implementation function (the ability to follow through or implement the solution). The agency which performs the intelligence function resides in the individual and involves entrepreneurship (see paper by Bjerke, in this collection), and firms, in terms of their ability to make innovations in products, production, marketing and distribution (see papers by Wong in this collection).

However, once we move away from the concept of entrepreneurship and firm strategies, competitiveness has to be increasingly discussed as place competitiveness. This is an important qualification, since place competitiveness may often differ from the competitiveness of firms. While one could argue that highly

* Key ideas from this paper were presented at an ISA conference titled "Cities in Transition", Berlin (Panel on "Politics of Urban Economic Development"). The author gratefully acknowledges NUS financial support to attend this conference.

competitive places attract competitive firms, in an era of economic restructuring firms may often choose to abandon places in order to maintain competitiveness.

The discussion of place competitiveness requires an analysis of government policies. In a globalising economy, capital has become hypermobile, creating elaborate geographically dispersed production chains to maximise place advantages. Likewise, financial and business services are dispersed to support manufacturing capital. Labour is in turn more mobile, responding to job opportunities in different regions and as a result company transfers. Within this environment of capital and labour flows, only governments remain anchored to places, and it is in the interests of governments to devise place based competitive strategies.

My purpose in this chapter is not an examination of different types of government competitiveness policies as this has been discussed in Tan and Toh's paper in this collection. My argument in this paper is that the nature of state and society relations matter in sustaining place competitiveness.

Competitiveness policies are only good solutions if they can be implemented fast. The implementation process thus requires some degree of societal consensus. In the case of firms, the employment contract guarantees basic consensus in the implementation process. However, for governments and their policies, public support is an element which has to be negotiated in the implementation process. Policy implementation makes demands on citisens. Or as Migdal (1988: 22) puts it, "state social control involves the successful subordination of people's own inclinations of social behaviour or behaviour sought by other social organisations in favour of behaviour prescribed by state rules".

We have only to mention Singapore's more successful policies to see why this is so. The Central Provident Fund, our transport policies, urban renewal, attempts to increase worker productivity all share one thing in common: its success requires an adjustment of citisens' economic and social behaviour in line with state policies. Thus, governments concerned with place competitiveness must not only ensure the right mix of capital and labour as Peterson (1981) argues, governments must also maintain a necessary degree of social cohesiveness defined in terms of the ability of a substantial segment of the population to identify itself with a set of state inspired goals and programmes. This is what Gamer (1972, p. 35) meant by the term "the political capacity to plan". I use the metaphor "social fabric" to refer to the degree of social cohesiveness in Singapore society, the degree to which different population segments are linked together, interwoven in terms of their identification with government initiatives.

We need to take a historical detour in order to see how this cohesiveness has been reshaped away from ethnic based governance structures to a more state dominated system.

2. The Transformation of Economic Governance

In colonial Singapore, the government essentially adopted a narrow housekeeping function which focused exclusively on trade and which placed economic priorities over social concerns. The maintenance of the physical infrastructure of trade was of paramount importance in ensuring the surplus which accrued to British interests. As early as 1933, the government had given some thought to local manufacturing and whether such activities should be given tariff protection to help them grow. Their reply, which is summarised below, reflects the government's narrow approach:

> *"Though the interests of the local manufacturer would be best served by protection, the interference with the freedom of the port which would be involved might be disastrous to be entrepot trade... The prosperity of Singapore has been built on its entrepot trade. Industrial development is a later growth and has not begun to approach the entrepot in importance. To disturb this merely for the sake of protecting still problematic industries would be to throw away the substance and grasp the shadow"*
>
> (Pang and Tan, 1981, p. 141)

With such a system of governance, ethnic based associations grew to assume important economic and social functions. The Chinese community can serve as an example. Among the Chinese, identity and alliances were divided along dialect lines (Lee, 1978; Huff, 1994, pp. 162–164). Lee's (1978) analysis showed how, towards the end of the 19th century, the organisational basis of Chinese society changed from secret societies to dialect based associations. It was in these associations that the mercantile class, nurtured under Singapore's entrepot trade regime, was linked with the rest of society. Dialect based associations were thus able to mobilise the support of prominent individuals and wealthier segments of the Chinese community for social development projects in education and health.

For Chinese merchants, the dialect associations were not only a source of social prestige, or a sign of one's social standing in society, it was also a source of influence within the merchant class. A clear evidence of this influence is that leadership in the Chinese Chamber of Commerce, formed in 1906, was linked to one's prominence in various dialect groups (Lee, 1978, p. 99). Moreover, successful merchants also exerted their influence as intermediaries between the government and Chinese society through their membership in the Chinese Advisory Board, set up in 1890 by the British (Lee, 1978, pp. 90, 91, 96). As in the case of the Chamber of Commerce, representatives were nominated in proportion to the size of the dialect associations (Wong, 1990, p. 15).

The period of the inter-war years saw the Chamber playing a crucial role in laying down business conventions among traders, arbitrating business disputes, and as a receiver of bankrupt firms. It also compiled trade information and data, and provided a place where product samples were inspected. The Chamber also acted as an inspector and guarantor for companies (Wong, 1990, pp. 31–32). Wong (1990, p. 35) argues that the Chamber's most important function was in the aggregation and articulation of Chinese business interests to the ruling class.

Beneath the Chamber and affiliated with it was a variety of trade guilds that were an adaptation of those that existed in China (Gamba, 1966). Gamba (1966, pp. 126, 127) citing Morse's work, pointed out these associations "never recognised civil law nor claimed protection from it". These associations performed a regulatory function, settling matters within the particular trade internally instead of through the courts. Guilds made representations to the government on matters such as taxation, and if harassed, they could even clash with the government through boycotts.

The close ties to the trade guilds meant that the Chamber could also claim a role as spokesperson for the Chinese working population in a period when the majority of workers were employed in small kinship based firms. However, this function disappeared with the rise of trade unions in the 1950s.

With the array of economic associations, it would be tempting to suggest that these associations went beyond their regulatory role and assumed a developmental or intelligence function in the sense described by Piore and Sable (1984). The majority of the active organisations described were small and linked to commerce, and the large numbers were because of the heterogeneity of commerce. Manufacturing in the form of rubber based products was still in its infancy, and there was not the concentration which created the critical mass for associations to take on the developmental function, as was the case of the industrial districts described in Piore and Sable's study.

Having said this, a case may be made for an emerging developmental role and innovative function among colonial economic associations. Evidence for this comes from Huff's (1994, p. 233) observation that there was evidence of personal links between those involved in rubber and pineapple plantations, early manufacturing concerns, and the development of local banking. The Chamber and the clan associations could have had a role in the facilitation of such links, since the interlocking nature of these organisations meant the high circulation of leading merchants and entrepreneurs.

The decline of the SCCC paralleled the decline of Chinese economic organisations which failed to modernise traditional business practices. Many SCCC members, the majority of whom were in traditional Chinese enterprises, did not and could not change (Wong, 1990, p. 37). By 1976, 84% of the trade and occupational associations in Singapore had a non-ethnic origin (Cheng, 1985, pp. 40–41).

However, this forms only part of the explanation. As noted by Huff (1994: 235) the group that gained political power comprised English educated professionals. These persons did not have the affiliations with the Chamber or the clan associations, and embarked on a development strategy which relied on Western multinational corporations. The absence of close ties meant that these individuals, after reading the economic signals and regional political situation and surmising that commerce was of limited value in ensuring continued development, could move rapidly onto an industrialisation strategy without worrying about the social and political costs of offending the trading community. Besides, the orientation of the new leaders was towards achieving mass support and this could be better ensured through new jobs that industrialisation would bring, and through other social development programmes.

Clan associations became obsolete in the post-colonial period, as the new government assumed the social development function that was necessary to gain and maintain legitimacy and popular support. Moreover, the task of nation building had begun, and this began to erode the ethnic communal identity, a vital resource for clan association support. The rise and popularity of English language education also made these traditional associations unpopular among the young (Chong, 1992, pp. 26–27).

The transformation of economic governance involved several characteristics. The economic governance structure in colonial society was essentially a two-tiered structure. The colonial government played an essential but narrowly defined housekeeping role in maintaining economic infrastructures and a free trade environment. The absence of an interventionist state meant that economic associations had to play a stronger role in both the regulation of internal matters as well as to fend for themselves and protect their interests by making representations to the government that ruled with "benign neglect". The new economic institutions which the PAP government created essentially replaced this two-tiered structure by diluting the role of trade based and ethnic based associations. The decline of these latter types of associations was partly due to their obsolescence as traditional functions disappeared. It was also due to the fact that state initiatives were directed towards the industrialisation effort, thereby bypassing the associations that historically played an important role in regulating commerce.

The transformation also involved a change in the capacity of the intelligence and monitoring process. Compared to trade and ethnic based associations, which were essentially voluntary organisations depending on the goodwill of individuals to contribute their time and money, the new state run institution had enormous resources and regulatory powers. While trade associations essentially governed and innovated within industry, agendas of state run institutions like the Economic Development Board spanned industries and sectors.

The rise of these institutions in turn influenced state-business relations. The focus of these new institutions was the multinational companies (MNC), which had started going global after the Second World War (Frobel, *et al.*, 1980; Dicken, 1986). Mirza (1986, p. 5) estimated the foreign share of Singapore's GDP increased from 9% in 1966 to 28% in 1980. New cohorts of school leavers were being absorbed into the industries developed by foreign direct investment. For example, within manufacturing, the largest generator of employment growth was the electronics industry, which was heavily dominated by MNCs. The presence of a pro-business government means that by and large, laws and regulations favour businesses. Businesses also benefit in more direct ways, such as having their training expenses subsidised by the government, and having the help of the government in finding new markets and even sites for manufacturing. This pro-business climate essentially means that the business community had few grouses and fights to pick with the state.

However, two qualifications have to be made. While the pro-business climate meant cordial relations between state and capital, the need by the government to ensure Singapore remained competitive meant that this relationship was strategic. The case of the textile and garment industry serves as an example. In the late 1960s, the textile and garment industry was one of the major employers of labour. However, by the late 1970s, rising labour costs had created severe problems for this labour intensive industry. In a 1987 speech urging the industry to upgrade, the deputy Prime Minister had referred to the industry in kinder terms as a "high noon" industry rather than facing the setting sun in Singapore.[1] But the meaning was clear: in a country which had a small labour force and land resources, the government would only continue supporting an industry if it remained competitive and continued to upgrade technology and skills.

[1] *Straits Times*, April 4, 1987.

Likewise, small and medium sized enterprises faced a similar response. In discussing the role of local capital as a political force, Chalmers (1992) made the distinction between the local business elite and the small and medium enterprises (SME), and had argued that the recession of the mid 1980s created a move to inclusionary corporatism, where the state included SME interests within political institutions. While this distinction is useful, it is doubtful whether SME interests have indeed been included in the apparatus, alongside business elite interests. Part of the continued marginalisation of SME interests have to do with the inability of the city-state to sustain large and small businesses, given limited land and labour resources. The important point to note here is that the state's interests in SMEs have to do with helping them to grow and be competitive (and by so doing, make the economy more resilient), but this does not necessarily mean, as Chalmers (1992, pp. 72–74) suggested, that SMEs have an important voice and a space in the political arena. In fact, the state's response to SMEs can be best described as "to shape up (with some help of course!) or ship out (to lower cost areas)".

For the rest, the orientation of the state towards development means that the interests of business and the state are not in conflict. Given this situation, where businesses are direct beneficiaries of government actions, it is difficult to imagine why economic associations would act in ways other than in tandem with the state. Moreover, unlike the non-economic segments of society, the logic of modern capital would dictate that it votes with its feet rather than its voice. The government is painfully aware of this footlooseness and seeks to incorporate business interests in its policies. The relationship between business and the state is thus best described as consultative. Prominent local businessmen and executives of multinational companies are often called to perform an economic advisory role when they sit on various government committees. One of the more prominent ones includes the economic planning committee, comprising business leaders and high ranking civil servants, formed to strategise new directions for Singapore. However, it is important to emphasise again that it is the state which sets the agenda, and that businessmen and executives are co-opted with the express intention of providing feedback, and then in largely a reactionary capacity.

This suggests an economic parallel of the state and civil society equation. Just as a strong state may weaken civil society, the presence of a developmental state may in turn weaken associational forms of economic organisation. While a more serious analysis of this relation is beyond the scope of this paper, it may be suggested that state intervention and co-optation of businesses at different levels (vertical linkages involving cross industry interests) may in fact hinder the formation of stronger ties within industry (horisontal linkages), thereby weakening associational tendencies within industries. One can argue, for example, that state intervention in the granting of incentives to favoured industries creates, by implication, disincentives for those not on the list, since the effect of incentives is to lower production costs for beneficiaries. The selective pricing of worker levies by industry is a more direct example of how the government can practice selective encouragement. It is this type of selective discrimination that weakens the associational power of industries. The second industrial revolution in the 1979/80 period is an instance of how some industries were encouraged over others (see Rodan, 1989). It is precisely because governments value place over industry that the organisational capacities of particular industries remain weak in the presence of a strong state.

If the presence of a strong state has weakened independent economic voices, has an important pillar of competitiveness been toppled? In a globalised world, place competitiveness and company competitiveness have grown increasingly distant from each other. In an era of global production, it is to the company's advantage to have weak place commitments, since place flexibility becomes a strategy for firms to maximise concessions for operating in a particular locality. A certain degree of footlooseness or place flexibility is imperative to maintain a company's competitiveness. I think we are to a great extent prisoners of our own institutional developments. Having grown the developmental state and its affiliate organs, the state has taken effective control of the monitoring process, actively engaging in the process of industrial targeting (Chia, 1989, pp. 273–274). Thus, having committed to industrial targeting, the best compromise is to have in place institutional structures where businesses can be co-opted in order to ensure timely market and industry intelligence so that the economic vitality of the place is maintained.

3. Globalisation and the Social Fabric of Competitiveness

If, historically, the transformation of economic governance from associational to state-based institutions has enabled Singapore to compete more effectively in the global marketplace, we should also address the question of whether, in the contemporary period, Singapore's increasing embeddedness in the global economy has allowed in influences which fray the social fabric of Singapore society, and whether this fraying in turn dampens our competitiveness.

Globalisation and Workers

The effects of globalisation on workers have been mediated through the relations workers have with the government and with the firm. The effect of having in place a government that has been oriented towards maintaining place competitiveness has been the transformation of the labour movement from its left wing beginnings in the 1950s to progressively becoming an element in the competitiveness process. This transformation has been remarkable. In the plural society that was created under the British, the sentiments of the Chinese speaking community became increasingly articulated through the Chinese middle school students and the workers. Under the influence of the communists, the Singapore Chinese Middle Schools Union (SCMSSU) was closely allied with the labour unions.

The strength of this alliance is well known. In 1955 alone, there were 277 strikes, resulting in a loss of a million man-hours, a seven-fold increase over the previous year. The most famous strike was the Hock Lee Bus strike. The ineffectual handling of the strike by the fledging Labour Front resulted in the resignation of Singapore's first Chief Minister and had set back talks for internal self-government.

In 1959, when Singapore finally won internal self-government, the government's main agenda was the tackling of the unions. In 1959 and 1960, it deregistered 106 unions and absorbed the rest into the newly formed Trade Union Congress (Gamer, 1972, pp. 28–29). The deregulation of militant unions continued throughout the 1960s, and in 1968 the passing of the Employment Act and the Industrial Relations Ordinance curtailed the unions' right to strike and gave management sole jurisdiction over hiring, firing and transfers (Buchanan, 1972, p. 298). The now pro-government union underwent further restructuring in the 1980s and became a partner in the development process acting as an important vehicle for increasing worker productivity (Chiu, Ho and Lui, 1997, pp. 147–152).

While labour has become increasingly responsive to state policies, the relationship between labour and capital has grown strategic as the employment relationship moved from mutual obligations within a family firm framework to more contractual relationships. Weak company loyalties have in part been caused by the absorption of the workforce into globalised industries, which undergo retrenchment exercises to cope with the volatility of global demand patterns. Retrenchment and the threat of retrenchment weaken worker attachment to any one company, and the labour response to this industrial environment has been to switch firms according to the financial incentives offered.

The electronics industry provides a good example of this process. In a review of the semi conductor industry, the Singapore Economic Development Board (1985, p. 18) recognised that the industry has "erratic growth" characteristics. In the 1980s, there were two "dips" in the otherwise continuous expansion pattern of the electronics industry. The first downturn occurred in 1981–1982 and the second in 1985. In both periods output fell between 5.5% to 7.5% over the previous year and the industry shed a total of between 10,000 to 13,000 workers. In the earlier downturn of 1974–1975, retrenchment of workers was estimated at 15,000 (Lim, 1978, p. 18).

Thus, the industrial culture which arose out of this type of volatility has been for weakened commitments. Firms retrench in downturns, workers job hop in upturns. The movement of labour within the electronics industry is so high that an electronics company can claim credit for being a good employer when 25% of its workforce have stayed with the company for more than two years (Committee on the Third Shift, 1986, p. 86).

A high rate of labour turnover poses a threat to the competitiveness of firms when its energies are spent on recruitment and training instead of increasing productivity of workers, and when the shortage poses a disruption to the company's operations (Task Force on Job Hopping, 1988, p. 9). However, there is less certainty whether labour turnover will hinder place competitiveness since one firm's efforts at training the worker have been appropriated by another firm offering better salaries and/or job prospects.[2] Early work done by Pang and Lim (1977) for the electronics industry show labour movements to be a rather dynamic process between local firms and multinational companies. Local companies were less likely to retrench workers compared to multinational companies because lower wage rates paid and anticipated difficulty in rehiring when the economic situation improves. These companies were in fact able to hire experienced and better skilled workers retrenched from MNCs during the recession. The reverse flow of workers to the better paying MNCs occurs when overseas demand picks up (Pang and Lim, 1977, p. 26).

In a period of weakened loyalties between capital and labour, the government has allowed for job hopping and retrenchment by not enforcing commitment on both sides, given the inherent difficulties of enforcement. Instead, by assuming part of the costs of worker training, it has kept employers happy by reducing the training costs borne by employers created by job hopping workers. At the same time, retraining schemes have also worked to minimise social problems of unemployment created by retrenching firms by retraining workers so that they can improve their chances of finding new jobs.

Globalisation and Stratification

Another outcome of globalisation is its impact on social economic statuses of local residents (Sassen, 1991; Graham and Marvin, 1996). On the one hand, the new rich are plugged into jobs in the international sector viz. MNCs with global and regional ties. On the other hand, economic restructuring is beginning to hurt the working class disproportionately, especially older workers and women. Thus, while Singapore in the 1950s and 1960s had a small elite with a large working class and urban poor, globalisation has resulted in a more elaborate stratification system. The point is that class is more than an economic category, since classes imply social attributes in terms of

[2] Associate Professor Lim Chin raised this point during the workshop discussions.

lifestyle, interests and concerns, as well as the ability to socially reproduce these characteristics in future generations.

Thus, if competitiveness requires a local population to move in tandem with place solutions to the changes that globalisation brings, then with globalisation and stratification, the task of maintaining the cohesiveness and collective identity of the local population becomes a more difficult task at several levels.

With the middle and professional class, the challenge is on how to create place loyalties with the professional class' regionalised and globalised orientation. The Prime Minister's 1997 National Day speech is an indication of our realisation that we cannot do it alone, and will require a more liberal foreign worker policy in order to prop up our workforce. However, because the demands placed by the state on our citisens are high, we cannot afford to entirely let the country be managed by hired professionals. Thus, the twin demands of attracting foreign talent and creating place loyalties will continue to be a challenge for the future.

With the working class, the challenge is quite different. Place competitiveness requires a "lean and mean" regime that maximises economic spending on infrastructure and developmental projects while minimising social expenditures.[3] This indeed has been the official position of the government, which is to spend in order to "help people to help themselves". Outright welfare payments remain very low. Social expenditures in education have been seen in terms of investment rather than welfare, while expenditures in health and housing have a co-payment character rather than a transfer payment. However, in the 1990s, a more diverse socioeconomic stratification system threatened popular support. Wealth sharing became an important mechanism for maintaining support, especially for the working class given their lower income capacities. With neighbourhood upgrading, public housing has moved beyond basic needs to investment. Recently, the government has moved into the area of meeting the medical needs of the elderly, which promises to be another area of insatiable demand as the population ages.

Thus, the government will have to maintain an increasingly mixed set of policy initiatives in order to deal with different interests

[3] I am grateful to Tan Ern Ser for pointing this out.

of the population. With the professional class, the challenge of maintaining competitiveness has to do with preserving interests of this group to stay and contribute, while with the working class, this challenge has to do with balancing economic expenditures with social expenditures in order to minimise local discontents and maintain cohesiveness across social groups.

Globalisation and the Commodification of Culture

A globalised economy also brings with it a globalised culture in terms of increasingly homogeneous forms of popular culture (fashion, entertainment, food, etc), particularly among the youth. What is new about the effects of globalisation on the cultural industry is that new enabling technologies (most importantly satellite broadcast, computer and telecommunication technologies) have allowed popular culture, both "western" and "Asian" forms to be marketed more effectively and to a bigger audience. Moreover, the emerging segment of young affluent consumers in Asia has created an effective market for things "Asian". The best indicator of these trends is the phenomenal success of STAR TV, which in turn has attracted a number of big American cable companies to Asia: MTV, HBO, ESPN, Disney, and NBC.

Both globalisation and the commodification of culture have meant for Singapore an increased diversity of popular cultural forms. The difference between youth cultures of the past and the present, is that nowadays, youth resistance is a flourishing industry. Unconventionality sells, adding economic power to resistance. It is important to see this emerging industry as creating opportunities for young Singaporeans, and perhaps even alternative sources of competitiveness. Thus, the important point to note is that youth cultures have to do with alternative productivity, not non-productivity. At the same time, because this provides an effective forum for alternative cultures and lifestyles, emerging youth cultures may challenge existing dominant modes of adaptation.

An example of alternative productivity and social criticism is Eric Khoo's 12 Stories, a collection of "funny, sometimes tragic, stories of unhappy families living in what seems on the surface like soul-less slabs of concrete" (Sandi Tan, film reviewer).[4] Darren McDermott and Fara Warner, writing for the Asian Wall Street Journal, pointed out that "though Eric Khoo and the film's producers deny that they set out to comment on Singapore society, they've nevertheless succeeded. Simply and elegantly, the film presents unadorned slices of life that challenges the myth of a people thriving on 'Asian values', the catch-all phrase for moral uprightness popularised by Singapore elder statesman Lee Kuan Yew."[5]

Besides winning the international critic's prize at the 1997 Singapore Film Festival, 12 Storeys had the honour of being invited to the prestigious Cannes film festival and recently won the top award at the Hawaii International Film Festival.[6] This film is now contracted to be shown in France, Japan and Hong Kong.

Are cultural entrepreneurs like film maker Eric Khoo an enigma for the Singapore government? Since the late 1980s, the government has become actively involved with the promotion of arts (Ho and Chua, 1995: 4–6). In its quest to become the regional hub of the arts, Singapore has more recently moved beyond its role as a host for "world class" arts activities to the more experimental function of actively nurturing local talent. The recent comment by Koh Buck Song on Eric Khoo gives a nice introduction to the brave new world of nurturing creative arts talent:

> *"It (Khoo's films) would probably also make it to Timbuktu, Kulusuk and Ulan Bator, if these places had film festivals.*
>
> *The movie will parade a side of the island that will never ever feature in a Singapore Tourist Promotion Board poster.*
>
> *But what strikes me as especially interesting is that, in an ironical way, Khoo's movie may even do more for Singapore's diplomatic relations... Like travelling Necessary Stage plays about dark themes such as social alienation, 12 Storeys and movies like it offer a different view of Singapore. The chief benefit would be to counter-balance the typical breast-beating*

[4] *Straits Times*, March 31, 1997.

[5] *Asian Wall Street Journal*, June 25, 1997.

[6] *Straits Times*, November 21, 1997.

and hard-nosed straight-talking picture that Singaporean businessmen, diplomats and tourists may project abroad...there is much to win back, from the ground lost because of the Republic's uninviting reputation for arrogance and self-righteousness which, some fear, is already entrenched in the minds of too many outsiders. Singapore may have the world's No. 1 port, airline, government, workers and what have you. But it also has prostitutes and pimps with their problems and perversions. And the Republic may not be No. 1 in arrogance after all, since it has no qualms about showing its warts to all the world to see, even as its movies hit No. 1 in a film festival here and there."[7]

4. Discussion and Conclusion

This paper introduced several themes pertaining to globalisation and place competitiveness in the Singapore context. In the wake of decolonisation and to meet the challenges of a global economy, state institutions have emerged to replace a variety of associational governance structures which existed in the past. This transformation had to some extent tightened the social fabric by strengthening vertical ties between state and society. This tightening, I argue, has allowed Singapore to become more competitive, since the task of maintaining place competitiveness requires the population to move in tandem with the state's economic restructuring/competitiveness policies in order to ensure fast response and successful implementation. The success of this particular type of competitiveness can be seen in the transformation of the labour movement and various business-government partnerships which facilitated a number of relatively problem free economic adjustments over the last two decades (the second industrial revolution in 1980, regionalisation efforts in the 1990s).

However, these vertical linkages between state and society have resulted in a more varied package of government policies aimed at tying capital to place and keeping labour motivated, and in balancing

[7] *Straits Times*, May 12, 1997.

middle class and worker class interests. The increasing penetration of popular cultural forms, made possible by developments in broadcast media, computers and telecommunications, creates new avenues of competitiveness and alternative productivity not directly under the control of the government. It is important to stress again that these are alternative productivities, not non-productivities. The tension is that such efforts may, as reviewers of Eric Khoo's film have pointed out, show a dark side of Singapore which is less than flattering of Singapore. However, Singapore's arts policy, together with similar policy initiatives to develop electronic commerce and broadcasting, signals a new direction away from direct control and perhaps with a tolerance of unconventional creativity.

My belief is that in the next century, as Singapore moves away from manufacturing to services, it will become much more a key city in the regional, and the cultural and services industries will mean less government action, and more alternative sources of competitiveness. The social fabric of this city-state will grow to become more like a patchwork rather than a seamless piece of cloth. Such a patchwork fabric will create many sources of alternative productivity. The spotlight for the social scientist in the first years of the next millennium will be to see how state-society relations will be transformed such that these alternative productivities will be harnessed to its fullest degree.

References

Buchanan, I. (1972) *Singapore in Southeast Asia*, London: Bell.

Chalmers, Ian (1992) "Loosening State Control in Singapore: The Emergence of Local Capital as a Political Force", *Southeast Asian Journal of Social Science*, Vol. 20, No. 2, pp. 57–84.

Cheng, Lim Keak (1985) *Social Change and the Chinese in Singapore*, Singapore: Singapore University Press.

Chia, Siow Yue (1989) "The Character and Progress of Industrialisation", in Sandhu, K.S. and Wheatley, P. (eds.) *Management of Success*, Institute of Southeast Asian Studies, pp. 250–279.

Chiu, S., Ho, K.C. and Lui, T.L. (1997) *City States in the Global Economy*, Boulder, Colorado: Westview.

Chong, Grace (1992) "The Chinese Clan Association in Singapore: Survival or Demise?", *Unpublished Academic Exercise*, Dept. of Sociology, Faculty of Arts and Social Sciences, National University of Singapore.

Committee on the Third Shift (1986) *Report of Findings*, Singapore: National Productivity Board.

Dicken, Peter (1986) *Global Shift: Industrial Change in a Turbulent World*, London: Harper and Row.

Economic Development Board (1985) *A Review of Singapore's Semiconductor Industry*, Singapore: EDB.

Froebel, F., Heinrichs, J., Kreye O. (1980) *The New International Division of Labour*, Cambridge: Cambridge University Press.

Gamba, Charles (1966) "Chinese Associations in Singapore", *Journal of the Malayan Branch of the Royal Asiatic Society*, Vol. 39, pp. 123–168.

Gamer, R. (1972) *The Politics of Urban Development*, Ithaca, N.Y.: Cornell University Press.

Graham, S. and Marvin S. (1996) *Telecommunications and the City*, London: Routledge.

Ho, K.C. and Chua, B.H. (1995) *Cultural, Social and Leisure Activities in Singapore Census of Population 1990 Monograph No. 3*, Singapore: Department of Statistics.

Huff, W.G. (1994) *The Economic Growth of Singapore: Trade and Development in the Twentieth Century*, Cambridge: Cambridge University Press.

Lee, Poh Ping (1978) *Chinese Society in Nineteenth Century Singapore*, K.L., Malaysia: Oxford University Press.

Lim, Linda (1978) "Women Workers in Multinational Corporations: The Case of the Electronics Industry in Malaysia and Singapore", *Occasional Papers in Women's Studies*, Women's Studies Program, University of Michigan.

Migdal, J.S. (1988) *Strong Societies and Weak States*, Princeton, N.J.: Princeton University Press.

Mirza, H. (1986) *Multinationals and the Growth of Singapore Economy*, Andover: Croom Helm.

Pang, Eng Fong and Lim, L. (1977) *The Electronics Industry in Singapore*, Singapore: Economic Research Centre.

Pang, Eng Fong and Augustine Tan (1981) "Employment and Export-led Industrialisation: The Experience of Singapore", in R. Amjad (ed.) *The Development of Labour Intensive Industry in ASEAN Countries*, Geneva: ILO, pp. 141–174.

Peterson, Paul (1981) *City Limits*, Chicago: University of Chicago Press.

Piore, M.J. and Sable C. (1984) *The Second Industrial Divide: Possibilities for Prosperity*, N.Y.: Basic Books.

Rodan, G. (1989) *The Political Economy of Singapore's Industrialisation*, London: Macmillan.

Sassen, S. (1991) *The Global City*, Princeton: Princeton University Press.

Task Force on Job Hopping, (1988) *Report of the Task Force on Job Hopping*, Singapore: National Productivity Board.

Wong, Chow Ming (1990) "The Singapore Chinese Chamber of Commerce 1906–1942", *Unpublished Academic Exercise*, Dept. of History, Faculty of Arts and Social Sciences, National University of Singapore.

10

Human Resource Management for the New Competitive Environment

William Koh

1. Introduction

The objective of this chapter is to discuss some of the implications that the new competitive environment has for Human Resource (HR) practitioners and policy makers. The very fact that this chapter exists is a testimony to the fact that more and more people recognise the important role of HR in the new competitive environment. In fact, there is a growing body of management scholars who believe that employment practices, once mastered, can give an entity a sustainable advantage that is difficult to duplicate (Pfeffer, 1994; Dessler, 1997; Thurow, 1992; Quinn, Doorley & Paquette, 1990). And companies are beginning to buy this argument. As Greer (1995) puts it:

> *"In a growing number of organisations, human resources are now viewed as a source of competitive advantage. There is greater recognition that distinctive competencies are obtained through highly developed skills, distinctive organisational cultures, management processes, and systems. This is in contrast to the traditional emphasis on transferable resources such as equipment which can be purchased by competitors. Increasingly, it is being recognised that competitive advantage can be obtained with a high quality workforce that enables organisations to compete on the basis of market responsiveness, product and service quality, differentiated products, and technological innovation."*

In Singapore, top level decision-makers have always viewed the quality of the workforce as something central to economic development and competitiveness. Deputy Prime Minister, BG Lee Hsien Loong, noting the high costs of labour in Singapore, highlighted the need for Singapore workers to have better technical skills, and to be more productive than those of neighbouring countries.[1] Mr Lim Boon Heng, the Minister without Portfolio, mentioned the need to develop a world class workforce with critical skills.[2]

Singapore's labour force was judged as the best in the world in 1996 by the US-based Business Environment Risk Intelligence (BERI). This makes it two years in a row since 1995 when BERI included Singapore in the advanced economies category. However, it should be noted that while Singapore topped the overall ranking — as well as the two sub-categories of legal framework and relative productivity — it ranked third for worker attitude and eighth in technical skills. For worker attitude, it ranked behind Japan and Switzerland; for technical skills, it ranked behind Denmark, Switzerland, Japan, the United States, the Netherlands, Germany, and Sweden.[3] This shows that there is still room for improvement. One should not pop the champagne bottle just yet!

This chapter looks at a range of the latest techniques, principles, and practices in Human Resource Management (HRM). Emphasis is placed on the training and development of employees. This reflects the author's belief that training plays a critical role in making Singapore competitive, both at the national and organisational levels. To quote Dr Richard Hu, the Finance Minister,[4]

> *"Manpower is our most important resource. It is the main driving force behind Singapore's economic development. To ensure that we have the necessary manpower to support our economic growth, the Government has, and will continue, to*

---

[1] *Business Times*, April 30, 1997.

[2] *Straits Times*, March 2, 1997.

[3] *Straits Times*, April 7, 1997.

[4] *Straits Times*, July 23, 1997, p. 39.

invest heavily in the training and education of our workforce."

It is assumed that the reader has adequate basic grounding in the area of HR management. As such, I will be touching on the latest developments in the area of HRM pertaining to the enhancement of Singapore's competitiveness either at the national level or the organisational level.

2. Major Changes with Impact on HRM

I would start off this chapter by identifying certain key changes in the macro business environment that would create an impact on Singapore businesses. First and foremost is that of globalisation. This trend has been given impetus by the success of the World Trade Organisation (WTO), which led to the breakdown of trade barriers, lowering of tariffs, and other barriers to entry.

For the countries concerned, globalisation means free movement of goods and services across national borders leading to what has been termed a "borderless" world. For organisations, globalisation means that they must be able to compete on a worldwide basis. Organisations must either shape up or ship out. There is no choice in between.

Competition takes place on several fronts: the marketing of products and services worldwide, the sourcing of raw materials worldwide and the manufacturing of products worldwide. Such activities inevitably lead to intense competition for customers, raw materials, as well as human resources. The entry of two big supermarket chains into the local scene over the past several months illustrated succinctly what would happen when competitors come knocking at your door. Prices fall as consumers are given more choices. Smaller retailers must learn to be more competitive through better services or by banding together to get better prices from suppliers, or they risk being strangled by the bigger players.

One direct result of increased competition is to force companies to place greater emphasis on quality issues, which leads to the increased importance of *Total Quality Management (TQM)*. Many companies that are used to world class competition, such as Motorola and Xerox, have implemented TQM programmes as a means to attain world class quality both in terms of product and service. And with the added importance of TQM, the HR function is pushed into the forefront of organisational strategy. HR professionals play a critical role in providing training, facilitating work changes that help to improve work methods, implementing team based reward systems, instituting employee empowerment, and communicating new organisational vision to employees (Greer, 1995).

Companies in Singapore that are facing world class competition will have to do no less. As they learn to compete in the world marketplace, they would have to grapple with issues related to service and product quality, productivity, and technological changes. These issues have critical implications for employee recruitment, training and development. Employees will have to be trained in new skills, operate new kinds of machines (for example, computer aided design and manufacturing equipment) and learn to work in teams instead of working alone. Companies will also have to get their workers to understand the importance of quality, both in terms of product and service, and take part in company organised quality activities such as Quality Circles (QC).

The importance of providing quality service in the service sector led the civil service to come up with Public Service 21 (PS21), an initiative that is intended to bring public service into the 21st century. The emphasis is on the provision of first class service to all its customers. Since the start of the initiative in 1995, more public sector employees have seen the importance of service quality. The Civil Service itself, which provides jobs in areas such as education, defence, construction, engineering, police work and civil defence, has seen the need to grant more openness to its employees, more training opportunities (the target is 100 training hours per year per employee by the year 2000), better benefits and fair appraisal.[5] The PS21 initiative serves as a good model for all companies in the service sector such as those in the transport, retail, and hospitality industries.

Another change that has a great impact on organisations is the fast pace of *technological change* over the last decade. The advent of

---

[5] *Straits Times*, November 10, 1997.

powerful personal computers and computer software has changed the way products and services are sold, the way work is carried out, and the whole organisational landscape. Take for instance, the banking industry. By the end of 1997, the Post Office Saving Bank started Internet banking which permits cashless transactions such as payment to companies and checking of account particulars. The SMRT talks about a new smart card that permits contactless entry for commuters. Companies in the manufacturing sector are increasingly turning to Computer Aided Design (CAD) and Computer Aided Manufacturing (CAM). These are samples of the way technology has affected the conduct of business, which in turn affects the way HRM is being practised. Heavier usage of high tech equipment like CAD/CAM and information technology like Internet means that a completely new set of skills will be needed for employees. Employee recruitment, selection, training, performance evaluation, and career management will all have to be re-evaluated in the light of these changes.

Rapid technological change brings with it one critical HR problem: rapid skill obsolescence, particularly in engineering, science and other professions. This is a problem which HR professionals must tackle with great care and urgency, because technological obsolescence can cause a firm to lose its competitiveness by limiting its strategic alternatives (Greer, 1995). The end result could be devastating for a company. This is an area that our top level leaders are very much aware of and concerned with.[6] Training and retraining seem to be good strategies in handling this problem.

Globalisation and technology change bring with them a third related impact on HRM, namely the *change in the nature of work*. In North America and Western Europe, more jobs have been shifted from manufacturing to services. Take the United States for instance. The manufacturing sector gave up 12% of its workforce during the 1980s. New jobs added in the 1990s were in service industries like fast food, retailing, consulting, teaching, etc. (Dessler, 1997). What this means is that work in the future will be more knowledge intensive. As Peter Drucker (1988) predicted, "the typical business

[6] *Straits Times*, March 1, 1997.

will be knowledge based, an organisation composed largely of specialists who direct and discipline their own performance through organised feedback from colleagues, customers and headquarters."

This change in the nature of work, and perhaps in the very shape of organisations, brings with it an added blessing for HR professionals. The emphasis on knowledge workers has forced organisations to focus on human capital instead of merely physical capital. More emphasis is now placed on the knowledge, education, training and skills of a firm's workers instead of merely the machines that it has.

> "*Brainpower has never before been so important for business. Every company depends increasingly on knowledge – patents, process, management skills, technologies, information about customers and suppliers, and old fashioned experience. Added together, this knowledge is intellectual capital.*"
>
> (Steward, 1991)

The greater need for knowledge workers has propelled the HR function into the forefront of business strategy instead of taking a back seat compared to marketing or manufacturing. Companies will have to pay more attention to recruitment and selection as well as training and development. The greater need for knowledge workers is not lost on our top level decision-makers. They have frequently stressed the need for our workers and employees to be creative, innovative and up-to-date with the latest changes.[7]

With regard to the service sector, our top economic planners have certainly realised its importance. The EDB has attracted many service oriented companies to set up their business headquarters here and it intends to develop Singapore into a service hub for the region.[8]

Increased competition as a result of globalisation has led many companies to *downsize* their workforce, place greater reliance on teamwork, and employee empowerment, all of which bring with them tremendous HRM implications. Others resort to the greater use

---

[7] *Straits Times*, July 2, 1997.

[8] *Sunday Times*, October 26, 1997.

of part-timers. Take Seagate Technology Singapore for instance. It shed 500 contract workers at one go in a bid to cut cost during slack periods.[9]

Downsizing in Singapore

In Singapore, the urge to downsize and retrench workers as a proactive strategy to deal with increased competition is still rare among indigenous local companies. Most of such companies retrench workers in reaction to increased competition rather than using downsizing as a proactive strategy to cut labour costs. Good examples of this nature are the cutbacks by Tangs Studios in the retail sector and Singatronics in the electronics sector. The retail sector is being subject to intense competition while the electronic sector fell prey to the falling demand for electronic products worldwide in 1996.

Compared to the widespread downsizing and retrenchment of staff carried out by many US firms, the local response has been rather muted. This could be due to the fact that in a tight labour economy, many companies are already working with lean staff strength. Hence downsizing is rather unnecessary. Others choose to cut back on hiring, shorten the work week and cut overtime work as a means of coping with business slowdown rather than outright retrenchment. Still others choose to retrain redundant staff to take on other jobs in the same organisation. The Port of Singapore Authority (PSA) Corporation, for instance, announced that no staff would be retrenched when it was recently corporatised on October 1, 1997. Employees whose jobs were made redundant by corporatisation would be trained by the organisation to take on other duties. And when the neighbourhood policing system was restructured recently, the Minister for Home Affairs, Mr Wong Kan Seng, mentioned that there would not be any cut in manpower. In fact, manpower might be added to fill new job requirements due to the restructuring.[10]

Most of the downsizing done here is by foreign companies, particularly the US MNCs. Good examples are the retrenchments of

[9] *Straits Times*, September 30, 1997.

[10] *Straits Times*, July 25, 1997.

100 workers at GE Motors in July 1997, 150 workers at Whirlpool in September 1997 and 250 workers at Apple Computers in June 1997.[11] In fact, Cascio (1995) has noted that the practice of workforce juggling — laying people off when business dips and calling them back when it rises again — is uniquely American. These MNCs have business operations worldwide and would not hesitate to close down a plant in one country and move it to another just to take advantage of some cost differentials. The Japanese and Europeans, on the other hand, prefer to let natural attrition and voluntary early retirement take care of excess labour (Carrell, Elbert & Hatfield, 1995).

Most indigenous Singaporean companies seem to be following the more paternalistic measures used by their European or Japanese counterparts. The question is, how long can Singaporean firms hold out? Already, Japanese employers are beginning to shed workers,[12] and Europe is moving towards labour market deregulation. It is too early to tell, but firms in Singapore, and perhaps even those in the region, may have no choice but learn to operate with leaner staff. Already a top union leader warned that the liberalisation of the financial sector may result in mergers and acquisitions that could lead to more layoffs and downsizing.[13] Indonesian firms, affected by the recent currency and stock market turmoil have asked their government for permission to lay off some 10,000 workers.[14]

To be sure, American MNCs are not the only ones who have retrenched staff in order to cut costs. Others like Singatronics, a Singaporean firm, and Sinoca, a Taiwanese firm, have done the same thing.

In this connection, the Singapore Government, through the Economic Development Board (EDB), has done a great job by bringing in new businesses to absorb the retrenched workers. Take for instance, the electronics industry. Despite the great number of people being retrenched from 1990 to 1995, more jobs have been created in this sector to the extent that the unemployment rate in this

[11] *Straits Times*, July 11, 1997; September 12, 1997; June 5, 1997 respectively.

[12] *Asian Wall Street Journal*, September 30, 1997.

[13] *Straits Times*, October 25, 1997.

[14] *Straits Times*, November 1997.

sector is only 2%. With such new foreign direct investments, it is no wonder that out of the employees retrenched in the first nine months of 1996, 71% of them took an average of a mere 1.6 months to find a new job.

3. Employee Recruitment and Selection

The competitive environment means that there is a need for organisations to recruit workers who are flexible and adaptive. Such employees should have the following characteristics:

- be comfortable with new ways of work,
- willing to learn new skills,
- willing to work with new technology,
- willing to be deployed worldwide,
- willing to work with others, and
- willing to try new things.

It implies that during the recruitment process, employers should not only be looking for academic qualifications but also for the development potentials of prospective employees. In other words, such employees should have a full range of life interests, be active in extracurricular activities at different stages of their school life, and not just examination experts skilled in scoring A's in examinations.

How do we know if the employees have the above characteristics? A thorough examination of their resumes and skilful interviews should do the job.

Another school of thought advocates the selection of employees who can fit into the organisational culture. Needless to say, this is very important in the context of Japanese organisations. Take for instance, the comments by Fujio Cho, president of Toyota Motor Manufacturing, USA: "You might be surprised, but our selection and hiring process is an exhaustive painstaking system designed not to fill positions quickly but to find the right people for those positions. What are we looking for? First, these people must be able to think for themselves ...problem solvers and second, work in a team atmosphere. Simply put, we need strong minds, not strong backs. We consider the selection of a team member as a long-term investment decision. Why go the trouble of hiring a questionable employee only to have to fire him later?" (Dessler, 1997).

Mr Fujio spoke for many progressive HRM professionals. Indeed it would be a waste of the company's as well as the employees' time and money should there be a mis-match due to the lack of conscientiousness on the part of employers. They should spare no time and effort to ensure that the right employees are employed.

And Toyota USA puts its money where its mouth is. It is prepared to spend up to 20 hours of interviewing and screening before a decision is made to hire or not to hire someone. The company ensures that potential employees understand and fit into its core cultural values of *Kaizen* (Japanese for continuous improvement), teamwork, flexibility, and problem solving. This is done through an extremely rigorous hiring process which begins with Toyota showing a video on what it is like to work for the company. The use of such realistic job previews enables potential employees to engage in self-selection and thus ensures a better match between the employee, the job and the company. Its ultimate commitment to hiring the best employees is the major reason why Toyota cars have won numerous quality awards in the US and are selling like hot cakes around the world.

Another idea worth exploring is that of *value-based hiring* (Dessler, 1997). What it means is that employers should hire with an eye for the future. In short, they should hire people with long term potential in the company and not just to fill a position. Such employees would be trained and retrained by the company, promoted in the company and stay with the company for the long term.

Dealing with Worker Shortfall and High Turnover

Two major HR issues that organisations in Singapore have to contend with are the shortage of staff and the related issue of high staff turnover. The tight labour market is brought about by the small size of the skilled labour force coupled with a booming economy. Declining birth rates in the 1970s and 80s have further aggravated the situation.

The tight labour market encourages employees to be choosy,

hence bringing about high job turnover, which in turn worsens labour shortage at the firm level. The latest figures from the Ministry of Labour showed that the average monthly resignation rate was 3.2% in the first quarter of 1997. This works out to an average turnover of 38.4% per year![15] The high turnover rate has helped to push hiring decisions to the forefront of HRM in most organisations.

As HR managers juggle desperately to fill the head count requested by line managers, some of them end up hiring less than qualified staff. The high labour turnover, tight work schedule and training budget conspire to make HR managers cut back on training. Employees frustrated by a lack of competence and the company's unwillingness to train leave, thereby increasing the firm's labour turnover, and once again the HR managers have to search desperately for workers. This vicious cycle is left to repeat itself until the HR managers realise the folly of careless recruiting and reluctance in training. The only way to break this vicious cycle is through careful hiring, training, compensating and planning for the careers of their staff.

At the national level, one way Singapore has responded to this problem of labour shortage is look at how a big segment of the unemployed could be enticed to rejoin the workforce: housewives and healthy retirees. A tripartite effort by Ministry of Labour, the Productivity and Standards Board (PSB), the National Trade Union Congress (NTUC) and Singapore National Employers' Federation (SNEF) to woo these people resulted in a programme called "Back to Work" which was launched in September 1996.[16] The goal of the effort is to entice about 150,000 housewives and retirees back to work through training and transport subsidies from the Skills Development Fund (SDF). For each employee hired, the employer will receive $350 subsidy for pre-employment training. Once on the job, further training subsidies will be given to the employers. This is to encourage employers to change the design of jobs to suit these two major categories of economically inactive Singaporeans.

As another step in alleviating the shortage of workers, the retirement age will be raised from 60 to 62 from January 1, 1999.

---

[15] *Business Times*, August 28, 1997.

[16] *Straits Times*, September 14, 1996.

However, the proposed package permits employers to make lower CPF contributions, cut the pay of these older workers by 10%, and share the medical expenses with their employees. Some have voiced concern that this could mean that older workers would be worse off by retiring at 62 as compared to 60. They also urged the government to provide more incentives for skills training for older workers as well as tax rebates for employers who want to pay older workers more than the maximum amount of CPF contribution legislated.

While many are convinced that older employees do want to work beyond 60, the key question is, given the current package approved by the Government, will there be sufficient older workers who want to do so?[17] Those who are relatively healthy would certainly consider staying on in the workforce. How about those who may suffer from illnesses from time to time as a result of old age? Such people may find it more worthwhile to retire early. Since the measure will only come into effect in January 1999, the Government still has time to fine tune the package.

As another key strategy in making up for the shortfall in manpower, the Singapore Government did an about turn in its policy regarding foreign workers. More will be said about this in a later section.

At the firm level, most organisations have tried to solve the worker shortage problem by resorting to employing part-timers as well as hiring foreign workers. Take the local hospitals for instance. It is a well known fact that all of them rely on foreign nurses to make up for the shortfall of nurses in Singapore. A recent report indicated that the healthcare industry needs about 2,200 nurses in 1997. There are only 9,000 nurses presently. Although the Nanyang Polytechnic will continue to churn out qualified nurses, there will still be a shortfall that has to be filled in by overseas nurses from countries such as China, India, and the Philippines.[18] While the manufacturing sector could possibly make up for the shortfall of workers through greater automation and better job design, the service sector, which includes industries such as hotel, transport, and retail, will have little choice but to resort to foreign workers to make up for the shortfall.

[17] *Straits Times*, October 30, 1997.

[18] *Straits Times*, July 31, 1997.

After all, it is not likely that we can develop a robot to drive buses or serve drinks in the near future!

And how have organisations responded to the employee turnover problem? Careful hiring strategies, not unlike some of those mentioned previously. They do not want to rush into hiring someone, only to fire the employee six months later! Some of the strategies adopted are:

- Giving free personality tests to students
- Paying them to attend training programmes even before they start work
- Letting new recruits bargain for the jobs they prefer, instead of pushing them into vacancies

The Singapore National Employers' Federation (SNEF) plays an important role in helping to match employees with employers. For example, in 1996 it administered free personality tests to help more than 3,000 students understand what jobs are really suitable for them. In turn, they would make wiser decisions by joining the right organisation, thereby cutting down on wasteful labour turnover. These tests assess a job seeker's basic skills such as thinking and communication as well as personality. The tests are made available on the Internet to provide greater accessibility to foreign as well as local students.[19]

The use of psychological or personality tests is not new to organisations in Singapore. In June 1996, the Singapore Police Force announced the use of psychological tests to assess the suitability of candidates applying for junior officer positions. Since 1994, applicants for senior positions and the elite police commando squad have had to take similar tests. The Public Service Commission has plans to set up a testing unit to assess personality, intelligence and ability of those applying for certain categories of service under its administration.[20]

One local bank that has tried out the training programme technique is DBS. It has a scheme called DBS Earn-And-Learn (Deals), in which tertiary undergraduates and A-level students are paid $5 a day to attend an eight-day training programme in banking,

[19]*Straits Times*, February 22, 1996.

[20]*Straits Times*, September 6, 1996.

after which they are given vacation jobs at the bank's branches. If they finish the work stint, they would be given a bonus of $200. This method has helped the bank to have a steady stream of temporary staff. More importantly, the scheme helps students make suitable career choices by gaining more insight into banking careers while being paid for it.

OCBC, on the other hand, has tried the third technique with great success. Out of an average batch of 34 graduate trainees, 10 would be allowed to negotiate for the postings they want in the bank. Upon the completion of their job rotation training, the trainees will hear from the bank's Trainee Bank Officers Development Committee about available positions. Managers who have worked with them will make bids for the trainees they want and the recruits will also put up their case for the jobs and departments they want. Although it sounds chaotic to the outsider, OCBC mentioned that this technique has helped them retain about 32 out of 34 recruits each year.

In summary, it should be borne in mind that no one method of selection is perfect. A shrewd employer would do well to rely on a pool of selection devices to help look for the "right" employees and hence cut down on employee turnover. These devices could include the use of appropriate tests, realistic job previews, internship, work samples or simulations. Besides careful hiring and selection processes, others have resorted to the use of training programmes and attractive employee benefits or even promotions from within as means to curb high labour turnover (Dessler, 1997).

Attracting Foreign Talent

An issue that is related to the shortfall of workers, and which is currently a hot topic for debate and discussion, is the Prime Minister's call for the import of more foreign talent. This is a quantum reversal of the policy expressed in 1991 when Mr Goh talked about the dangers of being too dependent on foreign labour.[21] Then, it was feared that importing too many foreign workers would

[21] *Straits Times*, August 31, 1997.

dilute work values. Now, the wisdom is to draw from the best in the world. Not just people at the top but across-the-board, embracing of blue collar workers such as technicians, bus drivers and counter staff.

With about 560,000 foreigners here, and about 30,000 of them making their way here annually, there are those who wonder whether they will take away job opportunities from Singaporeans.[22] There would also be housing and education problems as these foreigners would also compete with the locals for rental housing and their children will compete for places with Singaporeans in the better schools.

The Ministry of Labour's recent statement that locals would be given priority in terms of jobs has certainly helped to calm some nerves of Singaporeans concerning their job prospects. There have also been assurances from the top that all things being equal, Singaporeans would be preferred over foreigners.[23] The PM has reiterated the fact that well educated and well trained Singaporeans need not fear competition from foreign talents. Singaporeans can still maintain their edge through improvements to the schools and universities, and the provision of assistance for older Singaporeans to upgrade their skills.[24]

One critical issue is: can we attract the best of the foreigners here? Only then can there be some form of technology transfer. If this is not feasible, we should attract only those categories of employees in which we have a severe shortfall. Clerical workers and bus drivers would be good examples.

One organisation that has not failed to attract foreign talents is the Institute of Molecular and Cell Biology. The Institute has about 250 scientists, of whom 160 have doctorates. Out of these 160, only 31% are Singaporeans. Many of the foreign scientists have taken up Singapore citizenship. What attracted some of these top professionals to Singapore in the first place? Good money, a good place to live, and an efficient government. These were some of the reasons quoted by many who have decided to live and work here.[25]

---

[22] *Straits Times*, September 13, 1997.

[23] *Ibid.*

[24] *Straits Times*, September 28, 1997.

[25] *Straits Times*, August 31, 1997.

Another interesting issue is: how much diversity should we have, given the findings that there is a curvilinear relationship between diversity and performance? For instance, it has been suggested that too much diversity can lead to communication problems and greater levels of conflict (McLeod & Lobel, 1992). In this connection, the recent currency and stock market turmoil seems to have worked in Singapore's favour in so far as attracting Malaysian workers is concerned. More of them are flocking to Singapore to find jobs.[26] Since they are culturally very similar, this pool of foreign talents should prove to be very helpful in alleviating manpower problems.

4. Employee Training and Development

In Singapore, high level policy makers view employee training or retraining as an extremely important issue. A well trained workforce is perceived to be a quality workforce. And a quality workforce is one of the keys to Singapore's competitiveness as a nation and the organisations that operate in this island republic. As a matter of fact, employee training and development is specifically mentioned as one of the keys to successful economic restructuring in Singapore.

As an indication of the Government's commitment to training and educating the workforce, the construction of a national training centre is in the pipeline. The goal is to use the training centre to train up to 50% of the workforce in Singapore. The centre might also provide regular updates on the types of jobs in demand as well as career guidance for workers.[27]

Training is carried out with several motives in mind:

- to improve workers' skills so as to enhance their productivity
- to improve workers' skills so as to enhance product and service quality
- to improve workers' skills so as to reduce accident rates
- to improve workers' skills so that they would not become redundant due to new technology
- to curb high labour turnover

[26]*Straits Times*, December 11, 1997.

[27]*Straits Times*, July 23, 1997.

General versus Specific Training

Human capital theorists, such as Becker (1964), have long contended that organisations are reluctant to invest in general training, since the employees can transfer such skills at the employers' expense to other employers. On the other hand, they are rather willing to invest in specific training, as such skills cannot be easily transferred to other organisations.

However, sceptics of the theory have argued that the differentiation between transferable and non-transferable skills is unclear (Brown, 1990) or, at best, misleading (Greer, 1995). They argue that in reality, very few skills are absolutely specific such that they have no use to other employers, and very few skills are absolutely general such that they can be easily transferred to another employer. Furthermore, employers also do not seem to see the difference between general and specific training (Mitchell, 1989).

Recent evidence seems to point in favour of the sceptics. The 1994 BLS survey found that among employers that provided formal training, more than half indicated that they did not fear losing trained employees to other employers. In fact, for these employers, training was used to retain valued employees and they also did not distinguish between transferable and non-transferable skills in their training programmes (US Bureau of Labor Statistics, 1994). Interestingly, even among firms that did not provide any formal training, only 3.1% responded positively to "fear of losing newly trained employees to other firms."

Although the research was done in the United States, one suspects that the findings may well be applicable to the Singapore situation. Perhaps even more so, due to our tight labour situation. Surely, it would make better sense for a company in Singapore to spend on training and hence get to keep their best employees than to risk losing them by ignoring training for fear of poaching.

Be that as it may, Singapore is doing all it can to provide for basic literacy skills, such as reading, writing, and mathematics, through the school system. Hopefully, for the majority of employers, this would have provided their employees with basic general skills at the point of employment so that they merely need to train employees on company specific skills.

Training at the National Level

The Productivity and Standards Board (PSB)

The Productivity and Standards Board (PSB) has been encouraging companies to spend more on training their employees. They have various schemes to do this, the oldest being the Skills Development Fund (SDF) set up in October 1979 with the aim of defraying training costs for employers. All employers who have employees earning $1,000 or less per month have to pay the Skills Development Levy (SDL) of 1% of their employees' remuneration or a minimum of $2, whichever is greater. From this fund collected, training grants are given to employers to mount training programmes for employees to improve their basic literacy and functional skills. This would contribute to higher productivity at the firm level. Ultimately, when sufficient firms do the same thing, productivity at the national level would increase.

Increasing workers' skills and productivity are key elements of the government's economic restructuring effort, the aim of which is to move away from labour intensive industries into high value added industries requiring higher levels of skills and advanced technology.

With the encouragement of the SDF, employers' expenditure on training as a percentage of payroll has risen from 1% in 1986 to 3.6% in 1995. The long term goal of the SDF is to reach the 4% level. Training places offered were 466,000 in 1996, up from 356,000 in 1990. Mr Lim Boon Heng, the Minister without Portfolio and Chairman of the PSB, mentioned that SDF has aimed to reach the goal of 900,000 training places in five years.[28]

One interesting new scheme introduced in early 1997 is the Small and Medium Enterprises (SME) Manager Scheme, which subsidises training costs for managers in such companies. Noting the lack of formal business management knowledge among managers in such organisations, the SDF came up with this scheme with the aim of helping such managers experience for themselves the benefits of training. If their own performance could be improved, they may want to send more of their employees for training.

[28] *Straits Times*, March 2, 1997.

Besides all the training schemes administered through the SDF, the PSB also encourages corporate quality and training excellence by giving annual awards to companies who excel in quality and training. For instance, the PSB certifies the quality process through the various ISO certifications. It also hands out the Singapore Quality Award (SQA) to excellent companies. Winners of the SQA in 1997 were Baxter Healthcare and the Housing and Development Board (HDB). It has been noted that both organisations have a strong foundation for training and developing its employees.[29]

Since 1988, organisations that have excelled particularly in training and developing its employees are given the National Training Award, and past winners of this award include Tan Tock Seng Hospital, New Changi Hospital, IBM Storage System Division, Anglo-French Travel, Sembawang Shipyard, and the HDB. The purpose of this award is for the winners to serve as a role model for other companies to invest in their human resources. Employees in the winning companies have received training which is substantially above the national average of 39 hours per employee.[30]

To top it all, the PSB is heavily involved with private organisations in providing training opportunities for workers. For instance, it started the Service Quality (SQ) Centre jointly with Singapore Airlines (SIA) to provide frontliners, supervisors and managers with training in service quality; the Anderson Consulting-PSB Training Technology Centre to promote the use of training technology in Singapore.

In connection with worker retraining, the PSB has an existing scheme introduced in 1994 called the Retraining Voucher Scheme. Retrenched workers are trained in PSB's Start Training and Retraining (START) programme, which aims to help such workers learn new skills and develop self-confidence in order to regain employment in the shortest possible time. Companies who put their affected workers through this scheme can have all the training costs absorbed by the SDF.

---

[29] *Business Times*, July 17, 1997.

[30] *Straits Times*, December 11, 1997.

The Institute of Technical Education (ITE)

The Institute of Technical Education (ITE) also plays a critical national role in the training and education of our workers. It provides training opportunities for students who could not proceed to take the "A" levels after their "O" level examinations. The ITE, through its many campuses, provides training and education in mechanical and electronics engineering. Graduates from the Institute are given National Training Certificates that certify them as skilled workers, thus enabling them to get the better skilled and salaried jobs. For instance, it provides for the training of workers under the BEST and WISE programmes. Both programmes are aimed at increasing the language and mathematical skills of workers in order to help them cope with the fast pace of change in the workplace. The BEST programme provides courses up to the Primary Six level and the WISE programme up to "N" levels.

Besides the ITE, the various polytechnics in Singapore also provide technical training of workers in Singapore. The two local universities also play an important role in worker education by turning out graduates with appropriate skills and knowledge to help make the nation more competitive.

The National Trade Unions Congress (NTUC)

At the national level, the National Trade Union Congress (NTUC) is currently concerned with the retraining of workers. This is in the context of corporate downsizing and relocation of factory premises by MNCs. Such activities often lead to massive employee layoffs.

A good case in point is the recent decision of International Video Products Private Limited — a joint venture between Toshiba of Japan and Thomson Multimedia of France — to close the Singapore plant. The company announced that by the end of 1997, it will relocate to Thailand and China, thus putting some 1,350 workers out of job.[31] Affected workers who are willing to be retrained will find it easier to find an alternative job while those who wish to stick to their previous jobs may find it more difficult to seek similar employment.

[31] *Straits Times*, August 29, 1997.

In some of these cases, retraining for a new job in the same or different organisation actually results in an increase in salary for the workers.[32] The NTUC plays a critical role by making known and creating training opportunities for affected workers as well as "matchmaking" these workers with appropriate companies. For instance, it is currently looking into the possibility of having wafer fabrication companies absorb retrenched workers from International Video Products.

Training at the Organisational Level

Given the high employee turnover in Singapore, some companies might be tempted to ignore training in order to avoid the "free rider" problem. There is the fear that once the employee is trained, he or she would be "poached" by competitors. This fear has been well documented (Stern & Ritzen, 1991). However, research in the US showed that only a small proportion of employers actually refrained from training their employees because of this reason. A great majority actually used training as a means of retaining valued employees (U.S. Bureau of Labor Statistics, 1994).

One suspects that the same fear of employee poaching may be happening here. Companies that are afraid to train their employees for fear of poaching may be encouraging the very behaviour that they hope to avoid. Employees who quit due to a lack of training opportunities could well signal a less caring employer.

Orientation and Socialisation

When a new employee joins a company, particularly a big one, he is likely to be given orientation training and socialisation. This phase of training is important because it provides the employee with his first real contact with people and work in the company. The employee is then given a chance to understand the company's culture, norms, and values. This phase is also important because turnover frequently occurs during the early months of employment (Greer, 1995).

In this regard, De Cenzo and Robbins (1996) suggested that all

[32]*Straits Times*, May 4, 1997.

company personnel, from the CEO to the HR department, have a critical role to play. The CEO's presence during this period will signal to the new recruits that they are treated as an important part of the organisation, while the HR department's role is to familiarise the new recruits to the organisation and coordinate orientation activities.

Interpersonal Skills

An issue related to the greater import of foreign talents would be diversity training. More foreign talents would mean a workplace of greater diversity. This is not to say that firms in Singapore are new to workplace diversity. Already many of our firms are using workers from Malaysia, Indonesia, Thailand, Bangladesh, India, and China. Industries that are heavily dependent on foreign labour are construction, hotel, healthcare, marine and shipbuilding. The recent call to attract more foreign talents can only mean that an even greater number of skilled foreigners would be enticed to work here.

Such an influx of foreigners, when it does happen, would create mini-melting pots all over the organisational terrain. An organisation that has employees from three different nationalities may well find the racial mix increase to five or even six different nationalities. This makes it imperative for employers to train their employees to work well with others from different backgrounds and cultures. The goal of creating a productive and harmonious workforce will have to be accorded a high level of importance by HR professionals.

Many American MNCs, such as Hewlett-Packard, Motorola and American Express, which have operations worldwide for a great number of years, are investing heavily in diversity training. There is no reason why Singaporean firms, who are likewise exposed to workplace diversity, should not do the same thing.

The greater need to work in teams would naturally lead to a greater need for interpersonal skills among employees. This implies more training for employees in interpersonal as well as team-building skills. Such skills do not come naturally but can be diligently acquired through training instituted by organisations, and informally through insightful self-examination and reflection.

Team-building skills can be acquired through adventure or

outdoor training that usually involves trainees being taken into a jungle terrain. Trainees would go through exercises that highlight the importance of trust and reliance on others in order to get things done. One of the exercises involves trainees being carried through a hole in a man-made spider web. Another involves falling from a height of 1.5 metres into the waiting arms of fellow trainees. Absolute trust and cooperation is necessary if the task is to be carried out effectively by the team. To make the training more exciting, it is usually carried out by a trainer who will divide the trainees into competitive teams. Though no prizes are offered, the mere fact of competition is enough to generate excitement among the trainees. This also helps to bring across the point that teamwork is needed to beat the competition in the real world.

In Singapore, outdoor training has been given a much needed boost when the new $35 million dollar Outward Bound School (OBS) complex in Pulau Ubin was opened on September 28, 1997. Since its inception in 1967, the school has trained 130,000 people in various skills such as leadership and teamwork. With the new facilities, the annual training intake will be increased from 8,000 to 13,000 by the year 2000.[33] The brainchild of Dr Goh Keng Swee when he was the Minister of Defence in 1967, OBS has evolved over the years, from being an adventure camp for students on vacation to a youth leadership camp, and finally to what it is today. Now, it trains trainees not only from Singapore, but also around the region like Brunei, Cambodia and Sri Lanka. Intangibles like a spirit of adventure, enterprise, leadership, confidence and trust are taught besides the importance of teamwork.[34]

One organisation that has used adventure or outdoor training aggressively is PSA Corporation. A $4 million outdoor training programme which started in 1995 resulted in more than 7,000 of its employees being sent for outdoor training conducted by Singapore Training and Development Association, Service Quality Centre and OBS. The outcome? Improved communication, trust, understanding and teamwork. PSA is now extending the training to its subsidiaries. Take Raihan Yusof, 55, a safety officer and a father of four children,

---

[33] *Straits Times*, September 28, 1997.

[34] *Straits Times*, September 27, 1997.

for instance. Outdoor training has helped Yusof to be more vocal and to understand his younger colleagues better.[35]

Technical Skills

Bearing in mind that the Singapore workforce was ranked eighth in the world by BERI in terms of technical skills, employers here must surely perceive the need to spend more on technical training and upgrading of their workers. Employees' technical skills would have to be continually upgraded in order to cope with technological changes in the workplace as well as customers' demand for higher quality goods. Upgrading of machines, equipment, and facilities must be accompanied by upgrading of workers' skills.

This pertains particularly to technical employees such as technicians and engineers. Such employees would need to be trained to use new and better equipment to get their jobs done. For instance, auto mechanics will have to be trained to use the latest equipment to check and repair newer cars. I recently visited a local cable manufacturer who had just invested in a US$5 million machine imported from the United States to make high grade cables. In the process, quite a few technicians, engineers, and machine operators were sent for training on how to use and maintain this new machine in order to get the most out of it.

In this age of continual technological upgrading in order to provide better service or to churn out better quality products for customers, continual upgrading of technical skills is no longer a luxury. It is an absolute necessity. Failure to do so could mean the loss of market share and long term competitiveness.

As an illustration, consider the battle between the two US retail giants Wal-Mart and K-Mart. It is now well documented that Wal-Mart won the battle principally through its superior information technology and satellite network. The satellite system transmits sales information from the retail stores to its headquarters, and merchandising and training programmes from the headquarters to the stores. Computers keep track of inventory round the clock so that the stores are rarely out of items that customers are looking for.

---

[35]*Straits Times*, November 3, 1997.

Investing in such technologies has enabled Wal-Mart to operate at lower costs. These savings are then passed on to consumers through lower prices, which ultimately spelt doom for its competitors.

Ironically, when K-Mart tried to hit back using the same strategy by investing in sophisticated information systems, it was found wanting because its workers were not trained to use the latest equipment before they were installed! (Robbins, 1997, p. 218 and Schmerhorn, 1996, p.158)

Training in the use of latest equipment is also essential for non-technical workers. Postal workers need to be trained to use auto sorters to speed up mail processing and cut mail delivery time. Bus drivers need to be trained to drive new generation buses or use new electronic gadgets installed on existing buses. Even cab drivers are not spared the brunt of technological advancement in Singapore.

The Comfort group of companies, which owns the largest fleet of taxis in Singapore with a fleet strength of 10,000 taxis, has invested heavily in new technology such as the Comfort Cablink and Global Positioning System (GPS). The latter system enables its fleet of 7,500 taxis to relay information on road congestion to the Land Transport Authority which then posts the information on the Internet for all road users.[36] Investing in such systems naturally means that cab drivers will have to be trained and informed of their new role and new ways of attracting customers. Gone are the days when the only way to pick up a fare was by zooming towards the frantic hands of customers waving by the roadside. With the GPS, a customer could just dial for a cab; the GPS will enable the company to track the taxi that is nearest to the caller's location. The nearest cab driver would then be despatched to fetch the customer. The cab drivers play a critical role, in that they must know how to read the digital readout on their in-cab computer panel. In short, they must be literate.

Evidently, technology has even caught up with the durian sellers. The enterprising ones are now taking orders through the fax and even over the Internet! In a luncheon talk I delivered not too long ago, a 60-year-old senior manager approached and asked me about using the Internet. So, who says technology only affects technicians and engineers!

[36] *Straits Times*, September 23, 1997.

Conceptual and Analytical Skills

Apart from interpersonal and technical skills, employees must also be trained in conceptual and analytical skills. One of the key areas is problem-solving skills. This is needed so that employees can carry out empowerment effectively. As a case in point, at Saturn Corporation, a major division of General Motors, each employee receives about 320 hours of training to develop his problem-solving and analytical skills as part of the employee empowerment programme. Typical tools that are taught include basic statistics and accounting.

Customer Service Skills

In today's economy, the service sector — comprising major players such as hotels, departmental stores, airlines, and the transportation companies — is growing to be just as important as the manufacturing sector. Companies in this sector will have to train their employees to provide excellent customer service so that they would return or even recommend the services to their friends. In an economy that depends on tourism to drive our economic growth, providing excellent customer service would seem like a natural thing to do.

As an indication of how seriously our national policy makers view customer service excellence, the PSB, together with some other organisations, have presented annual awards to individuals who provide excellent service to their customers. Called the Excellence Service Awards, they are given out to individuals who are nominated by their companies for providing excellent service to customers. Some excellent service providers are even singled out and given national publicity in the local newspapers.

As an example of how customer service training can play a role in providing better service, consider the Trans-Island Bus Company. Besides its normal fleet of buses and taxis, it also operates two premium services, the London Cab service and the Bus Plus service. Before the drivers of such services are put on the road, they are given extensive customer service training. For instance, London Cab drivers are trained in basic courtesy and strongly encouraged to help customers with their luggage or any bulky items. After all, if customers are paying more, they do expect a higher level of service.[37]

All this just goes to show that an organisation that wishes to be around well into the next century must be willing to invest, and invest generously, in training and educating its employees. Anecdotal evidence on the returns on training abounds.

Cross-Functional Training

With the increasing likelihood that the traditional organisation, with its rigid and specialised work functions and detailed job descriptions is increasingly becoming a thing of the past, HR professionals must set their sights on training their workers to be multi-skilled. This is sometimes known as cross-functional training.

The underlying logic is that the more adaptable the workers, the more valuable they become to the organisation. Cross-functional training also provides a company with a broad talent base so that if an employee resigns, there are others who can take over the duties. This gives the employer added depth in manpower deployment, thus ensuring that business operations can proceed smoothly without any hiccups.

One local manager mentioned to the author that in order to encourage more workers to go for cross-functional training, he was prepared to increase their wages upon completion of training. The advantage of having a flexible workforce far outweighs the training costs and higher wages that the company has to pay the multi-skilled workers.

From the workers' standpoint, being multi-skilled also enables them to have greater choices in career development. In short, it is a win-win situation. The workers win, by having greater latitude in career choices. The company wins, by having greater flexibility in work scheduling.

Training in Creativity

Creativity is another type of training that is gaining popularity in today's competitive environment. In the US, the number of

[37] *Straits Times*, September 22, 1997.

organisations with 100 or more employees that offer creativity training doubled from 1986 to 1990. It jumped from 16% to 32% and further to 35% in 1995 (Training, 1995).

In Singapore, creativity training is taken very seriously at the national level. There has been a lot of discussion about producing the kind of creative graduates that the economy will need for the 21st century. The curricula at the two local universities are being reviewed to produce graduates who can think and are innovative.[38] What does this national effort mean for the HR professionals? In future, employees would go to them well trained to think, to be creative and innovative. If the national effort is successful, and there is no reason to doubt why it should not be, the ultimate beneficiaries will be the employers.

Training for Global Deployment

Next, organisations must also train their employees for worldwide deployment. Many Singaporean companies have expanded regionally, and therefore managerial workers and technicians will have to be sent there periodically. Such employees need to be trained in foreign language and culture in order for them to function effectively overseas. Take an assignment to Thailand for instance. There is little doubt that a Singaporean based in Bangkok is likely to be more effective if he or she can speak the Thai language and hence relate to the Thai people more effectively.

Management Development

Finally, in these times of great uncertainty and change, it is imperative that company executives are well trained. Particularly important is the executives' ability to learn and make decisions under conditions of rapid change (Fulmer & Graham, 1993). In short, companies must develop the conceptual skills of their managers to enable them to find new ways of improving quality, service, and prices. In order to do this, they would have to be schooled in global economics, foreign markets and cross-cultural negotiations.

---

[38]*Straits Times*, March 24, 1997.

Furthermore, in the context of today's flatter organisational structures, staffed with better educated employees, managers would have to learn to become teachers, coaches, and consultants rather than bosses who go around barking orders (Conger, 1993).

Popular methods in management development are university courses like the executive MBAs or short two-week executive development programmes conducted by various organisations in Singapore. Other methods like coaching, job rotation and on-the-job training are also very popular.

As more and more Singaporean firms go regional or global in their business outlook, they may have to consider what some MNCs are doing: rotating managers globally or regionally. Shell and British Petroleum are two of the MNCs using this approach to train their managers (Dessler, 1997).

A study in the US (Fenwick-MacGrath, 1988) showed that for executive development to be successful, the following five key factors must be present:

1. Extensive and visible involvement by the CEO
2. Clearly articulated and understood executive development policy and philosophy
3. Executive development policies and strategies which are directly linked to the corporation's business strategies, objectives, and challenges.
4. An annual succession planning process; planned OJT development assignments; customised internal executive programmes supplemented by the selective use of university programmes
5. Executive development being the responsibility of line management rather than the HR function.

Training Methods

Computer Based Training (CBT)

More and more companies are turning to computer based training, which is basically nothing but textbook learning put into a computer. This can take the form of programmed learning, which permits the trainees to learn at their own pace. Computer based programmed learning also permits immediate feedback and is certainly more interesting than learning from a textbook. With the advancement in computer technology, text can be combined with graphics, video and audio components to create a multimedia learning environment.

A wide variety of software is currently available in areas such as mathematical skills, language skills, and statistics. It has been shown that CBT can also be used to train employees in interviewing or sales skills.

Teletraining

New technology makes training possible and indeed cheaper. A trainer could train trainees based at different locations miles away through a television hookup, a process popularly known as teletraining. This is made possible through satellite communication, which even allows two-way interactions between trainers and trainees. This would cut down travelling expenses and the need for large training facilities.

Vestibule or Simulated Training

Another popular training method is the use of vestibule or simulated training. Trainees use the actual equipment they will handle on the job, not in a real life situation but in a simulated environment. This form of training can be used in conjunction with computer technology and is particularly useful for jobs in which training at actual equipment in real life situations can be extremely dangerous and costly. A good example will be the use of simulation for training aeroplane or ship pilots. With simulated training, mistakes committed by trainees do not come with a price. In real life situations, such mistakes could be astronomically costly, both in terms of money and life.

Video Conferencing

Defined as "a means of joining two or more distant groups using a combination of audio and visual equipment " (Emery & Schubert, 1993), video conferencing allows people from different locations to communicate live with each other. In particular, two-way video conferencing, which permits the instructor to see the learners, is likely to emerge as an effective training tool for companies with employees who are spread out geographically. It permits two-way interaction between instructor and students and closely emulates the traditional classroom (O'Connor, Bronner & Delaney, 1996).

On The Job (OJT)

This technique is not new. However, in the Singapore context, it has taken on a whole new dimension. The PSB has been aggressively promoting structured OJT as *the* method of training, viewing it as the most appropriate method given the tight labour market. Organisations can barely afford employees the time off for formal training. The best compromise would be to have some form of "structured" OJT.

Structured OJT, which is very popular with Japanese firms, refers to the training of employees on-site in a systematic manner, using designated trainers, and carefully designed materials along with a plan for certification (Brown & Reich, 1997). The training is done one-on-one till the trainees are certified to carry out the jobs themselves.

To encourage more companies to use structured OJT, the PSB has, as at September 1996, allowed a training subsidy of $4 per worker, provided the training leads to national certification. The subsidy is $3 per worker if it leads to industry certification. In the local context, companies that have adopted structured OJT for their workforce include YCH Distripark, Kinderworld Educare Centre, AIA, NTUC Fairprice, Westin Stamford, Konica Singapore, and Keppel Shipyard. Under the National On-The-Job Training 2000 Training Plan, the objective is to get 200,000 workers trained under the structured OJT method by the year 2000. As at February 1997, 90,000 workers had already been trained.

By and large companies who have spent generously on training have reported their meeting of key objectives. For instance, Seiko Instruments, a watchmaker in Woodlands, pledged to spend at least 2% of company time and 4% of payroll on skills training for its staff of 850. The results? Lower labour turnover, higher productivity and increased company flexibility due to multiskilled workforce.[39]

[39]*Straits Times*, May 24, 1996.

5. Performance Appraisal

In this information technology age, even the traditional human resource practice of performance appraisal is not spared the brunt of technological invasion. Computer software have been written to take performance appraisal on-line and take the administrative chore out of the process. Computerised versions even allow for the use of sophisticated behaviourally anchored rating scales and storage of critical incidents for later use by the assessors.

As more and more firms rely on teams instead of individuals to get the job done, it would seem natural that appraisal of group or team performance should take precedence over performance appraisal of individual employees.

Some firms have resorted to what is called a 360-degree performance evaluation, in which one's peers, subordinates, superiors and even internal and external customers evaluate an individual. This method is being used in US MNCs such as Du Pont, General Electric, Motorola, UPS, and Johnson and Johnson.

The new delayered workplace has resulted in employees given greater work responsibilities. In some instances, this has meant that superiors no longer have a complete picture of all the employees' tasks and duties. Hence, it makes sense for a more well rounded look at a person's performance by using a 360-degree of evaluation instead of the conventional supervisor rating. Though it is a relatively new technique, empirical data has shown positive effects of such an evaluation system due to more accurate feedback, employee empowerment, removal of subjectivity, and the development of leadership skills.

As an illustration of the benefits, take the case of Jerry Wallace, Saturn plant's head of human resource. 360-degree evaluation helped him to realise his tendencies to control others, thus making him an undesirable team member. This resulted in him having to do everything by himself, thus reducing his effectiveness. The new evaluation method thus helped to bring out a side of him which he was blind to, with the end result that a major barrier to his career progression at Saturn was removed.

6. Pay and Compensation

Pay and reward systems should also be modified to suit the new competitive environment. In tandem with performance appraisal, the pay package should increasingly be team or group based. One simple method of implementing a team or group based reward system is by using *gainsharing*. Basically, it means that a great proportion of employees' take home pay is tied to a company's performance. If employees work hard, the company is likely to do well. This would result in greater company profits, which are to be shared by the employees in some sort of gainsharing formula. In a way, it results in a win-win situation by tying employee motivation to company performance rather than individual performance.

In the context of today's competitive and fast changing business environment, Belcher, a compensation expert, has suggested that the gainsharing formula should reward behaviours such as quality of goods or services provided to customers, customer satisfaction, safety, environmental compliance, support for and involvement in organisational change initiative, and cost control (Belcher, 1995).

One of the latest trends in the area of compensation is the use of *broadbanding*. This involves the reduction of salary grades and ranges from ten or more down to three to five. A recent study in the United States showed that about a third of the 3,400 employers surveyed indicated that they had already used or were considering using broadbanding (Bulletin to Management, BNA Policy and Practice Series, 1994).

Broadbanding of jobs fits nicely into a firm of the future, with its flattened hierarchy and greater emphasis on self-managing teams and boundarylessness. With the broader bands of salary grades, an employee who spends time in a lower level job to develop a certain skill set need not suffer any pay cut. This would have been impossible under the traditional pay system. Furthermore, broadbanding of pay encourages employees not to think too narrowly about their jobs, but to view their careers from a broader perspective. After all, the new workplace needs employees to be less specialised and to engage in many cross-functional activities, all of which call for expanded job duties. Two international MNCs which have broadbanded their jobs are General Electric and Toyota.

Besides the above trend towards broadbanding, firms that are progressive in their compensation practices also experiment with the following techniques:

1. Offer packages of above average pay combined with incentives and extensive benefits
2. Build a compensation package that puts a significant portion of pay at risk.
3. Build a pay plan that encourages employees to think of themselves as partners. This means that they should have a healthy share of the profits in good years, and less share during bad times.
4. Provide a package of benefits that makes it clear that employees are viewed as long term investments.
5. Emphasise self-reporting hours worked rather than devices like time clocks.
6. Paying employees for their competencies rather than just for responsibilities and activities. This means that employees will be paid for their performance.
7. Pay system will move away from focusing on creating order, reinforcing the hierarchy, and directing behaviour — through job descriptions, job evaluations, and salary structures — to focusing on encouraging involvement and commitment, and rewarding positive results through competency or skilled based pay, spot awards, team incentives, and gainsharing.

7. Employee Benefits

There is little doubt that every employee treats the benefits package as part of the total compensation package. Therefore, HR professionals should pay as much attention to their benefits programme as they do to the compensation package.

Apart from granting the legally binding annual, sick, and compassionate leave, overtime pay, workman compensation, retrenchment benefits, etc., some employers are increasingly experimenting with newer concepts such as the flexible benefits system and family friendly benefits. This is done to better meet the needs of their employees, to contain future costs of the benefits as well as to help in the retention of staff. Local firms that use the flexible benefits system include the Westin Stamford, Western Digital, IBM Singapore, DBS Land, Singapore Telecom and Singapore Post.

Although the rate of usage is extremely low compared with companies in the US, one could foresee that as more and more employers and employees see the advantages of having such a benefits scheme, the flexible benefits scheme will increase in popularity among organisations and HR professionals in Singapore. A recent survey among 50 Asian, European, US and Australian companies in Singapore indicated that 86% of them were interested in developing flexible benefits for their employees. 5% indicated that they already had some sort of flexible benefits plan in use.

Basically, the flexible benefits system permits employees to choose from among a basket of benefits. Employees are given points with which they can purchase the benefits of their choice. A single individual, for instance, may view membership in a country club as important and thus use her points to purchase this item and have the company pay for the monthly membership fee. A married employee, on the other hand, may prefer to spend more on holidays or purchase of textbooks. The key feature of the system is of course, flexibility. Given the choice, employees would prefer to choose those benefits that are of greater value to them than to be forced to take benefits that do not really benefit them. For instance, of what use is childcare allowance to an unmarried employee?

Others use what could be termed as family friendly benefits in order to attract and keep employees. Such benefits are so named because they help employees to care for their dependants. They are offered because companies recognise the fact that when employees are faced with a choice between their jobs and their family, a vast majority of them place their job second (De Cenzo & Robbins, 1996). Family benefits have been used in the United States to cut down on staff turnover, absenteeism and to improve productivity (Peterson & Massengill, 1988). Some companies in Singapore are beginning to adopt the scheme. For instance, Glaxo-Wellcome offers health insurance not only for its 458 employees, but also for their spouses and dependants. Employees receive optical benefits and female employees even get obstetrics and gynaecological consultations paid for by the company. Other employers provide school holiday care for children of their employees, before and after school care facilities, and fully paid holiday packages.[40] To encourage more employers to be family friendly, starting from 1998, qualifying companies could be given the Pro-Family Company Awards jointly administered by the SNEF and NTUC.[41]

Some companies turn to the use of generous benefit packages in order to keep their workers. In the local scene, we can think of Hewlett Packard. Another example is Canon Corporation of Japan. Employees at Canon are given an average of eight weeks leave a year — which includes periods when the whole company is shut down and four weeks of fully paid personal leave — extensive training. Employees are also allowed to take leave of absence from work for up to a year in order to do volunteer work in Japan or overseas. During this period, they get 20% of their normal pay.

8. Career Development

The shortfall of workers coupled with the high labour turnover in the local context makes it essential that organisations provide a clear career path for their employees if they want to entice workers and keep them. Take the healthcare industry, for instance. Almost all the hospitals use clear career paths as a means to entice nurses to join them. New Changi Hospital, for example, explicitly stated that a clear career path is present which could lead a student nurse all the way up to director of nursing, depending of course, on his or her attitude, effort and skill. The statement is supported by numerous training schemes offered to nurses who joined the hospital.[42]

At the other end of the spectrum, we have industries that have been downsized to meet up with the competition. With lesser managerial positions available, how do we handle the career aspirations of young and well qualified employees? One way is to

[40] *Straits Times*, October 27, 1997.

[41] *Straits Times*, November 9, 1997.

[42] *Straits Times*, July 31, 1997.

create a dual career track. The first for those with managerial capabilities to be put on track for a management career, and the other for outstanding "individual contributors". Those in the second category can aspire to be "senior engineers" or "senior sales representatives" (Dessler, 1997).

Overseas Job Postings

In line with the government's call to go regional, many Singapore organisations have done so. However, many are finding it difficult to entice their staff to work overseas. Some have resorted to giving hefty cash incentives, while most rely on having an attractive benefits package to do the job. A recent survey by the SNEF on benefits given to employees on overseas postings revealed that most give some form of hardship allowance for the inconvenience of having to live away from home. Others provide generous housing and transport allowance.[43]

Promotion

There is little doubt that from a motivational standpoint, promotion decisions are important. It would seem extremely logical to promote people based on competence and performance. This can be done using past or current performance as a gauge, or using assessment centres to assess management potential. Many large Japanese organisations use promotion from within, and increasingly, many US firms such as FedEx and Delta Airlines are also adopting this HR strategy.

Pfeffer (1994) suggested that the best way is to promote people from within. The rationale being that it would give people a sense of loyalty to the organisation. In turn, organisations would also have greater incentives to train their employees.

It would appear that promotion from within work well with value based hiring described earlier. An employee who has been employed by a company for the long term would certainly appreciate promotion from within.

---

[43]*Straits Times*, January 1, 1996.

9. What More Can Companies Do?

Redesign Jobs to Fit Part-timers and Allow Job Sharing and Flexitime

It would seem that while firms in the advanced economies have changed, management style in Singapore remains particularly archaic. Not many employers have redesigned jobs to fit people who want to work part-time. Neither have they redesigned jobs to fit older people who have retired from the full-time workforce.

A Labour Member of Parliament, Mrs Yu-Foo Yee Shoon, has noted that the participation rate of healthy older workers is dropping. Coupled with the declining participation rate of the older married housewives, this has meant that we have two major pockets of employable Singaporeans who could be tapped on to increase the labour force participation rate. She rightly commented that in order to entice such people to come back to work, employers must be willing to redesign jobs to allow for part-time work or job sharing.[44] Flexitime and a compressed work week are other options that employers can turn to.

A recent survey by the SNEF shows that out of 350 companies, only 31 companies (or 8.8%) offered flexible work arrangements. More than half (58.3%) have a five-day work week; five allow job sharing and only one offered alternative workplace arrangements.[45] These findings reinforce the view that employers need to be bolder in the way work is arranged and designed.

On this aspect, I suggest that the government, through its many organisations and agencies, should take the lead in employing part-timers and older people. This has already taken place at HDB, the Ministry of Education, Singapore Telecom, The Singapore Post and the Inland Revenue Authority of Singapore. The POSB Bank has also been cited for having work flexibility. Private companies like Esso Singapore, McDonald's PepsiCo Restaurants, Citibank, Compaq, Western Digital, etc., are among those offering part-time work. However, these are mainly for lower level positions like

---

[44]*Straits Times*, March 22, 1997.

[45]*Straits Times*, October 27, 1997.

clerks, production workers and bank tellers. Employers must be willing to staff higher level positions with part-timers as well. More can be done.

Once this happens, more and more housewives would be willing to come back to work. Older but healthy workers would also be enticed to rejoin the workforce. A combination of these strategies should make Singapore less dependent on foreign workers.

Emphasise Lifelong Learning

In the context of a fast changing world, it is imperative that a company creates a culture that highlights the importance of systematic problem-solving, experimentation, learning from experience, learning from others and transferring those knowledge quickly and efficiently throughout the organisation. These five activities form the core of what has been dubbed as learning organisations (Dessler, 1997), which are skilled at creating, acquiring, and transferring knowledge, and at modifying its behaviour to reflect new knowledge and insights (Garvin, 1994).

To this end, a company must emphasise lifelong learning among its frontliners as well as managers. Lifelong learning entails extensive continuing training from basic remedial skills to advanced decision-making techniques throughout an employees' career. A good example of such an approach is provided by Honeywell, which puts its employees through basic language courses, literacy, numeracy, and computer literacy. This is then followed up by college level courses for all factory employees to earn diplomas and certificates. Finally, employees are given job related training every other week for two hours, focusing on concepts such as just-in-time inventory system, team effectiveness, interpersonal and communication skills, conflict resolution, problem-solving and dealing with a diverse workforce (Nopper, 1993). Such a culture would be able to prevent a company from having employees with obsolete skills.

In this connection, there is the possibility that employees may want to adopt a life long attitude of learning and training but employers are unwilling to pay for the training costs. One MP has suggested that the government could perhaps consider giving tax incentives or the use of Central Provident Fund to pay for such courses.[46]

10. Conclusion

Thus far, the reader must surely have noticed the basic tenor of this chapter is that traditional HRM practices and policies are giving way to new and better ways of managing human resources. Ways that motivate employees to perform at higher levels and stay committed to the organisation are in line with new and harsher realities in the economic environment. Companies that have adopted these progressive HR practices are likely to have better performance from their employees, which, all things being equal, should lead to better organisational performance.

The careful reader would have noticed the multi-pronged approach towards some of the HR issues in connection with Singapore's competitiveness. Take the problem of insufficient labour, for instance. The solution is to tackle it at different levels with different methods. At the national level, the idea is to entice top foreign talents to work and live here in addition to encouraging those who have gone abroad to study to return home and find a job here.[47] Also at the national level, there is the tripartite effort to entice housewives and retirees to rejoin the workforce. At the firm level, the extension of retirement age and willingness to take in more part-timers should help to attract sufficient workers with appropriate skills and attitudes.

The reader must have also noticed that with the new competitive environment, the role of the HR professional has become more and more crucial in the running of an organisation. He or she needs to stay constantly in touch with managers at the highest level to ensure that HR strategies complement corporate strategies. In fact, HR strategies may well be instrumental in the fulfilment of corporate strategies. Take for instance, the greater use of part-timers.

---

[46] *Sunday Times*, July 20, 1997.

[47] *Straits Times*, October 28, 1997.

Many progressive US firms have turned to this HR strategy to meet the corporate objective of being more flexible and responsive to rapid changes in the external business environment.

There are also those who feel that with more and more traditional HR activities being outsourced to outside contractors, HR professionals will have to carve out new roles for themselves as veritable business partners, using their skills in people management and strategic planning to improve company performance. Particularly in the case of Singapore. Human resource is about the only kind of resource that we have in any meaningful supply. It is imperative that employers do not shortchange their human resources by under-investing in their HRM efforts to attract, retain, and utilise the best people in the best possible way for their companies.

Finally, it must be said that we have national leaders who do not sit idle and watch all the changes that go by. They have embraced the concept of globalisation, understanding that this is a necessity given Singapore's small size and lack of resources. They have embraced Information Technology (IT) and the concept of a high-tech economy, knowing that the Information Age is unstoppable and labour scarce Singapore has to go the high-tech way.[48] The big question is: how will our organisations in general and HR professionals in particular respond to those changes?

The writing is on the wall. The clock cannot be turned back. May our HR executives rise up to the challenge!

References

Becker, G. (1964) *Human Capital: A Theoretical and Empirical Analysis with Special Reference to Education*, New York: National Bureau of Economic Research.

Belcher, J.G. (1995) "Group Incentives: Improving Performance through Shared Goals and Rewards", in Risher and Fay (Eds.) *The Performance Imperative*, San Francisco, California: Prentice-Hall.

Brown, C. (1990) "Empirical Evidence in Private Training" in Ehrenberg, E., *Research in Labour Economics*, Greenwich, CT: JAI Press.

[48] *Straits Times*, October 3, 1997.

Brown, C. & Reich, M. (1997) "Developing Skills and Pay through Career Ladders: Lessons from Japanese and US Companies", *Californian Management Review*, Vol. 39, No.2, Winter, pp. 124–144.

Cascio, W. (1995) *Managing Human Resources* (Fourth Edition), New York: McGraw-Hill.

Carell, M.R., Elbert, N.F. & Hatfield, R.D. (1995) *Human Resource Management* (Fifth Edition), Engelwood Cliffs, New Jersey: Prentice-Hall.

Conger, J. (1993) "The Brave New World of Leadership Training", *Organisational Dynamics*, Vol. 21. No. 3, p. 49.

De Cenzo, D.A. & Robbins, S.P. (1996) *Human Resource Management* (Fifth Edition), New York: John Wiley.

Dessler, G. (1997) *Human Resource Management* (Seventh Edition). Upper Saddle River, New Jersey: Prentice-Hall.

Drucker, P. (1988) "The Coming of the New Organisation", *Harvard Business Review*, January–February, pp. 45–63.

Emery, M. & Schubert, M. (1993) "A Trainer's Guide to Video Conferencing", *Training*, June, p. 60.

Fenwick-MacGrath, J.A. (1988) "Executive Development: Key Factors for Success", *Personnel*, July, pp. 55–57.

Fulmer, R. & Graham, K. (1993) "A New Era of Management Education", *Journal of Management Development*, Vol. 12, No. 3, pp. 30–38.

Garvin, D.A. (1994) "Building a Learning Organisation", *Business Credit*, January, p. 20.

Greer, C. (1995) *Strategy and Human Resources*, Englewood Cliffs, NJ: Prentice-Hall.

Mitchell, D.J.B. (1989) *Human Resource Management: An Economic Approach*. Boston: PWS-Kent.

McLeod, P.L. & Lobel, S.A. (1992) "The Effects of Ethnic Diversity on Idea Generation in Small Groups", Academy of Management Best Papers Proceedings, pp. 227–231.

Nopper, N. (1993) "Reinventing the Factory with Lifelong Learning", *Training*, May, pp. 55–57.

O'Conner, B.N., Bronner, M. & Delaney, C. (1996) *Training for Organisations*. Cincinnati, Ohio: South-Western Publishing.

Peterson, D.J. & Massengill, D. (1988) "Childcare Programs Benefits Employers Too", *Personnel*, May, pp. 43–47.

Pfeffer, J. (1994) *Competitive Advantage Through People: Unleashing the Power of the Workforce*, Cambridge, Massachusetts: Harvard Business School Press.

Quinn, James, Thomas, B., Doorley, L. and Penny C. Paquette (1990) "Beyond Products: Services-Based Strategy", *Harvard Business Review*, Vol. 90, No. 2, pp. 58–67.

Risher, H. & Fay, C. (1995) *The Performance Imperative*, San Francisco, California: Prentice Hall.

Robbins, S. (1997) *Managing Today*. Upper Saddle River, New Jersey: Prentice Hall.

Schermerhorn, J.R. Jr. (1996) *Management* (Fifth Edition). New York: John Wiley.
Stern, D. & Ritzen, J.M.M. (1991) *Market Failure in Training? New Economic Analysis and Evidence on Training of Adult Employees*, New York, NY: Springer-Verlag.
Steward, T. (1991) "Brain Power", *Fortune*, June 3, p. 44.
Thurow, L.C. (1992) *Head to Head: The Coming Economic Battle Among Japan, Europe, and America,* New York: Morrow.
Training (1995) Vital Statistics. Issue 32, pp. 55–66.
U.S. Bureau of Labor Statistics (1994) *BLS Reports of Employer-Provided Formal Training*, Press Release, September 23, Washington, D.C.

www.ingramcontent.com/pod-product-compliance
Ingram Content Group UK Ltd.
Pitfield, Milton Keynes, MK11 3LW, UK
UKHW020400150926
8624IPUK00004B/264

9 789971 692148